Studies in
Monetary
Economics

Studies in Monetary Economics

Don Patinkin

The Eliezer Kaplan School of Economics and Social Sciences
The Hebrew University of Jerusalem

Harper & Row, Publishers
New York, Evanston, San Francisco, London

STUDIES IN MONETARY ECONOMICS

Standard Book Number: 06-045031-2

Library of Congress Catalog Card Number: 78-170625

TO DVORA

Contents

Preface

The major purpose of this book is to bring together, in a convenient form, various papers that I have written since the appearance of the second edition (1965) of my book *Money, Interest, and Prices*—and which represent a continuation and further development of the analysis there presented. Most of these papers have already been published, but two (Chapters 9 and 10) appear here for the first time.

The first four essays, however, are of pre-1965 vintage and thus do not fall within the preceding category. They are reprinted here for a variety of reasons. Thus, even though the analysis of Chapters 2 and 3 ("Price Flexibility and Full Employment" and "Financial Intermediaries," respectively) has largely been incorporated and further developed in the aforementioned book (see the Postscript to Chapter 3), these articles have continued to be cited in the literature. Chapter 1 deals with the basic methodological question of stocks and flows; the original discussion has been supplemented here by a Postscript that provides a further interpretation of the results. The analysis of Israel's monetary experiences (detailed in Chapter 4) is one to which I have frequently referred—and which was originally published outside the professional economic journals.

Chapters 5–11 are the more recent essays referred to in the opening paragraph. In Chapter 5 I have returned to a question that has interested me for many years—Wicksell's cumulative process. This time I have examined the process in terms of a simulated econometric model. Chapter 6 also reflects an old interest of mine: the doctrinal history of the quantity theory. The history that primarily concerns me here, however, is the relatively recent one of the Chicago school of the 1930s and 1940s.

As befits an encyclopedia article, Chapter 7—on the rate of interest—presents a general historical and theoretical survey of the relevant issues. Its emphasis on the monetary aspects of the interest rate reflects the terms of reference which were specified for this article.

The common subject of Chapters 8 and 9 is the real-balance effect. In Chapter 8 the nature of the real-balance mechanism is analyzed—with particular emphasis on balance-sheet adjustments, as contrasted with what I now feel are the less important direct effects on current consumption. Chapter 9 analyzes the relation between inside money and the real-balance effect, and deals with the issues that Pesek and Saving have raised in this connection recently.

Chapters 10 and 11 also have a common subject: namely, monetary influences on growth. Chapter 10 deals with this question in a somewhat heuristic manner, in terms of a simple Keynesian model. Chapter 11 (which was written together with David Levhari, to whom I am indebted for agreeing to have it reprinted here) represents a more rigorous and comprehensive approach in terms of a modified Solow growth model that explicitly provides for the functions of money in the economy.

For permission to reprint the articles previously published, I am indebted to *The American Economic Review*, Banca Nazionale del Lavoro, Crowell Collier and Macmillan Inc., *The Journal of Money, Credit, and Banking*, The Magnes Press of the Hebrew University of Jerusalem, and The Wicksell Lecture Society.

I would like to express my sincerest appreciation to Miss Susanne Freund, who prepared the essays for publication. I am also grateful to Mrs. Gwendoline Cohen, Miss Margret Eisenstaedt and Miss Adèle Zarmati for their technical assistance, and to Miss Toney Hart for preparing the indexes. Finally, I would like to thank The Hebrew University of Jerusalem, The Mills B. Lane Foundation, and The Israel Academy of Sciences and Humanities for the research grants that made this assistance possible.

Don Patinkin

1
On Stocks and Flows[1]

It is a commonplace that wealth is to income as a stock is to a flow—where the distinction between the latter two is that a stock is time-dimensionless, while a flow has the dimensions of 1/time. The details of the wealth-income relationship are, however, more complicated than usually realized. Indeed, they have been the source of some misunderstandings in the literature.[2]

These misunderstandings have to do with the dimensional aspects of the wealth-income relationship. For convenience in dealing with this question, let us denote the dimensions of any expression $g(x)$ by $D[g(x)]$. Similarly, let $\$$ denote the dimensions of money and T the dimensions of time (which, in turn, is denoted as usual by t). We also make use of the fact that the dimensions of a product are the product of the dimensions.[3]

If the rate of flow of income over time is represented by the continuous functions $f(t)$—where, by definition, $D[f(t)] = \$/T$—and if in addition compounding is assumed to take place continuously, then wealth W_0 can be defined as

$$W_0 = \int_0^\infty \frac{f(t)dt}{e^{rt}}, \tag{1}$$

From Money, Interest and Prices, *2nd ed., pp. 515–523 (Mathematical Appendix 11). Copyright © 1965 by Don Patinkin. Reprinted by permission of Harper & Row, Publishers, Inc.; material referring to the rest of the book has been deleted and a Postscript has been added.*

[1] Without wishing to burden them with responsibility for the emphasis and interpretation of this appendix, I would like to express my appreciation to Tsvi Ophir and Milton Friedman for their invaluable assistance on certain crucial points.

[2] See, for example, H. G. Johnson, "Monetary Theory and Policy," *American Economic Review*, LII (1962), 339. For my own sins on this question see *Money, Interest, and Prices*, 1st ed. (Evanston, Ill.: 1956), p. 25, note 17 and p. 147, note 16.

[3] Cf. G. C. Evans, *Mathematical Introduction to Economics* (New York, 1930), Chapter 2.

where e^{rt} is the continuous-discount factor.[4] Since $D[r] = 1/T$ and $D[t] = T$, this factor is a pure number and thus time-dimensionless. Similarly, the numerator $f(t)dt$—the amount of income received during interval dt—is also time-dimensionless: for $D[f(t)dt] = D[f(t)]D[dt] = (\$/T)T = \$.$[5] Thus the right-hand side of (1) has the dimensions of money. Clearly, this is also the case for the left-hand side: for, in accordance with the usual definition of wealth, $D[W_0] = \$$.

From (1) we can also compute a constant rate of income-flow K, whose discounted value equals W_0. This is

$$K = rW_0, \qquad (2)$$

which clearly has the dimensions of money per unit of time.

Let us now turn to the definition of wealth in the case of period analysis. For simplicity, consider first the Fisherine case of an individual maximizing his utility over a horizon of (say) two weeks. This individual's wealth is accordingly defined as

$$W_0 = R_1 + \frac{R_2}{1 + r}, \qquad (3)$$

where R_1 and R_2 are the respective incomes of the first and second week, and r is the weekly rate of interest. From this formula it is clear that R_1 must have the same dimensions as W_0, which is a stock. By analogy, R_2 must then also have the dimensions of W_0; and this in turn implies that $1 + r$ is a pure number. Thus the requirements of dimensional consistency in (3) seem to lead to the paradoxical conclusion that both income and interest are time-dimensionless!

The solution to this paradox lies in realizing that (say) R_1 in (3) represents not a *rate* of income (e.g., a wage rate), but the *amount* of income received during the week (e.g., wage payments during the week); that is, R_1 corresponds not to $f(t)$ in equation (1), but to $f(t)dt$. Correspondingly, the time-dimensionlessness of R_1, just like that of $f(t)dt$, reflects the fact that this amount is not affected by changing the time-unit in which the interval is measured. In other words, the individual in equation (3) receives R_1 dollars in the first week and R_2 in the second—whether we call a week a week, or seven days, or 1/52 of a year. Similarly, the time-dimensionlessness of $1 + r$ represents the fact that the amount by which we must discount R_2 is not affected by saying that this income will be received "seven days hence" instead of "one week hence." Another point that should be emphasized is that the time-dimensionlessness of R_1 and R_2 is also reflected in the fact that

---

[4] See R. G. D. Allen, *Mathematical Analysis for Economists* (London, 1938), pp. 232–234, 401–405.

[5] From certain mathematical viewpoints, dt can be considered only as the symbol of an operator; correspondingly, one can legitimately speak only of the dimensions of the right-hand side of (1) as a whole—and these dimensions are those of the sum which approaches it as a limit. Since, however, such a formulation does not affect the following conclusions, we have adopted the heuristically convenient device of treating dt as a separate variable with the same dimensions as t.

these payments must be considered as if they were concentrated at *instants* of time: namely, the beginning of the first and second week, respectively; that is, those instants for which 1 and $1 + r$ are, respectively, the correct discount factors.

More rigorously, we must take account of the fact that the proper time dimensions in equation (3) are obscured by the tacit assumption that certain time periods are of unit length. In order to bring this out, let us place (3) within a somewhat broader context by assuming that R_1 and R_2 are the income payments respectively received at the beginning of the first and second "payment intervals," each assumed to be h time-units long. Similarly, let us define the "compounding interval"—assumed to be m time-units long—as that period of time after which the interest obligation is compounded. Finally, let us represent by F_1 and F_2 the *rates* of income flow which would conceptually have cumulated, respectively, to R_1 and R_2. That is,

$$R_j = F_j h \qquad (j = 1, 2). \tag{4}$$

For simplicity, consider first the case in which the payment and compounding intervals are of equal length: that is, in which compounding takes place once each payment interval. Then the discounting formula corresponding to the foregoing assumptions is

$$W_0 = \frac{F_1 h}{1} + \frac{F_2 h}{1 + mr}, \tag{5}$$

where, by assumption, $h = m$. If in addition the payment (and compounding) interval is assumed to be one time-unit long, then (5) reduces in form to (3). Assume now that while the payment (and compounding) interval remains (say) a week, the time-unit is reduced to a day. This, of course, requires us to refer to a "week" as "seven days"; on the other hand, it clearly does not affect the value of either the numerators or denominators in (5): for the fact that the number associated with F_j will be reduced to one-seventh its former magnitude will be offset by the fact that the number associated with h will increase sevenfold—and a similar statement holds for r and m.[6] This time-dimensionlessness is, of course, a direct implication of the fact that $D[F_j h] = D[F_j]D[h] = (\$/T)T = \$$, and $D[mr] = D[m]D[r] = T(1/T) = 1$.

The foregoing discussion can be generalized to the case in which there are n equal payment intervals, assumed generally to differ in length from the compounding interval. If h/m is an integer greater than or equal to unity, wealth is then defined as

$$W_0 = \sum_{i=1}^{n} \frac{F_i h}{(1 + mr)^{(h/m)i}}, \tag{6}$$

[6] Note that if, say $(1 + 0.1)$ is the discount factor when the time-unit is one week, then changing this time-unit to a day will *not* change the discount factor to $(1 + 0.1/7)^7$. For the change in the time-unit has not affected the length of the compounding interval, and, by definition, interest within this interval accumulates in a simple manner. Hence the relevant discount factor remains $[1 + 7(0.1/7)] = (1 + 0.1)$.

where F_i is the conceptual rate of income flow during the ith interval, and where each of the actual income payments $F_i h$ is assumed to be made at the instant of time at the end of the interval.[7] We have already seen that the numerator of the right-hand expression is time-dimensionless and will now only note that F_i and h in this numerator obviously correspond respectively to $f(t)$ and dt in (1). We have also seen that $1 + mr$ is time-dimensionless, and this is clearly true for h/m as well. Hence it must also be true for the denominator in (6). In brief, since both the rate of discount *per compounding interval* and the relevant number of compounding intervals for any given income payment are unaffected by a change in the time-unit, so too is the discount factor that must be applied to any such payment.

Consider now the problem of determining a constant, perpetual income flow F whose present value equals W_0. This is obtained from (6) by setting $F_i = F (i = 1, \ldots, n)$ and $n = \infty$ and solving the resulting equation for F. This yields the (conceptual) flow

$$F = \frac{[(1 + mr)^{h/m} - 1] W_0}{h},\tag{7}$$

which clearly has the dimensions of $\$/T$. If $h = m$, this reduces to

$$F = rW_0,\tag{8}$$

which is the counterpart of (2). Clearly, the corresponding constant income *payment* is

$$R = Fh = (rW_0)h = (rh)W_0,\tag{9}$$

which is time-dimensionless.

Let us now consider the more general implications of the foregoing argument for the wealth-income relationship. The usual discussion of this relationship seems to interpret the role of the rate of interest as that of converting an income flow (with dimensions $\$/T$) into a stock (with dimensions $\$$) by dividing this flow by the rate of interest (with dimensions $1/T$). If the income stream is a constant, perpetual one, this is indeed a valid interpretation—both when the stream is continuous [equation (2)] and when it is discrete [equation (8)]. If, however, the income stream is not a constant one, then the interpretation is not correct—and again there is no difference between the continuous [equation (1)] and discrete [equation (6)] cases. This in no way affects the fundamental distinction between a capital asset and the flow of services which it provides, or the parallel distinction between the source of an income flow and the flow itself. The only point is the essentially semantic one that in computing the value of this source we are actually applying time-dimensionless discount factors to a stream (or, if we

[7] Note that equations (3) and (5) assume payments to be made at the beginning of the respective intervals.

Equation (6) can also be modified so as to take account of the case in which h/m is not an integer. This, however, involves certain complications which need not concern us here.

prefer, time-sequence) of time-dimensionless income payments—where these payments refer to either infinitesimal or finite time intervals.

On the other hand, it should be emphasized that there is a valid basis for our intuitive feeling that income payments are—and wealth is not—affected by a change in the "time-period." The relevant change, however, is not one in the time-unit, but one in the time-duration of the payment interval. This can be most easily seen in the case of the constant, perpetual income stream described by equations (8) and (9): a change in the time-unit leaves both R and W_0 unaffected; but a change in h, the time-unit being held constant, causes a proportionate change in R, while leaving W_0 invariant. Correspondingly, the accepted description of the distinction between W_0 and R as paralleling that between a "stock" and a "flow" should be understood as implicitly defining a "flow" not as a quantity whose dimensions are $1/T$, but as a quantity whose magnitude is directly proportionate to h; similarly, the implicit definition of a "stock" is that of a quantity whose magnitude is independent of h. Clearly, such "stocks" and "flows" can be added together.

This contrast between income payments and wealth also holds—though only as an approximation—in the case of the finite income stream described by equation (6). The essential point here is that the counterpart of the change in h discussed in the preceding paragraph is an equiproportionate change in the frequency *and number* of income payments which leaves invariant their (conceptual) rates of flow and *un*discounted sum.[8]

The nature of the argument here is illustrated in Figure 1.1. Let the

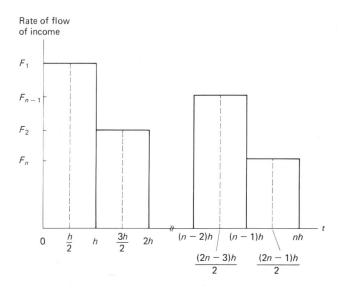

Figure 1.1.

[8] If, however, the frequency is (say) increased while the number of payments is kept constant—which corresponds to decreasing h in equation (6) while keeping n constant—then the undiscounted sum of payments and the value of W_0 will obviously also decrease. In particular, as h approaches zero, so must W_0.

stream of income payments in equation (6) be represented by the relevant rectangular areas under the step-function in this diagram, namely, the n rectangles corresponding to segments $(0, h)$, $(h, 2h)$, ..., $[(n - 1)h, nh]$ on the X-axis. Assume now that the (conceptual) rates and durations of income flow represented by the step-function remain unchanged, while the frequency and number of payments (and compoundings) are doubled. Then the stream of payments is now represented by the respective areas of the $2n$ rectangles corresponding to segments $\left(0, \frac{h}{2}\right)$, $\left(\frac{h}{2}, h\right)$, $\left(h, \frac{3h}{2}\right)$, ..., $\left(\frac{2n - 1}{2}h, nh\right)$. Clearly, each of these payments is half the corresponding original one. On the other hand, the measure of wealth is affected only to a relatively minor extent, as a result of the fact that slightly different discount factors are now being applied to the "same" income payments: i.e., payments which correspond to the same segments of the step-function in Figure 1.1.

This argument can also be presented analytically in a somewhat more general form. In doing so, we shall for simplicity regard compounding as if it were taking place continuously, so that (6) is rewritten as

$$W_0 = \sum_{i=1}^{n} \frac{F_i h}{e^{\rho h i}}, \tag{10}$$

where ρ is chosen so as to satisfy the relationship

$$e^\rho = (1 + mr)^{1/m}. \tag{11}$$

If the (conceptual) rates of flow of income F_i and their durations are left unchanged, while the frequency of payments is increased, say, k-fold, then the ith term in the summation of (10) is replaced by

$$\sum_{j=1}^{k} \frac{F_i \frac{h}{k}}{e^{\rho h[(i - 1) + j/k]}} \sim F_i \frac{h}{k} \sum_{j=1}^{k} \frac{1}{e^{\rho h i}} = \frac{F_i h}{e^{\rho h i}} \qquad (i = 1, \ldots, n). \tag{12}$$

This, then, is the proper sense in which it can be said that the measurement of wealth in (10) is unaffected by a change in the length of the payment interval.

Postscript[1]

The major point of the foregoing discussion can be stated as follows: The distinction between variables that have the dimensions of a stock and those that have the dimensions of a flow is of relevance only in a model in which time is continuous. By contrast, in a model in which time is discrete (that is, in period analysis), there cannot—by definition—be variables with the dimensions of a flow with respect to time. In such models, as shown by the preceding discussion, all variables have the dimensions of a stock.

[1] This postscript reflects the outcome of stimulating discussions with the late Miguel Sidrauski which took place while I was visiting at M.I.T. during the spring and summer of 1968.

As emphasized above (p. 4), this in no way changes the fact that there is a fundamental analytical distinction between, say, the stock of capital on the one hand and investment on the other. In particular, it in no way changes the fact that the marginal productivity of capital is determined by the former and not the latter. But what it does make clear is that—in period analysis— the difference between these two variables is not the time-dimensional one between a stock and a flow. Hence, to continue with this example, net investment during a period can be added validly to the initial capital stock in order to obtain the capital stock at the end of the period. Indeed, this is the type of accounting identity that manifests itself in the usual comparison that we make between balance sheets at different points of time.

2

Price Flexibility and Full Employment[1]

At the core of the Keynesian polemics of the past ten years and more is the relationship between price flexibility and full employment. The fundamental argument of Keynes is directed against the belief that price flexibility can be depended upon to generate full employment automatically. The defenders of the classical tradition, on the other hand, still insist upon this automaticity as a basic tenet.

During the years of continuous debate on this question, the issues at stake have been made more precise. At the same time, further material on the question of flexibility has become available. This paper is essentially an attempt to incorporate this new material, and, taking advantage of the perspective offered by time, to analyze the present state of the debate.

In Part I, the problem of price flexibility and full employment is presented from a completely static viewpoint. Part II then goes on to discuss the far more important dynamic aspects of the problem. Finally, in Part III, the implications of the discussion for the Keynesian-classical polemic are analyzed. It is shown that over the years these two camps have really come closer and closer together. It is argued that the basic issue separating them is the rapidity with which the economic system responds to price variations.

This article originally appeared in American Economic Review, *XXXVIII (1948), 543–564. It is here reprinted by permission of* The American Economic Review *in the modified and corrected version in which it appeared in F. A. Lutz and L. W. Mints (eds.),* Readings in Monetary Theory *(Philadelphia, 1951), pp. 252–283. The changes were made as a result of comments by Milton Friedman, Donald Gordon, Franco Modigliani, and Norman Ture; and also as a result of Herbert Stein's criticism in his "Price Flexibility and Full Employment: Comment"* American Economic Review, *XXXIX (1949), 725–726. For further details of the changes made at the time see the introductory footnote to the 1951 version (p. 252).*

[1] The author acknowledges having benefited in the process of writing this paper from stimulating discussions with Milton Friedman of the University of Chicago, and Alexander M. Henderson of the University of Manchester.

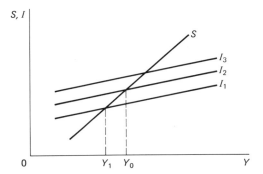

Figure 2.1.

I. STATIC ANALYSIS

1. The traditional interpretation of Keynesian economics is that it demonstrates the absence of an automatic mechanism assuring the equality of desired savings and investment at full employment. The graphical meaning of this interpretation is presented in a simplified form in Figure 2.1. Here desired real savings (S) and investment (I) are each assumed to depend only on the level of real income (Y). $I_1, I_2,$ and I_3 represent three possible positions of the investment schedule. Y_0 is the full employment level of real income. If the investment desires of individuals are represented by the curve I_1, desired savings at full employment are greater than desired investment at full employment. This means that unemployment will result: the level of income will drop to Y_1, at which income, desired savings, and investment are equal. Conversely, if I_3 is the investment curve, a situation of over-employment or inflation will occur: people desire to invest more at full employment than the amount of savings will permit. Only if the investment schedule happened to be I_2 would full employment, desired investment, and savings be equal. But since investment decisions are independent of savings decisions, there is no reason to expect the investment schedule to coincide with I_2. Hence there is no automatic assurance that full employment will result.

2. The classical answer to this attack is that desired savings and investment depend on the rate of interest, as well as the level of real income, and that, granted flexibility, variations in the interest rate serve as an automatic mechanism insuring full employment.

The argument can be interpreted as follows: the savings and investment functions (representing what people desire to do) are written as

$$S = \Omega(r, Y)$$
$$I = \Psi(r, Y)$$

where r represents the rate of interest.

Consider now Figure 2.2. On this graph there can be drawn a whole family of curves relating savings and investment to the rate of interest—one pair for each level of real income. In Figure 2.2, these pairs of curves are

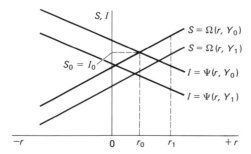

Figure 2.2.

drawn for the full-employment income, Y_0, and for the less than full-employ-ment income, Y_1. On the assumption that for a given rate of interest people will save and invest more at a higher level of income, the investment curve corresponding to $Y = Y_0$ is drawn above that corresponding to $Y = Y_1$; similarly for the two savings curves. The curves also reflect the assumption that, for a given level of real income, people desire to save more and invest less at higher rates of interest.

Consider now the pair of curves corresponding to the full-employment income Y_0. If in Figure 2.2 the interest rate were r_1, then it would be true that individuals would desire to save more at full employment than they would desire to invest. But, assuming no rigidities in the interest rate, this would present no difficulties. For if the interest rate were to fall freely, savings would be discouraged, and investment stimulated until finally desired full employment savings and investment would be equated at the level $S_0 = I_0$. Similarly, if at full employment desired investment is greater than desired savings, a rise in the interest rate will prevent inflation. In this way variations in the rate of interest serve automatically to prevent any discrep-ancy between desired full-employment investment and savings, and thus to assure full employment.

This argument can also be presented in terms of Figure 2.1: assume for simplicity that desired investment depends on the rate of interest as well as the level of real income, while desired savings depend only on the latter. Then downward variations in the interest rate can be counted on to raise the investment curve from, say, I_1 to I_2. That is, at any level of income people can be encouraged to invest more by a reduction in the rate of interest. Similarly, upward movements of the interest rate will shift the investment curve from, say, I_3 to I_2. Thus desired full employment savings and invest-ment will always be equated.

3.   The Keynesian answer to this classical argument is that it greatly ex-aggerates the importance of the interest rate. Empirical evidence has accu-mulated in support of the hypothesis that variations in the rate of interest have little effect on the amount of desired investment. (That savings are insensitive to the interest rate is accepted even by the classical school.) This insensitivity has been interpreted as a reflection of the presence of wide-

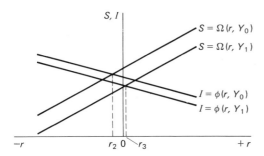

Figure 2.3.

spread uncertainty.[2] The possible effect of this insensitivity on the ability of
the system automatically to generate full employment is analyzed in Figure
2.3. For simplicity the savings functions corresponding to different levels of
income are reproduced from Figure 2.2. But the investment functions are
now represented as being much less interest sensitive than those in Figure
2.2. If the situation in the real world were such as represented in Figure 2.3,
it is clear that interest rate variations could never bring about full employment. For in an economy in which there are negligible costs of storing money,
the interest rate can never be negative.[3] But from Figure 2.3 we see that the
only way the interest rate can equate desired full employment savings and
investment is by assuming the negative value r_2. Hence it is impossible for
the full-employment national income Y_0 to exist: for no matter what
(positive) rate of interest may prevail, the amount people want to save at full
employment exceeds what they want to invest. Instead there will exist some
less than full-employment income (say) Y_1 for which desired savings and
investment can be brought into equality at a positive rate of interest (say)
r_3 (cf. Figure 2.3).

   Thus once again the automaticity of the system is thrown into question.
Whether the system will generate full employment depends on whether the
full-employment savings and investment functions intersect at a positive rate
of interest. But there is no automatic mechanism to assure that the savings
and investment functions will have the proper slopes and positions to bring
about such an intersection.[4]

4.   Sometimes attempts are made to defend the classical position by arguing
that the investment function is really higher (or the savings function lower)
than represented by the Keynesians—so that desired full-employment sav-

[2] Cf. Oscar Lange, *Price Flexibility and Employment* (Bloomington, Indiana, 1945), p. 85
and the literature cited there. For an excellent theoretical discussion of this insensitivity,
cf. G. L. S. Shackle, "Interest-Rates and the Pace of Investment," *Economic Journal*, LVI (1946),
1–17.

   [3] Note that in a dynamic world of rising prices, the effective rate of interest may become
negative. But even here the *anticipated* effective rate cannot be negative. For in that event
there would again be an infinite demand for money.

   [4] I have discussed this whole question of the contrast between the classical and Keynesian
positions in greater detail elsewhere. Cf. "Involuntary Unemployment and the Keynesian
Supply Function," *Economic Journal*, LIX (1949), 376–378.

ings and investment can be equated at a positive rate of interest (cf. Figure 2.3). But this is beside the point. The fundamental disagreement between Keynesian and classical economics lies in the former's denial of the automaticity of full employment posited by the latter. Hence a successful restatement of the classical position must demonstrate the existence of some automatic mechanism which will always bring about full employment. Thus to argue that *if* the investment or saving function is at a certain level, full employment will be brought about is irrelevant; what must be shown is that there exist forces which will *automatically* bring the investment or saving functions to the required level. In other words, the issue at stake is not the *possible*, but the *automatic*, generation of full employment.

5. To the Keynesian negative interest rate argument replies have been made by both Haberler and Pigou.[5] Just as the crude Keynesian argument of Section 1 was answered by introducing a new variable—the rate of interest—into the savings function, so the more refined argument of Section 3 is countered by the introduction of yet another variable—the real value of cash balances held by the individuals in the economy. Thus, denoting the amount of money in the economy by M_1 (assumed to remain constant) and the absolute price level by p, Pigou's saving schedule is written as

$$S = \Gamma\left(r, Y, \frac{M_1}{p}\right).$$

His argument is as follows: if people would refuse to save anything at negative and zero rates of interest, then the desired savings schedule would intersect the desired investment schedule at a positive rate of interest regardless of the level of income (cf. Figure 2.3). The willingness to save even without receiving interest, or even at a cost, must imply that savings are not made solely for the sake of future income (i.e., interest) but also for "the desire for possession as such, conformity to tradition or custom and so on."[6] But the extent to which an individual wishes to save out of current income for reasons other than the desire for future income is inversely related to the real value of his cash balances.[7] If this is sufficiently large, all his secondary desires for saving will be fully satisfied. At this point the only reason he will continue to save out of current income is the primary one of anticipated future interest payments. In other words, if the real value of cash balances is sufficiently

---

[5] G. Haberler, *Prosperity and Depression*, 3rd ed. (Geneva: League of Nations, 1941), pp. 242, 389, 403, 491–503.

A. C. Pigou, "The Classical Stationary State," *Economic Journal*, LIII (1943), 343–351; "Economic Progress in a Stable Environment," *Economica*, XIV (1947), 180–188. Although these articles deal only with a stationary state, their basic argument can readily be extended to the case in which net investment is taking place.

In the subsequent text, I shall follow the exposition of Pigou; but the argument holds also with respect to Haberler.

[6] Pigou, *op. cit.* (1943), p. 346.

[7] And all his other assets too. But the introduction of these other assets does not change Pigou's argument; while concentration on money assets brings out its (the argument's) basic aspect. Cf. below, Section 6.

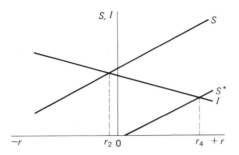

S, I

−r r_2 0 r_4 +r   **Figure 2.4.**

large, the savings function becomes zero at a positive rate of interest, regard-less of the income level.

A graphical interpretation of this argument is presented in Figure 2.4. Here S and I are the full-employment savings and investment curves of Figure 2.3 (i.e., those corresponding to $Y = Y_0$), and r_2 is again the negative rate of interest at which they are equal. Pigou then argues that by increasing the real value of cash balances, the full-employment savings curve shifts to the right until it is in such a position that no savings are desired except at positive rates of interest. This is represented by the savings curve S^*, which becomes zero at a positive rate of interest. (In fact, S^* shows dissaving tak-ing place at sufficiently low rates of interest.) The full-employment savings curve S^* clearly intersects the full-employment investment curve I at the positive rate of interest r_1. Thus by changing the real value of cash balances, desired full-employment savings and investment can always be equated at a positive rate of interest.

How can we be sure that real cash balances will automatically change in the required direction and magnitude? Here Pigou brings in his assump-tions of flexible wage and price levels, and a constant stock of money in circulation. If full-employment saving exceeds investment, national income begins to fall, and unemployment results. If workers react to this by accept-ing a decrease in their money wages, then the price level will also begin to fall. As the latter continues to fall, the real value of the constant stock of money increases correspondingly. Thus, as the price level falls, the full-employment saving function continuously shifts to the right until it inter-sects the full-employment investment function at a positive rate of interest.[8]

---

[8] The exact price level is determined when to our preceding four equations is added the liquidity preference equation, $M_0 = (r, Y, p)$, where M_0 represents the given amount of money in the system. (As will be shown in the next section, the "stock of money" relevant for the liquidity equation is completely different from the "stock of money" relevant for the Pigou analysis of the savings function; hence the use of two different symbols—M_0 and M_1.) We then have the complete system of five equations in five variables:

$$I = \Phi(r, Y)$$
$$S = \Gamma\left(r, Y, \frac{M_1}{p}\right)$$
$$I = S$$
$$Y = Y_0$$
$$M_0 = \Lambda(r, Y, p).$$

This is the automatic mechanism on which Haberler and Pigou rely to assure full employment. It is essential to note that it will operate regardless of the interest-elasticities of the savings and investment functions—provided they are not both identically zero. It should also be emphasized, as Haberler does, that although this argument has been presented above as an answer to Keynes, it is of much older origin. In particular, it is implicit in classical theorizing on the quantity theory of money. The crucial step in this analysis, it will be recalled, comes at the point where it is argued that as a result of increasing the amount of money in the economy, individuals' cash balances are larger than desired at the existing price level, so that they will attempt to reduce these real balances by increasing their money expenditures. The main contribution of Haberler and Pigou is to show how this set of forces must, and can, be introduced into the Keynesian analytical apparatus.

6. The inner mechanism and distinctive characteristic of the Pigou analysis can be laid bare by considering it from a larger perspective. It is obvious that a price reduction has a stimulating effect on creditors. But, restricting ourselves to the private sector of a closed economy, to every stimulated creditor there corresponds a discouraged debtor. Hence from this viewpoint the net effect of a price reduction is likely to be in the neighborhood of zero. The neatness of the Pigou approach lies in its utilizing the fact that although the private sector considered in isolation is, on balance, neither debtor nor creditor, when considered in its relationship to the government, it *must be* a net "creditor." This is due to the fact that the private sector always holds money, which is a (non-interest-bearing) "debt" of government. If we assume that government activity is not affected by the movements of the absolute price level,[9] then the net effect of a price decline must always be stimulatory.[10] The community gains at the "expense" of a gracious government, ready, willing, and able to bear the "loss" of the increased value of its "debt" to the public.

More precisely, not every price decline need have this stimulating effect. For we must consider the effect of the price decline on the other assets held by the individual. If the decline reduces the real value of these other assets (e.g., houses and other forms of consumer capital; stock shares; etc.)

Under the Pigovian assumptions this system is consistent; its equations are satisfied for a positive rate of interest.

The workings of a more general system of equations under the Pigovian assumption are described in detail in Parts IV and V of the reference cited in note 4 above. In this more detailed treatment, the full-employment level, Y_0, is not arbitrarily defined—as it is in the present paper—but emerges instead from the economic behavior functions themselves.

[9] Pigou makes this assumption when he writes the investment function (which presumably also includes government expenditure) as independent of the absolute price level. Cf. note 8 above.

[10] It must be emphasized that I am abstracting here from all dynamic considerations of the effect on anticipations, etc. These will be discussed in Part II below.

to an extent more than offsetting the increased value of real cash balances,[11] then the net effect will be discouraging. But the important point is that no matter what our initial position, *there exists* a price level sufficiently low so that the total real value of assets corresponding to it is greater than the original real value. Consider the extreme case in which the value of the other assets becomes arbitrarily small.[12] Clearly even here the real value of the fixed stock of money can be made as large as desired by reducing the price level sufficiently. Thus, to be rigorous, the statement in the preceding paragraph should read: "There always exists a price decline such that its effect is stimulatory." From this and the analysis of the preceding section, we can derive another statement which succinctly summarizes the results of the Pigou analysis: "In the static classical model, regardless of the position of the investment schedule, there always exists a sufficiently low price level such that full employment is generated." In any event, it is clearly sufficient to concentrate (as Pigou has done) on cash balances alone.[13]

This analysis is subject to at least two reservations, neither one of which has been considered by Haberler or Pigou. First of all, we have tacitly been assuming that the depressing effect of a price decline on a debtor is roughly offset by its stimulating effect on a creditor; hence the private sector, being on balance a creditor with respect to the government, can ultimately be stimulated by a price decline. But allowance must be made for the possibility of a differential reaction of debtors and creditors. That is, if debtors are discouraged by a price decline much more than creditors are encouraged, it may be possible that there exists no price decline which would have an encouraging effect on expenditures. In brief, the Keynesian aggregative analysis followed by Pigou overlooks the possibility of micro-economic "distribution effects."

Secondly, we have so far considered only the effects of a change in real balances on household behavior; that is, on the consumption (or, its counterpart, the savings) function. It seems only natural to extend the analysis to include the influence of real cash balances on firms, and, hence, on the investment function as well. However, this extension cannot be made automatically, inasmuch as the respective motivations of firms and house-holds are not necessarily the same. Nevertheless, it does seem reasonable to assume that investment decisions of firms are favorably influenced by a higher level of real balances. Once we take account of firms, the differential reactions mentioned in the preceding paragraph become increasingly significant. If firms are, on balance, debtors with respect to households and

---

[11] A necessary (but not sufficient) condition for this to occur is that the price level of assets falls in a greater proportion than the general price level.

[12] I am indebted to M. Friedman for this example.

[13] Cf. above, note 7. Another possible reason for Pigou's emphasis on cash balances to the exclusion of other assets is that the relative illiquidity of the latter makes them less likely to be used as a means of satisfying the "irrational" motives of saving. Hence the inverse relationship between other assets and savings out of current income might not be so straight-forward as that between real cash balances and savings.

government, then a persistent price decline will cause a wave of bankrupt-cies. This will have a seriously depressing effect upon the economy which may not be offset by the improved status of creditors. Furthermore, in most cases of bankruptcy the creditors also lose. For these reasons it is not at all certain that a price decline will result in a positive net effect on the total expenditures (consumption plus investment) function. On this point much further investigation—of a theoretical as well as an empirical nature—is required.

From the preceding analysis we can also see just exactly what con-stitutes the "cash balance" whose increase in real value provides the stimulatory effect of the Pigou analysis. This balance clearly consists of the net obligation of the government to the private sector of the economy. That is, it consists primarily of the total interest- and non-interest-bearing govern-ment debt held outside the treasury and central bank, plus the net amount owed by the central bank to member banks. Thus, by excluding demand deposits and including government interest-bearing debt and member bank reserves, it differs completely from what is usually regarded as the stock of money.

These same conclusions can be reached through a somewhat different approach. Begin with the ordinary concept of the stock of money as con-sisting of hand-to-hand currency and demand deposits. Consider now what changes must be made in order to arrive at the figure relevant for the Pigou analysis. Clearly, government interest-bearing debt must be added, since a price decline increases its value. Now consider money in the form of demand deposits. To the extent that it is backed by bank loans and discounts, the gains of deposit holders are offset by the losses of bank debtors.[14] Thus the net effect of a price decline on demand deposits is reduced to its effect on the excess of deposits over loans, or (approximately) on the reserves of the banks held in the form of hand-to-hand currency and deposits in the central bank. Finally, hand-to-hand currency held by individuals outside the banking system is added in, and we arrive at exactly the same figure as in the preceding paragraph.

For convenience denote the stock of money relevant for the Pigou analysis by M_1. Note that this is completely different from M_0 of footnote 8: for M_0 is defined in the usual manner as hand-to-hand currency plus demand deposits. This distinction is of fundamental importance. One of its immediate implications is that central bank open-market operations which do not change the market price of government bonds affect the economic system only through the liquidity preference equation. Since such operations merely substitute one type of government debt (currency) for another (bonds), they have no effect on M_1 and hence no direct effect on the amount of savings. Even when open-market purchases do cause an increase in the price of government bonds, the changes in M_0 and M_1 will not, in general, be equal.

[14] Cf. M. Kalecki, "Professor Pigou on 'The Classical Stationary State'—A Comment," *Economic Journal*, LIV (1944), 131–132.

The increase in M_0 equals the total amount of money expended for the purchase of the bonds; the increase in M_1 equals the increase in the value of bonds (both of those bought and those not bought by the central bank) caused by the open-market operations.[15] Corresponding statements can be made for open-market sales.

7. How does the Pigou formulation compare with the original classical theory?[16] Although both Pigou and the "classics" stress the importance of "price flexibility," they mean by this term completely different things. The "classics" are talking about flexibility of relative prices; Pigou is talking about flexibility of absolute prices. The classical school holds that the existence of long-run unemployment is *prima facie* evidence of rigid wages. The only way to eliminate unemployment is, then, by reducing *real* wages. (Since workers can presumably accomplish this end by reducing their *money* wage, this position has implicit in it the assumption of a constant price level—or at least one falling relatively less than wages.) Pigou now recognizes that changing the relative price of labor is not enough, and that the absolute price level itself must vary. In fact, a strict interpretation of Pigou's position would indicate that unemployment can be eliminated even if real wages remain the same or even rise (namely, if the proportionate fall in prices is greater than or equal to that of wages); for in any case the effect of increased real value of cash balances is still present.[17]

The Pigou analysis also differs from those interpretations of the classical position which, following Keynes, present the effect of a wage decrease as acting through the liquidity preference equation to increase the real value of M_0 and thereby reduce the rate of interest; this in turn stimulates both consumption and investment expenditures—thus generating a higher level of national income. To this effect Pigou now adds the direct stimulus to consumption expenditures provided by the price decline and the accompanying increase in real balances. Consequently, even if the savings and investment functions are completely insensitive to changes in the rate of interest (so that the effect through the liquidity equation is completely

[15] It might be argued that through their effect on the interest rate, open-market purchases affect the value of assets other than government securities; hence, this change in value should also be included in the change in M_1. This is a point which deserves further investigation. The main question is whether there exists an offset to this improvement in the position of bondholders of private corporations.

[16] Pigou, of course, introduces the absolute price level into the analysis of the real sector of the economy, whereas classical economics insists that this sector must be considered on the basis of relative prices alone. As I have shown elsewhere, on this point classical economics is definitely wrong. For, in a money economy, the demand for any good must, in general, depend on the absolute price level, as well as on relative prices. This is a direct result of utility maximization. Cf. my "A Reconsideration of the General Equilibrium Theory of Money," *Review of Economic Studies*, XVIII (1950), Section 3, and references cited there.

[17] The role of real wages in Pigou's system is very ambiguous. At one point he assumes that reduced money wages will also decrease real wages [*op. cit.* (1943), p. 348, bottom]. At another no such assumption seems to be involved. "As money wage-rates fall . . . prices fall and go on falling" (*ibid.*, p. 349, lines 20–38).

inoperative), a wage decrease will still be stimulatory through its effect on real balances and hence on savings.

8. Before concluding this part of the paper, one more point must be clarified. The explicit assumption of the Pigou analysis is that savings are directly related to the price level, and therefore inversely related to the size of real cash balances. This assumption by itself is, on *a priori* grounds, quite reasonable; indeed, in a money economy it is a direct implication of utility maximization (above, note 16). But it must be emphasized that even if we disregard the reservations mentioned in the preceding sections, this assumption is insufficient to bring about the conclusion desired by Pigou. For this purpose he *implicitly* makes an additional, and possibly less reasonable, assumption. Specifically, in addition to postulating explicitly the direction of the relationship between savings and the price level, he also implies something about its *intensity*.

The force of this distinction is illustrated by Figure 2.5. Here S and I are the full employment savings and investment curves of Figure 2.3 (i.e., those corresponding to $Y = Y_0$) for a fixed price level, p_0. The other savings curves, S_1, S_2, S_3, S_4, represent the full employment savings schedules corresponding to the different price levels p_1, p_2, p_3, p_4, respectively. In accordance with the Pigou assumption, as the price level falls, the savings function shifts over to the right. (That is p_1, p_2, p_3, p_4 are listed in descending order.) But it may well be that as the real value of their cash balances continues to increase, people are less and less affected by this increase. That is, for each successive increase in real balances (for each successive price level decline) the savings function moves less and less to the right, until eventually it might respond only infinitesimally, no matter how much prices fall. In graphical terms, as the price decline continues, the savings function might reach S_3 as a limiting position. That is, no matter how much the price level might fall, the savings function would never move to the right of S_3.[18] In such an event the declining price level would fail to bring about full employment. The validity of the Pigou argument thus depends on the additional assumption that the intensity of the inverse relationship between savings

---

[18] Mathematically this may be stated as follows. Write the savings function as

$$S = \Gamma\ (r, p, Y).$$

(Cf. note 8, above.) Pigou's explicit assumption is

$$\Gamma_p(r, p, Y) > 0$$

where Γ_p is the partial derivative of S with respect to p. Let $Y = Y_0$ represent the full-employment income. Then the argument here is that the savings function, Γ, may still be of a form such that

$$\lim_{p \to 0} \Gamma(r, p, Y_0) = \Gamma^*(r, Y_0)$$

for any fixed r—where Γ^* is any curve which intersects the investment curve at a negative rate of interest. (In the argument of the text, Γ^* is taken to be S_2 in Figure 2.5.) Pigou tacitly assumes that the savings function approaches no such limit; or that if it does, the limiting function intersects the investment function at a positive rate of interest.

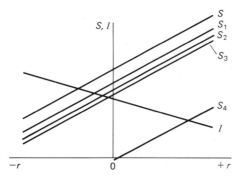

Figure 2.5.

and real cash balances is such that it will be possible to shift over the savings function to a position where it will intercept the investment function at a positive rate of interest: say, S_1 (cf. Figure 2.5).

What is at issue here is the reaction of individuals with already large real balances to further increases in these balances. Consider an individual with a cash balance of a fixed number of dollars. As the price falls, the increased real value of these dollars must be allocated between the alternatives of an addition to either consumption and/or real balances.[19] How the individual will actually allocate the increase clearly depends on the relative marginal utilities of these two alternatives. If we are willing to assume that the marginal utility of cash balances approaches zero with sufficient rapidity relative to that of consumption, then we can ignore the possibility of the savings curve reaching a limiting position such as in Figure 2.5. That is, we should be maintaining the position that by increasing the individual's balances sufficiently, he will have no further incentive to add to these balances; hence he will spend any additional real funds on consumption, so that we can make him consume any amount desired. If, on the other hand, we admit the possibility that, for sufficiently large consumption, the decrease in the marginal utility of cash balances is accompanied by a much faster decrease in the marginal utility of consumption, then the individual will continuously use most of the additional real funds (made available by the price decline) to add to his balances. In this event, the situation of Figure 2.5 may well occur.

9.   I do not believe we have sufficient evidence—either of an *a priori* or empirical[20] nature—to help us answer the question raised in the preceding paragraph. The empirical evidence available is consistent with the hypothesis that the effect of real balances on savings is very weak. But even granted the truth of this hypothesis, it casts no light on the question raised here. What we

---

[19] I am abstracting here from the possible third alternative, investment.

[20] Empirical studies on the effect of real balances on savings have been made by L. R. Klein, "The Use of Econometric Models as a Guide to Economic Policy," *Econometrica*, XV (1947), 122–125. Klein's procedure was incorrect in that he used a series for M_0, instead of M_1, in fitting his equations (cf. last paragraph of Section 6 above).

want to know is what happens to the effect of real balances on savings as these real balances increase in size. Even if the effect were arbitrarily small, but remained constant regardless of the size of real balances, there could be no convergence of savings functions like that pictured in Figure 2.5. In the face of this lack of evidence, we have to be satisfied with the conclusion that, subject to the reservations of Sections 6 and 8, Haberler and Pigou have demonstrated the automaticity of full employment within the framework of the classical static model[21]—the main mechanism by which this is brought about being the effect of a price decline on cash balances.

The statement of this conclusion immediately raises the interesting question of how this set of forces, emphasized by Haberler and Pigou, could have been overlooked by Keynesian economists, in general, and Keynes himself, in particular. Questions of this type can rarely be answered satisfactorily—and perhaps should not even be asked. Nevertheless, I think it is both possible and instructive to trace through the exact chain of errors in Keynes reasoning which caused him to overlook these factors.

I submit the hypothesis that Keynes recognized the influence of assets on saving (consumption), but unfortunately thought of this influence only in terms of physical capital assets. This was his fundamental error.[22] From it immediately followed that in his main discussion of the (short-run) consumption function, where he assumed a *constant* stock of capital, the possible influence of assets was not (and could not) even be considered.[23] But as soon as Keynes discussed a period sufficiently long for noticeable capital growth, the influence of assets on savings was immediately recognized.[24] Even here, Keynes could not come to the same conclusion as Pigou. For Keynes restricted himself to physical assets, and thus rightly pointed out that it would be "an unlikely coincidence" that just the correct amount of assets should exist—i.e., that amount which would push over the savings function to a position where full employment could be generated. Compare this with the determinate process by which just exactly the "correct amount" of real cash balances is brought into existence in the Pigou analysis. (See above, Section 5, paragraph 4.)

This exclusion of physical assets from the short-run consumption function was subconsciously extended to all kinds of assets. Here was the last link in the chain of errors. For later when Keynes began to examine the effects of increased real cash balances (brought about either by price declines or increases in the amount of money), he did not even consider their possible influence on consumption. Instead, he concentrated exclusively on their

[21] It must be re-emphasized that this conclusion holds only for static analysis. The modifications that must be introduced once dynamic factors enter are discussed in Part II.

[22] Note that there are really two distinct errors involved here. The first is the obvious one of the exclusion of monetary assets. The second is that what is relevant for the influence on saving is not the *physical* asset, but its *real* value in terms of some general price level.

[23] J. M. Keynes, *The General Theory of Employment, Interest and Money* (New York, 1936), Chapter 8. See especially pp. 91–95 where Keynes considers the possible influence of other factors besides income on consumption, and does not even mention assets.

[24] *Ibid.*, p. 218, second paragraph.

tendency, through the liquidity function, to lower interest rates.[25] (Cf. above, Section 7, last paragraph.)

Looking back on the nature of these errors, we cannot but be struck by the irony that they should have emanated from the man who did most to demonstrate the fundamental inseparability of the real and monetary sectors of our economy.

II. DYNAMIC ANALYSIS: THE QUESTION OF POLICY

10. The Haberler-Pigou analysis discussed in Part I makes two contributions. First, in its emphasis on the effects of a price on savings *via* its effects on real balances, it introduces into the Keynesian analytical apparatus a set of forces hitherto overlooked by the latter. (For convenience this will be referred to as the Pigou effect—though, as mentioned at the end of Section 5 above, it is of much older origin.) Secondly, it proceeds to draw the implications of this set of forces for static analysis, and summarizes its results in the following theorem (cf. Sections 5 and 6): *There always exists a sufficiently low price level such that, if expected to continue indefinitely,*[26] *it will generate full employment.*[27] (For convenience this will be referred to as the Pigou Theorem.) The purpose of this part of the paper is to accomplish a third objective: viz., to draw the implications of the Pigou effect for dynamic analysis and policy formulation. It must be emphasized that the Pigou Theorem tells us nothing about the dynamic and policy aspects which interest us in this third objective. (This point is discussed in greater detail in Section 12.)

Specifically, consider a full-employment situation which is suddenly terminated by a downswing in economic activity. The question I now wish to examine is the usefulness of a policy which consists of maintaining the stock of money constant, allowing the wage and price levels to fall, and waiting for the resulting increase in real balances to restore full employment.

At the outset it must be made clear that the above policy recommendation is *not* to be attributed to Pigou. His interest is purely an intellectual one, in a purely static analysis. As he himself writes: " . . . The puzzles we have been considering . . . are academic exercises, of some slight use perhaps

---

[25] *Ibid.*, pp. 231–234, 266. The following passage is especially interesting: "It is, therefore, on the effect of a falling wage- and price-level on the *demand for money* that those who believe in the self-adjusting quality of the economic system must rest the weight of their argument; though I am not aware that they have done so. If the quantity of money is itself a function of the wage- and price-level, there is, indeed, nothing to hope for in this direction. But if the quantity of money is virtually fixed, it is evident that its quantity in terms of wage-units can be indefinitely increased by a sufficient reduction in money wages. . . ." (*Ibid.*, p. 266. Italics not in original.)

[26] This qualifying phrase incorporates in it the restriction of the Pigou argument to static analysis.

[27] I am overlooking here the reservations discussed in Sections 6 and 8 above.

for clarifying thought, but with very little chance of ever being posed on the chequer board of actual life."[28]

In reality, Pigou's disavowal of a deflationary policy (contained in the paragraph from which the above quotation is taken) is not nearly as thoroughgoing as might appear on the first reading. The rejection of a price decline as a practical means of combating unemployment may be due to: (a) the conviction that dynamic considerations invalidate its use as an immediate policy, regardless of its merits in static analysis; (b) the conviction that industrial and labor groups, sometimes with the assistance of government, prevent the price flexibility necessary for the success of a deflationary policy. A careful reading of Pigou's disclaimer indicates that he had only the second of these alternatives in mind; i.e., that he felt that the policy would not work because it would not be permitted to work. What I hope to establish in this part of the essay is the first alternative: namely, that even granted full flexibility of prices, it is still highly possible that a deflationary policy would not work, due to the dynamic factors involved.

Nevertheless, nothing in this part of the paper is intended (or even relevant) as a criticism of Pigou, since the latter has clearly abstained from the problem of policy formulation. If sometimes the terms "Pigou effect" and "Pigou Theorem" are used in the following discussion, they should be understood solely as shorthand notations for the concepts previously explained.

11.   The analysis of this section is based on the following two assumptions: (a) One of the prerequisites of a successful anti-depression policy is that it should be able to achieve its objective rapidly (say, within a year). (b) Prices cannot fall instantaneously; hence, the larger the price level fall necessary to bring about full employment via the Pigou effect, the longer the time necessary for the carrying out of the policy. (If no price fall can bring about full employment, then we can say that an infinite amount of time is necessary for the carrying out of the policy.)

There are at least two factors which act toward lengthening the period necessary to carry out a policy based on the Pigou effect. The first is the possibility that the effect of an increase in cash balances on consumption is so small, that very large increases (very great price declines) will be necessary. Certainly there is a burden of proof on the supporters of a policy of absolute price flexibility to show that this is not so; that the economic system is sufficiently responsive to make the policy practical. So far no one has presented the required evidence.

The second factor is a result of the price decline itself. In dynamic analysis we must give full attention to the role played by price expectations and anticipations in general. It is quite possible that the original price decline will lead to the expectation of further declines. Then purchasing

[28] *Op. cit.* (1947), p. 188.

decisions will be postponed, aggregate demand will fall off, and the amount of unemployment increased still more. In terms of Figures 2.1 and 2.3, the savings function will rise (consumption will be decreased) and the investment function fall, further aggravating the problem of achieving full employment. This was the point on which Keynes was so insistent.[29] Furthermore, the uncertainty about the future generated by the price decline will increase the liquidity preference of individuals. Thus if we consider an individual possessing a fixed number of dollars, and confronted with a price decline which increases the real value of these dollars, his uncertainty will make him more inclined to employ these additional real funds to increase his real balances, than to increase his expenditures.[30] In other words, the uncertainty created by the price decline might cause people to accumulate indefinitely large real cash balances, and to increase their expenditures very little if at all. Finally, the bankruptcies caused by the inability of creditors to carry the increased real burden of their debt (above, Section 6) will strengthen the pessimistic outlook for the future. The simultaneous interaction of these three forces will further exacerbate these difficulties. For as the period of price decline drags itself out, anticipations for the future will progressively worsen, and uncertainties further increase. The end result of letting the Pigou effect work itself out may be a disastrous deflationary spiral, continuing for several years without ever reaching any equilibrium position. Certainly our past experiences should have sensitized us to this danger.

Because of these considerations I feel that it is impractical to depend upon the Pigou effect as a means of policy: the required price decline might be either too large (factor one), or it might be the initial step of an indefinite deflationary spiral (factor two).

On this issue, it may be interesting to investigate the experience of the United States in the 1930s. In Table 2.1, net balances are computed for the period 1929–1932 according to the definition in Section 6. As can be seen, although there was a 19 percent *increase* in real balances from 1930 to 1931, real national income during this period *decreased* by 13 percent. Even in the following year, when a further increase of 19 percent in real balances took place, real income proceeded to fall by an additional 18 percent. For the 1929–1932 period as a whole there was an increase in real balances of 46 percent, and a decrease in real income of 40 percent.

It will, of course, be objected that these data reflect the presence of "special factors," and do not indicate the real value of the Pigou effect. But the pertinent question which immediately arises is: To what extent were these "special factors" necessary, concomitant results of the price decline itself! If the general feeling of uncertainty and adverse anticipations that marked the period is cited as one of these "special factors," the direct

---

[29] See his discussion of changes in money wages, *op. cit.*, pp. 260–269, especially p. 263. Cf. also J. R. Hicks, *Value and Capital* (Oxford, 1939), and O. Lange, *op. cit.*

[30] Cf. above, Section 8, last paragraph.

Table 2.1

Year	Money in Circulation Outside Treasury and Federal Reserve System (1)	Market Value of Government Interest-bearing Debt Held Outside Government Agencies and the Federal Reserve System (2)	Member Bank Deposits in the Federal Reserve System (3)	Non-member Bank Deposits in the Federal Reserve System (4)	Other Federal Reserve Accounts (5)	Reserve Bank Credit Outstanding Excluding that Based on Reserve Bank Holdings of U.S. Government Securities (6)	Treasury Deposits in Member and Non-member Banks (7)	Postal Savings (8)	Net Balances (M_1) $(1) + (2) + (3) + (4) + (5) - (6) - (7) + (8)$ (9)	Cost of Living Index (p) (10)	Net Real Balances $\frac{M_1}{p}$ $(9) \div (10)$ (11)	Real National Income (12)
1929	4.5	14.5	2.4	0.0	0.4	1.3	0.4	0.2	20.2	1.22	16.6	89.9
1930	4.2	13.9	2.4	0.0	0.4	0.5	0.3	0.2	20.4	1.19	17.1	76.3
1931	4.7	15.1	2.3	0.1	0.4	0.6	0.4	0.6	22.1	1.09	20.3	66.3
1932	5.3	16.0	2.1	0.1	0.4	0.6	0.4	0.9	23.7	0.98	24.2	54.2

NOTES: All money figures are in billions of dollars.

Data for series (1), (3), (4), (5), (6) were obtained from *Banking and Monetary Statistics*, p. 368. On pp. 360–367 of this book their interrelationships are discussed. For (7) see *ibid.*, pp. 34–35. For (8) see *Statistical Abstract of the United States, 1947*, p. 419.

Being unable to find an official series for (2), I used the following procedure: Total outstanding government debt at face value was classified according to maturities (0–5 years, 5–10, and over 10) on the basis of *Banking and Monetary Statistics*, p. 511. These classifications were multiplied by price indexes for government bonds with maturities of more than 3 and less than 4 years, more than 6 and less than 9, and more than 10, respectively (Standard and Poor, *Statistics: Security Price Index Record*, 1948 edition, pp. 139–144). The sum of these products was used as an estimate of the market value of the total government debt. The ratio of this to the face value of the total debt was computed, and this ratio applied to the face value of government debt held outside the Treasury and Federal Reserve System (*Banking and Monetary Statistics*, p. 512) to yield an estimate of the required series.

Series (10): Bureau of Labor Statistics, cost of living index, *Survey of Current Business*, Supplement, 1942, p. 16.

Series (12): National income in billions of 1944 dollars. J. Dewhurst and Associates, *America's Needs and Resources* (New York: The Twentieth Century Fund, 1947), p. 697.

relationship between this and the decline in price level itself certainly cannot be overlooked. Other proposed "special factors" must be subjected to the same type of examination. The data of the accompanying table are not offered as conclusive evidence. But they are certainly consistent with the previously stated hypothesis of the impracticability of using the Pigou effect as a means of policy; and they certainly throw the burden of proof on those who argue for its practicality.

12.   The argument of the preceding section requires further explanation on at least one point. In the discussion of the "second factor" there was mentioned the possibility of an indefinitely continuing spiral of deflation and unemployment. But what is the relation between this possibility and the Pigou Theorem (cf. Section 10) established in Part I? The answer to this question may be expressed as follows:

   On the downswing of the business cycle it might be interesting to know that there exists a sufficiently low price level which, if it were expected to continue existing indefinitely, would bring about full employment. Interesting, but, for policy purposes, irrelevant. For due to perverse price expectations and the dynamics of deflationary spirals, it is impossible to reach (or, once having reached, to remain at) such a position.

   The implication of these remarks can be clarified by consideration of the cobweb theorem for the divergent case. Assume that a certain market can be explained in terms of the cobweb theorem. It is desired to know whether (assuming unchanged demand and supply curves) the designated market will ever reach a stationary position; that is, whether it will settle down to a unique price that will continue indefinitely to clear the market. This question is clearly divided into two parts: (a) does there exist such a price, and (b) if it does exist, will the market be able to attain it. In the case of the cobweb presented in Figure 2.6 it is clear that such a price does exist. For if the price P_0 had always existed and were expected to exist indefinitely, it would continuously clear the market. But Figure 2.6 represents the case of a divergent cobweb; hence the market will never be able to reach the price p_0. In brief, even though p_0 exists, it is irrelevant to the workings of the mar-

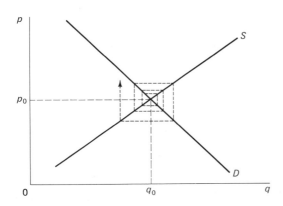

Figure 2.6.

ket. The analogy to the argument presented in the preceding paragraph is obvious.[31]

III. CONCLUSIONS

13.   The conclusions of this paper can be summarized as follows: in a static world with a constant stock of money,[32] price flexibility assures full employment. (I abstract here again from the difficulties raised in Sections 6 and 8.) But in the real dynamic world in which we live, price flexibility with a constant stock of money might generate full employment only after a long period; or might even lead to a deflationary spiral of continuous unemployment. On either of these grounds, a full-employment policy based on a constant stock of money and price flexibility does not seem to be very promising.

All that this means is that our full-employment policy cannot be the fairly simple one of maintaining a constant stock of money and waiting for the economic system to generate full employment automatically through price declines. Other policies will be required. One possible alternative policy can be inferred from the Haberler-Pigou analysis itself: there are two ways to increase real balances. One is to keep the money stock constant

---

[31] The distinction of this section can be expressed in rigorous mathematical form using the dynamic system which has become familiar through the work of Samuelson and Lange [P. A. Samuelson, "The Stability of Equilibrium: Comparative Statics and Dynamics," *Econometrica*, IX (1941), 97–120; Lange, *op. cit.*, pp. 91 ff.]. Consider a single market and let D, S, and p represent the demand, supply, and price of the particular good, respectively. Let t represent time. Then we can write this system as

(a) $D = f(p)$ demand function
(b) $S = g(p)$ supply function
(c) $\dfrac{dp}{dt} = h(D - S)$ market adjusting function

The last equation has the property that

(d) sign $\dfrac{dp}{dt}$ = sign $(D - S)$

i.e., price rises with excess demand and falls with excess supply. Consider now the static system identical with (a)–(c), except that it replaces (c) by
(e) $D = S$
As long as (e) is not satisfied, we see from (d) that the system will not be in stationary equilibrium, but will continue to fluctuate. Thus the existence of a solution to the static system (a), (b), (e) [i.e., the consistency of (a), (b), (e)] is a *necessary* condition for the existence of a stationary solution for the dynamic system (a), (b), (c). But this is not a sufficient condition. For the static system (a), (b), (e) may have a consistent solution which, if the dynamic system is not convergent, will never be reached.

Thus Pigou has completed only half the task. Setting aside the difficulties of Section 8, we can accept his proof of the *consistency* of the *static* classical system. But that still leaves completely unanswered the question of whether the classical *dynamic* system will converge to this consistent solution. In this and the preceding section I have tried to show why such convergence may not occur in the real world. (I have discussed these issues in greater detail elsewhere. Cf. note 4 above.)

[32] Throughout Part III, unless otherwise indicated, "stock of money" is to be understood in the M_1 sense of the last paragraph of Section 6.

and permit prices to fall. An equally effective way is to maintain the price level constant, and increase the stock of money by creating a government deficit.[33] This method of increasing real balances has the added advantage of avoiding one of the difficulties encountered previously (Section 11), for a policy of stabilizing the price level by increasing money stocks avoids some of the dangers of uncertainty and adverse anticipation accompanying general price declines. Nevertheless, there still remains the other difficulty— that individuals may not be very sensitive to increases in real balances. If this turned out to be true, we would have to seek still other policies.

14. On the basis of the analysis presented in this paper it is possible to re-examine the question which has been a favorite one of economists these past years: namely, what is the distinctive characteristic of Keynesian analysis? It certainly cannot be the claim to have demonstrated the possibility of the coexistence of underemployment equilibrium and flexible prices. This, in its day, served well as a rallying cry. But now it should be definitely recognized that this is an indefensible position. For flexibility means that the money wage falls with excess supply, and rises with excess demand; and equilibrium means that the system can continue on through time without change. Hence, *by definition*, a system with price flexibility cannot be in equilibrium if there is any unemployment;[34] but, like any other proposition that must be true by definition, this one, too, is uninteresting, unimportant, and uninformative about the real problems of economic policy.

Nor should Keynesian economics be interpreted as asserting that just as an underemployment equilibrium is impossible, so, too, in a static system may a full-employment equilibrium be impossible. That is, the static system

---

[33] Considered from this perspective, the Pigou analysis presents in a rigorous fashion part of the theoretical framework implicit in the fiscal-monetary policy of the Simons-Mints position. Cf. the recently published collection of essays of Henry C. Simons, *Economic Policy for a Free Society* (Chicago, 1948); and Lloyd W. Mints, "Monetary Policy," *Review of Economic Statistics*, XXVIII (1946), 60–69.

[34] This can be expressed mathematically in the following way: let N^S and N^D be the amounts of labor supplied and demanded, respectively; w, the money wage rate; and t, time. Then a flexible dynamic system will, by definition, contain an equation of the general type

$$\frac{dw}{dt} = f(N^D - N^S)$$

where

$$\text{sign} \frac{dw}{dt} = \text{sign} (N^D - N^S).$$

If by equilibrium is meant a situation such that

$$\frac{dw}{dt} = 0$$

then clearly this system cannot be in equilibrium unless

$$N^D - N^S = 0$$

i.e., unless there is full employment.

may be at neither an underemployment equilibrium, nor a full-employment equilibrium. In other words, the static system may be inconsistent. (This is the negative interest rate argument of Section 3.) For Pigou's and Haberler's discussion of the effect of a declining price level on real balances shows how this inconsistency is removed. It is, of course, still possible to maintain this interpretation of Keynes on the basis of the reservations of Sections 6 and 8. But I think this is neither necessary nor advisable. For the real significance of the Keynesian contribution can be realized only within the framework of *dynamic* economics. Whether or not an underemployment equilibrium exists; whether or not full-employment equilibrium always will be generated in a static system—all this is irrelevant. The fundamental issue raised by Keynesian economics is the *stability of the dynamic system*: its ability to return automatically to a full-employment equilibrium within a reasonable time (say, a year) if it is subjected to the customary shocks and disturbances of a peacetime economy. In other words, what Keynesian economics claims is that the economic system may be in a position of underemployment *dis*-equilibrium (in the sense that wages, prices, and the amount of unemployment are continuously changing over time) for long, or even indefinite, periods of time.

But this is not sufficient to characterize the Keynesians. Everyone agrees that there exist dynamic systems which will not automatically generate full employment. What distinguishes one economic school from the other is the system (or systems) to which this lack of automaticity is attributed. If the Keynesian message is applied to an economic system with no monetary policy (if such a thing is possible to define), then it is purely trivial. For few would claim automaticity of full employment for such a system. Keynesian theory acquires meaning only when applied to systems with more intelligent monetary policies. Here an element of arbitrariness is introduced; for what is termed "Keynesian" depends entirely on the choice of the monetary policy to be used as a criterion.

On the basis of Keynes' writings, I believe it is clear that he was primarily interested in attacking the policy of assuring full employment by manipulation of the interest rate through open-market operations.[35] But to Keynes, this policy was equivalent to one of wage flexibility;[36] for (he erroneously thought) the only effect of a wage decline was to increase the real value of the stock of money (in the M_0, not M_1, sense; cf. above, last paragraph of Section 6) and thereby decrease the rate of interest—just as in open-market operations. As we have pointed out above (end of Sections 6 and 7), these policies are really not equivalent. For open-market operations may change only M_0, whereas a wage and price decline change the real value of M_1 as well. Hence, open-market operations may act only through the liquidity prefer-

[35] Cf. Keynes, *op. cit.*, pp. 231–234; 266–267.

[36] "There is, therefore, no ground for the belief that a flexible wage policy is capable of maintaining a state of continuous full employment;—any more than for the belief that an open market monetary policy is capable, unaided, of achieving this result. The economic system cannot be made self-adjusting along these lines." (*Ibid.*, p. 267.)

ence equation, whereas a policy of price flexibility acts also through the savings function (cf. above, note 8 and end of Sections 6 and 7).

Let us now assume that even if Keynes had recognized the distinction between open-market and wage flexibility policies (i.e., if he had recognized the Pigou effect) he still would have continued to reject the latter as a means of assuring full employment. This is not an unreasonable assumption; for most of the objections cited above (Section 11) against the use of a policy based on the Pigou effect are the very same ones that Keynes uses in arguing against open-market operations.[37]

Granted this assumption, I believe it is useful to identify the Keynesian position against one which maintains that full employment can be automatically achieved via the Pigou effect by maintaining a constant stock of money, and providing for wage and price flexibility. It is now possible to delineate three distinct theoretical formulations of the Keynesian position—differing in varying degrees from the classical one: (a) Most opposed to the classical position is the Keynesian one which states that even if there were no problem of uncertainty and adverse anticipations (that is, even if there were a static system), and even if we were to allow an infinite amount of time for adjustment, a policy of price flexibility would still not assure the generation of full employment. (This is the negative interest rate argument of Sections 3 and 8; or the argument based on differential creditor-debtor responses of Section 6.) (b) Then there is the position which states that, in a static world, price flexibility would always assure full employment. But in a dynamic world of uncertainty and adverse anticipations, even if we were to allow an infinite adjustment period, there is no certainty that full employment will be generated. That is, we may remain indefinitely in a position of underemployment disequilibrium. (c) Finally, there is the Keynesian position, closest to the "classics," which states that even with uncertainty full employment would eventually be generated by a policy of price flexibility; but the length of time that might be necessary for the adjustment makes the policy impractical.

Although these positions are quite distinct theoretically, their policy implications are very similar. [In what way would the policies of a man advocating position (a) differ from those of a man advocating (c) and stating that the adjustment would take ten years?] The policies would in general be directed at influencing the consumption and investment functions themselves, in addition to manipulating the amount of money. Thus the policies may advocate tax reductions to stimulate consumption and investment (the Simons-Mints school); or may insist on direct government investment to supplement private investment (Hansen *et al.*). In this way we could cross-classify Keynesian positions according to their advocated policies, as well as their theoretical foundations.

Finally, it should be noted that none of the preceding three formulations of the Keynesian position is dependent upon the assumption of wage rigidities. This assumption is frequently, and erroneously, attributed to Keynesian

[37] Cf. the passages cited in note 35 above.

economics as a result of two related misconceptions as to its nature. First of all, as we have seen, the attempt to interpret Keynes' analysis of unemployment within a static equilibrium framework makes it mandatory, by definition, to assume the existence of wage rigidities. The dynamic approach followed in this paper obviates this necessity.

A second implication of restricting ourselves to static equilibrium analysis is that *involuntary* unemployment can, *by definition*, exist only if there are wage rigidities. For if there were no wage rigidities, the wage level could assume any value; and for each such value there would be a corresponding, and presumably, different, amount of labor supplied. Thus at the intersection point of the demand and supply curves—the only point of interest in static equilibrium analysis—workers are providing all the labor they wish to at the equilibrium wage. There can be no question of involuntary unemployment. Only if there are wage rigidities—a minimum wage w_0, below which the workers refuse to go—can the situation be different. For then the supply curve of labor is parallel to the quantity axis at the height w_0 until a certain point (say) N_1 is reached; only afterwards does the curve begin to rise. If the demand curve is now assumed to intersect the supply curve in its horizontal portion at, say, the quantity N_0, then we can say that *involuntary* unemployment to the extent $N_1 - N_0$ exists; for at the equilibrium wage rate, w_0, workers desire to provide a maximum of N_1 units of labor, and are instead providing only N_0.

However, once we throw off the restrictions of static equilibrium analysis, we also free ourselves of the necessity of assuming wage rigidity as a necessary precondition of involuntary unemployment. For, during any given period of time, the dynamic workings of the system may well keep the workers at a point *off their supply curve*. In this departure from the supply curve lies the *involuntariness* of the unemployment. The important point here is that this situation can exist regardless of the shape of the supply curve; that is, even if wages are not rigid. One's view on the length of time such a situation can continue clearly depends on one's choice of the three alternative Keynesian positions delineated above. All this has been dealt with at length elsewhere,[38] and there is no need for any further repetition here.[39]

---

[38] Cf. reference cited in note 4 above.

[39] It might be added that in the light of Chapter 19 of the *General Theory*—the chapter which provides the climax to Keynes' argument, and which explicitly examines the effects of wage flexibility—it is difficult to understand how wage rigidities can be considered a basic assumption of the Keynesian theory of unemployment. From this chapter it is quite clear that wage rigidities are *not* an *assumption* of Keynes' analysis, but rather a policy conclusion that follows from his investigation of the probable effects of *wage flexibility*.

Further explicit evidence that Keynes, in his theory of unemployment, was concerned with a regime of flexible prices is provided by the following passage from the *General Theory* (p. 191): "in the extreme case where money wages are assumed to fall without limit in face of involuntary unemployment . . . there will, it is true, be only two possible long period position—full employment and the level of employment corresponding to the rate of interest at which liquidity preference becomes absolute (in the event of this being less than full employment)."

3
Financial
Intermediaries
and the Logical Structure
of Monetary Theory

Specialization is the essence of economic life. And the particular aspect of specialization which John G. Gurley and Edward S. Shaw have undertaken to analyze in their recent—and long-awaited—book[1] is that between earning income and disposing of it. It is this specialization that is "the basis for debt, financial assets, and financial institutions" (p. 17). Conversely, the existence of such financial arrangements is a necessary condition for the transfer of funds from savers to investors. Thus the ability of an economy to draw resources to their most efficient uses depends in a crucial way on the efficiency of its financial system (p. 56).

The workings of this financial system are studied by Gurley and Shaw (henceforth referred to as G-S) in a fresh and provocative way. Indeed, this is their major contribution: the detailed presentation of a conceptual framework from which they fruitfully reconsider old and familiar problems, and fruitfully undertake the analysis of new and unfamiliar ones.

I. THE MAIN ARGUMENT

The main theme of the book is the development of "a theory of finance that encompasses the theory of money, and a theory of financial institutions that includes banking theory" (p. 1). By this first objective is meant the presentation of the theory of money as part of a general theory of optimum portfolio selection (p. 57). Similarly, by the second objective is meant the presentation of the theory of the banking system as part of a general theory of the choice of optimum portfolios of assets and debts by financial institutions of various kinds.

Reprinted by permission from American Economic Review, *LI (1961), 95–116, with the addition of a postscript.*

[1] John G. Gurley and Edward S. Shaw, *Money in a Theory of Finance,* with a Mathematical Appendix by Alain C. Enthoven (Washington, D.C., 1960). [See Postscript.]

In accomplishing their first objective, the authors follow in the footsteps of Keynes, Joan Robinson, Hicks, and Tobin—to whom they make explicit acknowledgment (p. x). In this connection they provide a wealth of instructive and illuminating detail on the overriding objective of risk-avoidance which leads individuals to diversify their portfolios (p. 117), and on the comparative advantages and disadvantages of the various assets amongst which this diversification is carried out [tangible assets, short- and long-term bonds, constant-purchasing-power bonds, stocks, and "blue chips" (pp. 32–33, 159–173)]. G-S then go on to show that there are forces leading to security differentiation on the supply side as well. In brief, "excess demands, positive or negative, for current output are of necessity excess supplies of securities, and the sectoral location of excess demands partly determines the types of primary securities that will be issued. . . . Share-croppers cannot issue commercial paper, or farmers corporate bonds, or business firms Treasury bills. . . . The real world and the financial world are one world" (pp. 120, 122–123).

At the same time, G-S explicitly disclaim any intention to "advance in the least the theory of risk and uncertainty" (p. 10; also p. 92). Furthermore, their statement of the conditions that define an optimum portfolio is, to say the least, vague. This optimum is merely described (for a portfolio consisting of tangible assets, bonds, and money) as a situation which obtains when there exists a certain imprecisely specified relationship among the "marginal rental rate" (i.e., marginal productivity of capital—p. 26), the rate of interest, and the "implicit deposit rate" (pp. 32–33; also bottom of p. 119, and p. 127). By this last is meant some measure of the traditional transactions, precautionary, and speculative benefits of holding money, in addition to the possible benefits to be derived from a decrease in the price level (pp. 31–33, 70–71, 151–153). But nowhere is this rate explicitly defined. Indeed, there is not even an unambiguous statement of its dimensions! At one point (p. 32, top) it seems to have the dimensions of utility, while at another (p. 152) it seems to have those of a percentage, or even of money.[2]

Thus it is not in the direction of the pure theory of portfolio selection that G-S's contribution lies. This, instead, is to be found in the accomplishment of their second objective: namely, the analysis of "financial intermediaries," that is, "financial institutions whose principal function is the purchase of primary securities and [by?] the creation of claims on themselves" (p. 363). Here G-S are breaking new ground all the way. First, they bring "nonbanking" or "nonmonetary" financial intermediaries [e.g., insurance companies, savings and loan associations, mutual savings banks, pension funds (p. 193)] out of the limbo to which they have been relegated by most economic theory, and analyze them both from the view-

---

[2]This dimensional confusion is particularly noticeable on p. 66 where we are told that an optimum position obtains when there exists "a balance among marginal utility of consumption, the rate of interest, and the marginal implicit deposit rate for real money." This passage also illustrates the imprecision of G-S's description of the optimum—for what is the meaning of "balance"?

point of their influence on the "real" variables of the system (namely, the rate of interest, and thereby the levels of savings and investment), and from the viewpoint of their impact on the banking system.

Second, they most stimulatingly show (and this is one of their main themes) that the banking system itself is only one (albeit, usually the most important one) amongst many different kinds of financial intermediaries. In one of those striking passages that recur throughout the book they write:

> There are many similarities between the monetary system and nonmonetary intermediaries, and the similarities are more important than the differences. Both types of financial institution create financial claims; and both may engage in multiple creation of their particular liabilities in relation to any one class of asset that they hold (p. 202).
>
> The difference between the monetary system and nonmonetary intermediaries in this respect, then, is not that one creates and the other does not, but rather that each creates its own unique form of debt. . . . Money is unlike other financial assets, for it is the means of payment. Corporate stocks are unlike other financial assets, too, for they carry ownership rights in corporations. And policyholders' equities in insurance companies are different because they are linked to certain insurance attributes (pp. 198–199).

Similarly, G-S insist on analyzing the economic behavior of the banking system—like that of any other intermediary—in terms of its attempts to achieve an optimum portfolio of assets and debts within the restrictions imposed upon it. This approach is to be contrasted with the usual tendency of economists to treat the banking system as the Cinderella of monetary policy: as a parasitic member of the community, permitted to earn its living by doing something which—if it only wanted to—the government could do without cost (namely, creating money); as a member whose existence is accordingly suffered, and on whom we can therefore impose without compunction any restrictions deemed necessary by monetary policy. What G-S have shown is that the banking system has a purpose and a soul, and that if its welfare is not properly considered, it will wither up and die. The acceptance of G-S's approach should go far toward eliminating that War of Amalek between economists and bankers with which we feel it our duty to indoctrinate our beginning students.

One of the main questions that concern G-S is the relationship between the real and the financial in the growth process. On the one hand, they emphasize that improvements and innovations in "financial technology" can speed up this process by expediting the flow of funds from savers to investors, and thereby reducing the rate of interest. Under the heading of such technological improvements come improved distributive techniques (better communications, lower transactions costs, and generally the perfection of a well-developed securities market) and the emergence of financial intermediaries, primarily of the nonmonetary type (pp. 123–126).

On the other hand, G-S continuously stress that an integral part of the growth process is an increasing demand for real financial assets—in the form of both money and securities. Correspondingly, one of the questions to which they repeatedly return is the "neutrality" of money in this process: whether it makes any difference to the economy whether the increased real money balances it demands are supplied by an increase in the nominal quantity of money or by a decline in the absolute price level. Here the authors reconfirm the conclusion that, in the absence of money illusion, distribution effects, and rigidities, it does not make any difference. At the same time, on the familiar grounds that these assumptions are not likely to prevail in the real world, they make clear their own preference for accompanying the growth process with a concomitant growth in the nominal money supply (pp. 179–187). They also nicely emphasize that by adopting a policy of increasing nominal money at a constant price level, the government is in effect borrowing from the private sector at a zero interest rate, and can make use of these borrowings to finance an investment program that will further speed up growth (pp. 41–42). Alternatively, it can accomplish the same result by injecting the new money into the economy in such a way as to lower the rate of interest (pp. 185–187).

G-S also provide a formal analysis of the implications of the balanced-growth process for the stock of securities in the economy (pp. 95–112). There are, however, some loose ends to this analysis.[3] But my main reaction is to attach considerably less importance to this analysis than the authors seem to: for the balanced-growth assumption precludes from the outset just those possibilities of changing portfolio compositions and changing money velocities that should be of primary interest to monetary theorists (cf., e.g., pp. 110–111).

A recurrent and basic theme of G-S's book is that the growth in the totality of financial assets has a "scale effect" on the demand for any one given financial asset, and for money in particular (pp. 167, 170, 174, 177–178, 203). It is here that I find some of the most questionable aspects of G-S's argument. First, this totality of assets is measured in a gross way, without netting out any concomitant increase in debt. Second, the influence of these assets is conceived as something distinct from the influence of real wealth (p. 173, bottom). All this is part of G-S's repeatedly emphasized "gross money doctrine," which will be discussed in detail in the next section of this review. There it will be shown that G-S's "doctrine" stems from a basic misunderstanding. It will also be argued that the proper variable for the analysis of

---

[3] I have in mind the following points: (a) In their analysis of the debt-income ratio in equation (6) on p. 105, G-S do not even advert to the possibility of n (the rate of growth) being less than i (the rate of interest). Nor do they consider the case in which the marginal productivity of capital equals the rate of interest, so that the debt-income ratio reduces to the capital-output ratio. (b) It is contended that the existence of cyclical movements "is a drag on the growth of primary securities and financial assets" (p. 115). But it is not explained why this should cause the growth to be smaller over the period as a whole than that which would have taken place if the economy had expanded smoothly at the average rate of growth which obtained. (c) Ambiguity also surrounds the discussion of "mixed asset-debt positions," e.g., the position of a firm which issues securities in order to finance the holding of money (pp. 112–113). This will clearly increase the *absolute* supply of securities. But it should have been made clear that as long as the degree of "mixedness" remains constant there is no effect on the *rate* of growth of outstanding securities.

demand for any good, including money and securities, is total *net* wealth, including wealth in the form of financial assets.[4]

A great virtue of G-S's book is that the authors tie in their theoretical analysis with policy recommendations. Furthermore, it is abundantly clear to the reader that the authors have built their theoretical structure on the basis of a close and intimate knowledge of the realities of a modern financial system. Indeed we are explicitly told (p. vii) that the book is the outgrowth of an empirical study of financial institutions in the United States, the complete version of which is yet to be published.

One of G-S's policy conclusions is that there should be a greater integration—if not consolidation—of monetary and government-debt management. "Government debt, on the one hand, and debts of the monetary system on the other, are each so important a segment of total financial assets that management of them by different authorities working for dissimilar goals must be expensive in real interest costs to the Treasury, in monetary stability, or in real earnings of the banking system" (p. 280). This is not an unfamiliar contention, but it receives new force when viewed from the conceptual framework which G-S provide.

More novel conclusions are that monetary policy does not require either a legal or a customary minimum reserve ratio; that, indeed such a ratio forces the private banking sector frequently to become a "disequilibrium system"—for it is forcefully prevented in this way from achieving its optimum portfolio; and that, accordingly, a policy of paying banks a variable rate of interest on their deposits at the central bank (including the possibility of imposing negative rates) is a more desirable, and more flexible, means of influencing the banking system so as to contract and expand in accordance with the desiderata of monetary policy (pp. 266–271, 289).

Finally, and most interestingly, G-S argue that the choice of the banking system as the sector through which monetary policy is usually effected has worked to the disadvantage of this system as compared with other types of financial intermediaries. It is to this that they attribute the declining net profit-asset and capital-asset ratios of the banking system. Their suggested solutions for this state of affairs range from 100 percent money and a nationalized bank system to the spreading of controls over nonbanking financial intermediaries as well, "so that the burden of control is distributed more evenly among issuers of financial assets." These controls "may also be extended to ... issuers of primary securities, as illustrated by consumers credit regulations or by private capital issues restrictions" (pp. 288–291).

Whether or not one accepts these conclusions, there can be no doubt that future discussion of these problems will have to consider the points

[4] I hasten to add that my own treatment of this question in *Money, Interest, and Prices*, 1st ed. (Evanston, Ill., 1956), is not satisfactory: for there too demand is *not* represented as being dependent on the aggregate value of physical and monetary assets together (p. 126; see also pp. 205–206). On the other hand, it is not, strictly speaking, always correct to assume that the dependence of demand is on total wealth—that is, solely on the discounted value of the income stream. Under certain assumptions, it can be shown that the time-shape of the income stream also affects demand.

raised by G-S, and can also profitably make use of the analytical framework they have provided for this purpose. In brief, their book is one that must be read by every serious student of monetary theory and policy.

At the same time I must note that G-S's book suffers from some serious failings. First of all, its language is occasionally woolly and imprecise, and too frequently tends to the overdramatic (cf., e.g., pp. 39–40, 118, and especially 141–142). More important, the book is much too repetitious—to a degree that goes far beyond the degree of "judicious repetition" dictated by the authors' perfectly justified plan of proceeding from simple to more complicated models. What is accomplished by describing the nature of the demand for money in essentially similar ways first on pp. 32–33, then on pp. 70–71, and finally on pp. 150–153? And the same may be asked for the triple discussion of the neutrality of money on pp. 39–46, 82–88, and 179–187. Why is security diversification discussed under three separate headings on pp. 70–72, 117–119, and 150–152, respectively? This repetition is not only tiring but at times actually confusing. There is no doubt that *Money in a Theory of Finance* would have been a better book, and one with a much sharper impact, if it had been cut considerably.

On the other hand, despite the repetition, the reader is sometimes left in the dark as to the nature of the assumptions on which the argument at specific points is based. Thus he must infer for himself that the discussion of Chapter 4 is based on the assumption that all money is of the "inside" variety (see next section), and the same is true for Chapter 7. Similarly, only later does it become clear that the argument on pp. 79–81 assumes a balanced-growth process. And he is left to extend for himself the flow-of-funds table of p. 22 to the discussion on pp. 58–59, where it is really essential for a full understanding of the argument.

The second failing of the book stems from G-S's straining at "iconoclasm" (p. ix). This is what leads them to some of the stylistic excesses already noted. More important, it prevents them from lending a sufficiently understanding ear to some of the teachings of the Old Gods, including the Keynesian ones. As a result G-S sometimes misinterpret these teachings. And sometimes they fail to see the deeper relationship between these teachings and their own, a fact which prevents the reader (and frequently the authors too!) from seeing the full significance of the argument. We will see the main examples of this in Sections II and III below.

The last failing of the book is that it is involved in serious error at some points which are fundamental to its theoretical structure. This is what will be shown in Sections II and IV below.

Not much will be said here of the Mathematical Appendix to the book, which was written by Alain C. Enthoven. This gives a good deal of emphasis to the problem of balanced growth. I might, however, point out that this appendix makes repeated use of Samuelson's "Correspondence Principle" without really answering the criticisms which have demonstrated its limited applicability (p. 328, note 25). My main criticism, however, is on the grounds of omission: there is not always full communication between appendix and text. More important, the appendix does not treat just those crucial and incorrectly analyzed issues referred to in the preceding paragraph; and what makes this omission particularly unfortunate is that the errors are of a type that might have been caught by a mathematical cross-checking of the argument. All this will become clear from what follows.

II. "INSIDE" AND "OUTSIDE" MONEY

One of G-S's significant contributions is in bringing to the fore the distinction between money based on private domestic debt ("inside money") and money of a fiat nature or based on any other asset ("outside money"). Nevertheless, as already indicated, the analytical developments which G-S base on this distinction are themselves involved in error. In order to show this, we must first describe G-S's model in somewhat greater detail.[5]

In a familiar fashion, this model divides the economy into three sectors (consumers, business firms, and government) and four markets (labor services, current output, bonds, and money). Two additional notions crucial to G-S's analysis are that of "nonfinancial spending units" and "primary securities." By the former is meant "spending units whose principal function is to produce and purchase current output, and not to buy one type of security by issuing another" (p. 59). Correspondingly, "primary securities" are defined as "all liabilities and outstanding equities of nonfinancial spending units" (*ibid.*). All consumers and firms in the preceding models are assumed to be nonfinancial spending units. Only firms, however, are assumed to issue primary securities, and these for simplicity are assumed to have the form of a homogeneous perpetuity paying $1 annually, so that its price is the reciprocal of the rate of interest, or $1/i$.

Since money is a type of security, and since the government (assumed to consist of both a Policy and a Banking Bureau) can acquire primary securities by issuing money, it is not a spending unit but a financial intermediary. Correspondingly, the debt of government, like that of any such intermediary, is referred to as an "indirect security." In this simple model the only such security is money. The term "financial asset" refers to both direct and indirect securities. Purchase of primary securities by consumers is referred to as "direct finance"; purchase by financial intermediaries (government, in this case), as "indirect finance" (pp. 59–61; 93–95).[6]

Each of the three sectors has a budget restraint, showing the sources and uses of its funds: this is essentially what is shown by the flow-of-funds account (p. 22). Each of these restraints states that the excess of receipts over spending (on capital as well as current account) must equal the sector's

---

[5] What the following actually describes is G-S's "modified second model" (pp. 82 ff.). This includes features present only in the "rudimentary model" of Chapter 2.

[6] Actually, the classification of the government is ambiguous, though G-S do not recognize it as such in their discussion on p. 94. To the extent that it issues inside money, it is a financial intermediary. But to the extent that it issues fiat outside money to cover a deficit on current account, it is just like any other nonfinancial spending unit.

net accretion of financial assets (bonds and money). Every economic unit is classified as "surplus" or "deficit" according to whether this excess is positive or negative (p. 21). For the most part, households are surplus units and firms deficit units.

The nature of the relationships among the sectors of this economy can then be illustrated by the sectoral balance sheets of Table 3.1—where the symbols M^b, B, M^h, B^h, B^g and M are defined as indicated. From the definition given at the beginning of this section, it is clear that the economy described by this table has 100 units of inside money (corresponding to the value of the bonds held by the government and monetary sector) and 25 of outside money (corresponding to the fiat money issued to finance the cumulated deficit of this sector).

In order to evaluate G-S's further analysis of this model, it will first be necessary to depart somewhat from their description of the demand functions. In particular, assume for simplicity's sake, and in accordance with recent developments,[7] that the household demand functions depend on its total wealth. The essential point for monetary theory is that this wealth also consists of the household's initial holdings of financial assets. This, indeed, is the origin of the real-balance and real-indebtedness effects. In particular, it is assumed that these demand functions depend upon—in addition to the rate of interest, i—household wealth, W, where

$$W = T + \frac{\dfrac{B_0^h}{i} + M_0^b}{p}, \tag{1}$$

where T represents the discounted value of the income stream; p represents

Table 3.1 Sectoral Balance Sheets

Business Sector				Consumer Sector			
Assets		*Liabilities*		*Assets*		*Liabilities*	
Money (M^b)	50	Bonds (B/i)	500	Money (M^h)	75	None	
Tangible assets	900			Bonds	400		
		Net worth				*Net worth*	
		Accumulated				Accumulated	
		savings	450			savings	475
	950		950		475		475

Government and Monetary Sector			
Assets		*Liabilities*	
Bonds (B^g/i)	100	Money (M)	125
		Net worth	
		Accumulated	
		savings	-25
	100		100

[7] Milton Friedman, *A Theory of the Consumption Function* (Princeton, 1957), pp. 7–10.

the price level; and where the subscript 0 indicates given, initial quantities. Since the present discussion is restricted to a stationary state, T is constant and so can be disregarded in what follows. In a similar way it is assumed that businesses' demand functions depend on:

$$\frac{-\dfrac{B_0}{i} + M_0^b}{p}.$$

Let us now make the further assumption that in the economy as a whole there are no distribution effects; that is, that the aggregate demand of the economy depends only on the total of assets, and not on their distribution as between households and businesses. This means that these functions depend upon:

$$\frac{\left(\dfrac{B_0^h}{i} + M_0^h\right) + \left(-\dfrac{B_0}{i} + M_0^b\right)}{p}. \tag{2}$$

Making use of the definitions:

$$M_0 = M_0^h + M_0^b \quad \text{and} \quad B_0 = B_0^h + B_0^g, \tag{3}$$

we can reduce this to:

$$\frac{(M_0^h + M_0^b) + \dfrac{1}{i}(B_0^h - B_0)}{p} = \frac{M_0 - \dfrac{1}{i}B_0^g}{p}. \tag{4}$$

This last is clearly identified as the net real debt of the government sector to the private sector, or alternatively as the real value of outside money.

Making use of the preceding, let us write the following demand and supply functions:

$$E = F\left(Y_0, i, \frac{M_0 - \dfrac{1}{i}B_0^g}{p}\right) \tag{5}$$

$\qquad$ = aggregate demand for commodities;

$$\frac{B^d}{rp} = H\left(Y_0, i, \frac{\dfrac{B_0^h}{i} + M_0^h}{p}\right) \tag{6}$$

$\qquad$ = households' demand for real bond holdings as a stock;

$$\frac{B^s}{rp} = J\left(Y_0, i, \frac{-\dfrac{B_0}{i} + M_0^b}{p}\right) \tag{7}$$

$\qquad$ = businesses' supply of real bond holdings as a stock;

$$\frac{M^d}{p} = L\left(Y_0, i, \frac{M_0 - \frac{1}{i}B_0^g}{p}\right) \tag{8}$$

= aggregate demand for real money holdings as a stock.

The foregoing system of equations has ignored the market for labor, for this is assumed to be in full-employment equilibrium (pp. 10, 26). In order to keep the discussion here related to the G-S one, the functions are also assumed to depend on national income, Y, though the assumption that they depend on wealth might be taken to imply that this additional dependence on Y is otiose. Since in any event Y is assumed to be constant at Y_0, this issue will not affect the subsequent argument.

Assume that all demands are positively dependent on income[8] and net financial assets. On the other hand, business supply of bonds is negatively dependent on these variables; for the higher are a business's financial assets, the less it need be dependent on debt financing. What must now be emphasized is that the assumed absence of distribution effects implies that if households' financial assets increase by the same amount that firms' decrease, then the former's increased demand for bonds is exactly offset by the latter's increased supply. That is, the absence of distribution effects implies that at the level of aggregate behavior it is only the sum total of financial assets in the economy that matters. Hence the private sector's *excess* demand function for bonds—defined as the households' demand minus firms' supply—must have the form:[9]

$$B\left(Y_0, i, \frac{M_0 - \frac{1}{i}B_0^g}{p}\right) \tag{9}$$

$$\equiv H\left(Y_0, i, \frac{\frac{B_0^h}{i} + M_0^h}{p}\right) - J\left(Y_0, i, \frac{-\frac{B_0}{i} + M_0^b}{p}\right).$$

On the basis of the foregoing discussion we can now write our general-equilibrium equations as:

Equilibrium Condition   *Market*

$$F\left(Y_0, i, \frac{M_0 - \frac{1}{i}B_0^g}{p}\right) - Y_0 = 0 \qquad\qquad \text{commodities,} \tag{10}$$

[8] For reasons which are never explained G-S assume that the income elasticity of demand for money is greater than that for bonds (p. 71). This unexplained assumption is an important component of their subsequent argument (pp. 157–158).

[9] In mathematical terms, absence of distribution effects implies that $H_3(\ ) + J_3(\ )$ $\equiv 0$, where $H_3(\ )$ and $J_3(\ )$ represent the partial derivatives with respect to the third argument.

$$B\left(Y_0, i, \dfrac{M_0 - \dfrac{1}{i} B_0^g}{p}\right) + \dfrac{B_0^g}{ip} = 0 \qquad\qquad \text{bonds,} \qquad (11)$$

$$L\left(Y_0, i, \dfrac{M_0 - \dfrac{1}{i} B_0^g}{p}\right) - \dfrac{M_0}{p} = 0 \qquad\qquad \text{money.} \qquad (12)$$

If all money is of the outside variety, then $B_0^g = 0$, and the foregoing system reduces to a very familiar form. G-S, however, are primarily interested in the opposite case, in which money is entirely of the inside variety. This means that:[10]

$$M_0 = \dfrac{B_0^g}{i}, \qquad\qquad (13)$$

which in turn implies that the net financial assets of the private sector are zero. Hence system (10)–(12) reduces to:

$$F^*(Y_0, i) - Y_0 = 0, \qquad\qquad (14)$$

$$B^*(Y_0, i) + \dfrac{M_0}{p} = 0, \qquad\qquad (15)$$

$$L^*(Y_0, i) - \dfrac{M_0}{p} = 0, \qquad\qquad (16)$$

where M_0/p simultaneously represents the government's real holdings of bonds and the total real quantity of money in the economy—and where the asterisks remind us that these functions differ from those of system (10)–(12).

The foregoing analysis has made use of what G-S call the "net-money doctrine": the "approach to monetary theory [which] nets out all private domestic claims and counterclaims before it comes to grips with supply and demand on the money market" (p. 134). This they contrast—very unfavorably—with the "gross-money doctrine" which "avoids such consolidation of financial accounts" (*ibid.*). Thus in the case of Table 3.1, according to G-S, the net-money doctrine would say that the quantity of money is 75, while the gross-money doctrine would say that it is 175 (pp. 134–136). Against the net-money doctrine G-S then bring to bear a detailed and elaborate criticism (pp. 134–149). But as we shall now see, this criticism is quite beside the point and stems simply from a misunderstanding of the fundamental distinction between dependent and independent variables of the analysis, a misunderstanding which mars G-S's argument at other points in their book as well.[11]

[10]Strictly speaking, the following relationship implicitly assumes that all government capital gains from a reduction in interest are returned to the private sector as transfer payments financed by printing money. A corresponding statement holds, *mutatis mutandis*, for capital losses.

[11] See, for example, top of p. 29; see also the discussion in note 20 below.

In particular, G-S fail to distinguish properly between bond and money holdings as dependent variables (B^d, B^s, and M^d) and these holdings as independent variables (B_0^h, B_0, M_0^h and M_0^b).[12]

More specifically, G-S fail to realize that even though it is the *net aggregate value* of financial assets which is the proper *independent* variable of the demand functions of the private sector, it is the *individual financial assets* which are the proper *dependent* variables of the analysis. Thus in the special case of all money being inside money, system (14)–(16) shows that net financial assets disappear as argument (i.e., *independent* variables) of the demand functions; but this in no way affects the fact that in back of system (14)–(16), lies a system like (5)–(8) in which the individual demands and supplies for financial assets remain the *dependent* variables of the analysis. Though it is necessarily the net-money doctrine which is relevant for considerations of the wealth effect on demand functions, it is equally necessarily the gross-money doctrine which is relevant for considerations of the optimum amount of money which an individual wishes to hold in his portfolio. There is no contradiction between these two "doctrines": they simply refer to two completely different things.[13]

It should be emphasized that there is nothing unusual about this distinction: thus, consider the familiar case of an economy consisting of individuals who receive their income in the form of initial endowments of two commodities, x and y. If we abstract from distribution effects, the demand functions of this economy depend upon (among other things) the *aggregate* value of the initial quantities of x and y (i.e., total income); but this in no way affects the fact that the economy has *separate* demand functions for x and y. This example brings out the further point that the net-money doctrine does not represent an additional and optional assumption, but is the logical consequence of assuming at one and the same time that (a) the demand of an individual depends on his total wealth and (b) there are no distribution effects. G-S explicitly accept the second of these assumptions— and give no indication of rejecting the first. Hence, if they are to be consistent, they themselves cannot reject the net-money doctrine.

From all this it is clear that, contrary to the contentions of G-S, the net-money doctrine does *not* imply that an economy with only inside money is "money-less and bond-less" (p. 138), so that its price level is indeterminate (pp. 142–144). Indeed, the determinacy of such a system is immediately evident from equations (14)–(16) above. For though an arbitrary (say) increase in p will not affect any of the *demand* functions in this system, it will, by decreasing M_0/p, create an *excess* (or, in G-S's terminology "incremental") demand for money; alternatively, it will create an excess supply of

---

[12] This distinction is quite clearly made in the Mathematical Appendix, especially on p. 320. But unfortunately there is no communication between the appendix and the text on this crucial point.

[13] At one point (p. 320, top), the Mathematical Appendix does write the demand functions as dependent upon total financial assets. But this procedure is not carried over to other parts of the appendix—and its implications for the argument of the text are not seen.

On my own confusion on related points in earlier writings, see note 4 above.

bonds. This will increase i, thereby [from (14)] creating an excess supply of commodities, and thereby driving the price level down again.

This is how the "traditional argument" would be stated. It can also be stated, in G-S's conceptual framework, in terms of the fact that the increased price level disturbs the portfolio equilibrium of the private sector by decreasing its real money holdings relative to its bond holdings, and that the attempt of the private sector to re-establish equilibrium will cause the system to return to its original position.[14] This may be a more sophisticated way of describing the matter, but it certainly does not differ substantively from the argument of the preceding paragraph. And there is certainly no basis for G-S's contention that the "net-money doctrine overlooks the bearing of portfolio balance on real behavior" (p. 144).

I would conjecture that what misled G-S in all this discussion is the fact that the *demand* functions of a purely inside-money economy are independent of the absolute price level (note their emphasis on this fact on pp. 73–74). From this (I suspect) they incorrectly inferred that the system of equations of such an economy is ensnared in the price indeterminacy of the invalid dichotomy. They did not realize that what involves a system in such a dichotomy is instead the quite distinct assumption that all (nonmoney) *excess demand* functions are unaffected by the price level. And they particularly did not realize that, as shown by equations (14)–(16), a purely inside-money economy is actually a particular instance of the special case in which the system can be validly dichotomized by virtue of the fact that, though the commodity excess-demand equation is independent of the price level, the bond excess-demand equation is not.[15]

Looking at the inside-money model in this way also enables us quite simply to deduce one of G-S's main conclusions: namely, that open-market purchases in such a model (i.e., government acquisition of private securities) will not affect the rate of interest. Equation (14) shows us that, under the assumption of full employment, there is only one rate of interest at which the commodity market can be in equilibrium. Hence nothing that happens in

[14] Pp. 74–75, 79, and 143. There is some confusion in G-S's presentation of the argument. For they assume that the amount of bonds firms supply goes up proportionately with the price level, and state that such an assumption is necessary in order "to avoid distribution effects" (p. 75). Now, first of all, by G-S's own assumption as to the behavior of firms (pp. 63–64), an increase in the price level will *not* cause a proportionate increase in the supply of bonds—for it will have an encouraging "debt effect." Secondly, as shown above, what is necessary for the argument is that the *excess* demand function for bonds be free of distribution effects—and this can obtain even if the amount of bonds outstanding remains constant. For, as emphasized in equation (9) above, all that absence of distribution effects means is that the indebtedness effects of firms and households offset each other.

This confusion recurs throughout G-S's book (cf., e.g., pp. 88, 234, and 251). They may, of course, be thinking of changes in the *initial* quantities of bonds. But since, as just emphasized, they do not distinguish properly between initial and demanded quantities, their argument is not clear.

[15] See *Money, Interest, and Prices, op. cit.*, pp. 109–110 [see Postscript]. The validity of dichotomizing the system in this case has recently been emphasized by Franco Modigliani in the postscript attached to the reprinting of his well-known article on "Liquidity Preference and the Theory of Interest and Money" in H. Hazlitt (ed.), *The Critics of Keynesian Economics* (Princeton, 1960), pp. 183–184.

the bond or money markets alone can affect the equilibrium rate of interest. Once again, we can equivalently carry out the argument—as G-S do—in terms of "portfolio balance" (pp. 76–77). But in this case I believe that the G-S argument is less revealing than the "traditional one": for it fails to bring out the crucial nature of the dichotomy between the real sector and monetary sector which is implicit in the assumption of a purely inside-money economy.

By way of contrast, consider the case in which there is both inside and outside money, so that the more general system (10)–(12) obtains. It is immediately evident that the commodity market in this case can be in equilibrium at an infinite number of combinations of interest rate and price level. Hence the equilibrium condition in this market does not uniquely determine the rate of interest, so that there is room for changes in the interest rate to result from changes originating in the bond or money markets (the monetary sector). In particular, an increase in outside money in this case will *raise* the interest rate (pp. 85–86)[16] while an increase in inside money will *lower* it (pp. 84–85, 144–147). On the other hand—as the reader can readily verify from system (10)–(12)—a proportionate increase in both inside and outside money will cause a proportionate increase in prices and leave the interest rate invariant (p. 85).

Two comments must be made here. First—and related to our earlier discussion—the open-market purchase of bonds in the preceding case does not *initially* (i.e., before the interest rate change) affect the net obligation of the government to the private sector as represented by equation (4) above; correspondingly, it does not initially affect the *demand* functions in system (10)–(12). But by generating corresponding increases in B_0^g and M_0, it does create an *excess* demand for bonds and an *excess* supply of money—thus driving the interest rate down. In this way we see the untenability of G-S's contention that the "net-money doctrine ... implies that management of inside money cannot come to grips with the rate of interest" (p. 147).

My second comment is more a question of emphasis. G-S have done a real service in making explicit the distinction between inside and outside money. At the same time I think it is unfortunate that they have chosen to refer to the foregoing results as proving "that money is not neutral, within a neo-classical framework, when there is a combination of inside and outside money" (p. 232). For G-S repeatedly recognize that the "neo-classical framework" implies the absence of distribution effects—which means, among other things, that the increased money supply is injected into the system so as not to disturb "the pattern of demand for current output" (p. 41). Why, then, is there any essential difference between this and assuming that the money is injected so as not to disturb the pattern of demand for financial assets? And is it not this latter condition that we are implicitly fulfilling when we assume that the monetary increase is accomplished in such a way as not

---

[16]This rather surprising conclusion results from the assumption that the government is a creditor of the private sector. If it were a debtor, interest would fall. See Enthoven's analysis, pp. 330–333. See also *Money, Interest, and Prices, op. cit.*, Chapter 12, Section 5, and Mathematical Appendix, 9:e.

to disturb the proportions between inside and outside money? [See Post-script.]

Before concluding this section I must voice a more fundamental objection, though not to an analytical aspect of the book. G-S have explicitly adopted the procedure of "no footnotes and no bibliography" (p. x). There is much to be said for such a procedure. But it would seem to me that the "ground rules" (to use one of G-S's pet phrases) of scholarship then require the authors to forswear the pleasures of *Dogmengeschichte*, and particularly the pleasures of casting anonymous shafts at "traditional" and "neoclassical" economics. Unsupported *obiter dicta* on the nature of the latter can only add confusion to an already complicated issue.

Thus I for one would have been much happier not to have been unequivocally told, with respect to an economy all of whose money is of the inside variety, that "the traditional answer would be that the price level is not determinate, and that any price level would be compatible with general equilibrium" (p. 74); or that "the quantity-theory solution"—for the case of an increase in inside money when there exists money of both varieties—is "a new equilibrium at doubled levels of commodity prices, money wage rates, and nominal primary securities—with the rate of interest unchanged" (p. 145; see also p. 147). And I would have been happiest to have been informed who were the culprits responsible for such statements, and how far back in the literature one has to go in order to find signs of their activity.

III. THE INFLUENCE OF FINANCIAL INTERMEDIARIES

Within the confines of one book G-S have admirably transformed the analysis of financial intermediaries from a hitherto neglected question in the literature to one which will now have a recognized place in the corpus of monetary theory. My only objection to their analysis is that it is not sufficiently integrated into this corpus, and that as a result its full significance is not brought out. This is what will now be shown. At the same time it should be made clear at the outset that from the substantive viewpoint the following merely repeats G-S's analysis. It gives it only a slightly different twist—a slightly different emphasis. But it seems to me that this emphasis is of importance in simplifying and clarifying the analysis.

G-S fruitfully conceive of financial intermediaries (especially of the nonbanking type) as processing plants whose function it is to "turn primary securities into indirect securities for the portfolios of ultimate lenders" (p. 197). Intermediaries are able to profit by this transformation process by exploiting

> economies of scale in lending and borrowing. On the lending side, the intermediary can invest and manage investments in primary securities at unit costs far below the experience of most individual lenders. The sheer size of its portfolio permits a significant reduction in risks through diversification. It can schedule maturities so that chances of liquidity crises are minimized. The mutual or cooperative is sometimes favored with tax benefits that are not

available to the individual saver. On the borrowing side, the intermediary with a large number of depositors can normally rely on a predictable schedule of claims for repayment and so can get along with a portfolio that is relatively illiquid (p. 194).

In other words, the result of developing nonbanking financial intermediaries (like that of improving distributive techniques) is to provide ultimate lenders with the possibility of purchasing a security which is more attractive (more "liquid") than the primary securities issued by the ultimate borrowers (pp. 123–126). If G-S had followed up this aspect of their argument, they could have simply and instructively presented it as analytically equivalent to the case of an assumed increase in the liquidity of bonds within a standard Keynesian model. Such an increased liquidity makes bonds a better substitute for money, and thus causes the demand curve for money both to shift leftwards and to become more elastic. This is represented by the shift from D to D' in Figure 3.1, which essentially reproduces G-S's Charts 5 (p. 163) and 8 (p. 216). It follows that if the real supply of money remains constant at OC, then the rate of interest must decline from i_1 to i_0.

This, within the familiar framework of Keynesian theory, is the why and wherefore of the influence of financial intermediaries on the rate of interest, and thence on the real variables of the system. And within this same familiar context G-S could also have simply, succinctly, and systematically placed their analysis of an assumed greater marketability of securities, or smaller risks of default, or a shift in the "mix" of securities in favor of shorter-term obligations (pp. 160–173); or of government's substituting its securities for private ones, or insuring the latter (pp. 224–227); or of government's decreasing the liquidity of bonds relative to money by insuring the latter (pp. 225–226; this, of course, would reflect itself as an opposite shift—from D' to D). In a similar way, we can see from the diagram that if the monetary authority wishes to raise the interest rate from i_0 to i_2 by open-market sales, then it must decrease the real money supply much more in the case of the elastic demand curve D', which characterizes a system with nonbanking financial intermediaries, than in the case of the less elastic curve D'', which characterizes a system without them (pp. 239–241, 286). [See Postscript.]

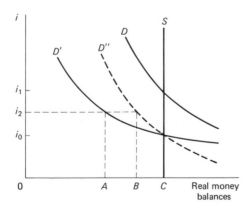

Figure 3.1.

Note that implicit in the foregoing exposition is the assumption that financial intermediaries are just that: namely, that they do not themselves change their money holdings in carrying out the full cycle of their activities. This, it seems to me, is the way the analysis should be carried out. Correspondingly, it also seems to me that G-S's attempt to achieve formal completeness of the argument by using as one of their standards of comparison a case in which intermediaries hoard money (pp. 217–218) simply confuses the nature of the real issues involved.

Finally, I should emphasize that in order to keep the foregoing exposition as close as possible to G-S's, I have carried it out in terms of the demand for and supply of money. Actually, however, I would have preferred to have carried it out in terms of a simultaneous general-equilibrium analysis of the commodity, bond, and money markets together. In particular, a parameter, t, can be introduced into each of the demand functions in system (10)–(12) to represent the degree of liquidity of bonds. An increase in t can be assumed to increase the demand for bonds, decrease that for money, and have either a positive or negative effect on that for commodities. This would have insured that we would not lose sight—as G-S sometimes do[17]—of the concomitant happenings in the commodity market as changes occur in those for bonds and money. [See Postscript.]

In this way it would also have been possible to bring out G-S's frequently emphasized point of the essential similarity between banking and nonbanking intermediaries (see Section I above). To speak somewhat loosely, both of these intermediaries influence the economy by affecting the terms on which bonds are demanded and supplied. But, in terms of the bond equation (11) above, the banking system does this by (say) increasing the second component of this demand (B_0^g/ip); whereas nonbanking intermediaries, by increasing the liquidity of bonds, and hence t, do so by increasing the first component $[B(\quad)]$. Alternatively, in somewhat more familiar terms, we can make the comparison in terms of the money equation (12) and say that the banking system affects the economy by changing the supply of money M_0/p; whereas nonbanking intermediaries do so by changing t, hence the demand for money $L(\quad)$, and hence the velocity of circulation. Note, however, that in both cases there are further endogenous changes in velocity caused by the change in the interest rate.

IV. THE MINIMUM REQUIREMENTS OF A MONETARY SYSTEM

G-S have reserved their most provocative question of all for their concluding chapter. Here they ask: What are the minimum prescriptions a monetary

---

[17] I am thinking primarily of G-S's discussion on pp. 153–158, which is based on the tacit assumption that the total demand for financial assets remains fixed. This discussion is then used as the basis for analyzing changes in the maturity of bonds, in their degree of risk, and so forth (pp. 159 ff.)—despite the fact that all of these changes will in general also affect the demand for commodities and hence the total demand for financial assets.

Note, too, that in their discussion of financial intermediaries, G-S explicitly assume "that there is no change in spending units' demand for current output" (p. 214, note 3).

authority must set in order to assure the determinacy of the price level in a monetary system? Alternatively, and somewhat more pointedly, I would prefer to ask the question in the following way: In most discussions of monetary theory the nominal quantity of money supplied is taken as an exogenous variable. But though we continuously shy away from this fact in our theoretical work, we do nevertheless know that in the real world this is not the case: for money is largely the creature of a banking system which responds to such endogenous variables as the rate of interest, the wages of clerks, and so forth. How then can we take account of these responses? And, in particular, is there a limit to the extent to which such endogenous influences can be assumed to operate? Conversely, must a determinate monetary system necessarily retain some exogenous element?

One cannot read G-S's concluding chapter without being struck by the success with which the authors have refreshingly broken through the traditional confines of thought, and by the fruitfulness with which they apply their analytical apparatus to problems of banking theory. But once again their exposition is marred by imprecisions and errors, and by a consequent failure to see the full and deeper significance of the argument.

G-S's discussion of this question is carried out almost entirely in terms of the purely inside-money model. They begin by introducing two new assumptions: first, that the banking system pays an "explicit deposit rate," d, on the money which it has issued (e.g., on its demand deposits); second, that the behavior of the banking system, like that of any other sector, is free of money illusion—i.e., that it is determined only by real variables (pp. 248–257).

Introducing the first of these changes into the inside-money system (14)–(16) above converts it into:

$$F(Y_0, i, d) - Y_0 = 0 \qquad \text{commodities,} \qquad (17)$$

$$B(Y_0, i, d) + \frac{M_0}{p} = 0 \qquad \text{bonds,} \qquad (18)$$

$$L(Y_0, i, d) - \frac{M_0}{p} = 0 \qquad \text{money.} \qquad (19)$$

In other words, in formulating their demand decisions in this economy, individuals take account of the rate of return on the asset money (d), as well as the rate of return on the asset bonds (i).

It is immediately evident that the foregoing system is indeterminate. For assume that we begin from an initial equilibrium position with d at a certain level, and that d is then increased. This is analytically equivalent to an increase in liquidity preference: money balances become more desirable at an unchanged rate of interest. Hence the system will reach a new equilibrium position which will reflect this shift in liquidity preference. It will not return to the original equilibrium position (pp. 248–252).[18]

_____

[18]In technical terms: system (17)–(19) has three variables—i, d, and p, and (by Walras' Law) only two independent equations. Hence it is generally indeterminate.

G-S, however, assume that the new equilibrium position differs from the original one only in the price level, while the rate of interest remains the same. This results from their assumption that the foregoing shift in liquidity preference is a neutral one as between bonds and commodities (p. 252). This assumption, however, is quite unreasonable within the given context. For the change in d primarily affects the relative desirability of bonds and money as liquid assets. Correspondingly, the shift in liquidity preference which takes place is primarily at the expense of bonds—and little, if at all, at the expense of commodities. Hence such a shift causes a permanent increase in the interest rate,[19] even when money is entirely of the inside variety. G-S do recognize this as a possibility (p. 252, bottom); but they do not see that this is what should normally be expected to happen.

Let us now proceed to G-S's second change—namely, that the quantity of money is no longer the exogenous variable that it is in system (14)–(16), but an endogenous one determined by the profit-maximizing behavior of the banking system. In brief, we now have a money-supply function of the banking system (which is simultaneously its bond-demand function) that states (and here I differ from G-S[20]):

$$\frac{M}{p} = S(i, d).$$
$$(20)$$

More specifically, the real amount of money the banking system wishes to supply (the real amount of bonds it demands) depends directly on the interest rate it receives and inversely on the deposit rate it pays. Substituting this into (17)–(19), we obtain:

$$F(Y_0, i, d) - Y_0 = 0, \tag{21}$$

$$B(Y_0, i, d) + S(i, d) = 0, \tag{22}$$

$$L(Y_0, i, d) - S(i, d) = 0. \tag{23}$$

Now, it is reasonable to assume that this system of two independent equations can determine the equilibrium values of its two variables, i and d. However, it clearly cannot determine the equilibrium price level (p. 255). This is

[19] *Money, Interest and Prices, op. cit.*, pp. 169–170.
[20] G-S write this function (p. 254) as:

$$\frac{M}{p} = S\left(\frac{B^g}{ip}, i, d, \frac{w}{p}\right).$$

For simplicity, the argument w/p—representing the real wage rate—has been omitted here in accordance with the assumption (made by G-S as well) that the labor market is always in equilibrium. On the other hand, G-S's inclusion of B^g/ip as an argument of the function is not explained by them—and seems to me again to reflect their failure to distinguish properly between dependent and independent variables (see Section I above). For by the inside-money assumption, $B^g/ip = M/p$, so that what G-S have essentially done is to write a supply function in which the same variable, M/p, appears simultaneously as a dependent and independent variable! This confusion has consequences for their later argument which will be noted in a moment.

obvious from the fact that p does not even appear as a variable of the system. Due to the incorrect way in which they write the money-supply function—a way in which p does ostensibly appear in the function[21]—G-S do not realize this crucial fact. Nor, accordingly, do they realize the full significance of the foregoing indeterminacy. This, in brief, is that in order for the absolute price level to be determined by market-equilibrating forces, changes in it must impinge on aggregate *real* behavior in *some* market—i.e., must create excess demands in some market. Now, the joint assumptions of a purely inside-money and the absence of distribution effects implies that there is no such impingement on the real demands of the private sector for commodities, bonds, or money, respectively. Similarly, we have assumed that there is no impingement on the real demand and supply functions of the banking sector. Hence the economy does not generate resistance to any arbitrary change in the price level. Accordingly, there is nothing to prevent the frictionless flow of prices from one level to another.

G-S now move one step closer to reality and assume that there is a central bank which creates reserves solely by purchasing primary securities. Reserves are thus a type of security issued by one financial intermediary (the central bank) and, by assumption, acquired only by another (member banks) (pp. 257–258). In terms of the sectoral balance sheets of Table 3.1 above, this means that though there is no effect on the household and business sectors, the government and monetary sector is now divided into two sectors, as in Table 3.2.[22]

Table 3.2   Sectoral Balance Sheets—Member Banks and Central Bank

Member Banks		*Central Bank*	
Reserves 25	Money (demand deposits) 100	Bonds (primary securities) 25	Reserves 25
Bonds (primary securities) 75			

It is further assumed that like any other security, reserves, too, provide a rate of return, namely, the "reserve-balance rate," d'. It is first assumed that member banks are not subjected to reserve requirements. Instead, they are free to choose their optimum portfolio of assets and liabilities—including, of course, reserves. Like any other economic unit, the private banking system's optimum portfolio depends only on real variables—and, in particular, on the alternative rates of return of the three assets (and liabilities) on which it must formulate its decisions: namely, i, d, and d'. Thus the private banking system's real supply function of money is now assumed to be:

$$S(i, d, d'), \tag{24}$$

[21] See preceding footnote.
[22] Because of the assumption that all money is inside money, Table 3.2 disregards the 25 units of outside money in Table 3.1.

and its real demand function for reserves,

$$G(i, d, d').^{23} \tag{25}$$

At the same time, the private banking system's supply of money is clearly no longer identical with its demand for bonds. The latter is instead now represented by, say, $U(i, d, d')$ where, by the banks' balance sheet of Table 3.2,

$$U(i, d, d') \equiv S(i, d, d') - G(i, d, d'). \tag{26}$$

On the other hand, the central bank's real supply of reserves, which is also its real demand for primary securities, is:

$$\frac{R}{p}, \tag{27}$$

where R is the nominal quantity of reserves. Correspondingly, system (21)–(23) becomes:

$$F(Y_0, i, d) - Y_0 = 0 \qquad \text{commodities,} \tag{28}$$

$$B(Y_0, i, d) + U(i, d, d') + \frac{R}{p} = 0 \qquad \text{bonds,} \tag{29}$$

$$L(Y_0, i, d) - S(i, d, d') = 0 \qquad \text{money,} \tag{30}$$

$$G(i, d, d') - \frac{R}{p} = 0 \qquad \text{reserves.} \tag{31}$$

G-S summarize their argument in the following terms: "Of three indirect techniques—fixing nominal reserves [R], setting the reserve-balance rate [d'], and setting members' own deposit rate [d]—the Central Bank can get along with any two in regulating all nominal variables in the economic system" (pp. 274–275); and G-S themselves concentrate on showing how the system works when the first two are chosen (pp. 259–263). At the same time they contend that a central bank that can only regulate the reserve-balance rate, d', is in a weaker position than a monetary authority that can "directly" regulate the deposit rate, d (pp. 263–264).

These passages reveal G-S's failure to understand two basic aspects of the argument. First, and most important of all, it is *not* a matter of indifference to the central bank as to which two of the three variables—R, d', or d—it chooses to fix. The decision on R is *not* analogous to the decision on d or d'. Indeed, unless the central bank makes a decision on R (though not necessarily the one indicated by G-S) it can not achieve a determinant price level.

In order to show this, let us for the sake of contrast first assume that the central bank, too, is influenced only by real variables. Then, instead of (27),

---

[23] Once again, these equations differ from those of G-S (pp. 258–259) for the same reason noted in footnote 20 above. Note in particular that G-S's money-supply function depends on B_c^g/ip, equal to members' reserves (p. 258). But, as we have just seen, this is quite wrong: for reserves demanded and money supplied are both dependent variables—dependent on the same three variables, i, d, and d'.

its real supply function of reserves would be represented by, say,

$$T(i, d').\qquad(32)$$

Replacing R/p by this expression in system (28)–(31) would then yield a system completely analogous to (21)–(23) above: namely, one that could determine the rates of return, but obviously not the price level, which would not even appear in it!

In terms of our earlier argument, all that this means is that since in the aggregate no other economic unit in system (28)–(31) reacts to changes in the absolute price level, then, in order to assure the determinacy of the price level, the central bank must do so. This is the behavior denied by equation (32) but affirmed by equation (27). For the latter implies that the supply of real reserves is inversely proportionate to the price level. On the other hand, it is clear that the central bank need not operate in this way. If it acts in accordance with any supply function for *real* reserves which is dependent on the absolute price level—say,

$$W(i, d', p)\qquad(33)$$

—the same purpose will be accomplished. In brief, a necessary and sufficient condition for the price level to be determinate in the foregoing inside-money model is that the central bank be willing to suffer from money illusion in one form or another! This is the essential point.[24]

From this we move to our second criticism. Once it has decided to fix the level of nominal reserves [or, more generally, act in accordance with (33)], the central bank uniquely determines all the variables of the system by fixing in addition either one of the two rates d or d'—or for that matter (though G-S do not realize this) any one of the three rates $d, d',$ or i. Hence at the theoretical level at which G-S are carrying on their discussion it cannot make a particle of difference which rate is so fixed. Accordingly it is meaningless to say that a monetary authority that can choose d is in a "stronger position" than one that can only choose d'.

---

[24]This presentation enables us to solve a seemingly paradoxical aspect of G-S's argument. They emphasize that a system with competitive banks—but no central bank—is determinate in its rates of return but not in its price level. On the other hand, the introduction of a central bank renders the system indeterminate both in rates of return and the price level. This raises the puzzling question: Why should the introduction of one new equation (for reserves) and one new variable (d') make the indeterminacy so much greater?

But what we now see is that G-S's first system corresponds to (21)–(23), in which the "indeterminacy" of the price level is just a complicated way of saying that this variable does not appear in the system at all. Instead, there exists a system of two (independent) equations in two variables (i, d). And as just noted in the text, we would get exactly the same type of "indeterminacy" if we were to introduce the central bank in the illusion-free way described by equation (32).

On the other hand, once we assume that the central bank suffers from money illusion, we obtain a system like (28)–(31), consisting of three independent equations in four variables ($i, d, d',$ and p), each of which actually appears in the system. And since there is no reason to assume that this system had a determinate subsystem, indeterminacy prevails in all the variables. This, of course, is also characteristic of system (17)–(19), to which system (28)–(31) is essentially similar.

The general conclusion that we can draw from all this is that, in the absence of distribution effects, the necessary condition for rendering a monetary system determinate is that there be an exogenous fixing of (1) some nominal quantity and (2) some rate of return. It follows that if we were to extend the argument to an economy with both inside and outside money (something G-S do not do) it would suffice to fix the quantity of outside money and its rate of return (say, at zero). In such an economy the price level would be determinate even if the central bank were to fix nothing, and operate solely in accordance with the principle of profit-maximization [as represented, say, by equation (32)]—subject to the restriction that the quantity of outside money is fixed.

It is, therefore, unfortunate that G-S have so strongly tied their discussion of central bank policy with that of the conditions necessary to achieve a determinate price level. As can be seen from what has just been said, this is not the real issue at all. Instead, the analysis of central bank policy should concentrate on the behavior (obviously, of a non-profit-maximizing type) such a bank can adopt with reference to such decisions as (say) open-market purchases of bonds in order to bring about *desired* changes in a *determinate* price level and in other variables of the economic system. But it would carry us too far afield to explore these questions in any further detail here.

Postscript

I would like first of all to take advantage of this postscript to express my regret that the critical (if not hypercritical) tone of the preceding article may well have obscured the fact that I considered—and still consider—the Gurley-Shaw volume to be a major contribution to the field of monetary and banking theory. Indeed, I think it is one of the most important and stimulating works that have appeared in this field in the postwar period.

Many of the points discussed in this review article were further developed in the second edition of *Money, Interest, and Prices*. In particular, the analysis of financial intermediaries within a general-equilibrium framework referred to on p. 47 above is developed in Chapter XII:5 of this edition. One of the major conclusions that stem from taking account in this way of the interactions between the commodity and money markets is that the existence of financial intermediaries also affects the price level of the economy— and that the greater this effect, the smaller the effect of these intermediaries on the rate of interest.[1]

Another conclusion of this general-equilibrium analysis is that—within the framework of comparative-statics analysis—constancy of the proportion between inside and outside money is not the special case which it is considered to be on pp. 44–45 above, but is instead the necessary characteristic of a model in which (a) banks hold outside money as reserves against inside money (deposits); (b) all economic units—including banks—are free of money illusion; and (c) the initial exogenous change occurs in the quantity of outside money. On the other hand, the proportion between inside and outside

[1]*Money, Interest, and Prices*, 2nd ed. (New York, 1965), pp. 301–302 and 251–252.

money will be affected if the exogenous change occurs in the banks' reserve ratio or in the currency-demand deposit ratio.[2]

Yet another issue which is clarified is the nature of the valid dichotomy discussed on p. 43 above. In the treatment of this question in the second edition[3] it is emphasized that the pure inside-money model first presented by Gurley and Shaw enables us to provide an economically meaningful instance of the valid dichotomy which was described only as a formal—and not particularly reasonable—possibility in the pages from the first edition cited in note 15 above. I regret that this was not originally made clear in this footnote.

On the other hand, the foregoing review article does refer to one issue—that of monetary policy—which, unfortunately, was not discussed in the second edition. As shown on p. 47 above, the existence of financial intermediaries does not, in principle, impair the efficacy of open-market policy. Theoretically, it only affects the conditions under which the monetary authorities operate in the bond market: that is, it affects the volume of the operations that the authorities must carry out in order to establish a given rate of interest. All this, however, rests upon the assumption that the behavior functions of the financial intermediaries are fully known and taken into account by these authorities. Since, in reality, this is not the case, the existence of financial intermediaries may in practice impair the efficacy of monetary policy by virtue of the fact that it introduces another uncertain link between the actions of the monetary authorities, on the one hand, and their effects on the economy, on the other. This may especially be true with respect to the lags with which these effects manifest themselves—a question that has been much discussed in recent years.

[2] *Ibid.*, pp. 298–300.
[3] *Ibid.*, pp. 180 (note 43), and 297–298.

4

Monetary
and Price Developments
in Israel: 1949–1953

INTRODUCTION

From its inception in May 1948, the State of Israel had undergone a series of monetary and price transformations. A full analysis of these transformations can be carried out only as part of a detailed study of the contemporaneous general economic developments. Such a study is far beyond the scope of this paper. Instead, its purpose is to analyze briefly the salient features of these

Reprinted by permission of the Magnes Press from Scripta Hierosolymitana, *Vol. III, Roberto Bachi (ed.),* Studies in Economic and Social Sciences *(Jerusalem, 1956), pp. 20–52.*

[1] With one exception, this paper reproduces with minor revisions the contents of a study prepared by the writer at the request of the Ministry of Finance and submitted to it at the end of June 1953. This study was subsequently circulated in mimeographed form among various government ministries. The major modification lies in the emphasis the paper now gives to nonbudgetary government expenditures and letters of obligation, which were neglected in the original study. With the exception of a footnote at the end, no attempt has been made to bring this study up to date (April 1954).

I am indebted to the Ministry of Finance for its permission to publish the results of this study. Needless to say, the opinions expressed in this paper are those of the writer alone; they do not necessarily represent the views of the Ministry of Finance or any other government office.

The original study, and hence this paper, could not have been written without the kind assistance of various government ministries and private financial institutions. In particular, I am indebted to the officials of the Accountant General's Office, the Central Bureau of Statistics, the Office of the Controller of Banks, the Food Division of the Ministry of Commerce and Industry, the former Office of Economic Coordination, the Ministry of Labor, and the Bank Leumi Le-Israel and the Union Bank for the data they supplied and for their helpful discussions.

I wish finally to express my appreciation to my student, Mr Tsvi Goldberger [Ophir], for his conscientious and meticulous work in the compilation of data, carrying out of computations, and preparation of diagrams.

A general statement might be made about the data on which this study is based. Clearly, in many cases they are crude and even nonrepresentative. The more extreme examples of this are referred to in what follows. Nevertheless, they do seem to me to be the best data available; and they do seem to give a correct general picture of the developments of the period under study.

transformations, with particular attention to the implications of the policy officially initiated in February 1952.

The framework within which this analysis will be carried out is that of the traditional quantity theory of money. The paucity of national-income data for Israel leaves little choice in this matter. Furthermore, as I have shown elsewhere, the traditional and national-income approaches actually yield equivalent results.[2] This same paucity of data will lead us to neglect the changes in total production and the velocity of circulation. However, it seems likely that both of these increased during the period in question, so that there is some degree of offsetting. More important, the magnitude of these developments is undoubtedly small relative to the extensive monetary and price changes which took place. Hence the analysis of the latter is probably not significantly changed by the omission of these factors.

The background material needed for the following discussion can be set out briefly. Until 1948 Palestine was a British-Mandate territory and a member of the sterling bloc. Its currency—the Palestine pound—was issued by the Palestine Currency Board and was freely convertible into sterling at a one-to-one ratio. The assets of this Board were entirely in sterling.

Under its first currency law, the Government of Israel—no longer a member of the sterling bloc—made an agreement with the Anglo-Palestine Bank[3] setting up an Issue Department to issue Israel currency. The initial assets of this Department were the Palestine pounds converted by the public at a one-to-one ratio with the Israel pound. These Palestine pounds were then exchanged for the assets which they represented and the proceeds held in frozen sterling accounts. The Issue Department was also authorized to issue currency against 91-day Treasury Bills, provided that its ratio of foreign-exchange holdings to notes in circulation did not fall below 50 percent.

In 1949 an agreement was reached with the British Government for the release of the frozen sterling assets. In order to free these assets for the financing of imports, the Government of Israel then amended its currency law to permit the Issue Department to hold Land Bonds as well as foreign exchange as part of its minimum required 50 percent reserve ratio. These bonds were long-term ones issued to finance the Development Budget and (with minor exceptions) were sold only to the Issue Department. In this way the latter's foreign-exchange holdings diminished sharply in 1950 and almost entirely disappeared in the spring of 1951.[4]

The events of the period under examination must be seen against the background of the three fundamental influences which dominated it. First

---

[2] See my "Keynesian Economics and the Quantity Theory," in Kenneth Kurihara (ed.), *Post-Keynesian Economics* (New Brunswick, N.J., 1954), Chapter 5.

[3] The name of this bank was later changed to Bank Leumi Le-Israel. It is the largest of the private banks in Israel. There is as yet no central bank in Israel, though proposed legislation for the establishment of one is already under discussion.

[Since the above was written the Bank of Israel has been established as the central bank. It began its operations on 1 December 1954.]

[4] See Appendix Table 1, p. 74.

was the problem of defense. The War of Independence of 1948 and the failure to replace the truce agreements with a permanent peace treaty necessitated continuous large defense expenditures. Second was the policy of mass immigration—the "Ingathering of the Exiles." The magnitude of this enterprise can best be appreciated by noting that by the end of 1951 roughly half the inhabitants of Israel had arrived after the establishment of the State. The majority of these immigrants arrived without adequate means. Their integration into the community was the declared responsibility of the government and related agencies. Third, and related to the preceding, was an extended program of economic development, aimed at increasing the productive capacity of the economy, and financed to a large extent by a special governmental Development Budget.

All of these influences created a heavy burden both on the government budgets and on the balance of payments. Thus most of the period under study was marked by a significant degree of inflationary financing. As far as the balance of payments is concerned, we need only note that on the average during this period only 15–20 percent of imports were matched by exports. The resulting deficit was financed by unilateral transfers of various types.

We turn now to our investigation proper. It will be convenient to divide this up into three parts, corresponding to three periods: the first extending to the summer of 1951; the second to the summer of 1952; and the third, to the culmination date of this study—the spring of 1953.

I. THE PERIOD OF SUPPRESSED INFLATION

The first period can be most easily characterized as one of suppressed inflation. Government deficit spending financed by bank borrowing, together with a continuous expansion of bank credit to the nongovernment sector, greatly increased aggregate expenditures and the money supply. On the other hand, the government attempted to maintain a system of price controls and rationing to keep the cost of living down. These policies created two parallel forces: First, the relatively small expenditures with which families could satisfy their basic needs encouraged them to divert increasing portions of their incomes to nonessential goods and black-market purchases. Second, this tendency was reinforced by the great increase in the real value of liquid assets held by the public. Thus the system created ever-increasing pressures which ultimately led to its dissolution.

The following data provide the basis for the foregoing description. During fiscal year 1948/1949 the government sold IL 33.2 million of Treasury Bills to help finance its various budgets. Most of these were sold to the banking system, including the Issue Department. During fiscal 1949/1950 (the first year in which there was a Development Budget) the government sold IL 22.2 million of Treasury Bills and IL 16.7 million of Land Bonds. The corresponding figures for 1950/1951 were IL 13.6 and IL 40.8 million, respectively. These Land Bonds financed slightly over half of the total expenditure of the Development Budget during these two years, and a little less than one third of the combined expenditures of this Budget and the Ordinary one.

In addition to the preceding, there were other minor government borrowings from the banking system. The complete picture is presented in Appendix Table 2. This shows that total government securities held by banks and credit cooperatives increased from an estimated IL 27.6 million at the end of January 1949 to IL 46.0 million (January 1950), to IL 54.2 million (January 1951), and reached a peak of IL 62.6 million in November 1951. At the same time, Treasury Bills and Land Bonds held by the Issue Department increased from IL 6.8 million (January 1949) to IL 22.0 million (January 1950), to IL 65.7 million (January 1951), and reached IL 86.7 million and IL 92.1 million in August and September 1951, respectively. Thus total government securities held by the banking system (inclusive of the Issue Department) increased from IL 34.4 million in January 1949 to IL 144.4 million and IL 150.2 million in August and September 1951, respectively.

The dependence of the government on borrowing from the banking system during this period is shown most clearly by the following facts. The total government internal debt on December 31, 1950[5] was IL 137.8 million. Of this at least IL 112.6 million, or 82 percent were held by the banking system (including the issue Department). The corresponding figure for December 31, 1951[6] were IL 179.1 million, of which at least IL 157.5 million, or 88 percent, were held by the banking system. It was a recurring characteristic of the entire period under study that the government was not able to borrow to any significant degree from the nonbanking public.[7]

With the exception of roughly IL 25 million of government securities which were substituted for the original foreign-exchange holdings of the Issue Department, the banking system purchased these securities by making net additions to the money supply. In particular, banks and credit cooperatives extended this credit to the government without contracting their credit to the nongovernmental sector. Indeed, precisely the opposite occurred: their acquisition of government securities enabled them greatly to expand this credit. For due to the effective readiness of the Issue Department to discount them at a fixed rate, Treasury Bills were almost perfectly liquid.

These developments are shown most clearly by an examination of the reserve position of the banks. Total effective reserves (cash *plus* net deposits abroad *plus* Treasury Bills) grew from IL 36.8 million at the end of January 1949 to IL 46.0 million (January 1950), to IL 53.7 million (January 1951), and reached a peak of IL 60.9 million in July 1951. The figures for August and September 1951 were IL 57.8 and IL 54.7 million, respectively. As a result of these increased reserves, as well as of a drawing down of the reserve ratio, loans and discounts of the banks[8] grew from IL 37.9 million

---

[5] Exclusive of bearer bonds.

[6] Exclusive of bearer bonds and Jewish Agency Loan.

[7] This is referred to again below.

[8] Exclusive of loans made in connection with the government's administration of its Development Budget.

(January 1949) to IL50.3 million (January 1950), to IL75.8 million (January 1951), and reached IL93.7 and IL98.4 million, respectively, in August and September 1951. Correspondingly, total deposits (demand deposits *plus* time deposits up to and including 12 months) grew from IL70.1 million (January 1949) to IL90.3 million (January 1950), to IL123.2 million (January 1951), and reached IL141.6 and IL144.1 million respectively, in August and September 1951. Thus during the period January 1949–September 1951 bank reserves increased by roughly 50 percent, whereas deposits roughly doubled. Accordingly, the relevant reserve ratio decreased from 52 percent in January 1949 to 38 percent in September 1951.[9]

This credit expansion created a corresponding increase in the money supply. Net credit creation by the Issue Department during February 1949–September 1951 (excluding the IL25 million substituted for foreign exchange) was roughly IL60.3 million. The corresponding figures for banks and credit cooperatives were IL30.5 million in government securities and IL77.7 million in loans and discounts, for a total of IL108.2 million. Thus the net credit expansion of the banking system during this period equalled IL168.5 million. Correspondingly, the money supply during this period[10] increased from IL107.8 to IL252.0 million, i.e. by IL144.2 million.

During this period the official cost-of-living index was maintained by direct controls at a low level. In fact, by a series of administrative decrees prices were reduced during 1949 and 1950 from a high of 98 in April 1949 to a low of 86, a level maintained continuously for the eight months following November 1949. With the outbreak of the Korean War and the rise in international prices which followed it, this stability was disrupted. Beginning with August 1950 the index began to rise slowly and in the summer of 1951 was once again back around 100.[11]

This relative stability of the index did not, however, correspond to a stability of the "true" price level. In particular, 53 percent of the index's weights were devoted to food items, where price controls were especially concentrated. It almost completely ignored the prices of the growing black market, which became particularly important after the unanticipated overnight introduction of clothing and footwear rationing on August 1, 1950.[12] This act marked the first time that the Israel public was sharply confronted with the realities of its economic situation and made to realize the difficulties which lay before it. Its reaction was reflected in an immediate minor run on

---

[9] For further details see Appendix Table 3.

[10] Defined here as hand-to-hand currency outside banks and credit cooperatives *plus* demand deposits and time deposits up to and including 12 months of banks and credit cooperatives, excluding those of government.

[11] See Appendix Table 4, column 2.

A detailed study of the policy of administrative price reductions during 1950 has been made by the Nachum Gross, "Inflation and Economic Policy in Israel: First Phase: 1949–1950" (unpublished M. A. thesis, The Hebrew University of Jerusalem, 1954; Hebrew).

[12] Note that the distortion of the official index is due not to the mere *existence* of a black market, but to the *change* in its importance and price movements relative to those of the legal markets.

the banks, a merchants' strike which closed shops for several days, and a sharp rise in the black-market dollar rate.

Unfortunately, no good estimates of the extent of black markets are available. There are, however, some data on prices in these markets. For example, during the period in question the black-market rate on the dollar in Tel Aviv rose almost continuously from approximately IL 0.350 per dollar in January 1949 by an average rate of 4 percent per month to a level of IL 1.250 per dollar in September 1951.[13] This represents an almost fourfold increase during the period. Since to some extent real-estate prices and some black-market prices moved in sympathy with this rate, it also gives us some idea of the developments in these free markets.

Some information is also available on the relationship between black-market prices and official prices in September 1951. Thus the black-market rate for the dollar was roughly three-and-a-half times the official rate. This figure, however, somewhat overstates the realities of the case, since the official rate was frequently raised in practice by special levies on imports. The black-market price for fresh meat was roughly eight times the official one. The corresponding figures for eggs, edible oil, sugar, and potatoes were 3.2, 9.3, 25.0 and 5.7, respectively. Similarly, the ratios for a man's suit, utility trousers, undershirts, bedsheets, utility tables, and aluminium cooking pots were roughly 3.5, 2.5, 4, 3, 3, and 1.5, respectively.[14]

An idea of the magnitude of the pressures which were creating the black market can be obtained from the following figures: From January 1949 to September 1951 the real value of liquid assets of the public more than doubled. This represents an increase of roughly 2 1/2 percent per month (see Figure 4.1). Admittedly, the increase would be less if the deflator used were a somewhat more realistic index than the official one. Nevertheless, it seems a valid conjecture that even the former index would show a decided increase in these assets.

The picture that thus emerges at the end of the period is one of the breaking-up of a system of controls. Black-market prices were rising. Even the official index in the period July–December 1951 rose regularly at the rate of approximately 2 1/2 percent per month. It was becoming more and more difficult to assure the marketing of local production through official channels. The black-market rate on the dollar in Tel Aviv was rising precipitously, and the public was following it daily. The level of real balances had reached a peak and was exerting a pressure which could no longer be withstood. All these factors were further aggravated by the serious drought of the winter of 1950/1951, which greatly reduced the quantity of food supplies marketed during the following summer and caused corresponding increases in their prices. There was a general realization and anticipation that the policies which the government had attempted to carry out until then would have to be seriously modified.

[13] David Kochav, "Imports without Allocation of Foreign Exchange in Israel: 1949–1952" (unpublished M. A. thesis, The Hebrew University of Jerusalem, 1953; Hebrew), p. 38.
[14] See Appendix Table 5.

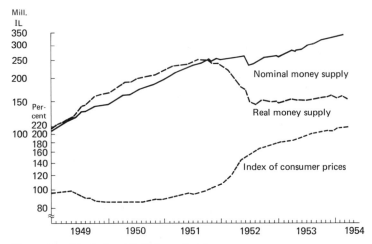

Figure 4.1.   Nominal and Ral Money Supply
SOURCE: See Appendix Table 4. Data after March 1953 based on new series; see *Statistical Bulletin of Israel*, Part B, V (April 1954), 247 (Hebrew).

II. THE "NEW ECONOMIC POLICY"

The period which follows can be described most easily as one during which there was an attempt to stop further inflationary credit expansion while, at the same time, the inflationary pressures which had been built up, but suppressed, during the preceding period were permitted to work themselves off in the form of price increases. During the eleven months over which this period extends, these price increases reduced the real value of the money supply in the economy by roughly 40 percent. Thus this period was marked by increasing reliance on "rationing by the purse."

In some respects this disinflationary policy began before September 1951. This is true, for example, in so far as the price increases are concerned. There are also indications prior to September 1951 of the desire to end inflationary financing. Thus the issue of Treasury Bills was discontinued in April 1951. But Land Bonds continued to be issued until the end of August. In this way the total of open government borrowing from the banking system continued to expand at roughly the same rate as before until September 1951.

Similarly, already on November 15, 1950 there was an attempt to restrict credit. Banks and credit cooperatives were requested[15] to keep a reserve ratio of 45 percent against demand deposits and time deposits up to and including 18 months. On March 31, 1951 the requested reserve ratio was raised to 50 percent on the level of deposits existing on that date, and 75 percent on any increase in deposits after that date. However, as will be argued below, these credit restrictions were at best qualitative in nature.

[15] In the absence of the necessary legislation, the banks could only be requested, not required.

Even after they were made, loans and discounts of banks and credit co-operatives continued to grow at the same regular rate at which they had grown since the beginning of 1949: roughly $2^1/_2$ percent per month.

On the other hand, the customary dating of the "New Economic Policy" as beginning on February 13, 1952 has little economic justification. On this date the Israeli pound was officially devalued from $2.80 = IL1.000, to a multiple exchange-rate system of $2.80 = IL1.000, $1.40 = IL1.000, and $1.00 = IL1.000. Actually, however, effective devaluation had begun several months before via administrative actions raising the valuation of imports for customs purposes and imposing other charges on importers. Thus it is not surprising that the action of February 13 evidences itself only to a minor extent in the data. Sharp price rises had already taken place in December and January—though it is true that the rise was somewhat sharper in February and March. Similarly, there were no significant changes in the black-market rate on the dollar following February 1952. The official depreciation seems to have been almost completely discounted in the precipitous rise of August–October 1951 mentioned at the end of the preceding section. Thus the devaluation of February 1952 merely reflects belated official recognition of developments that had started several months before.

September 1951 shows itself as the date on which the rate of increase in the money supply fell from roughly 2.5 percent per month to 1.5 percent per month. It shows itself even more sharply as a near-peak in the level of real money balances. From a level of IL252 million on this date, these balances fell steadily during the following ten months by a total of 40 percent, reaching a level of roughly IL150 million (in constant September 1951 Israel pounds) in July 1952. Similarly the real value of bank credit fell steadily during this same period by roughly 30 percent from an initial peak of IL122.5 million to roughly IL85 million (in constant September 1951 Israel pounds) in July 1952. In both cases the nominal amounts continued to rise, but the price index rose even faster.

Just as the behavior of the index during the first period exaggerated the rise in real balances, so its behavior in this period may well exaggerate the fall. Specifically, it may be that uncontrolled and black-market prices rose in a smaller proportion than the prices reflected in the index, and that in some cases they even fell. If this were true, the index would overstate the price rise. Unfortunately, the data on this question are inadequate. The contention seems to be less accurate for the present period than for the one after it. For the former, the data of Appendix Table 5 (p. 79) seem to show that the contention is not true for food items and most textiles but may be true for certain "luxury items." It is, however, known that there were definite decreases in real-estate prices.

On the other hand, the official index may underestimate the price rise. For the new index which came into effect on September 1951 gives a smaller weight to food items than did the preceding index (41 percent instead of 52.8 percent), and the rise in official food prices was somewhat higher than the average price rise during this period. In any event, there is some basis for thinking that the movements of the official index give a more accurate picture of the overall price rise from January 1949 to June 1952, or even better, from January 1949 to April 1953, than they do of the separate price rises of each of the three periods here delineated.

Let us now consider somewhat more systematically the actual price developments of this period as against the objectives that they could have accomplished. These objectives are two in number: first, a rise in the absolute price level in order to absorb the excess liquidity built up during the preceding inflationary period; second, changes in certain relative prices to correct serious distortions in the existing price structure.

We have already described how the first of these objectives was successfully accomplished. The reduction in real-money balances evidenced itself in a noticeable lowering of the pressure of excess demand on the markets. This is reflected in, for example, the relative stability of the black-market rate on the dollar throughout this period. From the viewpoint of general monetary theory, it is particularly interesting to note that despite the presence of all the psychological preconditions for a runaway inflation—a population many of whose industrial and commercial leaders had personally experienced post-World War I and II runaway inflations in Europe, a population which had experienced (by official indexes) a continuous fourfold increase in prices since 1939, and which had followed with close interest the continuous and precipitous deterioration of the Israel pound on local and foreign black markets over a period of two years—despite all this, a further rapid price increase of 62 percent was experienced within an eleven-month period without such an inflation being generated. Indeed, the developments of this period were accepted with relative calm. It would seem that despite the adverse expectations which undoubtedly existed, the constantly reduced real liquidity position of the public prevented it from acting on the basis of these expectations and thus prevented them from eventuating. It is true that there was not an ultimate levelling-off of prices; but the rate of their increase did finally drop off.[16]

The success in achieving changes in the relative price structure is much more difficult to judge. The relevant price data are for the most part either unavailable or inconclusive. Let us first list in a general way those price changes which might be considered desirable:

1. A decrease in money incomes relative to the cost of living;
2. A decrease in the real wage rate;
3. An increase in the price of goods whose import component is high relative to goods whose import component is low;

[16] It should, however, be noted that though the more extreme influences of expectations did not manifest themselves during this period (nor in any other), the presence of these expectations greatly restricted the desire to save. For this reason the government was never able successfully to float a popular anti-inflationary loan and had to resort instead to borrowing from the banking system; see above.

4. An increase in the prices of locally produced commodities which
    can best serve as import substitutes, as compared with prices of
    less efficient import substitutes;
5. An increase in the price realizable from exporting a commodity,
    relative to costs and to the price obtainable by selling it in the
    domestic market.

Though listed separately, there is a great deal of overlapping among
these five objectives, particularly among the last four. The first provides
for a reduction in the standard of living. This reduces the pressure on the
balance of payments and also enables the diversion of a greater proportion
of the economy's resources to development. There is a distinct difference
between the first objective and the second; through unemployment, the first
can be accomplished without any change in the real wage rate. It is also
possible that the real wage rate paid by employers remains the same, while
that received by the workers decreases because of increased taxation. In this
case there would be no incentive for the increased employment of labor.
Subsumed under the second objective is also that of increasing the cost of
using mechanized methods relative to nonmechanized ones. It has been a
frequent criticism of the Israel economy that the wage-price structure did
just the opposite. This is hardly the correct economic policy for a country
with a serious shortage of capital trying to absorb a greatly increased population.

The last three objectives all have the common purpose of improving
the balance of payments: they represent the description of a successful
depreciation. Accomplishment of the third objective would cut down on
imports through its influence on consumption; the fourth would do the
same through its influence on production. The latter is possibly more important than the former. For example, it has frequently been claimed that the
structure of agricultural prices does not promote this objective.

To the extent that the price increases during September 1951–July 1952
occurred uniformly, none of these objectives could be accomplished. In this
event, all that would happen is that the pressure of liquid assets would be
absorbed, but that the distortions in the price structure would remain. Before
we can definitely determine what actually did happen, thorough and extensive study will be needed. All that can be indicated here is the general and
provisional impression from the few data that are readily available. This
impression is that there were not too many significant changes in the relative
price structure during the period in question.

Thus a comparison of average official prices paid to agricultural producers for the crop year 1952/1953, as compared with 1950/1951, shows
that wheat, milk, eggs and poultry all rose in somewhat the same proportion.
On the other hand, there was a salutary rise in the relative price of potatoes.[17]
The data also show that in the period in question the retail prices of such

---

[17]Information received from G. Kadar.

import staples as flour, edible oils, and sugar all rose in a smaller proportion than did the general price level. Thus the relative subsidy given to these goods increased during this period. On the other hand, the prices of oranges, kerosene, and certain clothing items rose more rapidly than the general price level (see Appendix Table 6, p. 80).

Finally, the official data show no decline in the real daily wage rate. For purposes of this comparison February 1952 is taken as the base, in order not to include the increase in the basic wage rate of roughly 13 percent which occurred in January 1952. This increase was intended to compensate for preceding price increases which had not been fully reflected in the official cost-of-living index, and hence in the cost-of-living allowance. The index of the daily real wage rate in manufacturing industries was 103 in July, as compared with 100 in February 1952. The corresponding figures for construction were 101 in July as compared with 100 in January 1952 and 95 in February.

These latter data conflict with the general impression that one had during this period. They also seem to be inconsistent with the nature of the cost-of-living allowance system. For this allows a proportionate adjustment to the cost-of-living index (based on September 1951) only for the first IL 80 of the monthly wage. Hence the wage rate of any worker who received more than IL 80 during that month—and there were many such—should have increased in a smaller proportion than the cost-of-living.

There may be a tendency for the official wage statistics to underestimate the decline in real wages in industry. These statistics are based on payroll data of a sample of firms. It has been pointed out that due to the presence of unreported premiums, many workers received a higher compensation than appeared in these payrolls on the base date, and that these premiums disappeared on later dates. The relevance of this contention for our present data depends on the extent to which such premiums still existed in February 1952, when the level of employment in industry had already dropped. It has also been pointed out that due to this falling off in activity, firms let their unskilled workers go, while holding on to skilled ones. This would clearly tend to raise the average wage rates revealed by payroll data.

In any event, the picture with reference to the relative price structure is certainly not clear. The further developments that took place here will be discussed in the next section.

Let us turn now to the second declared objective of the "New Economic Policy"—that of putting an end to further inflationary credit expansion. As has already been pointed out above, after September 1951 the government was able to finance its budgets without recourse to additional net financing by Treasury Bills and Land Bonds. This, however, did not mean that there was no further expansion of bank credit due to the government. For the latter also had to meet a deficit generated by its nonbudgetary activities. Of particular importance here was the deficit generated by the system of multiple exchange rates through which the prices of many imports were subsidized. From February 13, 1952 until March 31, 1953 this amounted to IL14.9 million. On the other hand, the government had various nonbudgetary receipts which offset some of this deficit. On balance, by the end of March 1953 the government had borrowed outside its budget IL4.4 million from the banking system.[18]

In addition, the government issued Letters of Obligation to various semigovernmental and even private enterprises which were engaged in activities included in the Development Budget; and these Letters were for the most part used as a basis for obtaining bank credit. The total of such Letters issued as of March 31, 1953 was IL12.9 million.[19] Thus though the extent of government inflationary borrowing decreased as compared with the preceding period, it did not completely cease.

Even less success attended the attempts to institute credit restrictions. As indicated above, the requests for these restrictions were stated in quantitative terms. Actually, however, they were not intended for—and certainly did not accomplish—this purpose. Thus at each of the dates on which banks were requested to hold successively higher minimum reserve ratios, they were already below the requested ratio. Furthermore, as we shall see, total bank credit continued to expand throughout this period at a rate only slightly less than that which prevailed before.

The requests in question served only to give the government a certain degree of qualitative control over the expanding credit. Officially, banks could lend "beyond their reserve requirements" only with government approval, and such approval was given only for purposes considered essential. Actually, however, even this control was quite limited. For the computational procedure set out by the directive effectively enabled the banks to consider the authorized loans made outside the liquidity requirements as part of their legal reserves. Hence as long as they were not required to keep 100 percent reserves against the expansion in deposits caused by the authorized extension of credit, they were able to make additional credit expansions of their own. Thus the total of authorized bank credit (excluding credit cooperatives) outside the liquidity requirements on September 30, 1952 was IL18.7 million. But total bank credit from October 1950—shortly before the first directive went into force—until September 1952 grew by roughly IL45 million. This loophole was finally reduced by the directive of April 14, 1953, which required banks to hold in reserve 90 percent of net additions to deposits after December 31, 1952 or March 31, 1953— according to the choice of the bank. As seen in Table 4.1, it is true that since October 1, 1950 the percentage of bank credit going to the productive sectors of the economy has increased.

---

[18]*Summary of Accounts as of March 31, 1953 (Provisional Figures)*, Ministry of Finance, Accountant General's Office (Jerusalem, June 1953; Hebrew mimeograph). Earlier figures have not been published.

[19]*Financial Report for the Fiscal Year 1952/53 (Provisional Figures)*, Ministry of Finance, Accountant General's Office (Jerusalem, June 1953; Hebrew), p. 9. Earlier figures have not been published.

Table 4.1   Distribution of Bank Credit to Selected Sectors[a]   (percent)

End of	Agriculture	Industry	Construction	Trade
1948				
March	16.5	20.0	8.0	19.7
1949				
March	14.1	16.9	8.4	19.5
1950				
March	16.0	16.5	8.3	17.4
September	14.8	13.9	8.2	13.1
1951				
March	14.5	14.6	10.0	12.9
September	14.4	14.5	9.0	14.4
1952				
March	18.4	15.7	7.4	12.2
June	19.3	16.6	7.1	11.5
September	18.4	16.5	7.4	10.8
1953				
March	22.3	17.2	7.2	9.7

[a]Excludes credit of credit cooperatives; includes bank loans from government deposits in banks.
SOURCE: Office of the Controller of Banks.

Nevertheless, it is doubtful if the cause of this improvement lies entirely with the credit directives. The fact that on, say, September 30, 1952 "credit outside liquidity restrictions" constituted only about 13 percent of total bank credit, and that only 37 percent of the former were devoted to agriculture and industry, makes it clear that there must have been other factors at work, too.

The quantitative developments of this period can now be set out briefly. From 1949–1953 there was a definite linear trend downward—though with sharp fluctuations around the trend—in the ratio of demand deposits to hand-to-hand currency. This fell from an average of 2.3 in 1949 to 1.9 (1950), 1.8 (1951), 1.4 (1952), and 1.3 (January–April 1953) (see Appendix Table 7, p. 81). As long as the government financing described in the preceding section more than replenished their reserves, this internal drain was of no particular concern to the banks. But this type of financing ceased during the period in question. Hence the internal drain forced banks to discount their Treasury Bills with the Issue Department in order to meet the demand for cash. This caused a sharp and continuous decline in their reserves. They did not, however, respond to this reduction with a contraction in their credit. Indeed, as pointed out above, their loans and discounts continued to expand at the average rate of 2 percent per month. Thus the decrease in deposits that might have resulted from the internal drain was slightly more than offset by the expansion of credit. As a result, total deposits actually grew in the period

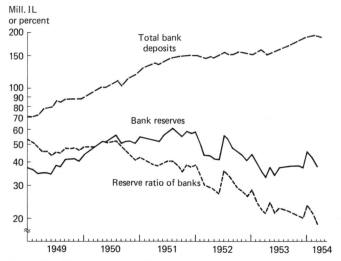

Figure 4.2.   Reserve Position of Banks
SOURCE: See Appendix Table 3, columns 1–4.

September 1951–May 1952. This is reflected in a corresponding growth in the money supply.

The data describing these developments appear in Figure 4.2 and Appendix Tables 2 and 3. These show a reduction in reserves of banks and credit cooperatives from IL 57.9 million in September 1951 to IL 44.5 million in May 1952. This reflects primarily the reduction in holdings of Treasury Bills from IL 45.5 million on the former date to IL 30.4 million on the latter. There is a corresponding increase during the same period in the holdings of Treasury Bills by the Issue Department from IL 26.1 to IL 38.3 million.

From September 1951 to May 1952 loans and discounts of banks and credit cooperatives increased from IL 122.5 to IL 140.0 million. Total deposits increased slightly from IL 180.2 to IL 180.5 million, and the reserve ratio dropped from 32.1 percent to 24.7 percent. The money supply during this period thus increased from IL 252.0 to IL 265.2 million, or roughly by the amount of the internal drain.

The period closed with an event which leaves a sharp, though transitory, impact on the data. This was the currency conversion of June 9, 1952. It should be emphasized that, in contrast with many European precedents, this conversion was not a means of monetary reform, but purely a fiscal operation. It was a forced loan of roughly 10 percent levied on individual money holdings. The government considered this loan just like any other receipt, and proceeded to use it to meet its authorized budget expenditures. Although the immediate consequence of the conversion was a sharp drop in the money supply, this was rapidly replenished as the government made use of the funds it had received. Thus a consideration of the money supply during the whole period September 1951–May 1953 shows the currency conversion as a temporary, though sharp, deviation from the expansionary trend which existed during this period. There seem to exist grounds for suspecting that if the fiscal nature of the conversion had been fully realized, a bolder policy as to the percentage deducted would have been taken.

The conversion also shows itself very clearly in the data on the banking system. The government deposited its cash receipts with the banks, and the latter used them to purchase Treasury Bills from the Issue Department. Thus the reserves and reserve ratios of banks and credit cooperatives were sharply increased. However, later, as the government spent the funds it had received, the downward trends in reserves and reserve ratios reasserted themselves (for details see Tables 2 and 3, in the appendix to this chapter, and Figures 4.1 and 4.2).

III. CONTROLLED INFLATION

Beginning with July 1952 the economy seems to have entered upon yet a third phase of its monetary development. In many ways this phase continued with the tendencies which had appeared during the preceding period. But in one aspect there was a distinct difference: The disinflationary impact of a sharply rising price level on real money supply and credit came to an end. From July 1952 to April 1953 these remained more or less on the same level.

Before getting on with the detailed analysis, two unrepresentative movements in the data should be noted. One is the apparent large expansion of credit deposits and money supply in January and February 1953. This is the result of operations concerning a certain large blocked account, and

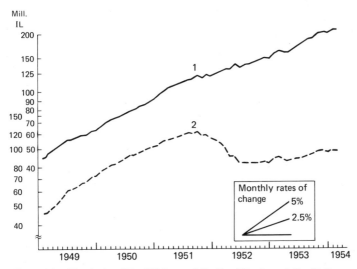

Figure 4.3. Nominal and Real Volume of Credit of Banks and Credit Cooperatives
1 Total Loans and discounts of banks and credit cooperatives excluding loans from government deposits
2 Same—in constant September 1951 Israel pounds
SOURCE: See Appendix Table 3, columns 6 and 9.

does not have any real economic significance. Hence it is better for our purposes to compare directly December, or even November, 1952 with March and April 1953, ignoring the intervening months. A second is the sharp decline in reserves at the end of March 1953. This was the result of an internal drain occurring in connection with the Passover holiday, which began on March 31.

The characteristics which this period shares with the preceding one can be briefly indicated. The volume outstanding of Treasury Bills and Land Bonds remained unchanged, but resort was still had to Letters of Obligation. During this period the internal drain continued, roughly in proportion to the increasing price level. With it continued the decline in the reserves and the reserve ratios of the banks and credit cooperatives. By April 1953 these had reached IL 41.1 million and 21 percent, respectively. Once again, most of the decline in reserves was due to the discounting of Treasury Bills at the Issue Department in order to meet the public's demand for cash. Bank credit continued to grow during this period at roughly the same 2 percent rate per month which had characterized the preceding period. This growth slightly more than offset the decline in deposits due to the internal drain, so that there was a slight increase in deposits. There was also an approximate 2 percent per month growth in the money supply—after adjustment is made for the aberrations in the data caused by the currency conversion and the blocked account noted above.

Most important, the period continued to reflect a greatly decreased pressure of excess demand on the markets as compared with the first one. Thus, as Appendix Table 5 (p. 79) shows, most black-market prices either did not rise, or actually fell. Correspondingly, the ratio between market and official prices decreased, primarily as a result of the continued rise in the latter. Similarly the black-market rate on the dollar showed relative stability and perhaps even a slight downward trend throughout this period. Outside the field of "essential" goods, there were continually recurring complaints that business was slow, and that merchants were having difficulty in moving their stocks. There was a falling off in some textile prices, and in the prices of "luxuries." But despite the complaints, there were no general price declines for consumers' goods and there were no bankruptcies. During this period the increase in unemployment which had begun toward the end of the preceding period became particularly noticeable. In the first quarter of 1953 this was roughly three times what it had been in the corresponding quarter of 1952. The percentage of un-employed construction workers increased most sharply. This reflected the sharp decrease in private construction and in the public works financed through the Development Budget.

The distinguishing feature of this period is the levelling-off of the real value of the money supply and bank credit. In the "ideal" case of a dis-inflationary policy, this occurs as a result of a cessation in the rise of the price level after such a rise has completed the task of absorbing the excess liquidity of a fixed, and originally excess, nominal money supply. This is not what occurred here. The constancy of the real value of the money supply and credit was achieved by proportionate increases in both of these items, as well as of the price level, at the average rate of 2 percent per month. This is, indeed, a sharp decline over the rate of increase which existed during the preceding period; but it is still very high.

Once again it should be pointed out that the official index during this period tends to exaggerate the price increase, since prices not fully reflected in it did not rise at the same rate, or even fell. This seems to have held much more for this period than the preceding one. As indicated above, most black-market prices either did not rise, or actually fell. It has also been estimated that during the period from the beginning of 1952 to April 1953 real-estate prices fell from 25–45 percent. But even after taking account of all these factors, it seems very likely that any realistic price index would show significant and continuous price increases since July 1952.

What seems to have happened during this third period is the following: There was a continuous process of (effective) devaluation carried out administratively by transferring goods to higher exchange-rate categories and levying special import charges. Hence the import-cost component of domestically consumed goods increased. Thus a necessary condition for stability in the price of these goods was that the per unit domestic-cost component decreased to a corresponding extent. This, in turn, could happen only as a result of greater efficiency of output, or lower costs per unit of domestic factor input, or both.

There are some indications that productive efficiency increased. On the other hand, it is quite clear that factor input prices increased even more. Specifically, the tying of the nominal wage level to a cost-of-living allow-ance makes it impossible to change relative prices without raising the absolute price level. In the period July 1951–February 1953 the daily nominal wage rate in manufacturing industry rose by roughly 17 percent, while the price level rose by 12 percent. It has already been indicated above that the data may overestimate both the rise in the wage level and in the price level. Hence, it is not clear that the real wage rate during this period had actually risen. It should also be noted that the data show a 5–10 percent reduction in the real daily wage rate for construction industries.

As indicated above, the rising price level from July 1952 onward was not accompanied by any further decreases in the level of real money bal-ances. It seems likely that the process at work was the following: The increased price level created a corresponding increased demand for credit from all sectors of the economy—industry, agriculture, labor unions, trade, etc.—which refused to submit to the disinflationary pressures on their activities that such a price rise would otherwise generate. This increased demand was satisfied by the banks expanding their credit at the expense of their reserve ratios. Not only was there an overall increase in credit in proportion to the price increase, but the specific real amounts allocated to agriculture and industry actually increased during the period June 1952– March 1953 by about 22 percent in the case of the former, and 9 percent in the case of the latter. On the other hand, the real credit extended to trade dropped by about 10 percent (see Appendix Table 8).

This increase in credit created a corresponding increase in the money supply, so that this, too, grew at roughly the same rate as the price level. Thus it seems likely that the increases in money supply in this period—in contrast with the first one—were not the immediate cause of the increased price level, but were rather called into existence by these increases, and enabled their maintenance.

Indeed, the popular rationale for the increased demand for credit was most explicit on this point. Despite the fact that credit was expanding at the rate of 2 percent per month—roughly the same rate of increase as that of the price level—the prevailing cry of the period was one of "deflation," "disinflation," "credit stringencies," and the "necessity for credit expansion to meet the increased needs of business resulting from the rise in prices." The reduction in the real volume of credit as compared with February 1952 was offered as evidence that credit must be expanded further. It was not recognized that it was precisely this reduction which was the objective and mark of success of the "New Economic Policy." Nor was it recognized that credit was expanding at a rate far greater than that of the *real* value of production, and that any attempt to make it expand at a rate equal to its *nominal* value could only lead to an inflationary spiral in which rises in prices caused expansions in credit, which caused further rises in prices *ad infinitum*.[20]

To summarize, there is no evidence that the continued price increase of this third period generated any further disinflationary pressures. Correspondingly, the only economic justification that can be advanced for this policy of continuously raising prices is that it may have improved their relative structure. There is some evidence that, at least temporarily, it did so (see Appendix Table 6, p. 80). But in the basic sense of providing a price structure that would have made viable the depreciation of February 1952, this justification, too, loses its validity; for in the spring of 1953 the government was already taking steps to depreciate the Israel pound once again.

CONCLUSION

The experience of the Israel economy in the period 1949–1953 shows the difficulties of achieving internal, and consequently external, equilibrium in the face of rigidities which prevent changes in relative prices and real incomes. These rigidities prevented the depreciation of early 1952 from being more than a temporary remedy for the serious overvaluation of the Israel pound which had resulted from the inflationary financing of 1949–1951. Specifically, within a little more than a year after February 1952 the new

[20]One cannot but be reminded here of the classical Bullionist and "Currency School"– "Banking School" controversies, and the "real bills" fallacy about which they centred. See L. W. Mints, *A History of Banking Theory* (Chicago, 1945), Chapter 3; J. Viner, *Studies in the Theory of International Trade* (New York, 1937), pp. 148–154, 234–243.

official values for the pound had once again become unrealistic because of the cost-price-credit spiral which moved on unimpeded. As long as the institutional structure which generated such a spiral continued to exist, no exchange rate could remain "realistic" for long.

Thus in the present institutional framework, long-run stability cannot be achieved in Israel by any policy which requires a prior raising of the price level. Nor can mere quantitative credit controls succeed. True, these do slow up the operation of the inflationary spiral just described and are therefore desirable from that viewpoint; but unless other actions are taken simultaneously, they cannot be expected to be maintained against the institutional pressures which have always brought about their effective dissolution in the past. Whatever the technical means used, long-run stability in Israel must involve as a prior condition the "coercion of individuals until they are willing" to reduce their real incomes. As in any other state, this coercion can come only as a result of government policy; but in order effectively to carry out such a policy the government must first arrange its own budgetary affairs so as to free itself of any dependence on the banking system.[21,22]

[21] These concluding observations also incorporate my remarks made as a member of the government Foreign Exchange Committee in June 1953, as well as the contents of a memorandum submitted to the Ministry of Finance shortly afterwards.

[22] As a postscript I might now (April 1954) add my general impression that the developments of the past ten months have been a direct continuation of those of the last period just described. Though the prevailing cry of the period remained "credit shortage" and "disinflation," the expansion of bank credit and money supply continued unabated at the rate of approximately $2\frac{1}{2}$ percent per month. Indeed, as Figures 4.1 and 4.3 show, this expansion was even more rapid than that of the price level. Banks now increased their credit to an extent more than offsetting the internal drain, so that total deposits also grew. Correspondingly, the reserve ratio of banks—with the exception of the end-of-the-year seasonal rise—continued to decline.

One possible significant difference between this period and the last one described in the text lies in the nature of the inflationary process. Though it is very difficult to define the distinction in quantitative terms, it does seem likely that the rapid rise in credit during the past ten months has not been purely a passive response to the rise in prices, but has to a certain extent led this rise. Another difference is that the direct responsibility of government for this credit expansion—by the processes described on p. 66 above—seems to have increased during the past ten months. These points require further study.

Statistical Appendix

Table 1   Bank Leumi Le-Israel Issue Department—Balance Sheet[a] (IL million)

End of	Foreign Exchange Holdings	Currency Notes of the Palestine Currency Board	Govern- ment Land Bonds	Treasury Bills and Other Government Obligations	Total Bank Notes in Circulation
	(1)	(2)	(3)	(4)	(5)
1948					
December	6.8	18.8	—	5.0	30.7
1949					
March	19.7	6.6	—	10.2	36.5
June	27.9	0.4	—	13.3	41.5
September	25.4	0.3	5.1	15.2	46.1
December	28.4	0.3	16.7	4.7	50.1
1950					
March	27.5	0.3	16.7	10.5	55.0
June	22.6	0.2	21.8	11.8	56.4
September	15.4	—	29.9	24.4	69.7
December	10.9	—	49.9	13.1	73.9
1951					
March	5.9	—	53.9	21.1	80.9
June	2.8	—	57.1	25.7	85.6
September	2.8	—	66.0	26.1	94.9
December	2.8	—	77.1	20.4	100.3
1952					
March	—	—	77.1	35.5	112.7
June	—	—	77.1	21.1	98.2
September	—	—	77.1	34.2	111.4
December	—	—	77.1	42.7	119.9
1953					
March	—	—	76.8	54.6	131.5

[a]Totals do not add up because of rounding off.

SOURCE: Central Bureau of Statistics and Economic Research, *Statistical Bulletin of Israel, et passim.*

**Table 2 Government Securities Held by the Banking System (Including the Issue Department)
(IL million)**

End of	Treasury Bills Held by Banks and Credit Cooperatives[a,b]	Other Government Securities Held by Banks and Credit Cooperatives[a]	Treasury Bills Held by Issue Department	Land Bonds Held by Issue Department	Total Government Securities Held by Banking System (1) through (4)
	(1)	(2)	(3)	(4)	(5)
1948					
December	24.2	0.9	5.0	—	30.1
1949					
March	23.4	2.8	10.2	—	36.4
June	26.8	3.2	13.3	—	43.3
September	30.3	3.2	15.2	5.1	53.8
December	36.2	3.4	4.7	16.7	61.0
1950					
March	44.9	3.4	10.5	16.7	75.5
June	48.4	3.3	11.8	21.8	85.3
September	42.3	3.3	24.4	29.9	99.9
December	42.9	6.7	13.1	49.9	112.6
1951					
March	42.3	7.6	21.1	53.9	124.9
June	43.2	8.0	25.7	57.1	134.0
September	45.5	12.6	26.1	66.0	150.2
December	46.2	13.8	20.4	77.1	157.5
1952					
March	32.8	14.2	35.5	77.1	159.6
June	46.1	14.6	21.1	77.1	158.9
September	35.4	15.5	34.2	77.1	162.2
December	26.4	15.4	42.7	77.1	161.6
1953					
March	15.1	16.4	54.6	76.8	162.9

[a] For December 1948 and all of 1949 the figure for credit cooperatives is based on estimates.
[b] For 1950 and 1951 includes also Land Bonds held by banks. During other years no Land Bonds were held by either banks or credit cooperatives.
SOURCE: Office of the Controller of Banks and *Statistical Bulletin of Israel*.

Table 3   Reserves, Loans and Deposits of Banking System (IL million)

End of	Reserves of Banks[a]	Loans and Discounts of Banks[b]	Total Deposits (Demand plus Time)[c]	Reserve Ratio of Banks Columns (1) ÷ (3), percent
	(1)	(2)	(3)	(4)
1948				
December	37.2	38.8	70.2	53
1949				
March	35.4	41.6	76.9	46
June	39.2	47.4	86.4	45
September	42.0	49.2	88.3	48
December	44.2	50.6	90.7	49
1950				
March	49.9	53.3	100.8	49
June	54.8	55.5	105.3	52
September	51.8	66.7	112.2	46
December	55.1	72.3	127.1	43
1951				
March	53.3	82.2	137.2	39
June	59.1	90.9	144.6	41
September	54.7	98.4	150.9	36
December	58.6	96.3	151.0	39
1952				
March	43.8	106.1	148.1	30
June	57.1	106.9	158.1	36
September	45.6	113.1	158.2	29
December	45.0	119.6	153.6	29
1953				
March	33.3	126.9	154.3	22

[a] Cash *plus* net deposits in banks abroad *plus* Treasury Bills and Land Bonds. Excludes deposits of credit cooperatives in banks which are considered by credit cooperatives as their major reserves.
[b] Does not include "Loans from government deposits."
[c] Excludes interbank and credit cooperative deposits.

Reserves of Banks and Credit Cooperatives[a]	Loans and Discounts of Banks and Credit Cooperatives[b]	Total Deposits (Demand plus Time) of Banks and Credit Cooperatives[c]	Reserve Ratio of Banks and Credit Cooperatives together Column (5) ÷ (7), percent	Real Value of Loans and Discounts[d] Column (6) ÷ Table 4, Column (2)
(5)	(6)	(7)	(8)	(9)
n.a.[e]	n.a.	n.a.	n.a.	n.a.
n.a.	49.4	n.a.	n.a.	50.4
n.a.	56.6	n.a.	n.a.	60.8
n.a.	59.0	n.a.	n.a.	67.0
n.a.	62.6	n.a.	n.a.	72.5
53.9	71.8	125.6	43	83.3
58.9	76.9	133.5	44	89.4
54.9	85.0	135.5	40	96.3
58.5	92.0	153.2	38	103.7
55.9	105.7	164.5	34	113.1
62.1	113.1	172.3	36	118.7
57.9	122.5	180.2	32	122.5
61.8	121.5	181.1	34	113.6
46.8	132.3	177.5	26	100.2
60.1	134.2	187.6	32	85.5
48.4	143.6	190.1	25	85.0
47.5	151.0	185.3	25	84.8
36.0	162.0	189.8	19	88.0

[d] Banks and credit cooperatives in September 1951 prices.

[e] Data not available.

SOURCE: Data on banks from Office of Controller of Banks; data on credit cooperatives from Ministry of Labor. See also *Statistical Bulletin of Israel.*

Table 4　Nominal and Real Money Supply

End of	Money supply[a] (IL million)	Consumers' Price Index[b] (September 1951 = 100)	Real Value of Money Supply in Millions of September 1951 IL Columns (1) ÷ (2)	Black-Market Rate on Dollar in Tel Aviv (index, June 1950 = 100)[c]
	(1)	(2)	(3)	(4)
1948				
December	103.0	96	106.9	62
1949				
March	116.6	98	119.0	58
June	132.7	93	142.4	65
September	141.0	88	160.2	67
December	145.1	86	168.1	84
1950				
March	162.9	86	189.0	90
June	172.2	86	200.1	100
September	184.3	88	208.7	127
December	199.3	89	224.7	130
1951				
March	220.5	93	236.0	235
June	235.4	95	247.1	178
September	252.0	100	252.0	194
December	251.7	107	235.2	428
1952				
March	257.8	132	195.3	405
June	236.4	157	150.6	408
September	259.1	169	153.3	389
December	263.0	178	147.8	366
1953				
March	286.7	184	155.8	384

[a] Notes in circulation + demand deposits in banks and credit cooperatives + time deposits up to and including 12 months in banks and credit cooperatives − cash held by banks and credit cooperatives − government deposits. (Last two items estimated for 1948/49.)

[b] As of September 1951: new Consumers' Price Index.

　　December 1950–September 1951: "Interim Index" transferred to base of September 1951 = 100 (the reading for September 1951 is the same as the New Consumers' Price Index).

　　December 1948–November 1950: Old Cost-of-Living Index adjusted as follows: Interim Index reading for December 1950 shows 337, while old Cost-of-Living Index shows 324. It was assumed that this difference of 13 points had occurred at the rate of $\frac{1}{2}$ point per month from November 1948 onward. A modified old c.o.l. index was constructed in this way and spliced to the Interim Index at December 1950.

[c] Rate in June 1950 was IL 0.650 = $1.00.

Data for May 1948–July 1949 inclusive, based on interpolation with rate for gold sovereigns in Tel Aviv.

Data for August–September 1951 and August–December 1952 based on rate in Zurich.

SOURCE: Office of Controller of Banks and *Statistical Bulletin of Israel*; Kochav, *op. cit.*

Table 5 Individual Black-Market Prices and Their Relationship to Official Prices[a]

		September 1951	January 1952	June 1952	August 1952	October 1952	December 1952	January 1953	February 1953	March 1953	April 1953	May 1953
Fresh meat												
black-market price		4.000	6.000	6.000	6.000	6.000	6.000	5.500	6.000	6.000	6.000	6.000
ratio to official price		7.7	6.8	3.75	3.75	3.75	3.75	3.4	3.75	3.75	3.0	3.0
Poultry	price	4.500	5.000	6.000	6.000	5.500	5.500	—	6.000	6.000	5.000	5.000
	ratio	4.5	4.5	3.75	3.0	2.75	2.75	—	3.0	3.0	2.1	2.1
Eggs	price	0.100	0.150	0.200	0.200	0.200	0.200	0.160	0.170	0.170	0.120	0.120
	ratio	3.2	4.6	4.4	4.0	4.0	4.0	3.2	3.4	3.1	1.7	1.7
Fish fillet	price	—	—	—	—	0.600	0.600	0.800	1.200	1.000	1.000	1.000
	ratio	—	—	—	—	1.4	1.4	1.8	2.7	2.3	2.3	2.3
White flour	price	—	—	—	—	—	—	0.400	0.450	0.400	0.300	0.300
	ratio	—	—	—	—	—	—	2.4	2.6	2.4	1.8	1.8
Margarine	price	1.500	2.000	3.500	1.500	1.500	1.500	1.500	1.750	2.000	1.750	2.000
	ratio	6.8	6.7	11.7	5.0	5.0	3.3	3.3	3.9	4.4	3.9	4.4
Edible oil	price	2.000	3.500	3.500	3.500	3.500	3.000	2.750	2.500	2.500	2.500	2.500
	ratio	9.3	11.7	11.7	11.7	11.7	7.5	6.1	5.6	5.6	5.6	5.6
Sugar	price	1.750	2.000	2.000	1.800	1.600	1.600	1.800	1.800	2.000	1.800	1.800
	ratio	25.0	22.2	22.2	20.0	17.8	11.4	12.8	12.8	14.3	10.0	10.0
Coffee	price	3.500	6.000	6.000	6.000	6.000	7.000	7.000	7.000	7.000	6.000	6.000
	ratio	2.7	4.6	2.8	2.8	2.8	2.4	2.1	2.1	2.1	1.8	1.8
Rice	price	0.600	1.000	1.500	2.100	2.100	1.800	1.800	1.800	2.000	2.000	1.800
	ratio	10.0	14.9	12.5	17.5	17.5	13.5	12.9	12.9	14.3	14.3	14.3
Potatoes	price	0.400	0.500	—	—	0.400	0.500	0.400	0.600	0.800	0.225	0.180
	ratio	5.7	7.1	—	—	3.3	3.3	2.7	4.0	5.3	1.5	1.2

[a]Prices are per kilogram except for eggs (per unit). Data refer only to Tel Aviv.
SOURCE: Central Bureau of Statistics and Economic Research.

Table 6 Price Changes of Individual Commodities[a] (in constant September 1951 IL per unit)

End of	Dark Bread[b] 1 kg	White Bread 0.750 kg	White Flour 1 kg	Frozen Fish 1 kg	Marga-rine 1 kg	Edible Oils 1 kg	Sugar 1 kg	Fluid Milk 1 liter	Eggs 10 units	Pota-toes 1 kg	Valencia Oranges 1 kg	Kero-sene 15 liter	Khaki Shirt	Shoes	Enamel Pot
1948															
May												0.372	1.060	3.665	0.620
December												0.415			
1949															
March	0.066	0.090	0.107	0.306	0.326	0.326	0.085	0.118	0.347	0.065	0.087				
June	0.057	0.086	0.113	0.252	0.300	0.322	0.089	0.125	0.300	0.063	0.091	0.391	1.073	4.186	
September	0.055	0.090	0.099	0.267	0.284	0.295	0.089	0.116	0.318	0.067	0.097		1.159	3.811	
December	0.056	0.092	0.101	0.250	0.290	0.301	0.090	0.118	0.290	0.068	0.098	0.348			
1950															
March	0.056	0.092	0.101	0.251	0.290	0.302	0.091	0.116	0.290	0.068	0.075	0.349	1.243	3.678	1.098
June	0.052	0.092	0.101	0.232	0.291	0.249	0.081	0.116	0.291	0.056	0.095				
September	0.051	0.089	0.099	0.227	0.249	0.242	0.079	0.113	0.283	0.054	0.093	0.345	1.207	3.569	1.111
December	0.051	0.089	0.098	0.226	0.248	0.241	0.079	0.113	0.282	0.054	0.092				
1951															
March	0.048	0.085	0.093	0.214	0.235	0.229	0.075	0.107	0.268	0.051	0.067				
June	0.047	0.083	0.091	0.210	0.231	0.225	0.073	0.105	0.262	0.061	0.094	0.357	1.197	3.821	1.158
September	0.050	0.085	0.095	0.200	0.220	0.214	0.070	0.102	0.310	0.070	0.090				
December	0.047	0.089	0.089	0.187	0.280	0.280	0.065	0.116	0.290	0.065	0.075	0.387	1.243	3.757	1.084
1952															
March	0.049	0.083	0.095	0.333	0.227	0.227	0.068	0.139	0.341	0.053	0.076				
June	0.048	0.073	0.080	0.280	0.191	0.191	0.057	0.127	0.318	0.076	0.115	0.602	1.726	6.398	1.255
September	0.044	0.068	0.074	0.260	0.178	0.178	0.053	0.118	0.296	0.071	0.107				
December	0.051	0.079	0.096	0.247	0.253	0.253	0.079	0.112	0.281	0.084	0.101	0.546	1.522	5.303	1.444
1953															
March	0.054	0.084	0.092	0.239	0.245	0.245	0.076	0.125	0.299	0.082	0.098				
April															
May	0.065	0.094	0.089	0.230	0.236	0.236	0.094	0.120	0.366	0.078		0.558	1.364	5.302	1.374

[a]Price obtained by dividing current price by index of retail prices presented in Table 4, column (2). [b]On February 3, 1952 weight of loaf reduced from 1 kilogram to 950 grams. On May 17, 1953, weight reduced to 900 grams. Data not adjusted to take this into account.

SOURCE: Food Division, Ministry of Commerce and Industry.

Table 7   Per Capita Money Supply (in constant September 1951 IL)

End of	Money Supply per capita[a] [Table 4, column (3) divided by population]	Cash Held by Public per capita[b]	Ratio of Demand Deposits to Cash Held by Public Columns $\frac{(1) - (2)}{(2)}$
	(1)	(2)	(3)
1948			
December	134.4	36.1	2.72
1949			
March	134.5	39.0	2.45
June	149.7	44.6	2.36
September	158.8	50.4	2.15
December	158.0	48.4	2.26
1950			
March	170.7	56.4	2.03
June	173.1	55.6	2.12
September	172.1	63.2	1.72
December	176.3	59.8	1.95
1951			
March	177.1	63.5	1.79
June	175.0	62.0	1.82
September	174.0	64.5	1.70
December	159.6	59.5	1.68
1952			
March	130.9	54.7	1.40
June	100.0	39.0	1.57
September	101.7	41.7	1.44
December	97.7	40.2	1.43
1953			
March	101.8	45.0	1.26

[a] Does not include time deposits.
[b] Excludes cash held by banks and credit cooperatives.

Table 8   Bank Loans and Discounts to Invidual Sectors[a] (IL million)

End of	In current prices			In constant (September 1951) prices		
	Agriculture	Industry	Trade	Agriculture	Industry	Trade
1948						
March	5.6	6.8	6.6	—	—	—
1949						
March	6.0	7.2	8.3	6.1	7.3	8.5
1950						
March	9.2	9.5	10.0	10.7	11.0	11.6
September	11.2	10.5	10.0	12.7	11.9	11.3
1951						
March	14.5	14.6	12.9	15.5	15.6	13.8
September	16.2	17.6	16.5	16.2	17.6	16.5
1952						
March	24.3	20.7	16.2	18.4	15.7	12.3
June	26.6	23.0	15.8	16.9	14.6	10.1
September	27.2	24.4	16.0	16.1	14.4	9.5
1953						
March	38.1	29.3	16.6	20.7	15.9	9.0

[a] Including loans from government deposits.

SOURCE: Office of Controller of Banks and *Statistical Bulletin of Israel.*

5

Wicksell's Cumulative Process in Theory and Practice[1]

It is for me a particularly gratifying experience to be able to lecture today within these halls. And I hope it will not be considered presumptuous on my part to take advantage of this opportunity to discuss the work of Knut Wicksell himself.

Let me begin with a few words of general background. One of the oldest of monetary theories is the Quantity Theory. By this I mean the theory which claims that—tastes and output remaining constant—changes in the quantity of money generate proportionate changes in the average price level. The rationale of this theory can be most simply presented in terms of the fact that if p represents the average price level—or the number of units of money that one must pay out in order to obtain an average basket of goods—then its reciprocal, or $1/p$, represents the proportion of that basket which can be obtained for one unit of money. That is, it represents the relative value of a unit of money as measured in terms of its purchasing power over commodities. Hence just as an increase in the supply of any commodity reduces its relative price in terms of other commodities, so an increase in the quantity of money reduces its relative price, $1/p$—which means that it increases the average price level, p.

This is one simple and familiar theme of classical and neoclassical monetary theory. Another and equally familiar one is that a change in the quantity of money is like a change in the monetary unit. Thus, for example, when the French government in 1960 introduced the New Franc—and defined it as equal to 100 Old Francs—it effectively reduced the number of units of money in the economy to 1 percent of its former quantity; corre-

Reprinted from Banca Nazionale del Lavoro Quarterly Review, *No. 85 (June 1968), 120–131, by permission of the publisher.*

[1] Lecture delivered at the University of Uppsala on May 5, 1967.

spondingly, prices (in terms of the unit of money) were also reduced to 1 percent of their former level.

There is, however, one fundamental difference between this case and that in which the monetary unit is left unchanged, but the quantity of money is reduced to 1 percent of its former level. For, to refer again to the French case, when the government issued its decree on the New Franc, it also effectively proclaimed the new level of prices: it effectively informed the grocers by how many places to move over the decimal point on their price tags. There was, thus, no need for these new prices to be determined by the market. In the case of a change in the quantity of money with an unchanged unit, however, the new level of market prices is of necessity determined by market forces. And it is the nature of these forces which was of primary concern to classical and neoclassical economists in general—and to Wicksell in particular.[2]

It will thus be seen that I have placed Wicksell squarely in the ranks of the adherents of the quantity theory—and in this I fear that I differ with other students of Wicksell's work. Wicksell, however, raised a specific problem with reference to the applicability of the quantity theory to an economy with a fractional reserve banking system. In particular, he claimed that the traditional quantity theory envisaged that monetary increases were received by individuals who—finding their cash holdings in excess of their needs—then spent them on goods, thus driving prices upward. But—Wicksell pointed out—in a modern banking economy an increase in money in the form of gold (and this is the form which was of primary concern to the traditional quantity theory) was usually deposited in the banks and was thus primarily devoted to increasing bank reserves. It was thus necessary to explain how this increase in reserves ultimately acted to raise the price level. And this was the role of Wicksell's famous "cumulative process."

A basic element of this process is Wicksell's equally famous distinction between the "money" or "market" rate of interest, on the one hand, and the "real" or "natural" rate, on the other. Since this material is all well known, I can summarize the process briefly.

Because of the pressure of excess reserves created by the monetary increase, banks will reduce the rate at which they are willing to lend money. This will reduce this rate below the natural rate—which reflects the unchanged marginal productivity of capital. Hence entrepreneurs will be induced to increase their borrowings and hence the demand for the goods and services which they purchase, thus driving their prices upwards. This process is "cumulative:" that is, it continues as long as the money rate is below the natural rate. And the former will continue to be below the latter as long as the banks have excess reserves; until finally—and this is the equi-

[2] For detailed evidence from the literature in support of this contention, see my *Money, Interest, and Prices*, 2nd ed. (New York, 1965), Supplementary Notes A, F:1, G:1, and J. On the specific interpretation of Wicksell's theory presented here and in what follows, see Note E:4.

librating mechanism of the process—this excess will disappear as a result of the internal drain on bank reserves caused by the price rise generated by the expansion of bank credit.

It should be noted—as Wicksell himself conceded[3]—that this type of interest-price interaction is to be found in Ricardo. Indeed, it is part of classical and neoclassical monetary theory in general—even though there are differences of opinion with respect to the forces which equilibrate the process. But Wicksell developed the theory with a degree of vigor and clarity—and with a clear specification of the problem—that are not to be found in the literature before him.

What is the empirical evidence on Wicksell's theory? Wicksell himself discussed in detail that finding which seems to be inconsistent with his theory: namely, the fact that historically interest rates and the price level have moved up and down together—or what Keynes was later to call Gibson's paradox. Wicksell's interpretation of these data, however, was that the prime mover here was the natural rate: that technological advances or other developments raised this rate, while banks lagged behind in making corresponding upward adjustments in their lending rate. Hence even though the money rate of interest was rising, it was still below the natural rate—thus causing an expansion of bank credit and hence a continuous rise in prices. Thus the facts, claimed Wicksell, accorded exactly with what his theory predicted.[4]

Wicksell's interpretation had recently been rejected by Phillip Cagan on the basis of his study of the United States experience. According to Cagan, Wicksell's interpretation implies that during the upward swing of prices and interest—and hence of bank credit and money—the reserve ratio of the banking system should be declining, while the opposite should occur during a downward swing. As against this implication, Cagan places "the facts for the United States before 1914, which provide the clearest evidence of the Gibson paradox"—and which show that changes in the banks' reserve ratios did not account "for any sizable part of the long-run movements in the United States money stock before 1914."[5] More specifically, Cagan shows that the growth in the United States money stock from 1875 and until World War I was due 90 percent to the growth in bank reserves, and only 10 percent to a reduction in the reserve ratio.[6]

It seems to me, however, that this criticism is not well taken. For Wicksell's interpretation implies a decline in banks' reserve ratios during the

---

[3] To Professor David Davidson; see Wicksell's *Lectures on Political Economy*, E. Classen, trans. (London, 1935), Vol. II, p. 200.

[4] *Ibid.*, pp. 205–207; *Interest and Prices*, R. F. Kahn, trans. (London, 1936), pp. 107, 167–168.

[5] Phillip Cagan, *Determinants and Effects of Changes in the Stock of Money, 1875–1960* (New York, 1965), p. 254.

[6] *Ibid.*, p. 19, Table 2. The 90 percent figure is the residual obtained after deducting from 100 percent the 10 percent increase provided by the change in the reserve ratio. Because of rounding errors, it differs from the sum of the relative contributions recorded in the table for "high powered money" (68 percent) and the currency ratio (25 percent).

expansionary period *on the assumption that total reserves are constant*: for then the expansion of bank credit which drives prices upwards can take place only if the banks reduce their reserve ratio. But, as Cagan's own work shows, total bank reserves in the United States during the prewar I period grew—as a result both of the growth in the gold stock and of a decrease in the ratio of currency to demand deposits.[7] Hence banks could have expanded their credit—in accordance with Wicksell's interpretation—even though the decline in the reserve ratio made only a minor contribution to the expansion in the money stock.

There is, however, a more fundamental point—one that revolves about the question of how we are to measure "importance" or "unimportance" of the role of changes in the reserve ratio. As a determinant of the change in the money stock, changes in the reserve ratio were indeed small. But what is really relevant for Wicksell's analysis is not "importance" in this sense, but the movement in the reserve ratio itself. And here Cagan's own data show that the average reserve ratio of commercial banks almost halved in the period 1875–1915—from approximately 20 percent to 11 percent.[8] Surely such a marked fall is consistent with Wicksell's argument.

I should like to emphasize that the evidence cited here does not prove that Wicksell's interpretation is correct. For we are all familiar with the basic methodological position that empirical evidence can only refute hypotheses, not establish them. Correspondingly, my main point here is that the evidence which Cagan cites does not provide such a refutation. At the same time I share with Cagan[9] the reluctance to believe that the explanation of the *long-run* trends described by the Gibson paradox lies in the continued failure of banks to adjust their lending rates upwards with sufficient rapidity. Thus the validity of Wicksell's interpretation of the Gibson paradox rests on the assumption that bankers never learn—even in the long run!

There are two other types of empirical evidence in support of Wicksell's cumulative process that I would like to present. The first is based on econometric investigations of the behavior of the banking system in the United States. These show that—other things being equal—banks respond to an increase in the demand for loans by raising their lending rates; and that this rise lags behind that of other short-term rates in the market.[10] This is precisely what we should expect on the basis of Wicksell's argument.

The second type of evidence stems from a simulation of the United States economy. Consider the cumulative process in the case in which the initial disturbance takes the form of an increase in bank reserves. As we have seen, Wicksell argues that—other things equal—this should in the first

[7]*Ibid.*, pp. 19 and 51.

[8]*Ibid.*, pp. 356–357.

[9]*Ibid.*, p. 255.

[10]S. M. Goldfeld, *Commercial Bank Behavior and Economic Activity* (Amsterdam, 1966), pp. 37–43, 62–68. See also Frank de Leeuw, "A Model of Financial Behavior," in J. S. Duesenberry and others (eds.), *The Brookings Quarterly Econometric Model of the United States* (Chicago, 1965), pp. 506–519, especially pp. 513–515.

instance drive interest down, which in turn strengthens the upward movement of prices; and that once prices have increased in the same proportion, interest will return to its original level. Now, in the real world, other things are never equal, and so it should not surprise us to find that the actual movement of the interest rate and the price level in times of monetary expansion actually differs from the foregoing. What is, then, a proper test of Wicksell's analysis is to see if the foregoing monetary expansion will cause the rate of interest to be lower—and the price level higher—*than they would otherwise be*. This, of course, is the same approach which Wicksell adopted in his discussion of the Gibson paradox.[11]

Obviously, we cannot rerun history in order to check the validity of this contention—though it might be noted that all empirical analysis of historical events is implicitly an attempt to describe how history would have been different, if only certain exogenous factors had been different. We can, however, obtain some answer to our question by simulating the effects of the foregoing monetary expansion in an econometric model. More specifically, we can compute from an econometric model the "control values"—or the values of the endogenous variables corresponding to the values of the exogenous variables which actually prevailed; and then compare these control values with the "simulated values"—or the values of the endogenous variables corresponding to exogenous variables whose values have been modified in a specified manner.

Such a simulation has been carried out with the Wharton Econometric Model, constructed by Professor Lawrence Klein and his associates at the University of Pennsylvania on the basis of quarterly data in the United States for the period from the third quarter of 1952 to the second quarter of 1964, inclusive.[12] This is a model of 47 equations, which decomposes the three major categories of aggregate demand (consumption, investment, and government expenditure) into more detailed subcategories (consumption of nondurable goods and services, consumption of durable goods, investment in plant and equipment, investment in housing, and the like), and which then specifies the income, wealth, price, and interest variables which in turn determine these components. For our purposes, the critical equation of the model is the one which states that

$$i_s = 0.42 + 0.994\, i_d - 0.0895\, FR,$$

[11] Cf. in particular the following passage from *Interest and Prices* (p. 107, italics in original):
> Our problem is, therefore, to show that in those periods when upward movements of prices have been observed, the contractual rate of interest—the money rate—was *low* relatively to the natural rate, and that at times of falling prices it was relatively *high*. It is only in this relative sense that the money rate of interest is of significance in regard to movements of prices. It can at once be seen that it is quite useless to try to demonstrate the existence of any direct relation between absolute movements of the rate of interest or of the discount rate and movements of prices.

[12] I am greatly indebted to Professor Klein and to Professor Michael Evans for carrying out the simulation, as well as for their invaluable advice and assistance at every stage.

where i_s is the short-term rate of interest, as represented by the rate on 4–6 month commercial paper; i_d is the Federal Reserve Discount rate; and *FR* represents the ratio of net free reserves of the banking system (i.e. excess reserves *less* member bank borrowings from Federal Reserve Banks) to total required reserves. A monetary increase in this model can only take the form of an increase in free reserves; conversely, the foregoing equation is the only one of the model which directly reflects the impact of such an increase.

Thus the direct impact of a monetary increase is on the short-term rate of interest. In the Wharton model, this in turn affects the long-term rate (as measured by Moody's average yield on bonds) in accordance with the equation

$$i_L = 0.21 + 0.086\, i_s + 0.889\, (i_L)_{-1},$$

where $(i_L)_{-1}$ represents, of course, the long-term rate in the preceding quarter. And through the effects on the long-term rate of interest, the effect of the monetary increase spreads to the rest of the system, and in particular to investment activity.

The specific simulation which I wish to consider is one in which the free reserves of the banking system are assumed to be $1.0 billion higher in 1952 than they actually were—and to remain at this higher level afterwards. This represents roughly a 5 percent increase in total member bank reserves at that time. It might be noted that total reserves during the period in ques-

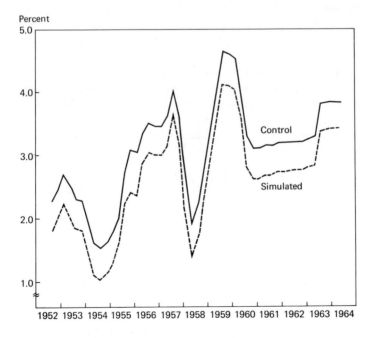

Figure 5.1.   Short-Term Rate of Interest

tion remained more or less at the same level; correspondingly, excess reserves in the simulated model are roughly 5 percent above the control values throughout the period.

As might be expected from the description of these equations, the immediate impact of this monetary increase is to reduce the short-term interest rate. Indeed, it falls sharply by roughly 20 percent of its control value—from 2.27 percent to 1.81 percent. And throughout the period 1952–1964 the simulated value of the short-term interest rate is (with a few exceptions) from 10–25 percent below the control value (Figure 5.1). Due to the lag in response, the long-term rate is at first barely affected (it falls from 3.22 percent to 3.18 percent in the quarter in which the monetary increase takes place); after a year, however, the differences between the control (3.41 percent) and simulated (3.28 percent) values is 0.13 percent, and after another half year it reaches 0.18 percent (= 3.47 percent − 3.29 percent), and by the second year it is 0.22 percent. This relative difference between simulated and control values continues to prevail in subsequent years as well (Figure 5.2).

According to the assumption of the model, the long-term rate of interest affects investment (in plant and equipment and in housing) with a lag of half a year; and in view of the lag of the long-term rate behind the short-term, it is not surprising that total gross investment is barely affected during the first three quarters after the monetary increase. A year afterwards, however, it is roughly 3 percent above the control value, and it remains 2–3 percent above the control value throughout the period. The level of consumption on the other hand (which, the model assumes, is not directly affected by the rate of interest) is accordingly insignificantly affected.

As a result of this increase in aggregate demand, real GNP is also

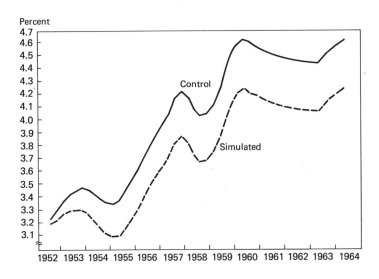

Figure 5.2. Long-Term Rate of Interest

greater in the simulated model. In particular, after a lag of three quarters, it increases by roughly 0.5 percent and remains at this relatively higher level throughout the period.

Let us now consider the price level, as measured by the implicit deflator of GNP. This is unaffected during the first three quarters in which, as we saw, investment was also unaffected. It then rises—though not by a significant amount—and remains 0.1 percent–0.2 percent above the control value throughout the period. This is represented in Figure 5.3.

Thus the results of the simulation are consistent with the Wicksellian cumulative process: the monetary increase depresses the rate of interest and raises prices. In connection with our earlier discussion of the Gibson paradox, it might also be noted that during a good part of the period in question, both the short-term and long-term rates of interest were rising together with the price level. But this in no way contradicts the validity of the Wicksellian contention as reflected by the comparison between the simulated and control models: a comparison which shows that the monetary increase makes interest lower—and prices higher—than they otherwise would have been.

There are, however, two aspects in which these results differ from the Wicksellian cumulative process: first, in the relatively minor upward pressure on prices, even after account is taken of the increase in real GNP; and second, in the fact that the difference between the rate of interest of the simulated and control models is not eliminated in the course of time, but after the initial phase remains more or less constant.

With respect to the second of these differences, let me point out that it is a reflection of the fact that bank reserves in the Wharton model are an

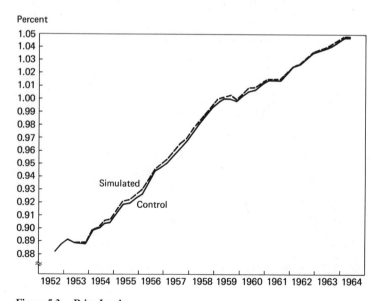

Figure 5.3. Price Level

exogenous variable. That is, the model provides no mechanism by which the developments in the economy can affect the level of these reserves. And in particular it does not provide for the Wicksellian mechanism in which the monetary expansion ultimately causes an internal drain which causes reserves to decrease and hence forces banks to raise their lending rates once again.

I might note that the same type of simulation (i.e., for an increase in reserves by $1.0 billion) was carried out with the revised Klein-Goldberger annual model for the United States for the period 1929–1941 and 1947–1964.[13] Because of the lower level of reserves in 1929, this increase then represented an increase of over 40 percent in total reserves. Once again, the pattern is one of a downward pressure on the short- and (with a lag) long-term rates of interest, a significant upward shift in real investment with little effect on consumption, a corresponding increase (after a lag of two years) in real GNP, and an almost insignificant upward effect on the price level.

At this point you might be asking yourselves: What, after all, is surprising in the fact that a model which assumes a Wicksellian monetary relation yields Wicksellian results? There is a point to the question. The answer, however, is that the support to the Wicksellian theory is directly related to the extent to which a model with a Wicksellian equation provides a good fit. That is, the validity of the model as a description of reality is what can give support to the contention that the Wicksellian analysis does indeed provide an accurate description of the real world.

Let me conclude by saying that the foregoing econometric models are not Wicksellian in the fullest sense of the term—for they provide for monetary influence only through the interest rate. This does indeed reflect Wicksell's thinking in his *Interest and Prices*, where he concentrated on this indirect effect of a monetary expansion. But in the concluding pages of his *Lectures* we find Wicksell referring to his earlier discussion of the indirect effects of a monetary expansion and saying:

> Only in so far as new gold is deposited in the banks in the form of "capital," i.e. without being drawn out in cheques and notes soon after, can it give rise to a lowering of interest rates and in that way affect prices. But this need not happen, and, contrary to Ricardo's view, does not happen as a rule. Rather most of the gold flows in payment for goods and should then, in proportion as it exceeds the demand for new gold, have a direct influence in raising prices without lowering interest rates.[14]

It would carry us beyond the subject matter of this lecture to discuss the implications of this revision in Wicksell's thinking.

---

[13] This model is described in L. R. Klein, *The Keynesian Revolution*, 2nd ed. (New York, 1966), pp. 230–231.
Once again, I am indebted to Professor Klein for providing the results of this simulation.
[14] *Lectures on Political Economy*, Vol. II, p. 215.

6

The Chicago
Tradition,
the Quantity Theory,
and Friedman [1,2]

I must begin this paper with an apology for being over a decade late; for I
should have written it as an immediate reaction to Milton Friedman's by
now well-known 1956 essay on "The Quantity Theory of Money—A Restatement."[3] But the recent appearance of Friedman's *International Ency-*

Reprinted by permission, from The Journal of Money, Credit and Banking, *I(No. 1, 1969).*
46–70. Copyright © 1969 by the Ohio State University Press. Appears here with minor modi-
fications and additions.

[1] This paper was written during 1968 while I was visiting at M.I.T. under a research
grant from the National Science Foundation (NSF Grant GS 1812). I am grateful to both
institutions for making this work possible.

I am happy to express my deep appreciation to Mr. Stanley Fischer of M.I.T. for
his invaluable assistance at all stages of the preparation of this paper—and particularly in
the examination of the relevant literature. In addition, I have benefited from discussions with
him and from his criticisms of earlier drafts.

I am also indebted to my Jerusalem colleagues Yosef Attiyeh, Yoram Ben-Porath, and
Giora Hanoch whose thoughtful suggestions have greatly improved the general organization of
this paper, as well as the discussion of specific points.

As usual, it is a pleasure to thank Miss Susanne Freund for her careful and conscientious checking of the final manuscript and its references.

Needless to say, responsibility for the interpretations and views presented in this paper
remain entirely my own.

[2] I would like to dedicate this paper to the memory of Miguel Sidrauski. His untimely
death in August 1968 was a great loss, not only to his family and friends, but to the economics
profession in general—and particularly to the development of monetary theory. Though I
do not think Miguel had a strong interest in the history of doctrine, I hope that—as a Chicago
graduate—he would have been interested in reading the final product of a work whose
beginnings he witnessed.

[3] In M. Friedman, ed., *Studies in the Quantity Theory of Money* (Chicago, 1956), pp.
3–21; referred to henceforth as "Quantity Theory I."

In self-defense, I might, however, note that I have on previous occasions discussed
in passing some of the points presented below—and have also emphasized the Keynesian
nature of Friedman's essay. Thus see my "Indirect-Utility Approach to the Theory of Money,
Assets, and Savings," in F. H. Hahn and F. P. R. Brechling (eds.), *The Theory of Interest*

clopedia article on the quantity theory[1] (though, as will be shown in Part IV below, it differs significantly in its doctrinal aspects from the earlier paper) provides an appropriate, if tardy, occasion to raise some basic questions— from the viewpoint of the history of monetary doctrine—about the validity of Friedman's interpretation of the quantity theory of money, and of its Chicago version in particular.

The argument of the present paper is as follows: In both of the foregoing articles, Friedman presents what he calls a "reformulation of the quantity theory of money." In Part IV I shall show that this is a misleading designation and that what Friedman has actually presented is an elegant exposition of the modern portfolio approach to the demand for money which, though it has some well-known (though largely undeveloped) antecedents in the traditional theory, can only be seen as a continuation of the Keynesian theory of liquidity preference.

The main purpose of this paper, however, is to describe (in Parts II and III) the true nature of the Chicago monetary tradition. In this way I shall also demonstrate the invalidity of Friedman's contention (in his 1956 essay) that this tradition is represented by his "reformulation of the quantity theory." As a minimum statement let me say that though I shared with Friedman—albeit, almost a decade later—the teachers at Chicago whom he mentions (namely, Knight, Viner, Simons, and Mints), his description of the "flavor of the oral tradition" which they were supposed to have imparted strikes no responsive chord in my memory.

Friedman offers no supporting evidence for his interpretation of the Chicago tradition. This is unfortunate. For questions about the history of economic doctrine are empirical questions. And the universe from which the relevant empirical evidence must be drawn is that of the writings and teachings of the economists in question. No operational meaning can be attached to the existence of a "tradition" which does not manifest itself in at least one of these ways.

From this it will be clear that my examination of this evidence in what follows should be interpreted as a criticism of the individuals involved. On the contrary, I would consider it unjustified to criticize them for not having fully understood and integrated into their thinking what we have succeeded in learning only in the course of the subsequent development of Keynesian monetary theory. My quarrel is only with those who imply that such an understanding and integration existed before, or independently of, this development.

Rates (London, 1965), p. 54, note 5 (this is the proceedings volume of an International Economics Association Conference held at Royaumont in March 1962); and *Money, Interest, and Prices*, 2nd ed. (New York, 1965), p. 81, note 8. See also the implicit criticism contained in my article on "Interest," *The International Encyclopedia of the Social Sciences*, VII (1968), 480b, reproduced as Chapter 7 on this book (p. 118 below). See also below, pp. 107–108.

    [1] "Money: Quantity Theory" in *The International Encyclopedia of the Social Sciences*, X (1968) 432–447; referred to henceforth as "Quantity Theory II."

I would like finally to emphasize that my concern in this paper is with the analytical framework of the Chicago monetary tradition, and not with its policy proposals as such. Correspondingly, I shall not—except incidentally—discuss the relation between these proposals and those of Friedman. Let me, however, note that though there are, of course, basic similarities, there are also significant differences—particularly about the degree of discretion to be exercised by the monetary authorities.[5]

I. FRIEDMAN'S CHICAGO

Friedman begins his 1956 essay with the explanation that:

> Chicago was one of the few academic centers at which the quantity theory continued to be a central and vigorous part of the oral tradition throughout the 1930's and 1940's, where students continued to study monetary theory and to write theses on monetary problems. The quantity theory that retained this role differed sharply from the atrophied and rigid caricature that is so frequently described by the proponents of the new income-expenditure approach—and with some justice, to judge by much of the literature on policy that was spawned by quantity theorists. At Chicago, Henry Simons and Lloyd Mints directly, Frank Knight and Jacob Viner at one remove, taught and developed a more subtle and relevant version, one in which the quantity theory was connected and integrated with general price theory and became a flexible and sensitive tool for interpreting movements in aggregate economic activity and for developing relevant policy prescriptions.
>
> To the best of my knowledge, no systematic statement of this theory as developed at Chicago exists, though much can be read between the lines of Simons' and Mints' writings. . . . It was a theoretical approach that insisted that money does matter. . . .
>
> The purpose of this introduction is not to enshrine—or, should I say, inter— a definitive version of the Chicago tradition. . . . The purpose is rather to set down a particular "model" of a quantity theory in an attempt to convey the flavor of the oral tradition. . . .[6]

Friedman then goes on to present this model. Since I am interested only in the doctrinal aspects of the question, it is sufficient to cite the model's basic features. In Friedman's words:

[5]This will become clear from a comparison of Friedman's policy (namely, expanding the quantity of money at a constant rate) with the contracyclical monetary policy advocated by Simons and Mints [see Propositions (4) and (5) on pp. 97–98 below; see also p. 99 and especially note 25]. One might also note Jacob Viner's criticism of Friedman's policy proposals in his (Viner's) "The Necessary and the Desirable Range of Discretion to be Allowed to a Monetary Authority," in Leland B. Yeager (ed.), *In Search of a Monetary Constitution* (Cambridge, Mass., 1962), pp. 244–274.

Friedman himself discusses some of these differences explicitly in his paper on Simons referred to in note 28 below—and implicitly in his *Program for Monetary Stability* (New York, 1960), pp. 86–90. See also M. Bronfenbrenner, "Observations on the 'Chicago School(s)'," *Journal of Political Economy*, LXX (1962), 72–73.

Another interesting question which lies beyond the scope of the present paper is the extent to which the policy views of the Chicago school in the 1930s represented those of other quantity theorists of the period.

[6]"Quantity Theory I," pp. 3–4.

1. The quantity theory is in the first instance a theory of the *demand* for money. It is not a theory of output, or of money income, or of the price level. Any statement about these variables requires combining the quantity theory with some specifications about the conditions of supply of money and perhaps about other variables as well.
2. To the ultimate wealth-owning units in the economy, money is one kind of asset, one way of holding wealth. . . .
3. The analysis of the demand for money on the part of the ultimate wealth-owning units in the society can be made formally identical with that of the demand for a consumption service. As in the usual theory of consumer choice, the demand for money (or any other particular asset) depends on three major sets of factors: (a) the total wealth to be held in various forms—the analogue of the budget restraint; (b) the price of and return on this form of wealth and alternative forms; and (c) the tastes and preferences of the wealth-owning units.[7]

From these and other considerations Friedman arrives at a demand function for money of the form

$$M = g(P, r_b, r_e, \frac{1}{P}\frac{dP}{dt}, w, Y; u),   \qquad (1)$$

where M is the nominal quantity of money; P, the price level; r_b is the interest rate on bonds; r_e, the interest rate on equities; $(1/P)(dP/dt)$, the rate of change of prices—and hence the negative of the rate of return on money balances; w, the ratio of nonhuman to human wealth; Y, money income; and u, "variables that can be expected to affect tastes and preferences."[8] Friedman then makes the familiar assumption that this function is homogeneous of degree one in P and Y, and hence rewrites it as[9]

$$\frac{M}{P} = f(r_b, r_e, \frac{1}{P}\frac{dP}{dt}, w; \frac{Y}{P}; u).   \qquad (2)$$

Alternatively, dividing (1) through by Y, he obtains

$$Y = v(r_b, r_e, \frac{1}{P}\frac{dP}{dt}, w, \frac{Y}{P}; u) \cdot M.   \qquad (3)$$

"In this form the equation is in the usual quantity theory form, where v is income velocity."[10]

As an aside, I might note that at no point in the foregoing exposition does Friedman mention the name of Keynes. Indeed, one cannot escape the impression that even the term "liquidity" is being avoided.[11]

Friedman does recognize that "almost every economist will accept the general lines of the preceding analysis on a purely formal and abstract level." But Friedman defines three distinguishing features of the quantity theorist, of which the first is that the quantity theorist

---

[7] *Ibid.*, p. 4.
[8] *Ibid.*, pp. 4–10; the quotation is from p. 9.
[9] *Ibid.*, p. 11, equation (11).
[10] *Ibid.*, p. 11; see equation (13).
[11] Cf., e.g., *ibid.*, pp. 5, 14, and 19.

> accepts the empirical hypothesis that the demand for money is highly
> stable. . . . The quantity theorist need not, and generally does not, mean
> that the . . . velocity of circulation of money is to be regarded as numerically
> constant over time. . . . For the stability he expects is in the functional rela-
> tion between the quantity of money demanded and the variables that
> determine it. . . .

The other two features are that the quantity theorist believes that "there
are important factors affecting the supply of money that do not affect the
demand for money" and that the demand for money does not become in-
finitely elastic (viz., absence of a "liquidity trap").[12]

There is no question that these last two features are generally found
(either explicitly or implicitly) in presentations of the quantity theory. But
it is equally clear to me that the first—which is crucial to Friedman's interpretation—is not. Correspondingly, one of the basic points that will be examined in the following discussion of the Chicago economists is whether they
did indeed think in terms of a stable velocity in Friedman's functional sense.

II. THE OTHER CHICAGO

As against the foregoing, let me now describe a Chicago tradition of monetary theory whose approach, contents, and language can be represented by
the following summary-propositions.[13]

1. The quantity theory is, first and foremost, not a theory of the de-
    mand for money, but a theory which relates the quantity of money
    (M) to the aggregate demand for goods and services (MV), and
    thence to the price level (P) and/or level of output (T); all this in
    accordance with Fisher's $MV = PT$.

2. V is not constant; on the contrary, a basic feature of economic life is
    the "danger of sharp changes on the velocity side"; or in other
    words, the danger "of extreme alternations of hoarding and dis-
    hoarding."[14] These "sharp changes" in turn are due to anticipa-
    tions of changing price levels, as well as to the changing state of
    business confidence as determined by earnings.[15] Thus if indivi-

---

[12]*Ibid.*, pp. 15–16.

[13]The following is primarily a summary of Simons' views, which were largely accepted
by Mints. Knight's analysis is the same, though—quite characteristically—he seems to have
had less faith than did Simons and Mints in the policy proposals. For Viner, I have been
able to find clear evidence only on the first proposition. Nevertheless, Viner (together with his
colleagues) did advocate government deficit financing as a means of combating unemployment.

For references to the relevant writings of the foregoing (as well as further comments
on Viner's position) see Appendix I below. Cf. also J. R. Davis, "Chicago Economists,
Deficit Budgets, and the Early 1930s," *American Economic Review*, LVIII (1968), 476–482.

[14]Simons, "Rule versus Authorities in Monetary Policy," *Journal of Political Economy*,
XLIV (1936), 1–30, as reprinted in *Economic Policy for a Free Society* (Chicago, 1948), p. 164
(this passage is cited in full in Appendix I below). That by "hoarding and dishoarding" Simons
means changes in velocity is clear from p. 165; see also the reference cited in the next footnote.

[15]See Simons, "Banking and Currency Reform" (unpublished memorandum, 1933),
as quoted in Appendix I below.

duals expect prices to rise and earnings to be good, they will dis-hoard—that is, increase the velocity of circulation. But the crucial point here is that these expectations will be self-justifying: for the very act of dishoarding will cause prices to rise even further, thus leading to further dishoarding, and so on. In this way a "cumulative process" of expansion is set into operation which "feeds upon itself" and which has no "natural" limit.[16] Conversely, an indefinite "cumulative process" of hoarding, price declines and depression, and further hoarding is set into operation by the expectation that the price level will fall and/or that earnings will be poor. Thus the economic system is essentially unstable.[17]

3. Such a cumulative process might possibly take place—albeit in a much less severe form—even if the quantity of money in the economy were to remain constant.[18] In the actual world, however, the process is highly exacerbated by the "perverse" behavior of the banking system, which expands credit in booms and contracts it in depressions. As a result the quantity of money (M) and near-moneys (and hence V) increases in booms, and decreases in depressions.

4. In accordance with (2) and (3), the government has an obligation to undertake a contracyclical policy. The guiding principle of this policy is to change M so as to offset changes in V, and thus generate the full-employment level of aggregate demand MV. If prices are downwardly flexible, the operational rule which will assure the proper variation in M is that of increasing M when P falls, and decreasing it when P rises. In any event, it is "inconceivable" that a sufficiently vigorous policy of (say) expanding M in a period of depression would not ultimately affect aggregate spending in the required manner.

5. The necessary variations in M can be generated either by open-market operations or by budgetary deficits. The latter method is more efficient, and in some cases might even be necessary. Budgetary deficits, in turn, can be generated by varying either government expenditures or tax receipts. From the viewpoint of contracyclical policy, this makes no difference—for either method changes M; but from the viewpoint of the general philosophy of the

[16] Knight, "The Business Cycle, Interest, and Money: A Methodological Approach," *Review of Economic Statistics*, XXIII (1941), 53–67, as reprinted in *On the History and Method of Economics* (Chicago, 1956), pp. 210–211, 223–224.

[17] For supporting quotations from Simons, *Personal Income Taxation* (Chicago, 1938), p. 222, and "Hansen on Fiscal Policy," *Journal of Policitcal Economy*, L (1942), 161–196, as reprinted in *Economic Policy for a Free Society, op. cit.*, p. 188, and from Knight's "The Business Cycle, Interest, and Money," *op.cit.*, pp. 211 and 224, see Appendix I.

[18] See the quotation from Simons, "Rules versus Authorities in Monetary Policy," *op. cit.*, p. 164, reproduced in Appendix I below. See also *ibid.*, p. 331, footnote 16, and Mints, *Monetary Policy for a Competitive Society* (New York, 1950), pp. 120–122.

proper role of government in economic life, the variation of tax receipts is definitely preferable. Hence, a tax system which depends heavily on the income tax is desirable not only from the viewpoint of distributive justice, but also from the viewpoint of automatically providing proper cyclical variations in tax receipts.

Before going on to bring out the flavor of these propositions as contrasted with that of Friedman's presentation, I would like briefly to indicate three reasons for the emphasis I have given in the foregoing to the writings of Simons. First, at the Chicago which concerns us, Simons was undoubtedly the dominant figure in dicussions of monetary and fiscal policy. (In Friedman's presentation too there is more emphasis on the writings of Simons and Mints than on those of Knight and Viner.) Second, Simons' writings on these questions were the earliest by far of the writers here considered. And, third, they were sufficiently early to represent the Chicago tradition in its pristine— and pre-Keynesian—form.

The significance of this last point will become clear from our discussion of Mints at the end of this part. In connection with the first reason, I might note that Mints repeatedly makes clear his indebtedness to Simons.[19] Again, I would conjecture that Knight's writings referred to above also reflect Simons' influence. Similarly, in my recollections of student days at Chicago—and I think I can safely speak for my fellow students at the time— it is Simons who stands out sharply as the major source of intellectual stimulation and influence in all that regards monetary and fiscal policy. In the slang of those days, most of us were "Simonized" to some degree or other.[20]

Let me turn now to the propositions themselves. The contrast drawn by Proposition (1) is that between the transactions approach to the quantity theory and the cash-balance approach emphasized by Friedman. Now, it is a commonplace of monetary theory that these two approaches can be made analytically equivalent. Indeed in his general discussion of monetary influences, Fisher himself vividly shows that he was thinking in terms of a demand for money.[21] Nevertheless, if we consistently find a treatment in terms of the transactions approach, we can take this as some indication that the economists in question did not primarily approach monetary theory from the viewpoint of the demand for money. Or at least we cannot take it as an indication that they did![22]

Indeed, it is a much closer approximation to the flavor of the Chicago

---

[19] Cf., e.g., *Monetary Policy for a Competitive Society, op. cit.*, p. vii.

[20] In a letter to me commenting on this paper, Martin Bronfenbrenner disagrees with this evaluation of Simons' influence and states that "Simons was wasted on the undergraduates; few graduate students other than tax technicians took his 'Fiscal Policy' course, 361."

My opinion is still that expressed in the text. But I must admit that—in contrast with most graduate students—I also did my undergraduate work at Chicago, and that my first impressions of Simons were accordingly formed in that context. I should also note (though again I am not sure that it is relevant) that Bronfenbrenner's recollections refer to the period 1934–1936 whereas mine are for 1941–1946.

[21] *The Purchasing Power of Money*, 2nd ed. (New York, 1922), pp. 153–154.

[22] Actually, Friedman draws a sharper distinction on this score between the transactions and cash-balance approaches than I would; thus compare his "Quantity Theory II," pp. 437–438 with my *Money, Interest, and Prices, op. cit.*, pp. 166–167.

tradition to say that basically it was not interested in a systematic analysis of the demand for money:[23] for it believed so strongly that "the supply of money matters" that—for the policy purposes which were its main concern—the exact form of the demand function for money did not matter at all, aside from the critical (though sometimes implicit) assumption "that additional money in unlimited amounts would [not] be hoarded in its entirety." For then no matter what the demand for money—in the language of Simons and Mints, no matter what the extent of hoarding—its adverse effects could be offset by a sufficient increase in M. "Much hoarding would simply require a larger addition to the stock of money."[24] The possibility that destabilizing lags could interfere with the efficacy of such a monetary policy—a problem which has received so much attention in recent years—was either not seen (Simons) or not given much weight (Mints[25]).

It should therefore not surprise us that Simons did not present a detailed analysis of the demand for money. Indeed, despite his frequent references to "hoarding," there does not seem to be any point in his writings in which he even uses the term "demand for money." Another, and related, manifestation of the lack of interest in such an analysis is the fact that Simons did not spell out the details of the mechanism by which an increase in the quantity of money was supposed to increase the volume of spending on goods and services. Instead, he sufficed with the simple, sometimes implicit, and frequently mechanical statement that an increase in M increased aggregate demand MV.

Again, even the influence of the rate of interest on the demand for money was not consistently recognized by the Chicago school of the 1930s and 1940s. Thus even though Knight discussed cyclical variations in the rate of interest, he did not take account of the possible influence of such variations on the velocity of circulation.[26] Similarly, though [as indicated in Proposition (3)] Simons and Mints did emphasize the influence of near-moneys on velocity, it was the *volume* of these money substitutes to which they referred, not to the *rate of interest* upon them.

Let me turn now to the "extreme alternations" in velocity described in Proposition (2). It is not clear from the writings of the Chicago school whether it believed that the very fact that prices were, say, increasing would cause an indeterminate flight from money—so that there could

---

[23] It is noteworthy that the work on the empirical nature of the demand function for money that was done at Chicago during the 1940s was carried out under the inspiration not of the "Chicago oral tradition," but of the Keynesian model builders at the Cowles Commission, which was then located at the University of Chicago. See in particular Lawrence Klein. "The Use of Econometric Models as a Guide to Economic Policy," *Econometrica*, XV (1947), 125 ff., and *Economic Fluctuation in the United States, 1921–1941* (New York, 1950), pp. 95–101.

[24] The last two quotations in this paragraph are from Mints, "Monetary Policy," *Review of Economic Statistics*, XXVIII (1946), 67. See also *ibid.*, p. 61 and *Monetary Policy for a Competitive Society, op. cit.*, pp. 48–49. Cf. in this connection the quotation (given in Appendix I below) from Viner's "Schumpeter's *History of Economic Analysis*," *American Economic Review*, XLIV (1954), as reprinted in *The Long View and the Short* (Glencoe, Ill., 1958) p. 365.

[25] Mints, *Monetary Policy for a Competitive Society, op. cit.*, pp. 138 ff. Mints ascribes the suggestion that such a destabilizing influence might occur to Milton Friedman, who by then was his colleague (*ibid.*, p. 138, footnote 8).

[26] See the discussion of Knight in Appendix I below.

exist no stable functional relationship between velocity and the anticipated rate of change of prices; or whether velocity was unstable because of the nature of the expectations function which generated a sequence of ever-increasing anticipated rates of price changes which operated through a stable demand function to generate ever-increasing (or decreasing) changes in the quantity of money demanded; or whether there were other forces in the economy [of which those described in Proposition (3) are an example] which generated such a divergent sequence—or whether it believed that a combination of some or all of these factors was at work. But in any event one point is clear: there is no place in their writings in which the aforementioned Chicago economists even hint that they were thinking in terms of Friedman's crucial assumption of a velocity which is a stable function of (among other variables) the anticipated rate of change of prices.[27,28]

There were other respects in which the Chicago tradition lacked some of the basic ingredients of the flavor of the "model" which Friedman has presented of it. In particular, whereas (as indicated above) this tradition was primarily concerned with the relation between the stock of money and the flow of expenditures, Friedman's primary concern is with the relation between the stock of money and the stocks of other assets. I shall return to this point in Part IV below. But let me now admit that with respect to this comment—and, even more so, with respect to much of what has been said above about the lack of interest at Chicago in the demand for money—Lloyd Mints was at least a partial exception. Thus even though it is not at all comparable—in either detail or precision—with Friedman's exposition, Mints' *Monetary Policy for a Competitive Society* contains a more explicit analysis of the asset-demand for money than any earlier Chicago discussion.[29] But it is

---

[27] See in this context the statement by Frank Knight [from his *Risk, Uncertainty and Profit* (New York, 1957), p. xlv] quoted in full Appendix I.

[28] I might at this point note that in his recent paper on Simons, Friedman cites the passage referred to in footnote 18 above and then concludes that:

> There is clearly great similarity between the views expressed by Simons and by Keynes—as to the causes of the Great Depression, the impotence of monetary policy, and the need to rely extensively on fiscal policy. Both men placed great emphasis on the state of business expectations and assigned a critical role to the desire for liquidity. Indeed, in many ways, the key novelty of Keynes' *General Theory* was the role he assigned to "absolute" liquidity preference under conditions of deep depression. ["The Monetary Theory, and policy of Henry Simons," *Journal of Law and Economics*, X (1967), 7.]

But Friedman gives no indication of the fact that this interpretation of Simons is hardly consistent with that of his 1956 essay, with its emphasis on the functional stability of V and, even more to the point, on the absence of a "liquidity trap" (cf. above, end of Part I).

In this paper, Friedman also contends that "had Simons known the facts as we now know them [about the monetary history of the U.S. during the Great Depression], he would, I believe," have been less concerned with "'the danger of sharp changes on the velocity side'" (*ibid.*, p. 12). Without discussing the validity of this conjecture, I shall merely note that it is not relevant to the question which concerns me here—namely, Simons' actual approach to the quantity theory.

[29] *Op. cit.*, Chapter 3; see also Chapter 9 and especially pp. 210–211. See also Mints' *History of Banking Theory* (Chicago, 1945) pp. 219–222 and "Monetary Policy," *op. cit.*, pp. 63 *et passim*.

highly significant that the chapter in which this analysis is presented (Chapter 3) is followed by a special appendix on Keynes' theory of liquidity preference. Similarly, as shown in Appendix II, it was in this context (and not in that of the quantity theory of money) that Mints' lectures on the asset-demand for money were given. It is also noteworthy that the few Chicago doctoral theses of the period 1939–1950 that were concerned with the choice of money as a component of a portfolio of assets generally took Keynes as their point of departure and gave no indication that they saw this approach as stemming from the Chicago tradition (see Part III below).

Thus the picture which emerges from all this is that by the 1940s the Chicago school itself had—quite understandably—been influenced by Keynesian monetary theory. Accordingly, not only did it begin to evince an interest in a systematic analysis of the demand for money, but it frequently did so from the Keynesian viewpoint of money as one component of an optimally chosen portfolio of assets. Indeed, it had to use this viewpoint in order to explain why it rejected some aspects of the Keynesian theory: namely, the Keynesian concentration on the choice between money and bonds, and the related interpretation of interest as a monetary phenomenon; and the emphasis on the possibility of indefinite hoarding (the "liquidity trap"), and the related Keynesian conclusion that money could not matter enough, so that only a policy of increased government expenditures could deal adequately with the problem of unemployment.[30]

III. THE ORAL TRADITION OF CHICAGO

The preceding discussion of the Chicago school has been based on its writings. It is, however, the "oral tradition of Chicago" which Friedman primarily claims to represent—and to which, accordingly, I shall now turn.

A priori it seems unlikely that scholars who had presented a consistent—and sometimes lengthy—statement of their views in print would have provided a significantly different presentation in their classroom discussions. Fortunately, there is no need to rely solely on such a priori considerations—or even on my memories of these classroom discussions as contrasted with those of Friedman. For there is concrete evidence on their nature in the form of lecture notes which I took during my graduate studies at Chicago in the period 1943–1945.

Of course, these lecture notes are subject to all of the standard reservations about the accuracy with which students understand their teachers. Furthermore, they constitute only one observation on these teachings. But at the present moment this is one more than has yet been provided on the question. It should also be noted that if we accept (as I do) the fact that there was a "tradition" at Chicago, then we can also assume that there was

---

[30] See again the references to Mints in the preceding footnote. See also the discussion of Knight in Appendix I.

a high degree of continuity between what was taught in my student days and what was taught before.

Mints devoted several lectures to the quantity theory at the beginning of his course on "Money." After presenting Fisher's equation of exchange (with no discussion of the determinants of V—or of the Cambridge K, to which he also referred), Mints went on to formulate the quantity theory of money in a way which has remained sharply etched in my memory—and which has always represented for me "the flavor of the Chicago tradition:"

> Some attempts [have been made statistically] to verify quantity theory by showing that $MV + M'V' = PT$ is true. But quantity theory says that P *is the dependent variable*. So [in order to verify theory] would have to show that exist consistent time lags. Have to establish *causal relationship*. Formula itself is a truism—doesn't need verification. Formula $\neq$ quantity theory.
>
> . . .
>
> Mints prefers following statement of quantity theory: P is the dependent variable (in the long run) of the equation $MV = PT$. But in the short run all the variables tend to move together.[31]

For our purposes (see end of preceding part), it is also most significant that Mints' discussion of the demand for money from a viewpoint which is closer to the portfolio approach did not occur in his lectures on the quantity theory, but a month later in the context of his discussion of Keynes' theory of liquidity preference. Here Mints said:

> Really four factors to be kept in equilibrium: (1) price level (2) rate of interest (3) demand for cash (liquidity preferences) and (4) quantity of money.
>
> Methods of disposing of cash:
> (1) Hold in cash
> (2) Purchase consumer's goods
> (3) Purchase producer's goods
> (4) Lend on short term
> (5) Purchase long-term bonds
> (6) Purchase corporation shares.
> Keynes assumes that doubts about the future affect only (5).
> But uncertainties affect (2) and especially (3). Demand will fall off for these, prices there will fall, profits decrease, and [hence] beginning of unemployment, etc.[32]

Mints then went on to present a discussion which closely parallels that of the first part of Chapter 3 of his *Monetary Policy for a Competitive Society*.

Some other notes from Mints' lectures, as well as relevant notes from the lectures of Knight and Simons, are reproduced in Appendix II. The evidence of these notes leads unmistakably to one simple and unsurprising con-

---

[31] Lecture notes from Lloyd Mints, "Money" (Economics 330), June 28 and July 3, 1944, italics in original.

It is noteworthy that this distinction between the quantity theory and the identity $MV + M'V' = PT$ is also emphasized by Friedman in his encyclopedia article; see "Quantity Theory II," pp. 434–436.

[32] Lecture notes from Mints, "Money" (Economics 330), August 4, 1944.

clusion: The oral tradition of the Chicago school of monetary theory was entirely reflected in its written tradition; whatever was not in the latter, was also not in the former.

Let me turn now to the doctoral theses written at Chicago during the period in question.[33] As we all know, students' theses reflect the interests, approach, and all too frequently even the views of their teachers. It is therefore interesting to see what we can learn about the Chicago tradition from this source. This is all the more legitimate in the present context in view of Friedman's assertion that "Chicago was one of the few academic centers at which the quantity theory continued to be a central and vigorous part of the oral tradition throughout the 1930s and 1940s, whose students continued to study monetary theory and to write theses on monetary problems."[34]

The list of relevant theses is presented in Appendix III. Even after taking account of the small number of theses which were being submitted in those days (a total of 46 for the 1930s and 52 for the 1940s), one is struck by the paucity of monetary theses written at Chicago during the 1930s. The fact that from 1931 through 1938 only one such thesis was submitted speaks for itself. The number is decidedly greater for the 1940s. Nevertheless, a casual comparison with the list of doctoral theses submitted at Harvard shows that even during the 1940s there were at least as many monetary theses being submitted at Harvard as at Chicago (though admittedly the total number of theses submitted at the former was three times as large).

Let me turn now to the far more important question as to the contents of the Chicago theses. The situation can be described quite simply: several of the theses are primarily descriptive and contain little, if any, analysis. To the extent that the theses refer to the quantity theory of money, they do so in terms of Proposition (1) on p. 96 above;[35] none of them do so in terms reminiscent of Friedman's "reformulation." Few theses even reflect a portfolio approach to the demand for money. Furthermore, those that do, draw their primary inspiration from Keynes or his supporters.[36] Similarly, the influence

---

[33] Without disclaiming any responsibility for what follows, I would like to express my appreciation to my assistant, Mr. Stanley Fischer, who has carefully gone through the monetary theses written at Chicago during the period 1930–1950—and on whose excellent notes I have relied heavily.

I would also like to thank Professor Lester Telser of the Department of Economics at the University of Chicago and his secretary Mrs. Hazel Bowdry for their help in obtaining a complete list of Chicago theses and microfilms of those discussed here, as well as information about theses committees.

[34] "Quantity Theory I," p. 3.

[35] Thus see, e.g., Benjamin F. Brooks, "A History of Banking Theory in the United States Before 1860" (1939), p. 354; Marion R. Daugherty, "The Currency School-Banking School Controversy" (1941), p. 54; Roland N. McKean, "Fluctuations in Our Private Claim-Debt Structure and Monetary Policy" (1948), pp. 51, 98, and 103. See also the references to Leland Bach's thesis in footnotes 39 and 40 below.

[36] Thus see, e.g., Martin Bronfenbrenner, "Monetary Theory and General Equilibrium" (1939), pp. iii, 43, 45, 156–157; McKean, op. cit., Chapter IV, and especially pp. 52 (footnote 5) and 57–59; and William W. Tongue, "Money, Capital and the Business Cycle" (1947), Chapters I and III.

of the rate of interest on the demand for money is rarely mentioned, even in appropriate contexts;[37] and when there is a mention, it is again largely inspired by Keynesian monetary theory.[38]

Of particular interest in the present context is Leland Bach's thesis on "Price Level Stabilization: Some Theoretical and Practical Considerations" (1940). In his general analysis and policy proposals, Bach presents the position of the Chicago school as summarized in the five propositions of Part II above.[39] Furthermore, in the process of so doing he refers explicitly to an "oral tradition" at Chicago which he describes in the following terms:

> The explanation of the cycle may, for our purposes, be ultimately reduced to the existence of two basic factors, the first redivisible into two more or less separate elements. These two sub-factors in the first are (a) psychological shifts by consumers, entrepreneurs, and investors, leading to changes in the propensities to hoard, consume, and invest, and (b) perverse fluctuations in the volume of money in the system (M plus M' in the Fisherian notation). The second basic factor is the existence of "sticky" prices throughout large sectors of the economy, of which many are cost-prices, so that costs have a tendency to move more slowly than do the more flexible selling prices.*
>
> *On this reduction to essentials I am indebted to Professor Mints, although it has been in the nature of an "oral tradition" at Chicago for some time and can be found in many writers, but only more or less obscured.[40]

It might be noted that at the time Bach wrote this footnote, the tradition was indeed largely oral: for all that then existed in print was Simons' brief discussions; the writings of Knight and Mints had yet to appear (see Appendix I).

In concluding this discussion of the Chicago school, I would like to emphasize once again that its purpose has not been either to praise or to criticize—and surely not to criticize the writers of the theses—but only to convey the flavor of the Chicago tradition as it really was.

---

[37] Cf., e.g., Arthur I. Bloomfield, "International Capital Movements and the American Balance of Payments, 1929–40" (1942), pp. 578–579; McKean, *op. cit.*, p. 80.

In all but the last chapter of his thesis (see especially Chapter IV), McKean follows Simons (to whom he repeatedly refers—pp. 3, 32, 52, 68, *et passim*), in being concerned with the volume of liquid assets and debts, and not the rates of return upon them (cf. above, p. 99). On the other hand, his discussion of 100 percent money in the last chapter (see especially pp. 174–177) explicitly takes account of the effect on the demand for money (and hence velocity) of changes in the rates of interest on money substitutes.

[38] See again the references cited in footnote 35. See also McKean, *op. cit.*, p. 100, who, however, refers to the influence of the quantity of money on the interest rate as "the very old argument, revived in the thirties" (*ibid.*, p. 99).

It might be noted that at some points McKean's thesis also reflects the influence of Milton Friedman, who had joined the Chicago staff in 1946. Thus see the reference to Friedman in McKean's discussion of the simultaneous influence of the interest rate on the demand for money and on savings (p. 101, footnote 1). Somewhat less relevant for our present purpose are McKean's many references in Chapters I–II and on p. 191 to Friedman's discussions of the problem of lags in monetary policy and of the proper framework for monetary and fiscal policy.

[39] See especially pp. 42–45 and 72–75 of his thesis.

[40] *Ibid.*, pp. 35–36.

IV. THE QUANTITY THEORY, FRIEDMAN,
AND KEYNESIAN ECONOMICS

As indicated in my opening remarks, the nominal occasion for the appearance of this paper is the recent publication in the *International Encyclopedia of the Social Sciences* of Friedman's article on the "Quantity Theory." From the substantive viewpoint, the "reformulation of the quantity theory" which Friedman presents on pp. 439–442 of this article is essentially the same as the one he presented in his 1956 essay (see Part I above). But from the doctrinal viewpoint which engrossed us in Parts II and III, there is a fundamental difference: for Friedman now makes no attempt to present this reformulation as a "model of the oral tradition of Chicago." Indeed, neither the Chicago school nor its individual members are even mentioned.

On the other hand, as just indicated, Friedman does continue to denote his presentation as a "reformulation of the quantity theory." The only support he adduces for this nomenclature is that "Fisher and other earlier quantity theorists explicitly recognized that velocity would be affected by, among other factors, the rate of interest and also the rate of change of prices."[41]

That such a recognition existed, there can be no doubt.[42] But—as I have indicated elsewhere[43]—the real question is the extent to which the "earlier quantity theorists" recognized the full and precise implications of these effects: the extent to which they consistently took account of these effects at the appropriate points in their discussions. For one of the fundamental facts of the history of ideas is that in general the full implications of a set of ideas are not immediately seen. Indeed—as has been frequently noted—if they were, then all mathematics would be a tautology; for its theorems are implicit in the assumptions made. The failure to see such implications is also familiar from many episodes in the history of economic doctrine: for example, from the tortuous and faltering manner in which the full implications of the marginal productivity theory were developed.[44]

Thus there is indeed a striking passage in Fisher's *Rate of Interest* about the "convenience" of money holdings which makes an individual willing to forgo the interest that he could earn.[45] But the only echo of this passage in *The Purchasing Power of Money* is a passing reference to the influence of the "waste of interest" on velocity.[46] Furthermore, it is clear that Fisher did not integrate this influence into the general analysis of this book. Indeed, this influence is not mentioned at any other point in it: neither in the

---

[41] "Quantity Theory II," p. 436b.

[42] For specific references to writings of Walras, Wicksell, the much neglected Karl Schlesinger, Fisher, and the Cambridge school (Marshall, Pigou, and especially Lavington) which discuss or at the least refer to the influence of interest on the demand for money, see my *Money, Interest, and Prices, op. cit.*, pp. 372, 545, 556, and 576–580.

[43] "Interest," *op. cit.*, p. 480b. Cf. also my *Money, Interest, and Prices, op. cit.*, p. 372.

[44] See G. J. Stigler, *Production and Distribution Theories* (New York, 1941).

[45] *The Rate of Interest* (New York, 1907), p. 212. This passage is slightly elaborated upon in *The Theory of Interest* (New York, 1930), p. 216, where Fisher refers to the "liquidity of our cash balances [which] takes the place of any rate of interest in the ordinary sense of the term."

[46] *The Purchasing Power of Money, op. cit.*, p. 152.

analysis of the effects of the higher interest rates which mark the "transition period" (Chapter IV), nor in the detailed description of the determinants of the velocity of circulation (Chapter V),[47] nor finally in the statistical investigation of the theory, with its description of how velocity varied during the periods examined (Chapters XI–XII).

I find this last omission particularly significant. For the empirical investigator is confronted with a concrete situation in which he is called upon to take account of the major theoretical variables which might explain the data (even if some of these variables will subsequently be rejected as statistically insignificant); hence this situation provides a proper and operationally meaningful test of whether the influence of a variable has been "fully recognized." It should therefore be emphasized that the failure even to mention the rate of interest as a possible explanation of the observed variations in the velocity of circulation also characterizes the writings of Carl Snyder,[48] to whose empirical work (as well as that of Fisher) Friedman refers.[49] And a similar picture obtains for the earlier studies by James W. Angell[50] and Clark Warburton[51] to which Selden refers in his survey of empirical investigations of the income velocity of circulation in the United States.[52] Furthermore, the fact that Angell and Warburton mention the influence of interest only in their later studies—and in explicit response to issues raised by Keynesian monetary theory[53]—reinforces my basic contention that the

[47] Fisher's discussion here is in terms of the "habits of the individual," the "systems of payments in the community," and "general causes"—by which he means "density of population" and "rapidity of transportation" (*ibid.*, p. 79).

[48] Thus see Snyder's "New Measures in the Equation of Exchange," *American Economic Review*, XIV (1924), 699–713; "The Influence of the Interest Rate on the Business Cycle," *American Economic Review*, XV (1925), 684–699; and "The Problem of Monetary and Economic Stability," *Quarterly Journal of Economics*, XLIX (1934/1935), 173–205.

[49] "Quantity Theory II," p. 436b.

[50] "Money, Prices and Production: Some Fundamental Concepts," *Quarterly Journal of Economics*, XLVIII (1933/1934), 39–76 and *The Behavior of Money* (New York, 1936).

Angell's detailed and systematic analysis of the velocity of circulation is almost entirely in terms of the timing and mechanics of the payment process. The passing references to interest on pp. 57–58 of the article and pp. 164–165 of the book do not change this basic picture. Note too the discussion of "idle balances" on pp. 140 ff. of the book, which is devoid of any reference to the interest rate.

[51] "The Volume of Money and the Price Level Between the World Wars," *Journal of Political Economy*, LIII (1945), 150–163; "Quantity and Frequency of Use of Money in the United States, 1919–45," *Journal of Political Economy*, LIV (1946), 436–450.

Warburton's primary concern is with the secular trend in velocity, which he explains in terms of the mechanism of the payment process and a greater-than-unity income elasticity of demand for cash balances (*ibid.*, pp. 443–444); see also pp. 86–90 of his 1949 article cited in note 53 below.

[52] Richard T. Selden, "Monetary Velocity in the United States," in Milton Friedman (ed.), *Studies in the Quantity Theory of Money* (Chicago, 1956), pp. 184–185. Nearly half of the studies surveyed by Selden are by Angell and Warburton.

[53] Thus see James W. Angell, *Investment and Business Cycles* (New York, 1941), Chapters VI and IX. Similarly, Warburton first deals with this influence in his reply to Tobin's criticism (from the viewpoint of Keynes' liquidity-preference theory) of his (Warburton's) earlier work; see Clark Warburton, "Monetary Velocity and Monetary Policy," *Review of Economics and Statistics*, XXX (1948), 304–314. It is against this background that one must also read Warburton's discussion of the rate of interest in his later "Secular Trend in Monetary Velocity," *Quarterly Journal of Economics*, LXIII (1949), 89–90.

"early quantity theorists" did not of themselves fully recognize this influence.

It is true that the aforementioned empirical studies were primarily concerned with explaining the observed price level in the market, and not the demand function for money. But to press this point too far in the present context is to admit that these "early quantity theorists" did not really have a major concern with the properties of this demand function. Furthermore, even within the context of these empirical studies it is quite appropriate to investigate the possibility that observed deviations from the hypothesized V (whether assumed constant or secularly declining) can be explained in terms of changes in the interest rate—provided the observed V is assumed to equal the desired V. In fact, this is what Warburton did in his later (1949) study, though he concluded that this possibility should be rejected.

In any event, it is significant that the first empirical study (to the best of my knowledge) which explicitly deals with the influence of interest on the demand for money is the 1939 Keynesian-inspired study by A. J. Brown on "Interest, Prices, and the Demand Schedule for Idle Money."[54] I might also add that this is the first such study which discusses a *functional relationship* between the demand for money and "the rate at which the general price-level has lately been changing."[55] This discussion can well be contrasted with Fisher's imprecise statement that when money "is depreciating, holders will get rid of it as fast as possible."[56] Furthermore, Fisher sees this as an unstable process which will cause a further rise in prices which will again increase V "and so on."[57] In my discussion of the Chicago quantity theorists (above, pp. 99–100), I have already stressed the difference between this view and the stable relationship between the demand for money and rate of change of prices described by Friedman—and by Brown.

I have dwelt at length on the treatment of the rate of interest in Friedman's "reformulation" as compared with the actual writings of the quantity-theorists because this difference can be well-defined and hence clearly observed in the literature. But I attach no less significance to other—and more subtle—differences, which also characterize Friedman's 1956 essay. Thus Friedman's presentation of the demand for money is first and foremost in terms of the demand for an asset; for him the income variable in the demand function is primarily "a surrogate for wealth, rather than [as in the quantity theory] a measure of the 'work' to be done by money."[58] Correspondingly, as I have noted elsewhere (see note 3 above), Friedman is primarily concerned with the optimal relationship between the stock of money and the stocks of other assets, whereas the quantity theorists were

[54] *Oxford Economic Papers*, II (1939), as reprinted in T. Wilson and P. W. S. Andrews (eds.), *Oxford Studies in the Price Mechanism* (Oxford, 1951), pp. 31–51.

[55] *Ibid.*, p. 34; unfortunately, Brown goes on to represent this rate by the absolute difference $p_t - p_{t-1}$, instead of the ratio of this difference to p_t (or p_{t-1}), where p_t represents the price level p at time t.

[56] *The Purchasing Power of Money, op. cit.*, p. 63.

[57] *Ibid.*

[58] "Quantity Theory II," p. 440a.

primarily concerned with the relationship between the stock of money and the flow of spending on goods and services. Furthermore, their discussions of this relationship either did not make the distinction between stocks and flows—or at least were imprecise about it. Similarly, quantity theorists paid little, if any, attention to the effects on the rate of interest and other variables of shifts in tastes as to the form in which individuals wished to hold their assets.[59]

And now to our main point: all of the foregoing are precisely the differentia of Keynesian monetary theory as compared with the traditional quantity theory. They are the basic components of a theory of portfolio choice of which there are undoubtedly antecedents in the Cambridge cash-balance school (particularly as represented by Lavington) and before, but whose analytical structure as it now exists stems from the publication during the 1930s of Keynes' *Treatise on Money*,[60] Hicks' "Suggestion for Simplifying the Theory of Money,"[61] and Keynes' *General Theory*.[62] Subsequent valuable contributions to this analysis were made—during the 1940s and early 1950s—by, among others, H. Makower and J. Marschak,[63] Franco Modigliani,[64] R. F. Kahn,[65] Joan Robinson,[66] Harry Markowitz,[67] and James Tobin.[68] And in direct continuation of this intellectual line of descent, Milton Friedman provided us in 1956 with a most elegant and sophisticated statement of modern Keynesian monetary theory—misleadingly entitled "The Quantity Theory of Money—A Restatement."[69]

Actually, a careful reading of Friedman's encyclopedia article would seem to indicate that he has taken account of criticisms of his earlier exposition and that—at least in part—he himself now recognizes this intellectual indebtedness. Thus, first of all, he now describes his reformulation as one "that has been strongly influenced by the Keynesian analysis of liquidity preference."[70] Similarly, the term "liquidity"—which had been avoided in

---

[59]These differences also prevail between Friedman and the Chicago tradition; see above, pp. 100–101.

[60]London, 1930, vol. I, pp. 140–146.

[61]*Economica*, II (1935) as reprinted in F. A. Lutz and L. W. Mints (eds.), *Readings in Monetary Theory* (Philadelphia, 1951), pp. 13–32. Note the reference to Lavington on p. 15, footnote 2.

[62]New York, 1936, pp. 166–172, 222–229.

[63]"Assets, Prices and Monetary Theory," *Economica*, V (1938), as reprinted in K. E. Boulding and G. J. Stigler (eds.), *Readings in Price Theory* (Chicago, 1952), pp. 283–310.

[64]"Liquidity Preference and the Theory of Interest and Money," *Econometrica*, XII (1944), as reprinted in *Readings in Monetary Theory, op. cit.*, especially pp. 190–201.

[65]"Some Notes on Liquidity Preference," *The Manchester School*, XXII (1954), especially pp. 236–243.

[66]"The Rate of Interest," *Econometrica*, XIX (1951), 92–111.

[67]"Portfolio Selection," *Journal of Finance*, VII (1952), 77–91.

[68]"A Dynamic Aggregative Model," *Journal of Political Economy*, LXIII (1955), especially pp. 104–107.

[69]For a somewhat more detailed intellectual genealogy, see again the references cited in note 3 above.

[70]"Quantity Theory II," p. 439b. Although Friedman refers to Johnson's 1962 *American Economic Review* survey article immediately after this statement, I think that it can safely be assumed to reflect his own view as well.

the 1956 essay—is now used.[71] Second, he admits that the Keynesian analysis of the demand for money lays "greater emphasis on current interest rates" than did the "earlier quantity theorists."[72] Third, Friedman now recognizes that the "earlier quantity theory" envisaged the process of monetary adjustment in terms of the relation between the stock of money and the flow of expenditures—"to the almost complete exclusion" of the Keynesian approach, which envisages it in terms of the relation between the stock of money and other assets, particularly bonds.[73] Furthermore, Friedman himself accepts as "plausible" the Keynesian approach that "any widespread disturbance in money balances ... will initially be met by an attempted readjustment of assets and liabilities, through purchase and sale"—though he goes on to explain how the resulting change in prices will also "establish incentives to alter flows of receipts and expenditures."[74]

In view of all this, one can only regret that Friedman has persisted—even within the confines of an international encyclopedia—in presenting his exposition of the demand function for money as a "reformulation of the quantity theory."

Appendix: The Empirical Evidence

I. THE WRITINGS[1]

The sources for the first four[2] summary-propositions at the beginning of Part II are as follows:

HENRY C. SIMONS

> *A Positive Program for Laissez Faire*. Chicago, 1934. As reprinted in *Economic Policy for a Free Society*. Chicago, 1948. P. 64.

> "Rules versus Authorities in Monetary Policy," *Journal of Political Economy*, Vol. XLIV (1936). As reprinted in *Economic Policy for a Free Society, op. cit.* Pp. 164–166, 170–172, 326 (footnote 5), 331 (footnote 16).

> *Personal Income Taxation*. Chicago, 1938. P. 222.
> "Hansen on Fiscal Policy," *Journal of Political Economy*, Vol. L (1942). As reprinted in *Economic Policy for a Free Society, op. cit.* P. 188.

> "Banking and Currency Reform," p. 3 and Appendix, p. 2.

---

[71] "... the services rendered by money relative to those rendered by other assets—in Keynesian terminology, ... liquidity proper" ("Quantity Theory II," p. 440b).
   Compare this with the corresponding passage on p. 14 of the 1956 essay, cited in note 11 above.
[72] "Quantity Theory II," p. 438b.
[73] *Ibid.*, p. 441b.
[74] *Ibid.*, pp. 441b–442a.
   Though he does not refer to it at this point, Friedman's discussion here essentially summarizes the analysis presented in his and Meiselman's paper on "Relative Stability of Monetary Velocity and the Investment Multiplier in the United States, 1897–1958," in *Stabilization Policies* (Englewood Cliffs, N. J., 1963), pp. 217–222. In this analysis, Friedman and Meiselman distinguish their approach from the Keynesian one in terms of the range of assets involved in the monetary adjustment.

[1] See note 13 of the text.
[2] I have not provided specific sources for Proposition (5)—which does not really bear on the issue at hand, and which has been included in the text only for the sake of completeness.

The last passage listed (cited in footnote 15) reads:

> But any general change in business earnings will affect promptly the specu-
> lative temper of the community. Larger profits breed optimism; they stimulate
> investment and induce dishoarding (reduction of idle cash reserves). Pro-
> ducers will become more anxious to borrow for purposes of increasing
> inventories, expanding production, and increasing plant capacity. Lenders
> will have fewer misgivings about the ability of borrowers to repay. People
> generally will increase their lending and investment at the expense of their
> idle reserves of cash. In a word, the velocity of circulation will increase. But
> this change, in turn, means a larger volume of business and higher product-
> prices, and thus still larger earnings. The further increase of earnings, more-
> over, will induce further increase in the velocity of money. And so on and
> on, until the initially sticky prices which govern costs do finally move upward
> markedly and rapidly—or until some fortuitous disturbance (perhaps a mere
> speculative scare) happens to establish a sharp reversal of the trend in product
> prices. On the other hand, once earnings begin to decline, forces will be set
> in motion to continue and accelerate the trend—and perhaps with more
> striking results, for the crucial, sticky prices are peculiarly resistant to down-
> ward pressure.

"Banking and Currency Reform" is an unpublished and unsigned
memorandum dated by Aaron Director as November 1933 and ascribed by
him largely to Simons. See the Bibliography in *Economic Policy for a Free
Society, op. cit.*, p. 313; see also Milton Friedman, "The Monetary Theory
and Policy of Henry Simons," *Journal of Law and Economics*, X (1967), p. 2,
footnote 1.

I am greatly indebted to Friedman and Director for providing me with
a copy of this memorandum.

Friedman describes this Appendix as a "partial exception to the statement that Simons nowhere set forth a consistent statement of his theory"
(*ibid.*). However, except for its explicit relating of velocity to business earnings, the theoretical presentation of the Appendix to this memorandum
seems to me to be no more detailed or systematic than Simons' other
writings.

The passages from Simons' writings referred to in notes 14, 17, and
18 above are as follows:

> Once a deflation has gotten under way, in a large modern economy, there
> is no significant limit which the decline of prices and employment cannot
> exceed, if the central government fails to use its fiscal powers generously and
> deliberately to stop that decline. Only great government deficits can check
> the hoarding of lawful money and the destruction of money substitutes once
> a general movement has gotten under way. [*Personal Income Taxation, op.
> cit.*, p. 222.]

> The bottom of an uncontrolled deflation, for all practical purposes, is non-
> existent—with adverse expectations causing price declines and with the actual
> declines aggravating expectations, etc. ["Hansen on Fiscal Policy," *op. cit.*,
> p. 188.]

> With all its merits, however, this rule [of holding the quantity of money
> constant] cannot now be recommended as a basis for monetary reform.

The obvious weakness of fixed quantity, as a sole rule of monetary policy, lies in the danger of sharp changes on the velocity side, for no monetary system can function effectively or survive politically in the face of extreme alternations of hoarding and dishoarding. It is easy to argue that something would be gained in any event if perverse changes were prevented merely as to quantity, but the argument is unconvincing. The fixing of the quantity of circulation media might merely serve to increase the perverse variability in the amounts of "near moneys" and in the degree of their general acceptability, just as the restrictions on the issue of bank notes presumably served to hasten the development of deposit (checking-account) banking. ["Rules versus Authorities in Monetary Policy," *op. cit.*, p. 164.]

LLOYD W. MINTS

A History of Banking Theory. Chicago, 1945. Pp. 218–222.

"Monetary Policy," *Review of Economic Statistics*, XXVIII (1946), especially 61, 63, 67.

Monetary Policy for a Competitive Society. New York, 1950. Chapter 3 (especially pp. 29, 32–35, 39–41, 48–49, 69–70), Chapter 6 (especially pp. 120–122, 138–142), and Chapter 9 (especially pp. 194, 202–203, 207, 210–211, 227).

FRANK H. KNIGHT

"Economics." *Encyclopaedia Britannica* (1951). As reprinted in *On the History and Method of Economics*. Chicago, 1956. Pp. 15, 30.

"The Business Cycle, Interest, and Money: A Methodological Approach," *Review of Economic Statistics*, Vol. XXIII (1941). As reprinted in *On The History and Method of Economics, op. cit.* Pp. 210–211, 213, 223–224.

Preface to 1948 reprint of *Risk, Uncertainty and Profit*. New York, 1957. Pp. xlii–xlv.

The passages from Knight referred to in footnotes 17 and 27 are as follows:

... in the case of money, just what does set a boundary to a movement of general prices in either direction, and especially the downward movement, becomes something of a mystery. ["The Business Cycle, Interest, and Money," *op. cit.*, p. 211.]

Up to a point, socialist critics have been right in regarding cycles and depressions as an inherent feature of "capitalism." Such a system must use money, and the circulation of money is not a phenomenon which naturally tends to establish and maintain an equilibrium level. Its equilibrium is vague and highly unstable. Its natural tendency is to oscillate over a fairly long period and wide range, between limits which are rather indeterminate. [*Ibid.*, p. 224.]

My chief ground for disagreement with the Keynesian theory of money is the belief that in view of these facts, [viz., the instability of V] —some, or most, or all of them well recognized by Keynes as well as others—supply and demand curves for "liquidity" have no solid foundation and are not a sound basis for action but are "theoretical" in the bad and misleading sense. [*Risk, Uncertainty and Profit, op. cit.*, p. xlv.]

It might be noted that in his discussion of Keynes' theory of liquidity preference in his 1941 article Knight readily recognizes that the rate of interest "must equalize the attractiveness of bonds and of money for holding;"[3] and earlier in this article he also describes the holding of money as an alternative to the holding of other assets.[4] Knight does not, however, take this dependence of the demand for money on the rate of interest into account in his discussion of variations in the velocity of circulation during the course of the business cycle—despite his discussion of the cyclical changes in the rate of interest.[5] All that is discussed in this context is the influence of price expectations.

JACOB VINER[6]

> *Studies in the Theory of International Trade.* New York, 1937. Pp. 40–45, 131, *et passim.*

> "Schumpeter's *History of Economic Analysis,*" *American Economic Review,* Vol. XLIV (1954). As reprinted in *The Long View and the Short.* Glencoe, Ill., 1958. P. 365.

> "International Aspects of the Gold Standard," in Harris Foundation Lectures, *Gold and Monetary Stabilization.* Chicago, 1932. As reprinted in *International Economics.* Glencoe, Ill., 1951. Pp. 137–140.

The discussion on pp. 40–45 of the *Studies* shows that Viner thought of the quantity theory as specifying a causal relationship between the quantity of money and its value. The effect of anticipations of price increases in increasing the velocity of circulation is indicated on p. 131.

The passage from Viner's review of Schumpeter is an instance in which it would have been most appropriate for Viner to have indicated (if he had so believed) that the quantity theory specified not the constancy of the velocity of circulation, but the constancy of the functional relationship between this velocity and the variables that determine it. Instead, he merely emphasizes that exponents of the quantity theory

> would not find variability of velocity disturbing for their theory, provided the variations in velocity were not inverse to those in quantity—or, perhaps, even if they were, provided the amplitude of variation of velocity was less than that of quantity.

It is also interesting to note that Viner goes on in this passage to say that

> the quantity theory of money [can be] understood as holding only: (1) that an authority powerful enough to make the quantity of money what it pleases can so regulate that quantity as to make the price level approximate to what it pleases, and (2) that the possibility of existence of such power is not inconceivable *a priori.*

---

[3] "The Business Cycle, Interest, and Money," *op. cit.,* p. 221.

[4] *Ibid.,* p. 210.

[5] *Ibid.,* pp. 219–220. On p. 223, Knight does refer to high "liquidity preference" and low interest rates in depressions; but he does not refer to a causal relationship between these two phenomena (i.e., to a movement along a demand curve for money), and instead presents them as parallel consequences of the same cause—namely, the depression.

[6] For methodological reasons, I have restricted myself to writings of the period in question (1930–1950)—or at least not too long afterward; hence I have not taken account of Viner's 1962 article on monetary policy cited above in note 5 of the text.

The foregoing writings thus reflect Viner's agreement with Proposition (1) in the text as well as his rejection of the constancy of V. At the same time, Viner did not develop the inconstancy of V into the cyclical theory presented by Proposition (2).

I might also note that in his 1932 Harris Foundation lecture on the gold standard Viner discussed the problem of price stabilization in the following terms:

> A country on the gold standard binds itself to all the vagaries of gold as a standard of value. . . . A standard of value fluctuating erratically in its own value must be an important factor in initiating and in accentuating the recurrent cycles of expansion and depression from which the modern world has suffered. [Pp. 137–138.]

He then went on to

> express [the] individual view [that] we know too little as yet of the possibilities of [price] stabilization to take immediately any major steps in that direction. [Pp. 138–139.]

What Viner did, however, advocate was "continuous experimentation . . . with the possibilities of stabilization . . . in the hope that something can still be made of the gold standard" (p. 139).

In concluding this discussion of Viner's views, I might note that in a letter to me commenting on the present paper as it first appeared, Professor Viner wrote:

> It was not until after I left Chicago in 1946 that I began to hear rumors about a "Chicago School" which was engaged in *organized* battle for laissez faire and "quantity theory of money" and against "imperfect competition" theorizing and "Keyensianism." I remained sceptical about this until I attended a conference sponsored by University of Chicago professors in 1951. . . . At no time was I consciously a member of it [i.e. the "Chicago school"], and it is my vague impression that if there was such a school it did not regard me as a member, or at least as a loyal and qualified member.

(Personal letter dated November 24, 1969—and cited here with Professor Viner's kind permission; emphasis in original).

II. THE LECTURES[7]

The only relevant passage I have been able to find in my notes from Simons' lectures are from his course on "Economics of Fiscal Policy." This passage reads:

> Only thing that has stopped deflationary movement is that government begins to get insolvent too. (Fears that cheap money really would set in.) So inevitably get government deficit which works to stop deflation. No automatic recovery—nothing in system to bring this about. This Simons' theory of business cycles: deflation [continues] until government action. No stability in economy—so that's why have fluctuations to begin with.

[7] See p. 56 above.

Should we obtain deficits by (1) revenue changes or (2) spending changes? Simons in favor of (1).[8]

My lecture notes from Mints' courses contain the following additional relevant passage, taken from his discussion of the Cambridge cash-balance approach:

> In modern theory, demand for money said to have unitary elasticity. Assume that V and T constant. Then P changes directly proportionate with M. [Real] value of total money remains the same. [A diagram of a rectangular hyperbola appears at this point].
> Some have said on basis of postwar I experience that η for money $\neq 1$. E.g., total quantity of money increased 10 times, while goods that could be purchased with this [i.e., a unit of money] decreased 1/15 (?). But in this case have been changes in V and T—contrary to our assumptions. So assume that has been shift from one demand curve to another (also with $\eta = 1$) according as V and T change. [More diagrams follow here].[9]

Mints concluded his course on "Money" with a discussion of policy, in which (among other things) he stated:

> If [government] stabilizes price level, will stabilize aggregate demand and thus prevent unemployment. Inconceivable that federal government couldn't so increase cash balances of public that it wouldn't want to purchase goods.[10]

Most of Mints' discussions of policy matters were, however, contained in his course on "Banking Theory and Monetary Policy" (Economics 331). The material presented here closely paralleled the corresponding discussions in his books on *A History of Banking Theory* and *Monetary Policy for a Competitive Society*.

There is nothing of relevance in my lecture notes from Viner's courses (economic theory, international trade). In my notes from Knight's lectures on economic theory there is a passage that repeats the analysis of his article on "The Business Cycle, Interest, and Money: A Methodological Approach" which had appeared a few years before (see Appendix I). Indeed, the notes refer explicitly to this article and read:

> Keynesian economics. The older viewpoint assumed ideal neutral money: money only an intermediary, so really have barter [economy]. Say's law— *loi des debouchés*. Under ideal competition [conditions?] wouldn't have any money used as medium of exchange—just as unit of account.
> Keynes didn't do anything not adumbrated in previous writings. Instead of saying: "Every supply of goods a demand for other goods"—said: "Every supply of goods a demand for money." [Keynes] hypostatizes money under name "liquidity preference." People want money as such—for its own sake— not as immediate purchasing power.
> Knight says demand for money highly speculative—especially in investors' market and even in consumers' market. If consider changes in prices relative to changes in interest rate—former much greater than latter. So if foresee

[8] Lecture notes from Henry Simons, "Economics of Fiscal Policy" (Economics 361), April 20, 1945.
[9] Lecture notes from Lloyd Mints, "Money" (Economics 330), June 30, 1944.
[10] *Ibid.*, August 11, 1944.

rising prices will borrow money to buy goods; and when foresee lower prices will hurry to sell now. And the anticipation itself will create the price change —and this is cumulative. "Every speculation on the future value of goods is a speculation on the future value of money." Essential fact in slump is just that. In a boom everybody begins to realize that prices are really too high—overcapitalization. All changes in the value of money tend to be cumulative—an unstable equilibrium.

In wheat futures markets have same thing—anticipation creates changes. But there, there is an equilibrium dependent on well-known objective facts. So damped oscillations. But no definite known equilibrium value of money. Everyone might know that [value of] money is too high—but question is whether it will continue to rise—don't know where the breaking point is.

Knight doesn't know how to stabilize price level—and at what height to stabilize it.[11]

I cannot resist citing in addition the following typical Knightian remark, which occurred at a later point:

In medieval times [men] didn't look for remedies since thought everything from God who was good—so everything good. Now science is the God—and we think that must be remedy for every disease. Maybe there is no answer to the business cycle: [maybe] have to let it take its course.[12]

[11] Lecture notes from Frank Knight, "Price and Distribution Theory" (Economics 301) July 24, 1945.
[12] *Ibid.*, July 26, 1945.

III. THE THESES

Doctoral Theses on Monetary Problems Submitted to the University of Chicago: 1930–1950

Author	Title of Thesis
Ernest R. Shaw	The Investment and Secondary Reserve Policy of Commercial Banks
Francis A. Linville	Central Bank Cooperation
Benjamin F. Brooks	A History of Banking Theory in the United States Before 1860
Martin Bronfenbrenner	Monetary Theory and General Equilibrium
Joseph E. Reeve	Monetary Proposals for Curing the Depression in the United States, 1929–1935
George Leland Bach	Price Level Stabilization: Some Theoretical and Practical Considerations
Mrs. Marion R. Daugherty	The Currency School-Banking School Controversy
Benjamin Caplan	The Wicksellian School—A Critical Study of the Development of Swedish Monetary Theory, 1898–1932
Arthur I. Bloomfield	International Capital Movements and the American Balance of Payments, 1929–1940
R. Craig McIvor	Monetary Expansion in Canadian War Finance, 1939–1945
Don Patinkin	On the Inconsistency of Economic Models: A Theory of Involuntary Unemployment
William W. Tongue	Money, Capital and the Business Cycle
Roland N. McKean	Fluctuations in Our Private Claim-Debt Structure and Monetary Policy
Joel W. Harper	Serip and Other Forms of Local Money
Raymond H. McEvoy	The Effects of Federal Reserve Operations, 1929–1936

[a]Where known, the committee chairman is designated by the superior letter[a].

Thesis Committee	Date of Submission
L. D. Edie[a], S. P. Meech, L. W. Mints	1930
H. D. Gideonse (?), L. W. Mints, J. Viner	1937
F. H. Knight, L. W. Mints,[a] J. Viner	1939
E. H. Knight, L. W. Mints, H. Schultz,[a] J. Viner	1939
G. V. Cox, L. W. Mints, J. Viner[a]	1939
L. W. Mints, H. C. Simons, J. Viner	1940
G. V. Cox, L. W. Mints, J. Viner[a]	1941
O. Lange, H. C. Simons, J. Viner	1942
O. Lange, L. W. Mints, J. Viner[a]	1942
R. Blough,[a] J. K. Langum, L. W. Mints	1947
P. Douglas, H. G. Lewis, J. Marschak,[a] T. Yntema	1947
O. Lange (?), H. G. Lewis, F. H. Knight, L. W. Mints[a]	1947
A Director, E. J. Hamilton, L. A. Metzler, L. W. Mints[a]	1948
S. E. Leland,[a] L. W. Mints, H. C. Simons (?)	1948
E. J. Hamilton, L. A. Metzler, L. W. Mints[a]	1950

7
Interest

Interest is one of the forms of income from property, the other forms being dividends, rents, and profits. Interest usually originates in the payment for a loan of money over a period of time—although it can also arise from loans in kind. Interest is essentially measured by the difference between the amount that the borrower repays and the amount that he originally received from the lender (which is called the principal).

The term *interest* sometimes has the broader connotation of all income from property. This is the case when we speak of "the interest charge on capital," which denotes the alternative income that can be earned on a given quantity of money capital. It is, however, with the narrower sense of the term that this article will almost exclusively be concerned.

Etymologically, *interest* stems from the medieval Latin word *interesse*, although the meaning of *interesse* was sharply distinguished by the medieval canonists from what is now denoted by *interest*. In particular, the canonists used *interesse* to refer to the compensation made by a debtor to his creditor for damages caused to the creditor as a result of default or delay in the repayment of a loan; as such the compensation evolved from the *quod interest* of Roman law, which was the payment for damages arising from the nonfulfillment of any contractual obligation. The canonists considered *interesse* to be conceptually distinct from the payment for the use of a loan, which they (and Roman law) denoted by the term *usura*.[1] Since canon law permitted *interesse* but forbade *usura*, the reason for the evolvement of the modern term *interest* is clear.

Reprinted by permission of the publisher from the International Encyclopedia of the Social Sciences, *David L. Sills, ed. Vol. VII. pp. 471–485. Copyright © 1968 by Crowell Collier and Macmillan, Inc.*

[1] John T. Noonan, *The Scholastic Analysis of Usury* (Cambridge, Mass., 1957), pp. 105–106.

In the case of a loan repaid in one lump sum, the total amount of interest that is due depends on the principal, P, on the percentage rate of interest per unit of time, r, on the number of time units over which the loan is outstanding, h, and on the number of time units after which the interest obligation is added to the debt of the borrower, m. If this obligation is added only once, when the loan matures (that is, if $h = m$), the interest is said to be simple. The total amount to be repaid at maturity, S, is then

$$S = P(1 + mr). \tag{1}$$

Correspondingly, the total interest payment is

$$S - P = P(1 + mr) - P = mrP. \tag{2}$$

If, in addition, the time unit with respect to which the rate of interest is measured is the same as that of the duration of the loan, then $h = m = 1$, and formulas (1) and (2) are further simplified.

If the interest obligation is added more than once, interest is said to be compounded. In this case h is usually a multiple of m, so that h/m represents the number of times that interest is compounded over the duration of the loan. The total amount to be repaid at the maturity of the loan in this case is

$$S = P(1 + mr)^{h/m}. \tag{3}$$

The shorter is the period after which interest is compounded (that is, the smaller m is), the larger is the amount payable, S. In the limiting case, one can conceive of compounding being carried out continuously over time, in which case the amount payable is derived from formula (3) by letting m approach zero, thus obtaining

$$S = Pe^{rh}, \tag{4}$$

where e is the transcendental number 2.71828. . . . The variable r in this case is frequently called "the force of interest per unit of time."

In order to compare the rates of interest effectively paid on loans with different arrangements for compounding, it is necessary to express the loans in a standardized form. This form is usually that of a loan granted at a rate of interest of i per year, compounded once a year. The standardized rate of interest, i, corresponding to any single-repayment loan extending for h years, is then determined by solving for i in

$$S/P = (1 + i)^h, \tag{5}$$

where S, P, and h are the actual terms of the loan. Alternatively—and frequently more conveniently—the standardized rate is the force of interest, ρ, as solved from

$$S/P = e^{\rho h}. \tag{6}$$

Loans need not be made in the form of money but can be made in the form of a commodity (for example, wheat, in ancient times). The rate of interest on such loans is frequently called "the own-rate of interest"—a term originated by Keynes.[2] Because the anticipated price movements of various commodities differ, their own-rates need not be equal to each other or to the rate of interest on money loans. If, however, there is perfect arbitrage, then in equilibrium we must have approximately $r_n = r_c + s_c$, where r_n is the rate of interest on money loans, r_c is the own-rate of interest on the loan of any commodity, and s_c is the anticipated rate of increase (net of carrying charges) in the money price of that commodity. For if (say) the right-hand side of the foregoing equation were to exceed the left-hand side, a profit could be made by borrowing money, using the proceeds to purchase wheat to be lent out at its own-rate, and subsequently selling the wheat received in repayment of the loan. Such arbitrage transactions would raise r_n and lower r_c and s_c until the foregoing equality was established.

If the formula is applied to commodities in general—so that s_c represents the anticipated increase in the general price level—it becomes an expression of Irving Fisher's celebrated distinction between the money rate and the real rate of interest. The real rate is the rate of interest as measured in terms of commodities and accordingly is approximated by $r_n - s_c$.[3] The logic behind this relationship explains the fact that money rates of interest tend to be high in periods of inflation. It also explains the appearance in inflationary economies of so-called linked or escalated bonds—that is, bonds whose principal and/or interest payments are proportionately adjusted in accordance with some price index.[4]

Since they are alternatives to one another, the different forms of property income must be quantitatively related. In a world of certainty and perfect markets, the ratio of the dividends paid by a stock (including net appreciation in the value of the stock) to the original price of the stock, the ratio of the rent of an asset (net of depreciation and other operating costs) to the original price of the asset, and the ratio of the profits of a firm to the amount invested in it all have a common value, equal to the rate of interest. This equality reflects the fact that in such a world the individual is indifferent to the form in which he receives his income from property.

Conversely, the preferences that individuals in the real world have for particular forms of property income reflect the differing degrees of risk and uncertainty attached to these various forms, the individual's own attitudes toward the risk and uncertainty, the differing degree of knowledge that individuals have of market conditions, differing anticipations of

[2]John Maynard Keynes, *The General Theory of Employment, Interest and Money* (London, 1936), p. 223; see also Abba P. Lerner, *Essays in Economic Analysis* (London, 1953), pp. 354–356.

[3]Irving Fisher, *The Theory of Interest* (New York, 1930), Chapters 2 and 19.

[4]Arthur J. Brown, *The Great Inflation: 1939–1951* (London, 1955), pp. 200–203; David Finch, "Purchasing Power Guarantees for Deferred Payments," *International Monetary Fund Staff Papers*, V (1956), 1–22; Peter Robson, "Index-Linked Bonds," *Review of Economic Studies*, XXVIII (1960), 57–68.

future price conditions, and the like. Of the four forms of property income, interest usually involves the least risk and the least necessity for acquiring detailed knowledge of market conditions. Assuming that the individual has an aversion both to risk and to the effort involved in acquiring information, we should on the average expect the rate of interest to be lower than the rates of return implicit in other forms of property income.

HISTORICAL ASPECTS OF THE INTEREST RATE

Credit arrangements go back to prehistoric times and may even have antedated the emergence of a money economy. Similarly, there is ethnological evidence of the existence of credit in kind in primitive communities having no trace of a medium of exchange.[5]

In prehistoric agricultural communities, loans of seed—to be repaid by a greater quantity of seed at harvest time—were undoubtedly a recognized type of arrangement. However, to the extent that repayment was not required in the case of harvest failure, such arrangements were not pure loans but had at least some aspects of what we would today call a partnership or, more generally, an equity investment. Such mixed arrangements complicate any attempt to compare modern credit arrangements with those of earlier periods. In any event, it seems possible that the natural productivity of agriculture suggested the concept of interest on loans to men in prehistoric—and then in historic—times.

Loans bearing interest are described in contracts from the Sumerian civilization (beginning about 3000 B.C.), and mentions of such loans are numerous in the descriptions of credit agreements that have come down to us from the Babylonian empire (beginning about 1900 B.C.). In the Sumerian period the customary annual rates of interest on loans of barley and silver were, respectively, $33\frac{1}{3}$ percent and 20 percent. These rates were later established as the legal maxima by the Code of Hammurabi (c. 1800 B.C.) as part of its general tendency to regulate prices, terms of contracts, and other aspects of economic life.[6]

An even greater development of the credit system characterized the Greek city-states of the seventh century B.C. and onward. Particularly popular were "bottomry loans," in which the money advanced by a lender was secured by the hull of a ship or by its cargo on a specific voyage. In the case of shipwreck the debt was usually canceled; if the voyage was successful the borrower paid from 22 to 100 percent interest, depending on the

[5] Raymond Firth, "Capital, Saving and Credit in Peasant Societies: A Viewpoint from Economic Anthropology," in Raymond Firth and B. S. Yamey (eds.), *Capital, Saving and Credit in Peasant Societies* (Chicago, 1963), p. 29.

[6] Fritz M. Heichelheim, *An Ancient Economic History: From the Palaeolithic Age to the Migrations of the Germanic, Slavic and Arabic Nations*, Vol. I, rev. English ed. (Leyden, 1958), pp. 55, 111–112, 134–136; Paul Einzig, *Primitive Money in its Ethnological, Historical and Economic Aspects* (London, 1949), p. 372; Sidney Homer, *A History of Interest Rates* (New Brunswick, N.J., 1963), Chapters 1 and 2.

length and hazardousness of the voyage. In contrast, loans secured by real estate and loans to cities frequently bore interest of 8 to 10 percent. Similar rates prevailed during the Roman era, which was characterized by legal maximum rates, first of 8.5 percent per year and subsequently of 12 percent.

Most loans in ancient times were granted for what would today be considered a short period: a year or a part of a year. Since there were no business firms in the modern sense of the term, the loans were necessarily to persons or partnerships. From this, however, we should not infer that these loans were predominantly for consumption purposes. It should also be noted that the Greeks and Romans looked down upon the earning of income from interest. According to certain authorities, this contrasts with the view of the peoples of the ancient Oriental civilizations, who (it is claimed) accepted interest as a normal feature of economic life.[7]

The absolute prohibition of interest was an outstanding feature of ancient Hebrew economic legislation, as incorporated in the well-known Biblical passages "If thou lend money to any of my people that is poor by thee, thou shalt not be to him as an usurer" (Exodus 22.25) and "Thou shalt not lend upon usury to thy brother" (Deuteronomy 23.19). The rabbis of the Mishnah (200 B.C.–A.D. 200) applied this proscription to commercial transactions as well. At the same time they accepted its effective evasion in certain instances by means of the legal fiction of considering the lender to be a partner entitled to profits from the enterprise financed by his funds (Mishnah: Baba Metzia V, 4).

In the Middle Ages the prohibition of interest (or, as it was then called, usury) was a central feature of canon law. But since the church did not prohibit income from property as a category, here too there rapidly developed legal fictions by which the prohibited interest from loans was converted into other—and permissible—forms of income from property. For some scholars this process represents an evasion and a vitiation of the canon law; for others it reflects the deliberate attempt of the church authorities to accommodate themselves to the business needs of the community and accordingly to place the main emphasis of the prohibition of usury on loans made for consumption purposes.[8]

An important aspect of the Reformation in the sixteenth century was the movement to abolish the legal prohibition of interest. The outstanding theological protagonist of this movement was Calvin. Toward the end of Henry VIII's reign in England, a law was enacted (1545) legalizing interest but limiting it to a legal maximum of 10 percent. In the first half of the

---

[7]Heichelheim, *op. cit.*, Vol. I, pp. 104–105, 219.

[8]Henri Pirenne, *Economic and Social History of Medieval Europe* (London, 1936), p. 146; Frank H. Knight, *The Ethics of Competition and Other Essays* (New York, 1935), p. 256; Noonan, *op. cit.*, pp. 169–170, 190–195.

(Knight's essay referred to here is his 1932 article on "Interest," which originally appeared in the *Encyclopedia of the Social Sciences*.)

nineteenth century, Roman Catholic authorities also publicly decreed that the interest permitted by law could be taken by everyone.[9]

With due allowance for the scarcity and imperfections of the data, there seems to have been a decline in interest rates in Europe from the medieval period to the Renaissance. The minimum interest rates on loans secured by land in the Spanish Netherlands from the twelfth century through the fifteenth century ranged from 8 to 10 percent, as compared with corresponding rates of 6 to 8 percent in the Dutch Republic during the sixteenth and seventeenth centuries. At the beginning of the eighteenth century in England, long-term government-bond yields were from 6 to 8 percent, declining to 3 percent in the midyears of the century and rising erratically toward the end of the century to 5 to 6 percent. These last rates continued during the Napoleonic wars at the beginning of the nineteenth century. Subsequently, the rate fell again to somewhat above 3 percent and declined even further toward the end of the century. Corresponding yields during the twentieth century have generally been higher and in 1955–1965 have again reached 6 percent. Thus, there may have been a slight downward secular trend in long-term interest rates in England over the past two hundred years, although it remains to be seen if this trend has not been reversed in the period since World War II.[10]

In any event, there does seem to have been a downward trend during the past fifty to one hundred years in the share of interest in the national income of developed countries. Thus, in the United States this share fell from 5.7 percent in 1899–1908 to 4.0 percent in 1954–1960. More generally, the data from the United Kingdom, France, Germany, and the United States all show a marked decline over this period in the share of property income (including that of unincorporated enterprises) in total national income. Kuznets attributes this finding in part to the fact that over the same period the ratio of total wealth to national income (the capital-output ratio) has moved downward in these countries; he also conjectures that the decline was reinforced by a secular downward trend in the yield on capital.

Similarly, Kuznets shows that in 1958 the share of income from assets (excluding those of unincorporated enterprises) in total national income was slightly higher in underdeveloped countries (20.6 percent) than in developed countries (18.4 percent). He attributes this finding to the much higher yield on capital in the underdeveloped countries, which more than offsets their lower proportion of corporate assets. Correspondingly, the extent to which the share of property income in the underdeveloped countries exceeds that of the developed ones is much greater when account is taken of all such income—including that of unincorporated enterprises. This finding, as well as that mentioned in the preceding paragraph,

[9] Benjamin N. Nelson, *The Idea of Usury: From Tribal Brotherhood to Universal Otherhood* (Princeton, 1949), Chapter 3; Noonan, *op. cit.*, Chapter 19.

[10] Homer, *op. cit.*, pp. 137–138, 193, 411, 504–506.

would, of course, be modified if we were to take account of the capital invested in the form of education in human beings and accordingly of that part of wages and salaries which reflects the return on this capital.[11]

Studies of the business cycle in the United States have shown that the rate of interest (as measured by the yield on railroad bonds) more or less conforms, with a lag, to the level of general economic activity. Similarly, it conforms, with a lag, to the movements of the price level—a fact (referred to generally by Keynes as the Gibson paradox) that raises certain theoretical questions discussed below, under "Interest in a money economy."[12]

THEORIES OF INTEREST

Interest in a barter economy

From the definition of the interest rate as the price paid for the use of a loan for one unit of time, it seems natural to analyze the determination of this rate in terms of the demand for and supply of loans. Although there are many theories that have not been explicitly formulated in terms of this "loanable-funds approach" to interest, they can nevertheless be examined from this viewpoint.

Investment and the demand for loans. For simplicity, let us define "households" as those economic units that engage solely in the sale of the services of factors of production and in the consumption of goods and services, and let us define "businesses" as the locus of all production and investment activity. Then in an economy in which money exists only as an abstract unit of account (and for the present purpose such an economy is equivalent to a barter economy) any savings that a household makes will be lent out. Correspondingly, the supply of loans by households to the business sector must equal the total amount that households save. (Consumption loans will be discussed later.) Similarly, under the assumption of a perfect capital market, the net investment of the business sector can be considered as being equal to its total demand for new loans (that is, net of refundings) from the household sector, for in such a market it can make no difference either to businesses or to households whether investment is financed by means of loans, stock issues, or undistributed corporate profits.

[11] Simon Kuznets, *Modern Economic Growth: Rate, Structure, and Spread* (New Haven, 1966), Tables 4.2, 4.3, 8.1, and accompanying text.

[12] John Maynard Keynes, *A Treatise on Money*, Vol. II: *The Applied Theory of Money* (London, 1930), pp. 198 ff.; Frederick R. Macaulay, *Some Theoretical Problems Suggested by the Movements of Interest Rates, Bond Yields and Stock Prices in the United States Since 1856* (New York, 1938), Chapter 6; Arthur F. Burns and Wesley C. Mitchell, *Measuring Business Cycles* (New York, 1946), p. 501; Arthur F. Burns, "New Facts on Business Cycles," in Geoffrey H. Moore (ed.), *Business Cycle Indicators*, Vol. I: *Contributions to the Analysis of Current Business Conditions* (Princeton, 1961), p. 28; Phillip Cagan, "Changes in the Cyclical Behavior of Interest Rates," *Review of Economics and Statistics*, XLVIII (1966), 219–250.

The basic fact that lies behind businesses' demand for loans is the productivity of capital. By this is meant the fact that an investment project can yield over time a stream of returns that exceeds the total costs of carrying it out. In particular, if a project is planned for n years, and if $S_1, S_2, \ldots,$ S_n represents its expected stream of net returns or, in more technical terms, of quasi-rents (that is, the expected receipts in each year from the sale of the output of the project *less* the corresponding current operating expenses in the form of wages, costs of raw materials, and the like—exclusive of depreciation), then the productivity of the capital invested in the project is reflected in the fact that $S_1 + S_2 \ldots + S_n$ (where S_n also includes the possible scrap value) is greater than the cost of the plant and equipment, V, involved in the project.

More precisely, the marginal productivity of capital—which for our purposes can be taken as synonymous with Keynes' marginal efficiency of capital—is defined as that rate which equalizes the present value of the stream of quasi rents with the cost of plant and equipment. It is the rate, ρ, which satisfies the equation

$$\frac{S_1}{1 + \rho} + \frac{S_2}{(1 + \rho)^2} + \ldots + \frac{S_n}{(1 + \rho)^n} - V = 0,$$

where it has been assumed that net positive receipts occur at the end of each period, whereas the total payment for plant and equipment is made at the beginning of the first period. In a world of certainty and a perfect capital market, potential investors will carry out any project whose marginal rate of return, ρ, exceeds or equals the interest rate, r, which is assumed to remain constant over the economic horizon and which measures the actual or imputed marginal cost of the funds invested in the project. Correspondingly, investors will not carry out any project whose rate of return is less than r. Thus, under these assumptions, the rate of interest serves as the rationing device that allocates scarce capital funds in an optimal manner among competing investment projects. From this it also follows that the lower the rate of interest, the larger the number of investment projects that it pays to carry out.

This relationship is frequently described by means of a negatively sloped curve relating increasing volumes of investment to a declining rate of interest. It should be emphasized that the concept of investment basic to this curve is that of *gross* investment. The firm's decision about a particular investment project can in no way be affected by whether this project represents "replacement" or "new capital"; nor, in a perfect capital market, can it be affected by the accounting distinction between funds made available from depreciation allowances and those made available from new loans. For our purposes, however, it will be more convenient to deal with the derivative concept "*net* investment," defined as gross investment less depreciation. As a first approximation (whose accuracy increases the shorter the life of the project) the calculation of this depreciation can be assumed to be unaffected by the rate of interest. Correspondingly, the net-investment

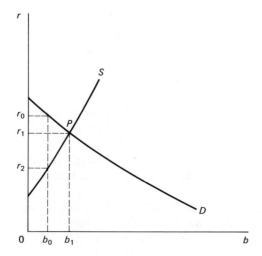

0   b_0 b_1 b **Figure 7.1.**

curve is obtained from the gross-investment curve by simply shifting the latter to the left by an amount equal to depreciation.

This, then, is the explanation of the negative slope of the demand curve for loans, D, in Figure 7.1, which under our present assumptions is identical with the net-investment curve. The vertical axis in this diagram represents the (real) rate of interest and the horizontal axis the real volume of new loans made during the specified period of time (say, a year) to which the analysis refers. By construction, any rate of interest on this curve (say, r_0) corresponding to a given volume of loans (say, b_0) equals the marginal productivity of capital after net investments of the designated volume have been carried out. In other words, if the stock of capital (and hence real volume of loans) in the economy at the beginning of the year in question is B_0, then r_0 measures the marginal productivity of a stock of capital of $B_0 + b_0$ units.

Another property of the demand curve that has been frequently assumed in the literature is that in the absence of uncertainty the demand for loans approaches infinity as the rate of interest approaches zero, for in such circumstances it would pay to carry out any investment project that would yield a perpetual stream of net income. Thus, at a zero rate of interest it would pay to level the Alps or to build a canal across the United States—if such activities would enable us to anticipate with certainty net savings in transportation costs through all future time.

It is clear from the foregoing presentation that b has the dimensions of a stock and is thus not affected by changes in the unit of time used to measure the period specified in the analysis. In other words, at the rate of interest r_0, firms will desire to contract b_0 units of new loans during the year— whether the year is called a year or 12 months or 52 weeks. Alternatively, however, b can be interpreted (as it frequently is) as the average rate at which new loans are contracted during the year. Under such an interpretation, b

clearly has the dimensions of a flow and is accordingly affected by the time unit used to measure the year. In this case the firm's total stock of borrowing at the end of the year (at the rate of interest r_0) is represented by $B_0 + \int_0^T b_0 dt = B_0 + b_0 T$, where T is the length of the year as measured in the stipulated time units and where $b_0 T$ thus has the dimensions of a stock. Clearly, $b_0 T$ in the preceding expression is equal, in both dimensions and magnitude, to the b_0 of the interpretation given at the beginning of this paragraph.[13]

Savings and the supply of loans.   The supply side of the loan market as described above represents the savings behavior of households. In the analysis of this behavior by, for example, Marshall and Cassel, it was pointed out that an individual who saved in order to assure himself a given level of income in the future (say, after retirement) would have to accumulate a smaller capital sum the higher the rate of interest; correspondingly, such an individual would respond to a rise in interest rates by saving less. More generally—and more precisely—a rise in interest rates generates a wealth effect which, in the case of a lender, tends to offset the substitution effect. The rise makes current consumption more expensive relative to future consumption (by decreasing the present value of the cost of a unit of future consumption). Hence, it generates a substitution effect that decreases current consumption and thereby increases current saving. At the same time, it makes lenders better off by virtue of the higher interest they can earn and thus generates a wealth effect that tends to increase current consumption. If the wealth effect were to predominate (as is implicitly assumed by Marshall and Cassel[14] in the case mentioned above), the individual's savings curve would, in the relevant region, be negatively sloped with respect to the interest rate.

It is, however, unlikely that such a negative slope could characterize the savings curve of the economy as a whole. To every lender in a closed economy there corresponds a borrower for whom the wealth effect works in the opposite direction. Hence, in the absence of distribution effects, these wealth effects will cancel out, leaving the aggregate savings curve to reflect solely the uniformly positive influence of the substitution effects. Correspondingly, the supply curve of loans, S, in Figure 7.1 has been drawn with a positive slope.[15]

In the standard Fisher case of an individual with a two-period horizon, the individual is in an optimum position when he adjusts his current consumption (and hence his savings) so as to equalize his marginal rate of substitution of future (C_2) for present (C_1) consumption with $1 + r$. In the

[13] See Chapter 1 above.

[14] Alfred Marshall, *Principles of Economics*, 8th ed. (London, 1920), p. 235; and Gustav Cassel, *The Theory of Social Economy*, new rev. ed. (New York: 1932), pp. 238–239.

[15] Martin J. Bailey, "Saving and the Rate of Interest," *Journal of Political Economy*, LXV (1957), 279–305; Donald V. T. Bear, "The Relationship of Saving to the Rate of Interest, Real Income, and Expected Future Prices," *Review of Economics and Statistics*, XLIII (1961), 27–35.

case of an individual with a horizon of n periods, the planned stream of future consumption $C_2, C_3, \ldots, C_n$ (where C_t represents consumption at the beginning of period t) can be considered as a single, composite good. The quantity of this good, C_F, is defined as equal to the constant level of per-period consumption over the future which has the same present value as $C_2, C_3, \ldots, C_n$; that is,

$$\sum_{t=2}^{n} \frac{C_F}{(1 + r)^{t-1}} = C_F \sum_{t=2}^{n} \frac{1}{(1 + r)^{t-1}} = \sum_{t=2}^{n} \frac{C_t}{(1 + r)^{t-1}}.$$

It can then be shown that the optimum marginal rate of substitution of future (C_F) for present (C_1) consumption in this case is

$$\frac{r}{1 - \left(\dfrac{1}{1 + r}\right)^{n-1}}.$$

For large values of n, this marginal rate can thus be approximated by r. That is, the individual in his optimum position can be induced to give up one dollar of present consumption by compensating him with a constant stream of future consumption of (approximately) r dollars per period.[16] In this sense, then, the rate of interest (say, r_2) on curve S corresponding to any volume of new loans made during the year (say, b_0) equals the marginal time preference of the individuals in the economy after they have carried out the savings that provide these loans.

    The equilibrium rate of interest. The equilibrium rate of interest for the year in question is determined in Figure 7.1 (interpreted as above in terms of either a stock or a flow) by the intersection of the demand and supply curves for loans at point P, corresponding to the rate of interest of r_1. As already indicated, for the barter economy now being discussed these curves can also be interpreted as respectively representing the *net* investment and savings curves of neoclassical interest theory. Correspondingly, by construction of these curves the equilibrium rate measures at one and the same time the marginal productivity of capital and the marginal rate of substitution between future and present consumption. (This analysis could just as well be carried out in terms of *gross* investment and saving—the curves in Figure 7.1 could be made to represent these magnitudes by simply shifting them to the right by an amount equal to depreciation allowances; hence they would continue to intersect at the rate of interest r_1.)

    The foregoing analysis can be recast in terms of demand and supply for the total stock of loans to be outstanding at the end of the year in question. Clearly, the amount of this stock demanded at the rate of interest

[16] Wassily W. Leontief, "Theoretical Note on Time-Preference, Productivity of Capital, Stagnation and Economic Growth," *American Economic Review*, XLVIII (1958), 105–111; Nissan Liviatan, "Multiperiod Future Consumption as an Aggregate," *American Economic Review*, LVI (1966), 828–840.

r_1 is $B_0 + b_1$, where, as before, B_0 represents the stock at the beginning of the year. Similarly, the stock supplied at the end of the year is also $B_0 + b_1$. Thus, this approach yields the same equilibrium rate of interest, r_1, as the preceding one and in this sense is equivalent to it.[17]

On the other hand, the elasticity (although not the slope) of the curves in Figure 7.1 at each point would be less if they referred to the total stock outstanding. This elasticity is the percentage change in the total stock of loans (say) demanded following a unit percentage decrease in the rate of interest; the same absolute increase in the amount demanded is a much smaller percentage of the total stock of bonds outstanding than of the net accretion during a year. Conversely, a one percent increase in this net accretion will require a much smaller fall in the rate of interest insisted upon by debtors than will a one percent increase in the total stock of bonds held.

Consumption loans can be incorporated into the analysis of Figure 7.1 either by adding them to the demand side or by deducting them from the supply side—in which case S would represent the net supply of loans by households to the business sector. From either viewpoint, in a modern economy the relative influence of such loans on the overall demand-and-supply situation—and hence on the equilibrium rate of interest—is a minor one. Correspondingly, it is a much better approximation of the truth to say that interest must be paid on consumption loans because the potential lender has the alternative of lending money at interest on productive loans than to say that the demand for consumption loans is the reason for the existence of interest.

It should also be emphasized that "impatience" or "time preference"—in the sense that an individual with a two-period horizon systematically prefers (say) ten units of consumption goods today and four tomorrow to the alternative combination of four units today and ten tomorrow—is not a necessary condition for the existence of interest. For the major manifestation of time preference in this sense—in an economy in which all individuals have a finite horizon and anticipate a constant stream of income payments—is that (strictly) positive savings will be forthcoming only at a (strictly) positive rate of interest. Conversely, absence of time preference manifests itself in the fact that if the rate of interest is zero, then savings are also zero.[18] Thus, the fact that individuals in such an economy insist on receiving interest in order to save is no evidence of a systematic preference for present

---

[17] [In the light of the Postscript to Chapter 1 above (pp. 6–7), I would now give much less emphasis to the stock-flow discussion of this and the following paragraphs.

I should also note that the approach in the text here slurs over a fundamental point which has been much discussed in the recent literature on capital theory: namely, the length of the period over which firms adjust their actual capital stock to the desired one. For a discussion of this issue as well as references to the relevant literature, see Dale W. Jorgenson, "The Theory of Investment Behavior," in Robert Ferber (ed.), *Determinants of Investment Behavior* (New York and London, 1967), pp. 129–155, especially pp. 132–133.]

[18] Kenneth E. Boulding, *Economic Analysis*, 2nd ed. (New York, 1948), pp. 746–752; Milton Friedman, *A Theory of the Consumption Function* (Princeton, 1957), p. 12.

goods over future ones. More generally, the fact that an individual will, at the margin, insist on receiving more than one unit of future goods to compensate him for forgoing one unit of present goods is not necessarily the *cause* of the existence of interest but its *effect*: he insists on receiving more because he has the alternative of obtaining more by lending out at interest the money that would be released from current consumption by saving.

Whether b in Figure 7.1 is interpreted as the net accretion to the stock of loans over the year or as the average rate of flow of new loans during the year, the equilibrium determined there is that of the short run. (Alternatively, in terms that derive from the second of the two interpretations, it is a "flow equilibrium.") The stock of capital (and hence the stock of outstanding loans) at the beginning of the subsequent year will increase, shifting both the demand and supply curves that could be drawn in Figure 7.1 for that year. In particular, if technology and the quantities of other factors of production are kept constant, the law of diminishing returns will cause a leftward shift of the investment curve and hence of D. At the same time, the increased capital will generate an increased stream of income, thus increasing the amount of savings forthcoming at any rate of interest and thereby shifting S to the right. The new equilibrium situation generated by these shifts is represented by the intersection at Q of the dashed curves D' and S' in Figure 7.2. For the same reason as before, point Q also represents a position of short-run equilibrium, so the curves will shift once again.

The stationary state. A question that has frequently been raised in the literature is whether the shifts just discussed can ultimately bring the economy to a position of long-run equilibrium (or "stock equilibrium," in the alternative terminology described above) in which no further capital accumulation will take place—and whether in this classical "stationary state" the rate of interest can be positive.

A situation in which both these conditions are met is illustrated in Figure 7.2 by the intersection of D'' and S'' at point R on the vertical axis.

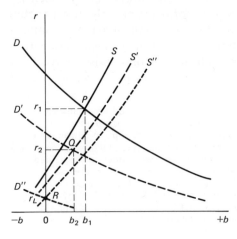

Figure 7.2.

At this point the marginal productivity of the existing stock of capital equals the prevailing rate of interest r_L, so firms have no inducement either to augment or to reduce this stock—and with it the stock of their outstanding loans from households. (The possibility of corresponding reductions in both of these stocks at rates of interest above r_L is represented by the extension of D'' to the left of the vertical axis.) Similarly, households have no inducement either to make new (net) loans to firms or to insist on the redemption of part of their outstanding loans in order to consume the proceeds.

A necessary condition for the existence of a stationary state with a positive rate of interest is that the individuals of this state (assumed to be of a given, finite life expectancy and to anticipate a constant stream of income) have a preference for present as against future consumption; for, as noted above, in the absence of such a preference these individuals would have zero savings only at a zero rate of interest—that is, their savings curve would always start at the origin of Figure 7.2.[19]

Growth models. We must now note that—as Frank Knight has particularly emphasized[20]—the concept of the stationary state has no relevance to the real world, which historically has been characterized by continuous growth in total capital and (as noted above, in "Historical aspects of the interest rate") relative stability of the rate of interest. These developments can in part be interpreted as reflecting the absence in the real world of the two basic assumptions that underlie the theory of the stationary state—namely, constancy in the quantity of other factors of production (that is, labor) and constancy of the state of technology. Indeed, a major concern of economic theory in recent years has been to analyze the growth patterns of economies in which one or both of these assumptions do not hold.

One case of a growing economy that has been particularly studied is that of a one-good, two-factor (capital and labor), perfect-competition economy with a given constant-returns-to-scale technology in which the labor supply is expanding at a constant, exogenously determined rate of n percent per year.[21] Assume for simplicity that the individuals in this economy save a constant proportion, s, of their incomes. Represent this behavior in some initial position by the vertical line S^* in Figure 7.3, where for convenience savings are measured as a percentage of the total existing stock of capital in that position. Similarly, let I^* represent the investment curve of the economy, also measured as a percentage of initial capital. The intersection of these curves at point A—corresponding to the rate of interest r^*—then represents the equilibrium position of the economy.

[19] Cf. Arthur C. Pigou, *The Economics of Stationary States* (London, 1935), Chapter 10.

[20] Knight, *op. cit.* (1935) pp. 262–264; Frank H. Knight, "The Quantity of Capital and the Rate of Interest," *Journal of Political Economy*, XLIV (1936), 614–619 and 626–630; Frank H. Knight, "Diminishing Returns from Investment," *Journal of Political Economy*, LII (1944), 26–47.

[21] Robert M. Solow, "A Contribution to the Theory of Economic Growth," *Quarterly Journal of Economics*, LXX (1956), 65–94; T. W. Swan, "Economic Growth and Capital Accumulation," *Economic Record*, XXXII (1956), 334–361.

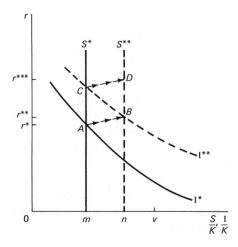

Figure 7.3.

It is clear, however, that this is only a short-run equilibrium, for the percentage rate of growth of capital (I/K) at point A equals m, which is less than the corresponding rate of growth of labor, n. Hence total output, total income, and (by assumption) total savings must all increase at some common rate greater than m and less than n; therefore, S/K must increase, shifting S^* to the right. Similarly, the fact that the ratio of labor to capital is increasing means (assuming that we are in the region of diminishing returns) that the marginal productivity of capital is increasing accordingly, so that I^* also shifts to the right. Furthermore, if we assume that the rate of interest throughout this adjustment process equals the marginal productivity of capital, then the investment curve must shift farther to the right than the savings curve, thus intersecting the latter at a higher rate of interest.

This process could continue indefinitely without the system's ever reaching a position of long-run equilibrium. However, under certain assumptions about the nature of the production function, such a position will be reached. In this case the rightward shifts of the vertical savings curve in Figure 7.3 continue until the curve reaches S^{**} at point n on the abscissa, where it is intersected at a higher rate of interest, say r^{**}, by an investment curve (I^{**}) that has also shifted to the right during the adjustment process. The point of intersection, B, between S^{**} and I^{**} represents a situation in which capital and labor—and hence total output, income, savings, and investment—are all expanding at the common rate n. Correspondingly, there will be no further shifts in the savings and investment curves of Figure 7.3. Point B thus represents a long-run moving equilibrium in which the labor-capital ratio and hence (by virtue of the properties of a constant-returns-to-scale production function) the rate of interest and the real wage rate remain constant. Clearly, per capita income and consumption also remain constant in this moving equilibrium.

The same argument holds, *mutatis mutandis*, if the initial equilibrium position in Figure 7.3 corresponds to a rate of capital accumulation v greater than n. In this case output (income) will increase at a rate less than v, so that S/K shifts to the left. Similarly, the increasing ratio of capital to labor will shift the investment curve to the left, and the equilibrium rate of interest will fall. Once again, long-run moving equilibrium will be reached only if the investment curve ultimately intersects the savings curve in the vertical position S^{**}, corresponding to a rate of growth of total output of n percent per year.

As might be expected, a special case of this long-run equilibrium is the classical stationary state represented in Figure 7.2, above. This can be represented in Figure 7.3 by setting the rate of growth of labor, n, equal to zero and drawing S^{**} accordingly to coincide with the vertical axis.

Returning to the nonstationary case depicted in Figure 7.3, let us assume that the long-run equilibrium position B is disturbed by an exogenous decrease in the savings ratio s that shifts the savings curve to S^*. The initial effect of this decrease is to shift the economy to short-run equilibrium position C. Here the forces described above will again come into operation, shifting the savings and investment curves to the right and thus generating the path of short-run equilibrium positions—say, CD—by which the economy is brought to the new long-run equilibrium position—say, D. Labor, capital, and hence total output at D are once again growing at the rate n. On the other hand, the decrease in the savings ratio has caused an increase (from r^{**} to r^{***}) in the long-run equilibrium rate of interest and (because of the constant-returns-to-scale assumption) a decrease in the real wage rate. Both of these changes reflect the fact that along path CD labor is expanding more rapidly than capital, so the labor-capital ratio is higher at D than at B. Similarly, along path CD output is expanding at a lower rate than labor, so per capita output is less at D than at B.

In brief, a decrease in the savings ratio in this model will decrease the long-run equilibrium ratio of capital to labor, with corresponding consequences for factor prices. The savings ratio, however, will not affect the equilibrium growth rate of the economy, which is uniquely determined by the exogenously given rate of growth of the labor supply.

It should be emphasized that the fact that per capita income is less at D than at B does not imply that per capita consumption is also less at D than at B. The lower level of income might be offset by the lower savings ratio (higher consumption ratio) that by assumption prevails at D. This suggests that among long-run equilibrium positions with alternative savings ratios there exists one specific ratio that maximizes per capita consumption. It can be shown that such a maximum is achieved when the savings ratio is such as to bring the economy to a long-run equilibrium capital-labor ratio that generates a marginal productivity of capital equal to the equilibrium rate of growth, n. The mathematical demonstration is straightforward: Per capita consumption equals

$$\frac{F(K, L)}{L} - \frac{S}{L},$$

where L is the quantity of labor and $Y = F(K,L)$ is the production function. By the assumption of constant returns to scale, this expression can be rewritten in terms of the capital-labor ratio, K/L, as where the second term

$$F\left(\frac{K}{L}, 1\right) - \frac{S}{K} \cdot \frac{K}{L},$$

has been multiplied and divided by K. Since only positions of long-run equilibrium are being considered, S/K can be replaced by the constant n. Maximizing the resulting expression by differentiating it with respect to K/L and setting the result equal to zero then yields

$$F_1\left(\frac{K}{L}, 1\right) - n = 0,$$

where $F_1(K/L, 1)$ is the partial derivative of $F(K/L, 1)$ with respect to its first argument and thus represents the marginal productivity of capital. The value of K/L that satisfies this equation is, thus, the capital-labor ratio that maximizes long-run per capita consumption.

An economy satisfying this equality between the marginal productivity of capital and the rate of growth is said to be growing in accordance with the "golden rule of accumulation." Under the assumption of perfect competition (in which case the marginal productivity of capital equals the rate of interest) this rule can be stated alternatively in terms of the equality between the long-run equilibrium rate of interest and the growth rate. This in turn implies that if point B in Figure 7.3 is on the golden-rule path, then it satisfies the relation

$$\frac{S}{K} = \frac{I}{K} = n = r^{**},$$

so that

$$S = I = r^{**}K.$$

That is, in a competitive economy growing in accordance with the "golden rule," total savings or investment during any period equals total income from capital. It should be noted that this is a macroeconomic relationship and does not imply that all income from capital is saved.[22]

The foregoing graphical analysis can be generalized to the case in which the savings ratio is an increasing function, $s = s(r)$, of the rate of interest, so that the savings function (expressed again as a percentage of the stock of capital) has the form

$$\frac{S}{K} = s(r)\frac{Y}{K}.$$

[22]Edmund S. Phelps, "Second Essay on the Golden Rule of Accumulation," *American Economic Review*, LV (1965), 793–814; Alvin L. Marty, "The Neoclassical Theorem," *American Economic Review*, LIV (1964), 1026–1029.

Such a function could be represented in Figure 7.3 by a positively sloped curve that would shift during the adjustment process in a manner analogous to that in which the vertical savings curve shifts.

The analysis can also be readily generalized to the case of technological change which is entirely labor augmenting (Harrod-neutral). In this case n can be considered as the rate of growth of the "effective quantity" of labor, where this rate equals the sum of the natural rate of increase of the labor force (say, n') and the rate of increase in labor efficiency per unit of labor (say, n''). The argument proceeds exactly as before, with the sole difference that the position of long-run equilibrium (in which savings, investment, capital, and output are once again all growing at the rate n) is characterized by an increase of n'' percent per period in per capita consumption.

Much attention has been given in the recent literature to more complicated growth models with more general kinds of technological changes or with more than one good, or both. These models are described elsewhere.[23]

Interest in a money economy

An economy in which money exists as a medium of exchange is not characterized by the identity that holds in a barter economy between planned investment and the demand for loans, on the one hand, and between planned savings and the supply of loans, on the other. In a money economy, firms can plan to finance investment in plant and equipment—and households can plan to supply loans—by reducing their money balances. Similarly, the supply of loans can be affected by changes in the quantity of money in the system. Another noteworthy difference between a barter economy and a money economy is that in a money economy the wealth of households includes the real value of their money holdings (or, more generally, of their net financial assets); correspondingly, an increase in wealth in this form will increase consumption and thus (*inter alia*) affect the rate of interest. This is a manifestation of what has been called the real-balance effect.

The stock of money that individuals want to hold is positively dependent on their total wealth (or income) and inversely dependent on the rate of interest, which measures the individual's opportunity cost of holding a unit of money instead of an income-yielding asset. Although the analysis of this dependence of money holdings on interest has its antecedents in the writings of the neoclassical economists, these economists did not really integrate the relationship into their expositions of the quantity theory of money, and into their analyses of the velocity of circulation in particular. This was indeed one of Keynes' major contributions.

In any event, individuals will not be willing to hold the existing stock of money in the economy unless the value they attribute to the liquidity service provided by the stock at the margin equals the rate of interest that

---

[23]See the *International Encyclopedia of the Social Sciences* article (Vol. IV, pp. 417–422) on Economic Growth, mathematical theory of.

could alternatively be earned by making a loan (or, in more familiar Keynesian terms, by holding a bond). It follows that when the system as a whole is in equilibrium, the rate of interest must at one and the same time equal the "threefold margin" of liquidity services, productivity of capital, and time preference.[24] Indeed, the money balances of a firm can be considered as part of its working capital—just like any other inventory that it holds—and must accordingly yield a corresponding marginal productivity.

The two major problems in the theory of interest that (by definition) are specific to a money economy are the effects of changes in the quantity of money and the effects of shifts in liquidity preference. These problems will now be discussed, first under the neoclassical assumptions of price flexibility and a constant full-employment level of income and then under the Keynesian assumptions of price rigidity and unemployment. For simplicity, it will be assumed that the economy's reaction to these monetary changes is rapid enough to make it possible to study them within the framework of short-run equilibrium analysis.[25]

A major theme of classical and neoclassical interest theory was that an increase in the quantity of money (generated by gold discoveries or by a government deficit) in the first instance increases the supply of loans and thus depresses the rate of interest. This is reflected by the shift from S to S''' in Figure 7.4. At the same time, classical and neoclassical economists argued that the increased quantity of money also raises prices and thus causes the real supply of loans to decrease once again. Ultimately—after prices have increased in the same proportion, restoring the real value of the public's money holdings—the supply curve returns to its original position, S, so that the rate of interest is once again r_1. Thus, the ultimate invariance of the rate of interest with respect to changes in the quantity of money

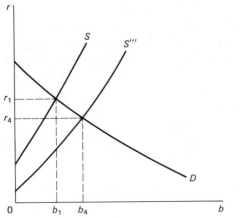

Figure 7.4.

[24] D. H. Robertson, *Essays in Monetary Theory* (London, 1940), pp. 16–17.
[25] On the rest of this section, see my *Money, Interest, and Prices*, 2nd ed. (New York, 1965).

(that is, the "neutrality of money") was an integral part of classical quantity-theory reasoning.

The details of the process just described were set out by classical and neoclassical economists in various ways. Among the best-known expositions is that of Wicksell, who referred to the rate of interest actually prevailing as the "money" or "market" rate—as distinct from the "real" or "natural" rate, which equates planned savings with investment (r_1 in Figure 7.4). By definition, the natural rate is also the rate equating the aggregate demand for commodities with the corresponding supply. The mechanism by which the money rate becomes equated with the natural rate was called by Wicksell the "cumulative process." The basic component of this process is the fact that the rising price level generated by the excess demand for commodities increases the demand for hand-to-hand currency, which the public satisfies by converting their bank deposits into cash. The resulting internal drain on bank reserves forces the banks to raise their lending rate until it is once again equal to the natural rate. Wicksell used the lag with which the market rate adjusts itself to the natural rate to explain the fact (noted above, at the end of the section "Historical aspects of the interest rate") that empirically the interest rate and the price level have tended to move together.[26]

It should be emphasized that the invariance of the equilibrium rate of interest holds even under the Keynesian assumption that the real demand for money also depends on the rate of interest. After prices have risen in the same proportion as the quantity of money, individuals will be willing to hold this increased nominal quantity—which will then represent an unchanged real quantity—at a correspondingly unchanged rate of interest.

However, classical and neoclassical economists did recognize that under certain circumstances monetary changes could have real consequences. Thus, they sometimes argued that—as a result, say, of the lag of wages behind prices—the inflationary process generated by an increase in the money supply could change the distribution of real income in favor of profit recipients and against wage earners. The profit recipients' presumed lower propensity to consume would then bring about a decrease in the total real consumption of the economy and hence an increase in its total real savings. Because of these "forced savings" (as they came to be called) the savings curve would not return to its original position even if prices were to increase in the same proportion as the quantity of money. In such cases these economists readily recognized that the monetary expansion was not neutral: it would increase the stock of capital in the economy and thus permanently depress the rate of interest.

Similarly, an increase in the quantity of money generated by an open-

[26]Knut Wicksell, *Interest and Prices* (London, 1936), pp. 107, 167–168; *idem, Lectures on Political Economy*, Vol. II: *Money* (London, 1935), pp. 205–207; Phillip Cagan, *Determinants and Effects of Changes in the Stock of Money, 1875–1960* (New York and London, 1965), pp. 252–259.

market purchase of bonds (instead of by the gold discoveries or the government deficit assumed until now) will also have a depressing effect on the equilibrium rate of interest. In the first instance, such a purchase merely replaces bonds by an equivalent amount of money in the public's portfolio and hence leaves undisturbed total wealth, the aggregate demand for commodities, and the initial equilibrium in the commodity market. But by simultaneously increasing the demand for bonds and the supply of money, it disturbs the equilibrium in both these markets and causes the rate of interest to decline. This decline reacts back on the commodity market, stimulating aggregate demand there and eventually causing prices to rise. It follows that if the reduction in the rate of interest stimulates investment relatively more than consumption, government open-market policy will have a long-run effect on the growth path of the economy.

Exactly the same reasoning can be applied to show that an increased supply of loans financed by a decrease in the desire to hold money balances (in Keynesian terms, by a decrease in liquidity preference) will also depress the equilibrium interest rate. The possibility of such an effect was not recognized by the neoclassical economists. This is another manifestation of the fact, which we have already noted, that although in their quantity-theory discussions these economists adverted to the holding of bonds and other productive assets as an alternative to holding money, they did not fully integrate this possibility into their thinking.

The initial impact of both the foregoing changes is again illustrated by means of the shift from S to S''' in Figure 7.4. The resulting decline in the interest rate generates an excess demand in the commodity market and hence an increase in the price level. This, in turn, reduces the real supply of loans and causes S''' to begin to shift to the left again. But in this case, unlike the case of an increase in the quantity of money generated by a government deficit, the supply curve cannot return to its original position. In that position the rate of interest would be the same as it originally was, but prices would be higher. Since the nominal value of the public's net financial assets is not affected by the open-market purchase or the shift in liquidity preference, this would imply the existence of a negative real-balance effect, which would preclude equilibrium in the commodity market. Thus equilibrium will be reached at a rate of interest below r_1 but above r_4.

The extent of the depressing effect on the equilibrium interest rate in both of the preceding cases clearly depends on the strength of the real-balance effect, which empirically has been shown to be fairly weak. Indeed, in an economy in which the net financial assets of the public are zero—and in which, accordingly, there is a unique rate of interest at which full-employment equilibrium in the commodity market can obtain—the equilibrium rate would be unaffected. Such an economy is one in which there is no government debt and in which the money supply is created entirely by the banking system in the process of extending loans to the private sector (the so-called "pure inside-money economy").

Under the Keynesian assumptions of price rigidity and unemployment, the rate of interest would be affected in all of the cases discussed above. For example, if the quantity of money was increased while prices remained unchanged or rose only slightly, then the economy would be brought to a new position in which the interest rate was lower—and hence the levels of aggregate demand and employment were higher—than before the monetary expansion. It should be noted that the decline in the rate of interest in this case is of the same nature as the short-run decline specified in the neoclassical analysis described in the last section.

Once we depart from the analytical framework of an economy with a given productive capacity and turn to growth models, there are additional reasons for the nonneutrality of money. For example, it will generally be true that a growing economy whose money supply is continuously expanded at a rate that stabilizes the price level will have a different growth path than one in which the quantity of money is kept constant and the price level declines over time. In general terms, the reason for this difference is that the declining price level increases the rate of return obtained by holding money balances (by virtue of the increase in their purchasing power that it generates), and thus increases the attractiveness of holding savings in this form. Hence, even if the overall savings ratio, s, should remain constant, the amount of savings (at any given level of output) that will take the form of physical capital goods will decrease; that is, the *physical* savings ratio will decrease. Thus, the effects of a declining price level can be analyzed in Figure 7.3 (which refers only to *physical* savings) in terms of a leftward shift of the (physical) savings curve from S^{**} to S^*; just as in the earlier analysis of such a shift, the long-run equilibrium rate of interest will then rise, and the long-run real wage rate will fall. More generally, the lower the rate of increase of the money supply, the greater the rate of decrease of prices and the smaller the long-run-equilibrium capital-labor ratio, hence the higher the corresponding marginal productivity of capital and the rate of interest. This result, however, need not obtain if the overall savings ratio is not constant, but instead depends directly on the respective rates of return of the various assets, including the rate of return on money balances (i.e., the rate of decrease of prices).[27]

General equilibrium analysis. Although the analysis of the determination of the equilibrium interest rate was presented above in terms of the demand and supply curves for loans (the so-called loanable-funds approach), it is clear from the discussion that these curves also reflect the forces at work in the markets for money and commodities, respectively. Correspondingly—and in a completely equivalent manner—it would be possible to present a

[27] John G. Gurley and Edward S. Shaw, *Money in a Theory of Finance* (Washington, D.C., 1960); Alain C. Enthoven, "A Neo-classical Model of Money, Debt, and Economic Growth," in *ibid.*, pp. 301–359; Patinkin, *op. cit.*, pp. 360–364; James Tobin, "Money and Economic Growth," *Econometrica*, XXXIII (1965), 671–684; Jerome L. Stein, "Money and Capacity Growth," *Journal of Political Economy*, LXXIV (1966), 451–465, [Cf. also Chapters 10 and 11 below.]

"liquidity-preference approach" that would depict the equilibrium rate of interest as occurring at the intersection of the demand and supply curves for money—and in which these curves would in turn reflect the forces at work in the markets for loans and commodities.

Thus, no substantive meaning can be attached to the choice of the particular market in which one carries out the analysis of the rate of interest. This choice does not alter the basic fact that the rate of interest influences behavior in all the markets of the economy and that accordingly its equilibrium value (like that of any other price) is determined by the necessity for all these markets to be in equilibrium. This fundamental point can best be brought home by actually carrying out the analysis within a general-equilibrium framework in which all these markets are considered simultaneously.[28]

A meaningful question, however, is the nature of the forces that have affected the equilibrium rate of interest over the course of time. The classical and neoclassical view has been that the major forces are changes in tastes, which affect the desire to save, and changes in factor proportions and technology, which affect the productivity of capital. On the other hand, this view attributes only minor importance to changes in the quantity of money and (by inference) to shifts in liquidity preference. It is in this sense that in the classical scheme interest is a "real" phenomenon. In contrast, the Keynesian view attaches much more importance to the monetary factors mentioned above and in this sense treats interest as a "monetary phenomenon."

The emphasis placed on monetary factors seems to have diminished in the more recent expositions of the Keynesian theory.[29] This might be interpreted as reflecting the fact that the Keynesian monetary theory of interest had its genesis in the great depression of the 1930s, when "excess savings" and extensive unemployment of plant and equipment discouraged thinking in terms of the scarcity and marginal productivity of capital. Conversely, the renewed emphasis on these traditional, real factors in recent years can be interpreted as a reflection of the widespread "capital shortage" of the post-World War II boom period in developed countries—and, even more so, of the key role played by the volume of capital formation and its productivity in the development plans of underdeveloped countries.

Interest differentials. The discussion thus far has been presented in terms of a single interest rate. Actually, however, there is a whole array of interest rates in the market. The major source of differentials in interest rates is the varying degree of risk associated with different loans. Two types of risk have received particular attention in the literature: the risk of default and the risk of illiquidity. "Illiquidity" refers to the risk that the

---

[28] J. R. Hicks, *Value and Capital*, 2nd ed. (Oxford, 1946), Chapter 12; Patinkin, *op. cit.*, pp. 258–260, 330–334, 375–381.
    [29] Joan Robinson, "The Rate of Interest," *Econometrica*, XIX (1951), 92–111, especially pp. 93 and 110.

lender may have to sell the bond under unfavorable circumstances before its maturity. This, indeed, is the basis of the Keynesian explanation of the fact that individuals hold money even though they have the alternative of holding interest-bearing bonds.[30] In any event, the actual rate of interest on any particular bond can be viewed as being composed of the "pure" rate of interest that would be paid on a riskless loan plus an appropriate risk premium.

Insofar as the risk of default is concerned, a study of corporate bonds of different quality classes in the United States for the period 1900–1943 showed that the bonds that were rated highest by investment agencies (for example, Moody's) yielded on the average 5.1 percent, whereas those rated lowest (and whose default rate was eight times as great) yielded 9.5 percent. It has been claimed that an important reason why this risk premium has been so large (4.4 percent) is the legal and traditional limitations on large institutional investors, which have prevented them from buying the larger quantity of high-yield, low-quality bonds appropriate to a rationally diversified portfolio.[31]

The risks of illiquidity have been analyzed particularly in connection with the tendency of the interest rate in most periods to increase with the duration of the loan. The formal analysis of this "term structure of interest rates" distinguishes between the long-term rate (say, the annual rate of interest, R, on a loan granted for n years), the forward short-term rate (the rate of interest r_t at which a one-year loan to be given in year t can now be contracted), and the spot short-term rate (the existing rate for a one-year loan). In equilibrium, $(1 + R)^n = (1 + r_1)(1 + r_2) \ldots (1 + r_n)$, for unless this equality obtains, individuals will find it advantageous to shift from long-term loans to an arrangement of refinancing by means of forward contracts for a series of short-term loans.

As can be inferred from the discussion above, a basic contention of liquidity-preference theory is that in order to induce lenders to make long-term loans—which in principle is equivalent to making forward contracts for short-term loans—the forward rate for year t must exceed the actually expected spot rate for that year by a "liquidity premium" that will compensate the lender for the risks involved in tying up his funds. This implies that if the short-term rate is expected to remain unchanged in the future, then the current short-term rate will be lower than the current long-term rate.[32]

Although the empirical evidence is not unequivocal, it does on balance seem to support the foregoing theory. It might also be noted that the yield on short-term government securities in the United States during the past forty years has typically been lower than the yield on corresponding long-

[30] James Tobin, "Liquidity Preference as Behavior Towards Risk," *Review of Economic Studies*, XXV (1958), 65–86.

[31] W. Braddock Hickman, *Corporate Bond Quality and Investor Experience* (Princeton, 1958), pp. 10–17.

[32] Hicks, *op. cit..*, Chapter 11.

term securities. Again, the history of business cycles in the United States during the past century has shown that the short-term rate has tended to rise relative to the long-term rate near the peak of the cycle. This can be interpreted in terms of the preceding equation as reflecting the market's opinion that the short-term rates at such a time are abnormally high and are due to fall. A corresponding interpretation holds, *mutatis mutandis*, for the symmetrical finding that the short-term rate falls relative to the long-term rate near the trough of the cycle.[33]

To return to the discussion of a single rate of interest, it should be emphasized that neoclassical and Keynesian economics, although they differ in their analyses of the equilibrating mechanism, are at one in equating the rate of interest with the value of the productive services of capital as determined by the market. However, as Knight emphasized many years ago in his fundamental and incisive critique of "productivity ethics," this does not constitute an ethical legitimation of the resulting income distribution and of its interest component in particular. Among other things, this distribution can be no more "just" than the distribution of the wealth that generates the interest income.[34]

In the Marxist theory of labor value, interest has a negative ethical connotation; it is one of the forms of "surplus value" that stem from the exploitation of labor in a capitalist economy. Because of this ideological connotation, interest costs were largely ignored in the economic planning of the U.S.S.R. in the 1930s and after. In more recent years, however, widespread agreement has developed among Soviet economists and practitioners on the theoretical necessity of making some sort of interest charge on capital (although usually under a different name) in order to make an optimal choice among alternative investment projects. There also seems to be increasing evidence of the actual use of such a charge by the planning authorities.[35]

[33]See Reuben A. Kessel, *The Cyclical Behavior of the Term Structure of Interest Rates* (New York and London, 1965) and references there cited.

[34]Knight, *op. cit.* (1935), pp. 41–75 and 255.

[35]Norman Kaplan, "Investment Alternatives in Soviet Economic Theory," *Journal of Political Economy*, LX (1952), 133–144; Alec Nove, *The Soviet Economy: An Introduction* (New York, 1961), pp. 209–217, 228–231; Abram Bergson, *The Economics of Soviet Planning* (New Haven, 1964), Chapter 11, especially p. 252; Haim Barkai, "A 'Recoupment Period' Model of Investment and Pricing in a Socialist Economy," in D. C. Hague (ed.), *Price Formation in Various Economies* (New York, 1967), pp. 183–202.

On the Nature
of the Monetary
Mechanism [1]

I

May I start by expressing my sincerest appreciation to the Wicksell Lecture Society for the honor they have bestowed upon me in inviting me to give these lectures. I hope that without being presumptuous I may be permitted to add that this invitation is a particular source of gratification to me in view of the specific and significant intellectual debt which I feel I myself owe to Wicksell's work in monetary theory.

But reading Wicksell was for me—as I am sure it has been for many others—not only a source of intellectual stimulation, but also a personal experience of contact with an individual of the highest sincerity and integrity, a man of simplicity and principles. These qualities even shine through his purely economic work, and it is therefore no surprise to find that they reflect the general characteristics of Wicksell as a man—as a determined fighter for intellectual and social freedom, as we can learn from Torsten Gårdlund's fascinating *Life of Knut Wicksell*.

The subject I have chosen for these lectures is a recurrent one of monetary theory, and was also one of Wicksell's primary concerns: namely,

These are the Wicksell Lectures of 1967 originally published by Almqvist and Wicksell, Stockholm. Reprinted by permission of the Wicksell Lecture Society.

[1] In the process of preparing these lectures for publication, I have taken the liberty of making various revisions. Basically, however, they remain in the form in which they were presented.

I am grateful to the Israel Academy of Sciences and Humanities for a grant which covered the costs of statistical and other technical assistance.

My thanks too to Dr. Karl-Olof Faxén for his kind and patient help in all the technical arrangements connected with the presentation of these lectures and their preparation for press. I am also deeply grateful to Professors Erik Lundberg and Assar Lindbeck for their warm hospitality during my most enjoyable visit to Stockholm.

the manner and extent to which a monetary expansion influences the economy directly—that is, as a result of the immediate impetus to aggregate demand which it may generate; and the extent to which it does so indirectly— that is, as a result of its prior effect on the interest rate and on relative prices, which in turn affect aggregate demand. In more modern terminology, this distinction can be described as that between the wealth effect of a monetary expansion, and its substitution effect.

Wicksell's name is usually associated with the view that only the indirect influence through the interest rate is of importance. This is undoubtedly a correct description of his analysis in *Interest and Prices*. It is however worth noting that by the time Wicksell published his *Lectures on Political Economy*, he had significantly revised his viewpoint. Thus we find him at the end of volume 2 of his *Lectures* explicitly referring to his earlier analysis of *Interest and Prices* and saying:

> Only in so far as new gold is deposited in the banks in the form of "capital," i.e. without being drawn out in cheques and notes soon after, can it give rise to a lowering of interest rates and in that way affect prices. But this need not happen, and, contrary to Ricardo's view, does not happen as a rule. Rather most of the gold flows in in payment for goods and should then, in proportion as it exceeds the demand for new gold, have a direct influence in raising prices without out lowering interest rates.[2]

In any event, emphasis on the indirect or substitution effect is one of the hallmarks of Keynesian monetary theory. The direct effect, on the other hand, is more in the tradition of the classical and neoclassical quantity theorists—though they also assigned a vital role in the dynamic adjustment process to the indirect effect of a reduction in interest. They emphasized however that this effect on the interest rate was only temporary, and that the rate would return to its original level once the full effects of the monetary expansion on prices had worked themselves out. In this, Wicksell was again in the neoclassical tradition, and indeed the role of his famous "cumulative process" in this context was precisely to explain how the rise in prices caused an internal drain on bank reserves, thus forcing the banks to raise the money rate of interest to its original level, at which it once again equalled the real, or natural, rate.[3]

In order to be able to deal more precisely with the problem at hand, it will first be necessary to make certain relevant distinctions and also to obtain some notion of the relevant empirical magnitudes. It is with this essentially preliminary material that we shall be almost entirely concerned today—leaving the more substantive analysis for the next lecture.

As the first stage of our argument, let me distinguish among three types of increases in the quantity of money:

1. Secular—or intercyclical—changes

[2]*Lectures on Political Economy*, Vol. II: *Money* (London, 1935), p. 215.
[3]For the relevant references to Wicksell and to the neoclassical literature, see D. Patinkin, *Money, Interest, and Prices*, 2nd ed. (New York, 1965), Chapter XV: 1.

2. Intracyclical changes—or changes within the business cycle
3. Once-and-for-all changes.

By secular change I mean, of course, the historical trend of an increasing money supply which has characterized most of modern history. The simplest way of measuring this trend is by approximating the data with an exponential curve, which rises at a constant rate. Where the data permit (and in the United States this is the case) we can also describe the trend in terms of the upward movement of the average quantity of money during each of the successive business cycles which the economy has experienced.

By intracyclical changes I mean changes in the money supply during the various phases of the business cycle. I will not be concerned much with such changes in what follows. Instead, my main concern will be with changes which represent strong deviations from the secular trend, but which are *not* hyperinflations. In order to bring out their basic characteristic, I shall refer to such changes as "once-and-for-all changes," though it is clear that since they represent deviations from a trend, the quantity of money continues to change afterwards as well. Such once-and-for-all changes are usually associated with wartime inflations or with serious depressions. Thus as we shall see below (Table 8.1), the average annual peacetime rate of increase of the total United States money supply (which is defined most simply for our purposes as hand-to-hand currency outside the banking system *plus* total bank deposits) was slightly less than 5 percent during the period 1875 to 1955; but during the periods of World Wars I and II, this rate more than tripled. Once-and-for-all decreases can also occur: thus the United States money supply fell from the peak of August 1929 to the March 1933 trough of the Great Depression by more than one third.

I have spoken so far of "money" in the singular. But in order to proceed with our analysis, it will be necessary to distinguish between two types of money: first, money in the sense that we have used until now—i.e. currency *plus* total deposits; and second, what has been called by Gurley and Shaw "outside money."[4] By this is meant that part of the money supply which is a net asset of the private sector—by virtue of its representing either the net debt of the government (including the central bank) or an international asset (gold or net foreign exchange).

A question which now arises (and which has been increasingly discussed in recent years)[5] is whether government interest-bearing securities should be considered as a net debt of the government—and hence a net asset of the private sector. The reason for this question is that these securities represent not only a stream of future payments of interest and principal by the government, but also a stream of future taxes to enable the government to finance these payments. Hence if the private sector discounts its future

[4] J. G. Gurley and E. S. Shaw, *Money in a Theory of Finance* (Washington, D.C., 1960), pp. 72–73.

[5] Cf. e.g., R. A. Mundell, "The Public Debt, Corporate Income Taxes, and the Rate of Interest," *Journal of Political Economy*, LXVIII (1960), 622–626.

tax liabilities to the same extent as its future receipts, the net value of these government securities is zero. Clearly, the discounting of the tax liability may only be partial—and it is indeed most reasonable to assume that it is. But only in the case where there is no discounting at all is it valid to consider the full value of government securities as a net asset of the private sector.

From this we can also see the special characteristic of fiat paper money. For though this too is nominally a debt of the government, it does not involve the payment of either interest or principal, and hence does not represent any future burden of "debt servicing." Hence it is a net asset of the private sector—even if the latter should take full account of its future tax liabilities.

To return to government interest-bearing debt, let us assume for simplicity that the discounting of future tax liabilities is complete. Then in the United States, for example, outside money should be defined as consisting of hand-to-hand currency (most of which is in the form of notes issued by the Federal Reserve Bank) *plus* that part of commercial bank deposits "backed" by reserves held in the Federal Reserve Bank *minus* Federal-Reserve-Bank credit to the private sector (i.e., reserve credit not based on United States government securities). Thus, if we ignore this last item (and in the present context of concern with secular and wartime changes, this might be forgiven), outside money (under the assumption of complete discounting) coincides with what Milton Friedman and Anna Schwartz have denoted as "high-powered money"—a term which they chose in order to underline the fact that this money represents the actual or potential reserves of the banking system, and hence the basis of a possible multiple expansion of the money supply.[6] However, for my present purposes—which are admittedly somewhat different from those of Friedman and Schwartz—I prefer Gurley and Shaw's earlier term "outside money," since it highlights the property that this money represents a net asset of the private sector—a property which, as already noted, will be a basic element of the analysis which follows.

In order to bring out the significance of this property, let us consider that part of the money supply which is *not* outside money—or what Gurley and Shaw have called "inside money." In slightly oversimplified terms, this represents that part of the money supply which is generated by a fractional reserve banking system in its normal process of creating deposits by credit expansion. Hence this money does not represent a net asset of this sector. For to every dollar of deposits thus created and held by some individual in the economy, there corresponds an offsetting debt of some other individual. Thus, in the case of expansion of bank credit to the private sector, the

---

[6] M. Friedman and A. J. Schwartz, *A Monetary History of the United States: 1867–1960* (Princeton, 1963), p. 50.

Actually, the Friedman-Schwartz definition of high-powered money does deduct part of Federal-Reserve-Bank credit: namely, the "float" (*ibid.*, p. 748, definition of column 2; and p. 808, definition of column 1).

offsetting debt is that of the borrower from the banking system. Similarly, under our present assumption that individuals fully discount their future tax liabilities, an expansion of bank credit to the government (i.e., the bank's acquisition of new government securities) will create both deposits for the private sector (after the government has spent the money borrowed from the banking system) and an offsetting debt of taxpayers. Thus deposits "backed" by commercial-bank holdings of government securities are also inside money.[7]

Since outside money includes the reserves of the banking system, there must be a relationship between it and the total quantity of money. But it is clear from the foregoing definition that such a relationship need not be a proportionate one. In particular—as we can learn from C. R. Phillips' classic work on *Bank Credit*[8]—the total quantity of money depends not only on the volume of reserves, but also on the reserve ratio which banks maintain and on the currency/deposit ratio which individuals maintain. An increase in either of these ratios (the other remaining constant) will cause a decrease in the total quantity of money—even though the quantity of outside money remains constant. A corresponding statement can, of course, be made for the effects of a decrease in these ratios.[9]

How important is outside money in a modern economy? Since one of the characteristics of such an economy is a well-developed fractional-reserve banking system, it can generally be assumed that outside money (as defined above) will constitute at most from 30–40 percent of the total money supply. This, however, is not a proper measure: for what really concerns us is how important outside money has been as a determinant of *changes* in the total money supply.

This, of course, is an empirical question. Let me answer it for the United States economy by first resorting to the aforementioned approximate equality between outside and high-powered money, thus making it possible to use for our purposes the data presented by Phillip Cagan in his recent interesting study.[10] The relevant findings of this study are presented—in a somewhat different classification and terminology—in Table 8.1. Column 4 of this table indicates the extent to which the growth of the total money supply can be explained by the growth of outside money—in the sense of indicating the percentage of the growth of the total money supply that would have taken place if the proportions between these two types of money had remained constant. Conversely, column 5 indicates the relative contribution of changes in the ratio of total money to outside money—which in turn reflect changes in the reserve ratio and/or currency/deposit ratio. Thus the

---

[7] Though I am using Gurley and Shaw's general distinction between outside and inside money, my specific definition differs from theirs (*op. cit.*, pp. 363–364) because of the differing treatment of government securities.

[8] New York, 1928, Chapters 3–4.

[9] These ratios play a central role in the Friedman-Schwartz analysis of changes in the money supply, *op. cit.*

[10] *Determinants and Effects of Changes in the Stock of Money, 1875–1960* (New York, 1965).

**Table 8.1   Changes in Total and Outside Money Stock in the United States:
Averages for Selected Periods, August 1875–December 1955 (Percent)**

	Average Annual Rate of Increase of		Total Growth in Money Stock[a]	Relative Contribution of	
				Changes in Outside Money $\frac{(2)}{(1)} \cdot 100$	Changes in Ratio of Total Money to Outside Money (3)–(4)
	Total Money Stock[a]	Outside Money[b]			
	(1)	(2)	(3)	(4)	(5)
All years	5.7	5.2	100	91	9
War years[c]	16.0	16.3	100	102	−2
Nonwar years	4.9	4.3	100	88	12
Pre-March 1917	6.3	4.3	100	68	32
Post-November 1918	3.2	4.4	100	138	−38

[a]Hand-to-hand currency *plus* total commercial-bank deposits.
[b]Coincides with Cagan's "high-powered money."
[c]March 1917–November 1918, and November 1941–August 1945.

SOURCE   Phillip Cagan, *Determinants and Effects of Changes in the Stock of Money, 1875–1960* (New York: National Bureau of Economic Research, 1965), p. 19.

data in the last line of the table show that if the total money supply had grown in the same proportion as outside money during the nonwar years after 1918, then it would have exceeded the actually observed growth by 38 percent—and that the reason this additional growth did not occur was that there took place an increase either in the reserve ratio and/or the currency/deposit ratio.

Thus the major impression which emerges from column 4 is the dominating importance of outside money in explaining changes in the total quantity of money—both in the once-and-for-all wartime context and in the secular context. In particular, we see that the monetary expansions of World Wars I and II can be interpreted in terms of an increase in the quantity of outside money causing an almost exactly proportionate increase in the total supply of money. A slightly less exact relationship—reflected by the figure 88 percent—holds for the secular increase in the money supply during the 75 peacetime years of the period. And an even less exact relationship holds when these peacetime years are divided into two subperiods. Indeed, the data for these subperiods show that the 88 percent is an average of the pre-World War I period, in which outside money grew at a rate which was roughly one third less than that of the total money supply—and of the post-World War I period, in which it grew at a rate which was roughly one third more. Nevertheless, the change in outside money remains the predominant explanation of the change in the total money supply in each of these subperiods as well.

Another indication of the importance of changes in outside money in a secular context is the extent to which such changes explain the changes in the average quantity of money during one business cycle as compared with that of the following one. Thus in 11 of the 18 National Bureau reference cycles from 1877 to 1953 examined by Cagan, changes in outside money were the major source of this intercyclical change in the quantity of money;[11] again, they played this major role in 9 of the 17 specific cycles over the same period.[12] It might, however, be noted that in both cases the cycle connected with the Great Depression of the early 1930s was a singular exception, with an increase in outside money (relative to the preceding cycle) being accompanied by an actual decrease in the total stock of money. More generally, the importance of peacetime intercyclical changes in the quantity of outside money as an explanation of corresponding changes in the total money supply was much greater before World War I (when it was the major source of the change in 6 out of the 7 intercyclical movements) than after (when it was the major source in only 2 of the 7 intercyclical movements).[13]

In any event, the foregoing picture is to be sharply contrasted with that which obtains for intracyclical changes. Here Cagan's data show that for the 18 specific cycles studied, changes in high-powered money explained on the average only 27 percent of the intracyclical changes in the total money supply—and that the percentage explained falls to 21 percent if only non-war periods are considered.[14]

As will be recalled, all of the foregoing data define money as including time deposits as well as demand deposits. Without entering into the substantive questions connected with this definition, we simply remark that it is the only one which can be used if we wish to analyze the United States money supply in the period before World War I—for which there exists no breakdown between these deposits. It is, however, worth noting that the secular relationship between outside and total money described by Table 8.1 holds (after World War I) even if money is defined to include only demand deposits. In particular, the total money supply so defined grew from November 1918 to December 1955 (excluding the period of World War II) at the average annual rate of 3.6 percent; hence the relative contribution of outside money to this growth was 122 percent $[= (4.4/3.6) \cdot 100]$—as compared with the 138 percent reported in Table 8.1 for the broader definition of money. Similarly, the wartime growth of the money supply (narrowly defined) was at the average annual rate of 18.6 percent; hence the relative contribution of outside money was 88 percent $[= (16.3/18.6) \cdot 100]$—as compared with the 102 percent recorded in Table 8.1.[15]

Let us now see how our findings are affected by dropping the assumption that individuals fully discount future tax liabilities. Indeed, let us for

---

[11] *Ibid.*, Table 28, p. 236.

[12] *Ibid.*, Table F–4, p. 332.

[13] *Ibid.*, Table 28, p. 236. The data in this table refer to reference cycles; a similar statement holds for the specific cycles described *ibid.*, p. 332.

[14] *Ibid.*, Table 4, p. 26.

[15] The rates of growth of money supply were computed from data provided in Friedman and Schwartz, *op. cit.*, Table A–1, column 7, pp. 709 ff.

Table 8.2   Changes in Total and Outside Money Stock in the United States: Averages for Selected Periods, June 1917–June 1966^a (Percent)

	Average Annual Rate of Increase of			Total Growth in Money Stock	Relative Contribution of Changes in Outside Money	
	Total Money Stock^b	Outside Money Narrowly Defined^c	Outside Money Broadly Defined^d		Narrowly Defined $\frac{(2)}{(1)} \cdot 100$	Broadly Defined $\frac{(3)}{(1)} \cdot 100$
	(1)	(2)	(3)	(4)	(5)	(6)
All years	5.5	5.1	6.0	100	93	109
War years^e	15.6	14.2	20.0	100	91	128
Nonwar years	3.3	3.2	3.1	100	97	94
1919–1939	2.3	5.0	6.9	100	217	300
1946–1966	4.3	1.5	−0.6	100	35	−14

^{a}Calculations based on end-of-June figures.
^{b}Hand-to-hand currency *plus* total commercial-bank deposits. The corresponding figures for the average annual percentage rate of growth of the total money stock excluding time deposits are 4.8 (all years); 17.1 (war years); 2.2 (nonwar years); 2.1 (1919–1939); and 2.4 (1946–1966).
^{c}As defined in Table 8.1, note b.
^{d}As defined in immediately following text.
^{e}June 1917–June 1919, and June 1939–June 1946.
SOURCE: Statistical Appendix.

simplicity go to the other extreme and assume that no discounting at all takes place, so that the total value of government securities is considered to be a net asset of the private sector. The appropriate definition of outside money for the United States is then hand-to-hand currency *plus* that part of commercial-bank deposits "backed" by reserves held in the Federal Reserve Bank or by commercial-bank holdings of United States government securities *minus* Federal-Reserve-Bank credit to the private sector *minus* government deposits in the commercial banks. The results of using this definition are presented in Table 8.2, which for comparison also provides calculations for the definition used in Table 8.1. Column 6 of Table 8.2 shows us once again that outside money (now defined broadly) was the major determinant of the secular and wartime[16] changes in the total money supply. As before, however, the overall relationship for peacetime years represents an average of two subperiods in which the relationship was much weaker. Indeed, if we use the broader definition of outside money, the relationship between it and the total money supply was even reversed in the post-World War II period. These findings require much further study. In any event, we note that all of the foregoing statements hold also for the total money stock defined so as to

[16] The period of World War II is defined in Table 8.2 as June 1939–June 1946. This seems to me to be a more appropriate definition than June 1941–June 1945—though the main results of the table hold for such a definition as well.

exclude time deposits—though in this case the differential pattern of the two peacetime subperiods (in which the total money stock exclusive of time deposits grew at the average annual rates of 2.1 percent and 2.4 percent, respectively) is somewhat less striking.

If outside money is narrowly defined, then there is no difference between a monetary increase generated by deficit financing on current account and one generated by an open-market purchase: in both cases there is an increase in outside money which corresponds to an increase in the net assets of the private sector. This, however, is no longer true if outside money is broadly defined. For then an open-market purchase from the nonbanking private sector (though *not* from the banking sector) will increase the quantity of outside money in the system; on the other hand, it will not—in the first instance—change the net asset position of the public; for all that has occurred is the replacement in the public's portfolio of government securities by an equivalent amount of money.[17] There will, of course, subsequently take place changes in the net value of this portfolio as a result of the changes in interest rate caused by the open-market purchase; but this is another question.

In the present context, however, the possibility of increasing the quantity of outside money in this way need not concern us. For the total volume of United States securities held by the nonbanking sector actually *increased* over the period 1917–1966—from a negligible level to roughly $155 billions, with the major increases taking place during World War I, the depression of the 1930s and (by far most important) during World War II.[18] Thus open-market purchases from this sector could not have been the source of the absolute increase in the quantity of outside money during the period in question.

All this is an overelaboration of the commonplace that monetary expansions have usually been the result of wartime government deficit financing on current account—and that the increased quantity of money so injected into the system remains there subsequently. Open-market purchases are undoubtedly of importance in explaining year-to-year or other short-term changes in the money supply. They are, however, not of importance in explaining the secular—and *a fortiori* the wartime—expansions of this supply.

In summary, then, the secular and wartime monetary expansions in the United States during the past 80 years can be largely explained by corresponding increases in the quantity of outside money, which have represented corresponding increases in the net worth of the public. We can accordingly conclude that the foregoing monetary expansions have generated positive wealth effects on the aggregate demand for goods and services—

---

[17] This is a specific example of the more general observation that—in the present context—outside money is of significance only as a component of net financial assets; cf. Patinkin, *op. cit.*, pp. 307–308.

[18] See Statistical Appendix.

and in that way could have exerted a direct upward pressure on prices and output. The task which thus awaits us in the next lecture is to analyze the nature of this wealth effect.

II

It was shown in the preceding lecture that secular and wartime expansions of money supply in the United States can be largely explained by expansions in outside money—and that the latter in turn represent an increase in the net-asset or net-wealth position of the private sector. The question to which we will now direct ourselves is the way in which such a monetary expansion can have a direct effect in increasing demand—that is, an effect which need not depend upon prior changes in the interest rate or in relative prices.

At first sight this question would seem to be related to the United States debates of the 1950s on the "availability doctrine"; namely, the doctrine that "the 'availability' of credit is a more important determinant of spending than is a variation of interest rates."[1] If, at the going rate of interest, there is an unsatisfied fringe of borrowers—businessmen who would like to borrow at the prevailing rate of interest and invest the money—then the expansion of outside money would provide banks with the necessary reserves to extend loans to these borrowers, and the latter would accordingly immediately increase their demand for goods and services at an unchanged rate of interest.

The question, of course, is why these potential borrowers were not able to obtain funds in the first place. If it was the result of credit rationing in an imperfect capital market, then the process can indeed be described in the foregoing way. But as has frequently been pointed out, it is difficult to believe that such a situation of rationing would not ultimately reflect itself in a rise in interest rates; and if the monetary expansion enables banks to extend their credit without raising interest in this way, then we should really interpret this credit expansion as reflecting the substitution effect of an interest rate which has been kept relatively low. And since we are interested in the long-run effects of a monetary expansion, this is indeed the only way we can look upon it.

The unsatisfied fringe of borrowers might also represent firms of lower credit-worthiness than those who do receive loans—and who would under ordinary circumstances receive such loans only at a higher rate of interest. But once again the extension of loans to such borrowers at an unchanged rate of interest is best regarded not as a direct effect, but as the result of a relative reduction in interest.

It is, therefore, not with the "availability doctrine" that I shall be concerned.

Another preliminary observation I would like to make is that there is

---

[1] Assar Lindbeck, *The "New" Theory of Credit Control in the U.S.*, rev. ed. (Stockholm, 1962), p. 14. The following paragraphs are based on Lindbeck's discussion.

one sense in which there has never been any real disagreement about the direct effect of a monetary expansion. For if, as assumed here, this expansion is the result of the government's printing money to finance a wartime deficit, then the very process of increasing the money supply is simultaneously a process of increasing the government's demand for goods and services. And this increased demand will affect not only current prices, but—as a result of the multiplier—prices in subsequent periods as well. That is, the increased incomes generated by the government's increased demand in the initial period will cause the new income recipients to increase their demand in turn, generating further increases in income and further increases in demand and so on. It should be noted that this multiplier process will be at work even if the government initially uses the new money it prints not to increase its demand for goods and services, but to make transfer payments; for the disposable income of the individuals who receive these transfer payments will increase, and with it their demand for goods.

I said that there has been no real disagreement about the foregoing process—and this is true insofar as the process itself is concerned. Indeed, this is the process involved in the direct effect of a monetary expansion as described by Wicksell in the passage cited at the beginning of the preceding lecture. But there might be disagreement about the description to be given to the process. For whereas Keynesians would describe it as reflecting what happens when one of the exogenous components of aggregate demand increases (namely, government expenditures), classical and neoclassical economists *might* have described it as the consequence of an increase in the quantity of money. I emphasize the word "might"—for I am not at all sure that they would have done so. For the effect of the monetary increase on prices which has just been described is not really the one which they had in mind in their discussions of the quantity theory.

The reason for this is simply that if we are concerned with a once-and-for-all increase in the quantity of money, then the process just described can only explain a *temporary* increase in the price level; it does not explain the *permanent* increase which (in the classical theory) is caused by the increased quantity of money. Thus in the case just considered, government expenditures in the period after the initial one will return to their original level. Furthermore, the multiplier effect set into operation by the initial increase in expenditure will—because of leakages—ultimately vanish. Hence if the only forces at work were those described above, then the price level too would return to its original level. That this is at variance with the real world is clear from the many historical experiences of wartime resort to the printing press, and the subsequent higher peacetime price levels which characterized the economies in question, even after their governments had ceased their inflationary financing.

Thus it was not on the foregoing flow of expenditures that quantity theorists based their reasoning. Instead we find Wicksell, Fisher, Marshall, Pigou, and others carrying out their analysis in terms of the increased real value of the stock of money in the hands of individuals generated by the monetary expansion; this makes the stock of money (to paraphrase Wicksell's words) "too large in relation to the level of prices"[2] or (in Fisher's words) too large with respect to the level "which his convenience had taught him to keep on hand."[3] And this excess—and the increased demand for goods which it was assumed to generate—would therefore continue to exist as long as prices had not risen in the same proportion as the quantity of money; that is, until the real value of the stock of money returned to its original level. Thus the emphasis of the quantity theory was not on the temporary *flow* of expenditures generated by the very act of increasing the quantity of money, but on the continued influence of an unduly large *stock* of money on the level of expenditures.

Let us now try to analyze this influence more rigorously. As already indicated, my point of departure is that monetary expansions of the foregoing kind have been accompanied by increases in outside money and hence in the net assets of the private sector; correspondingly, the effects of such expansions should be analyzed in terms of the wealth effect of demand theory.

At first sight there seems to be something artificial in talking about the wealth effect of a monetary expansion. Nevertheless, the representative individual who finds himself with a larger stock of money—all other things, including prices, being equal—surely does consider his wealth to have increased. True, when he—and all the other individuals in the economy—attempt to spend this increased wealth (and for the moment you will forgive me if I speak somewhat loosely in these terms), they will drive prices up. Indeed, under certain assumptions as to price flexibility and absence of money illusion, prices will continue moving upward until the real value of the money balances is the same as it originally was. Correspondingly, in the new equilibrium position that will thus be achieved, real wealth is unaffected by the monetary change. But in the dynamic process of reaching this new equilibrium position, a vital role is played by the very fact that—as long as prices have not risen in the same proportion as the quantity of money—the individual considers his wealth to have increased, and increases his demand for goods accordingly. It is indeed this very increase in demand which is the motive force of the upward price movement itself.

What, then, is the strength of this wealth effect? Consider first the effect on current consumption. If we assume that the rate of interest which the individual uses to compute the permanent income flowing from his wealth is 10 percent, and if we further assume that the marginal propensity to consume out of permanent income is 0.80, then the marginal propensity to consume out of wealth is the product of these two figures, or 0.08. And various empirical studies have indeed yielded estimates in this neighborhood.[4]

---

[2] See *Interest and Prices* (London, 1936), pp. 39–40.

[3] *The Purchasing Power of Money* (New York, 1911), pp. 153–154.

[4] Cf., e.g., Albert Ando and Franco Modigliani, "The 'Life Cycle' Hypothesis of Saving," *American Economic Review*, LIII (1963), 55–84; "The 'Life Cycle' Hypothesis of Saving: A Correction," *American Economic Review*, LIV (1964), 111–113; Patinkin, *op. cit.*, pp. 660–664.

In order to see what this means in more concrete terms, let us consider the United States economy in the full-employment year 1957, with (roughly) a GNP of $440 billion, a level of consumption of nondurables and services of $240 billion, and a volume of outside money (broadly defined) of $100 billion. If the quantity of outside money had then been increased by 10 percent, the wealth of individuals would in the first instance have increased by $10 billion, and the consumption of nondurables and services by $0.8 billion (= 0.08 × $10 billion). That is, an increase of 10 percent in outside money would have caused a direct increase of roughly 0.33 of 1 percent (= $0.8 ÷ $240.0) in the demand for current consumption goods. Thus it does not seem likely that the wealth effect in this form plays a major role in explaining the dynamics of an inflationary price movement. Correspondingly, if this were the only form of the wealth effect, then it would indeed be true that the major burden of dynamic adjustment process would be thrown on the interest rate, which—as a result of the increase in the total money supply—would temporarily decline.

But this need not be the most important form of the wealth effect in this context—though, if "my sins I recount today," I must admit that it is the major one to which I myself have given attention in the past.[5] For the direct wealth effect of a monetary increase can manifest itself not only in the demand for current consumption goods, but also in the demand for the goods which make up the individual's portfolio of assets.

Let me begin with some theoretical reflections. Consider the usual microeconomic analysis of a representative individual who comes to market with an initial endowment of goods X and Y. Denote this initial endowment in Figure 8.1 by X_0 and Y_0; that is, assume that point P on budget line AB—or, as it might be better denoted for our present purpose, wealth restraint AB—represents the individual's initial position. For simplicity,

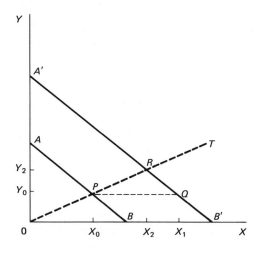

Figure 8.1.

[5] For this reason I would now reconsider the discussion on pp. 436–439 of my *Money, Interest, and Prices*.

assume also that point P is also the individual's optimum position when relative prices are those indicated by the slope of AB.

Assume now that the individual's initial endowment of X is increased to X_1, while that of Y remains constant. Then the individual's initial position shifts to Q and the wealth restraint (until the relative price of X begins to decline) to $A'B'$, parallel to AB. Assume finally that as long as relative prices are those represented by the slope of AB (or $A'B'$), the individual wishes to acquire X and Y in the fixed proportion represented by the slope of the ray from the origin, OT. Then the individual at point Q will plan to use part of his increased endowment of X to purchase Y, and in this way will begin to move to point R.

What must now be emphasized is that this movement from Q to R—this shift in the composition of the individual's basket of goods—is the consequence of a wealth effect, and not a substitution effect: for it takes place even at unchanged relative prices. More specifically, this shift is the consequence of the fact that the individual's wealth has increased in a manner which causes an initial discrepancy between the desired and actual composition of the goods which make up this wealth.

Clearly, in the process of eliminating this discrepancy in the economy as a whole, the relative price of X will also change. Indeed, this price will decline until the economy is willing to acquire the basket Q. Graphically, this means that the wealth line $A'B'$ will continue to rotate in a counterclockwise direction around Q, until this point becomes the equilibrium one. Thus the foregoing wealth effect must be looked upon as one of the components of this dynamic adjustment process.

Let us now apply this argument to the case at hand. Our representative individual is assumed to spend on current consumption a fixed proportion of the permanent income generated by his wealth—and we have already spoken of this. But we now also take account of the fact that he holds his wealth in the form of a certain portfolio of assets, and that an increase in wealth therefore also directly increases the demand for the various components of this portfolio. For simplicity, we shall continue to assume that these increases are equiproportionate; that is, that as long as relative prices are unchanged, the composition of the portfolio also remains unchanged.

Now, Keynesian theory implicitly visualizes the individual's portfolio as consisting only of money and bonds. Let these be represented in the preceding diagram (8.1) by X and Y, respectively. Correspondingly, an increase in the quantity of money is reflected initially in the shift from P to Q. Then insofar as the individual's portfolio is concerned, the wealth effect of this monetary increase reflects itself in the first instance only in a shift out of money and into bonds—represented by the movement from Q to R. From this follow the usual Keynesian conclusions that (1) there is no *direct* increase in demand for any physical asset, and (2) the only way in which the demand for these assets can increase as a result of a monetary increase is by the *indirect*, substitution effect of the decrease in interest caused by the increased demand for bonds.

These conclusions, however, no longer hold once we take account of the fact that the individual's portfolio consists not only of money and bonds, but also of such physical assets as real estate and consumers durables. For then the wealth effect generated by an increase in outside money will cause a direct increase in the demand for these assets as well. In terms of the diagram, the vertical axis now represents physical assets as well as bonds; correspondingly, the shift from Q to R also represents a shift out of money and into physical assets.

If we state this argument more rigorously, we see that it essentially makes use of the theory of the accelerator—or, more generally, stock-adjustment principle—so familiar from the theory of investment. For let A_i represent the ith asset and W total wealth. Then our assumption that—given the rates of return—the individual wishes to hold a portfolio of fixed composition, regardless of the level of wealth, is represented by the equation

$$A_i = k_i W,$$

where the k_i are constants for the given rates of return. Now, as long as the level of wealth is constant, the stock of (say) durable consumers goods which the individual wishes to hold is also constant. This means that his demand for new consumers durables equals his replacement demand. Alternatively, his demand for consumers durables, just like the demand for current consumption discussed above, can—under our present assumptions—be said to depend on the permanent income flow stemming from his wealth.

But we are interested not in a stationary situation, but in one in which an expansion of outside money has caused an initial increase in total wealth. From the assumption of fixed portfolio composition, it follows that in such a case there takes place a proportionate increase in the demand for the stock of each of the assets which make up the portfolio. Hence in addition to the foregoing replacement demand, there is—immediately after the monetary increase—a demand for new acquisitions of each asset equal to

$$\Delta A_i = k_i \Delta W.$$

As in the theory of investment, this induced element of demand can be assumed to operate with a lag—and I shall return to this point in a moment.

It should be noted that this increased demand for (say) consumers durables and housing will—in accordance with the theory of stock adjustment—eventually taper off as the stocks of these assets approach their respectively desired levels corresponding to the higher level of wealth. From this point on the only increased demand will be that associated with the larger replacement demand of these higher levels.[6]

---

[6] Another implication of this argument is that if the monetary expansion is not of the once-and-for-all variety, but is instead proceeding at a constant rate, and if total wealth is also growing at this rate, then the demand for new acquisitions of each asset grows at the same rate. In such a state of balanced growth, this flow demand for each asset could once again be described as a function of permanent income. This is indeed the assumption implicit in the growth model presented in J. Tobin, "Money and Economic Growth," *Econometrica*, XXXIII (1965), 671–684. See also Chapter 11, Section 3, below.

Another point that should be made about the foregoing argument is that it implicitly assumes that the increase in outside money accrues in the first instance to households. If instead it accrued in part to firms, then we would have also to take account of the portfolio adjustments carried out by the latter—which in this case would involve increased demands for plant and equipment, inventories, and other producers durables. This, however, raises some problems about the theory of the investment of the firm—and the nature of the capital market—into which we cannot go here.

So much for theory; how does it stand up against the facts? One implication of the theory is that an increase in the quantity of outside money should in the first stages increase the demand for consumers durable goods relatively more than that for consumers nondurables. Is this implication borne out by empirical studies of the respective consumption functions of these goods?[7]

Let me first of all say that to the best of my knowledge there have not yet been studies which have explicitly addressed themselves to this question, and which have made use of consumption functions specified in accordance with the foregoing discussion. In particular, to the extent that we find in the literature consumption functions which include "liquid assets" among their independent variables, (1) these assets are not defined as outside money and (2) it is usually the absolute level of these assets which is considered, and not their incremental change.

There are other, technical reasons why the consumption functions which appear in the econometric literature might not lend support to the foregoing theory. First of all, just those periods in which the stock of outside money has deviated sharply from the trend, and in which accordingly the effects of this deviation might be revealed by the data—namely, the periods of wartime deficit financing—are for the most part omitted from the time series analysis on the ground that they are "abnormal." Similarly, for example, the immediate post-World War II period—with its extremely high accumulation of liquid assets caused by the suppressed inflation which preceded it—is also claimed to represent "special" factors. But these "special factors" may be precisely those which are brought to light by the abnormal expansion of the money supply, an expansion which is sufficiently great to dominate other factors which obscure the workings of monetary influences during the more "normal" periods to which the time-series analysis is devoted.

Secondly, even if these "abnormal" periods are taken account of, the rapid expansion of outside money which characterizes them has—as indicated in the preceding lecture—usually been generated by a government deficit which comes to finance an additional demand for goods and services. Hence the monetary influence is confounded in the statistical analysis with the influence of this increased demand.

[7] A related implication which deserves study is that concerned with the relative movement of the prices of consumers durables and nondurables in the various phases of an inflationary process.

Finally, it is an essential contention of the foregoing theory that the process which it describes leads—to a certain extent at least—to an increase in the price level. Indeed, in a stationary economy this is the only effect it will have. Hence if the time-series analysis is based on annual data—and if the price adjustment is relatively rapid and indeed takes place during a period which is less than a year—then the data will reflect the value of real balances after they have (at least in part) already been reduced by the price increase which they have generated. Hence the analysis might not capture the possible effect on demand of the *temporarily* increased real value of cash balances which took place during the year.

This last consideration would suggest that time-series analysis based on quarterly data should yield more encouraging results. Unfortunately, this is not at all clear. Thus it is true that Goldfeld's aggregate quarterly model of the postwar United States economy yields a statistically significant coefficient for liquid assets in the consumers durable equation, but not in the consumers nondurable.[8] Again, the Suits-Sparks consumption study for the same period—carried out as part of the Brookings Quarterly Model— yielded an elasticity of expenditures with respect to liquid assets which was almost twice as high for durables (excluding automobiles) than for non-durables (excluding food). But the strength of this evidence is weakened by the fact that the elasticity for nondurables (excluding food) is also about twice as high as the corresponding elasticity for services.[9]

Actually, however, the relevant test of the foregoing hypothesis is not the absolute magnitudes of these elasticities, but their respective ratios to the corresponding elasticities of expenditure with respect to disposable income. In particular, these ratios should be higher for those goods into which (it is contended) the shift from money is made in the process of the portfolio adjustment. Thus the ratio should be higher for durable goods than for nondurables; but the opposite is true for the Suits-Sparks equations. As has, however, already been noted, the specification of these equations is not the correct one for our purposes.

It is, however, possible to adduce what I would consider to be strong evidence on the question at issue, not from time-series analysis, but from the savings surveys that have been carried out in recent years in Israel.

[8] S. M. Goldfeld, *Commercial Bank Behavior and Economic Activity* (Amsterdam, 1966), p. 129.

[9] Daniel B. Suits and Gordon R. Sparks, "Consumption Regressions with Quarterly Data," in J. D. Duesenberry and others (eds.), *The Brookings Quarterly Econometric Model of the United States* (Chicago, 1965), pp. 208–209. The coefficients of household liquid assets (lagged one quarter) in the consumption functions for durables (excluding automobiles), nondurables (excluding food), and services are 0.05, 0.07, and 0.06, respectively—with all coefficients being statistically significant (more than three times the standard error in each case). The average level of liquid assets in 1954 was approximately $200 billion (*ibid.*, p. 222). The levels of consumption of the foregoing three categories in 1954 were $21.1, $53.1, and $86.3 billion, respectively [*Historical Statistics of the United States, Colonial Times to 1957* (Washington, D.C., 1960), pp. 143 and 178; these are not the exact data used by Suits and Sparks]. Hence the elasticities of expenditure with respect to liquid assets in 1954 for durables (excluding automobiles), nondurables (excluding food), and services were approximately $0.50 [\approx 0.05 \cdot (200/21.1)]$; $0.27 [\approx 0.07 \cdot (200/53.1)]$; and $0.14 [\approx 0.06 \cdot (200/86.3)]$.

Indeed, it seems to me that the data of these surveys actually capture the very process in which households make portfolio adjustments after receiving an increase in wealth in the form of money.

One of the special characteristics of the Israel economy is the presence of many families which have received lump-sum restitution payments from Germany. These payments have constituted from 80–100 percent of the disposable income (exclusive of restitution payments) which the families in question received during the same year. Hence from *a priori* considerations (which, as we shall immediately see, are confirmed by the results of the survey) we should expect these families to consider the restitution payments not as receipts on current account, but as an addition to their wealth, which for the most part should accordingly be distributed in an optimum manner among the assets which make up their portfolios.[10]

Table 8.3   Use of Restitution Receipts by Israeli Families (Percent[a])

	Expenditure from Restitution Payments Received in 1957/1958[b]		Expenditure During 1963/1964 from Restitution Payments Received in:[c]	
	During 1957/1958	During 1958/1959	1963/1964	1962/1963
Current consumption	17	4	7	2
Net purchase of consumer durables	9	4	7	−1
Net purchase of real estate	20	25	21	21
Net purchase of securities	—	—	1	0
Net additions to liquid assets[d]	45	− 33	54	− 20

[a] Figures do not add up to 100 since not all uses are included in table.

[b] Figures for 1957/1958 are based on a sample of approximately 3,000 families, of which 5 percent received restitution payments.

The 1958/1959 figures are based on a reinterview sample of approximately 1,000 families drawn from the 1957/1958 sample. Of these 1,000 families, approximately 7 percent received restitution payments.

[c] The 1963/1964 figures are based on a sample of 3,166 families, of which 13 percent received restitution payments during 1963/1964, and 11 percent during 1962/1963. Average restitution payments in 1962/1963 were IL 6,788.

[d] In 1963/1964, defined as the net additions to demand, time, and saving deposits, and in some cases also the addition to cash holdings. In 1957/1958, also includes the addition to securities, which was presumably negligible.

SOURCE 1957/1958 and 1958/1959—Bank of Israel, *Annual Report 1959* (Jerusalem, 1960), p. 326, Table XVIII–4.

1963/1964—Based on figures from Central Bureau of Statistics and Bank of Israel, *Saving Survey 1963/64* (Central Bureau of Statistics, Special series No. 217; Jerusalem, 1967), pp. XXII–XXIV. The specific definitions of the various uses of the restitution payments are presented *ibid.*, pp. XLIII–LII.

---

[10] For empirical evidence (again based on the Israel Savings Survey) that the larger the ratio of the lump-sum payment to disposable income, the greater the likelihood that the household will treat the payment as being on capital, and not current, account—see the interesting note by Michael Landsberger, "Windfall Income and Consumption: Comment," *American Economic Review*, LVI (1966), 534–539.

In order to obtain detailed information on the ways in which the restitution families made use of these lump-sum payments, they were oversampled in the surveys. The results are summarized in Table 8.3. In each case, the percentage of restitution payments devoted to any given purpose was computed as the difference between the average expenditures of restitution families on the respective categories and the average expenditures of nonrestitution families (adjusted to the same income level, exclusive of restitution payments, as the restitution families). For simplicity, the average and marginal propensities to spend were assumed to be equal.

Consider first the data for 1957/1958. The first point that emerges is that only 17–18 percent of the restitution payments were used to increase current consumption. This is to be compared with the 90 percent of their disposable incomes which these families spent for the same purpose. This difference reflects the basic fact that these families did indeed consider these payments as receipts on capital account. In particular, the figure of 17 percent is consistent with the assumption that the families used an interest rate of 19 percent in evaluating the permanent income flowing from this addition to their capital, and then consumed on current account 90 percent of this additional income ($0.90 \times 0.19 = 0.17$). Note too the much smaller differential increase in current consumption recorded for 1958/1959: this can be interpreted as reflecting the fact that the increased wealth received in 1957/1958 generated interest payments which are included in the ordinary disposable income of 1958/1959.

Consider now the percentage expenditure on durable goods of 9 percent in 1957/1958. In order to see the significance of this figure, it must be compared with the percentage of disposable income devoted to this same purpose—which was around 5 percent. Thus the families spent roughly twice as much out of restitution payments on durable goods as they did out of current income. What is even more significant is the relative importance of these expenditures as compared with those on current consumption. In particular, whereas individuals spent out of restitution payments half as much on durable goods as on current consumption, they spent only 1/18 as much ($= 0.05 \div 0.90$) out of current income.

The most interesting aspect of the table is provided by the third and fifth rows. Here we see that the largest single use of the restitution payments was for the acquisition of real estate (primarily, new apartments in cooperative buildings, to be used as dwellings by the recipients of these payments), and that this acquisition was spread in almost equal portions over the two-year period following the receipt of the payments. Furthermore, the lag in acquiring real estate—which in turn can be interpreted as reflecting the time it takes to make a decision and the time necessary to complete construction—manifested itself in the temporary accumulation of liquid assets in the first year, which were largely liquidated in the second year to provide the necessary financing. In this way, restitution recipients had—by the end of the second year—directly invested half their receipts in real estate.

A similar picture is provided by Table 8.3 for the results of the 1963/1964 survey. Once again the pattern is revealed of a much larger relative expenditure (as compared with expenditures out of current income on durable consumers goods and real estate, with the expenditure on the latter constituting over 40 percent of the restitution payments and being stretched over two years—and this lag reflecting itself in the accumulation of liquid assets in the first year, and their subsequent liquidation (albeit to a lesser extent than in 1958/1959) in the second.[11]

These data undoubtedly reflect special circumstances: the backgrounds of the families which received the restitution payments; the general inflationary expectations of the Israel economy, which encourage individuals to invest in real estate; a rent-control act, which had led to a situation in which the construction of new apartments is carried out for sale, and not for rental; of a very thin stock market, which makes households reluctant to hold a large part of their wealth in the form of securities; of uncertainties as to the possible devaluation of the Israel pound. But even after taking account of these special circumstances—and their importance can also be exaggerated (thus, for example, fears of devaluation were much more rife in 1957/1959 than in 1963/1964)—it seems to me that the overall pattern of the operation of the wealth effect revealed by Table 8.3 can also be assumed to obtain in the general case of a wealth effect generated by a significant increase in outside money.

Let us now return to this general case and note that to the additional channels for the operation of the direct, wealth effect of a monetary expansion which it indicates, there correspond additional channels for the operation of the substitution effect. In particular, this effect will now operate not only through the increased demand for investment goods generated by a lowered interest rate (which in turn is caused by the shift out of money and into bonds—and which is the effect on which Keynesian monetary theory has concentrated exclusively), but also through an increased demand for nondurable consumption goods generated by the lowering of their price relative to that of durables (caused by the shift out of money and into durables), and through an increased demand for the services of housing generated by the lowering of their prices relative to that of buying a house (with the latter again caused by the shift out of money and into real estate). More generally, there will be a substitution effect generated by the lowering of the price of the services of durables relative to the price of the durable assets themselves.[12]

[11] An interesting question relates to the form in which the liquid assets were held. One of the relevant factors in determining this decision is, of course, the time that elapses before the planned expenditure takes place. Though they are not too reliable, unpublished data from the 1963/1964 survey indicate that—as might be expected—these assets mainly took the form of time deposits (and particularly those denominated in foreign currency), and not demand deposits. (I am indebted to Michael Landsberger of the Research Department of the Bank of Israel for providing me with these data.)

[12] Cf. Milton Friedman and David Meiselman, "The Relative Stability of Monetary Velocity and the Investment Multiplier in the United States, 1897–1958," in *Stabilization Policies* (Englewood Cliffs, N.J., 1963), pp. 218–220.

I have spoken until now of inflation. Let me, however, conclude with some brief comments on the problem of deflation. One of the implications of the foregoing argument is that some of the traditional techniques of monetary policy used to combat deflationary pressures generate (in the first instance) only a substitution effect, and not a wealth effect. This is certainly true for a reduction in the required reserve ratio of the banking system. And to the extent that individuals do not take account of future tax liabilities—and thus treat government securities as a net asset—it is also true for open-market purchases. On the other hand, a monetary expansion which does create a direct wealth effect is, by definition, one caused by an increase in outside money; and in the present context this means a monetary expansion generated by deficit financing. Hence such an expansion does not constitute monetary policy in the accepted sense of the term.

It is, of course, possible to generate a positive wealth effect not by deficit financing, but by permitting the price level to decline and thus generating an increase in the real value of the net financial assets held by the private sector. But as I have argued on many preceding occasions, the efficacy of this real-balance effect in combating deflation is likely to be greatly weakened—if not entirely offset—by the adverse expectations created by the declining price level and its concomitants. This general contention is reinforced by our argument that one of the major channels through which such a wealth effect works in inflationary situations is in the acquisition of consumers durables and other investment goods; and the aforementioned expectations are particularly likely to inhibit such purchases. Hence the real-balance effect in deflationary situations may—in Keynesian fashion—largely be diverted to the mere accumulation of money holdings, and not to increasing the aggregate demand for goods and services.

For these reasons, then, while obviously believing in the importance of monetary factors in the secular and once-and-for-all inflationary processes that I have described in these lectures, I continue to disbelieve in the efficacy of traditional monetary policy as a means of combating deflation and unemployment.

Statistical Appendix

Monetary Data for the United States ($ billions)

End of June	Outside Money Narrowly Defined[a] (high powered money)	Reserve-Bank Credit to Private Sector (excluding float)[a]	U.S. Government Securities Held by Commercial Banks	U.S. Government Balances at Commercial and Saving Banks	Outside Money Broadly Defined[b] (1) − (2) + (3) − (4)
	(1)	(2)	(3)	(4)	(5)
1914	3.482	0.010	0.750	0.061	4.161
1915	3.655	0.034	0.751	0.045	4.327
1916	4.129	0.090	0.753	0.036	4.756
1917	5.086	0.564	1.545	0.284	5.783
1918	5.892	1.423	3.251	1.562	6.158
1919	6.517	2.232	5.143	0.978	8.450
1920	7.214	2.909	3.751	0.191	7.865
1921	6.549	1.889	3.391	0.387	7.664
1922	6.321	0.731	3.985	0.153	9.422
1923	6.682	0.963	4.705	0.310	10.114
1924	6.851	0.547	4.435	0.181	10.558
1925	6.951	0.780	4.630	0.180	10.621
1926	7.130	0.857	4.555	0.228	10.600
1927	7.238	0.716	4.586	0.184	10.924
1928	7.150	1.171	5.165	0.235	10.909
1929	7.102	1.208	4.945	0.322	10.517
1930	6.908	0.494	4.981	0.224	11.171
1931	7.302	0.588	6.013	0.313	12.414
1932	7.788	0.606	6.218	0.430	12.970
1933	7.944	0.373	7.477	0.837	14.211
1934	9.260	0.066	10.313	1.649	17.858
1935	10.693	0.039	12.720	0.956	22.418
1936	11.698	0.040	15.272	1.077	25.853
1937	13.485	0.039	14.559	0.631	27.374
1938	14.609	0.027	14.043	0.543	28.082
1939	17.298	0.018	15.697	0.732	32.245
1940	21.814	0.013	16.552	0.792	37.561
1941	22.974	0.014	20.098	0.678	42.380
1942	25.233	0.019	26.410	1.848	49.776
1943	29.500	0.038	52.458	8.000	73.920
1944	35.600	0.145	68.431	19.500	84.386
1945	41.600	0.379	84.069	24.400	100.890
1946	44.300	0.319	84.268	13.400	114.849
1947	44.500	0.221	69.890	1.398	112.771
1948	45.200	0.333	64.499	2.720	106.646
1949	45.600	0.232	62.901	1.839	106.430
1950	43.100	0.131	65.597	3.680	104.886
1951	46.200	0.298	58.309	5.260	98.951
1952	48.200	0.806	61.005	5.076	103.323
1953	49.800	0.780	58.708	3.238	104.490
1954	49.100	0.218	63.501	4.420	107.963
1955	48.100	0.680	63.301	4.433	106.288
1956	48.600	0.857	57.011	4.366	100.388

Total Money Stock (including time deposits)	U.S. Government Securities Held by Private Sector	U.S. Government Securities Held by Non-banking Private Sector (7)–(3)	Total Money Stock (excluding time deposits)
(6)	(7)	(8)	(9)
16.146	0.910	0.160	11.504
17.144	0.908	0.157	12.119
20.351	0.913	0.160	14.348
23.942	2.645	1.100	16.875
25.839	11.675	8.424	18.287
30.320	24.784	19.641	21.390
34.708	23.503	19.752	23.592
32.212	23.119	19.728	20.955
33.646	21.724	17.739	21.618
36.411	21.487	16.782	22.653
37.992	20.157	15.722	23.226
41.691	19.328	14.698	25.362
43.539	18.341	13.786	26.082
44.384	17.122	12.536	25.796
45.861	16.229	11.064	25.761
45.918	15.507	10.562	26.189
45.303	14.330	9.349	25.293
42.598	15.387	9.374	23.883
34.480	16.776	10.558	20.449
30.087	19.470	11.993	19.232
33.073	23.291	12.978	21.068
38.049	27.344	14.624	25.199
43.341	32.957	17.685	29.630
45.195	34.355	19.796	30.587
44.100	34.087	20.044	29.173
47.681	36.899	21.202	32.586
54.328	38.338	21.786	38.763
61.296	44.081	23.983	45.349
68.998	63.249	36.839	53.382
90.360	117.948	65.490	72.826
104.568	167.061	98.630	83.324
124.631	210.034	125.965	97.467
139.300	214.862	130.594	106.800
146.000	201.670	131.780	111.400
146.900	193.329	128.830	111.300
146.400	193.257	130.356	110.400
149.400	199.247	133.650	112.800
154.000	189.439	131.130	117.600
163.200	190.032	129.027	124.300
169.600	191.920	133.212	127.800
174.400	195.037	131.536	129.200
181.300	198.314	135.013	133.900
184.700	193.587	136.576	135.600

Monetary Data for the United States ($ billions)

End of June	Outside Money Narrowly Defined[a] (high powered money)	Reserve-Bank Credit to Private Sector (excluding float)[a]	U.S. Government Securities Held by Commercial Banks	U.S. Government Balances at Commercial and Saving Banks	Outside Money Broadly Defined[b] (1) − (2) + (3) − (4)
1957	49.000	0.878	56.112	3.897	100.337
1958	49.000	0.335	64.799	5.691	107.773
1959	49.500	0.847	61.204	3.800	106.057
1960	49.000	0.475	55.513	5.781	98.257
1961	47.8[c]	0.172	62.402	6.638[c,d]	103.392
1962	49.7[c]	0.286	64.899	9.841[c,d]	104.472
1963	50.8[c]	0.410	63.401	11.306[c,d]	102.485
1964	53.5[c]	0.385	59.607	10.502[c,d]	102.220
1965	56.3[c]	0.471	57.810	12.062[c,d]	101.557
1966	59.4[c]	0.670	54.415	11.237[c,d]	101.908

[a]Float is already deducted from column 1; see footnote 6 above. Figures for 1914–1960 are annual averages of daily figures; figures for 1961–1966 are averages of average daily figures for December of year in question and December of preceding year.

[b]See pp. 149–50.

[c]Continuation of a revised version of the earlier figures.

[d](a) Figures for 1961–1966 are monthly averages of daily figures, whereas those up to 1960 are single-date figures. (b) Savings banks not included, but the effect is negligible.

SOURCES: Column 1—1914–1960: Milton Friedman and Anna Jacobson Schwartz, *A Monetary History of the United States, 1867–1960* (Princeton, 1963), p. 799, Table B–3, column 1.

1961–1966: Private communication from Anna Jacobson Schwartz; mainly Federal Reserve figures.

Column 2—1914–1916: *Banking and Monetary Statistics* (Washington, D.C., 1943), p. 368, Table 100 (sum of bills discounted and bills bought).

1917–1960: *Supplement to Banking and Monetary Statistics* (Washington, D.C., 1962), section 10, p. 14, Table 1A (sum of discounts and advances, acceptances, and all other).

1961–1966: *Federal Reserve Bulletin* (December 1967), p. 2078. (Sum of discounts and advances, and acceptances. Acceptances are estimated as difference between column headed "Total" and sum of columns headed "Total U.S. government securities"; "Discounts and advances"; and "Float." See *ibid.*, p. 2079, footnote 3.)

Total Money Stock (including time deposits)	U.S. Government Securities Held by Private Sector	U.S. Government Securities Held by Non-banking Private Sector (7)–(3)	Total Money Stock (excluding time deposits)
190.000	190.220	134.108	136.400
199.000	193.191	128.392	138.000
207.800	202.202	140.998	142.800
206.200	202.598	147.085	139.400
221.1^c	203.885	141.483	143.0^c
236.8^c	210.421	145.522	146.2^c
255.1^c	213.985	150.584	150.4^c
274.2^c	214.481	154.874	155.6^c
297.9^c	213.392	155.482	161.7^c
324.6^c	209.430	155.015	170.6^c

Column 3—1914–1941: *Banking and Monetary Statistics, op. cit.*, p. 512, Table 149 (column 6 "Member banks" *plus* column 7 "Other commercial banks").

1942–1966: *Federal Reserve Bulletin*, various issues. Figures for 1942–1945 are as in *FRB* sources. In June 1945 the notation system was changed, and thus the figures for 1946–1966 are those appearing in the *FRB* sources, multiplied by 0.99844—the ratio between the June 1945 figures according to the old and the new notation.

Column 4—1914–1960: Friedman and Schwartz, *op. cit.*, p. 749, Table A–3, column 2.

1961–1966: Private communication from Anna Jacobson Schwartz; mainly Federal Reserve figures.

Column 6—1914–1960: Friedman and Schwartz, *op. cit.*, p. 704, Table A–1, column 8.

1961–1966: Private communication from Anna Jacobson Schwartz; mainly Federal Reserve figures.

Column 7—1914–1941: *Banking and Monetary Statistics, op. cit.*, p. 512, Table 149, column 5.

1942–1960: *Federal Reserve Bulletin*, various issues. Figures arrived at by deducting "Federal reserve banks" column from "Total" column in source. For 1946–1960, data multiplied by 0.9902156; see above, sources to column 3 of this table.

1961–1966: *Federal Reserve Bulletin*, various issues, "Total" column of source only, multiplied by 0.9902156.

Column 9—1914–1960: Friedman and Schwartz, *op. cit.*, p. 704, Table A–1, column 7.

1961–1966: Private communication from Anna Jacobson Schwartz; mainly Federal Reserve figures.

9

Money
and Wealth[1]

Central to the discussions of the "Pigou" or "real-balance" effect during the
past quarter century and more is the assumption that the stock of money is a
component of the wealth of the economy, and that accordingly a change in
the absolute price level changes the real value of this component, hence total
wealth, and hence the level of consumption as well as other economic variables. But very early in these discussions—and, indeed, in a comment on
Pigou's original article—Kalecki pointed out that the stock of money relevant for the real-balance effect was not the usually defined concept of hand-
to-hand currency plus demand deposits, but the monetary base alone. In
Kalecki's words:

> The increase in the real value of the stock of money generated by a price
> decline does not mean a rise in the total real value of possessions if all the
> money (cash and deposits) is "backed" by credits to persons and firms, i.e. if

*This paper is based on one presented at the Far Eastern Meetings of the Econometric
Society, held in Tokyo in June 1969. Sections 1, 4, 6, and 8—which set out the main argument of
the paper—appeared as Part II of my "Money and Wealth: a Review Article,"* Journal of
Economic Literature, *VII (1969), 1140–1160; this is a review of the Pesek-Saving volume referred to in footnote 4. Reprinted by permission.*

[1] I have benefited greatly from discussions of earlier drafts of this paper in the Faculty
Seminar of the Department of Economics of the Hebrew University, as well as in the Monetary
Workshop there.

I owe a special debt to Peter Diamond and Tsvi Ophir, both for their comments during
these seminars and, even more, for their invaluable criticisms and suggestions during the many
hours afterwards in which we discussed the problems raised in this paper. Needless to say, the
responsibility for the views expressed remains mine.

Part of the work on this paper was done while I was visiting the Massachusetts Institute
of Technology in 1968 under a Research Grant from the National Science Foundation (NSF
Grant GS 1812). I am grateful to both institutions for making this possible.

I wish also to express my thanks to the Israel Academy of Sciences and Humanities for
a research grant to cover the costs of technical assistance.

all the assets of the banking system consist of such credits. For in this case, to the gain of money-holders there corresponds an equal loss of the bank debtors. The total real value of possessions increases only to the extent to which money is backed by gold.[2]

This view became accepted without question in the literature, and received its highest degree of formalization in the Gurley-Shaw distinction between "outside money—money that is backed by foreign or government securities or gold, or fiat money issued by the government" (which is part of the net wealth of the community) and "inside money—money based on private domestic primary securities" (which is not).[3]

More, recently, however, the validity of this distinction has been denied by Pesek and Saving in their much discussed book on *Money, Wealth, and Economic Theory*.[4] According to them, the quantity of money relevant for the real-balance effect should include inside money as well as outside: it should include demand deposits of banks as well as money issued by the government.

My reading of this book provided the initial stimulus for the analysis which follows. As will be seen, there are similarities with Pesek and Saving's conclusions—but there is also a basic difference in the analytical approach adopted. The details of these similarities and differences are described elsewhere in a review article which I have written of the Pesek-Saving volume—and except in Appendix I, I shall therefore not refer to them any further here (see introductory footnote above). On the other hand, I shall indicate below (see p. 184) how the approach of this paper differs basically from the one I have previously taken to the inside-money/outside-money issue.

1. Let us begin with an economy in which the government has a complete monopoly on the issuance—or, to use a term which is better for our present purposes, production—of money. Assume that this money is fiat paper money. Though there may be differences of interpretation, there can be no

Table 9.1

		Balance Sheet of Private Sector	
Assets		*Liabilities*	0
Government fiat money	$ 25,000		
Other assets	100,000	*Net worth*	$125,000
	$125,000		$125,000

[2] M. Kalecki, "Professor Pigou on 'The Classical Stationary State'—A Comment," *Economic Journal*, LIV (1944), 131–132. This is a comment on A. C. Pigou, "The Classical Stationary State," *Economic Journal*, LIII (1943), 343–351.

[3] J. G. Gurley and E. S. Shaw, *Money in a Theory of Finance* (Washington, D.C., 1960), pp. 363–364, *et passim*.

[4] Boris P. Pesek and Thomas R. Saving, *Money, Wealth, and Economic Theory* (New York, 1967).

doubt that money in this case should be considered as a net asset of the private sector, whose balance sheet can (for example) be represented as in Table 9.1.

Assume now that the government forgoes part of its monopoly powers and—without changing the quantity of its own money in circulation—grants to certain individuals the right to produce (issue) $5,000 of paper money. Since by assumption this does not involve costs of production, the balance sheet of the private sector *immediately* becomes that of Table 9.2. (Note that under the assumption of zero costs it is essential to assume that the right to issue money is quantitatively restricted in some form or other. For otherwise individuals would continue producing money until the value of the marginal product was also zero; that is, they would issue an infinite quantity of money which would be valueless in terms of purchasing power over commodities.)

Table 9.2

Balance Sheet of Private Sector			
Assets		*Liabilities*	0
Government fiat money	$ 25,000		
Monopoly rights to produce			
$5,000 of paper money	5,000		
Other assets	100,000	*Net worth*	$130,000
	$130,000		$130,000

Assume next that the individuals who have received this right establish a bank. That is, they exchange their monopoly rights for the common stock of the bank, so that Table 9.2 becomes Table 9.3.

Table 9.3

Balance Sheet of Nonfinancial Private Sector			
Assets		*Liabilities*	0
Government fiat money	$ 25,000		
Common stocks of bank	5,000		
Other assets	100,000	*Net worth*	$130,000
	$130,000		$130,000

Balance Sheet of Bank			
Assets		*Liabilities*	0
Monopoly rights to produce		*Net worth*	
$5,000 of paper money	$ 5,000	Common stocks	$ 5,000
	$ 5,000		$ 5,000

Assume finally that the bank exercises its rights to produce $5,000 and purchases debt instruments of the nonfinancial sector with this money. (Alternatively, in the language of Pesek and Saving, it sells its bank money in exchange for these debt instruments.) Then in the first instance Table 9.3 becomes Table 9.4.

Table 9.4

Balance Sheet of Nonfinancial Private sector			
Assets		*Liabilities*	
Government fiat money	$ 25,000	Debt to bank	$ 5,000
Bank money	5,000		
Common stocks of bank	5,000		
Other assets	100,000	*Net worth*	130,000
	$135,000		$135,000

Balance Sheet of Bank			
Assets		*Liabilities*	0
Debt of nonfinancial			
private sector	$ 5,000		
*Monopoly rights to			
produce money	5,000		
less *Monopoly rights			
used up (i.e. amount of			
bank money actually		*Net worth*	
produced)	5,000 0	Common stocks	$ 5,000
	$ 5,000		$ 5,000

(Note that if the bank had produced the money but not yet lent it, then the balance sheets could be left as in Table 9.3. Alternatively, the bank balance sheet could be left as in Table 9.4, except for the replacement of the asset "Debt of nonfinancial private sector $5,000" by "Bank money $5,000.")

Clearly, since the monopoly rights have been entirely used up, we could eliminate the starred entries in the bank balance sheet of Table 9.4. The disadvantage of this procedure, however, is that it would fail to specify one of the assets of the bank—and in fact that asset (namely, the monopoly rights to issue money) which represents the true origin of its net worth. Indeed, from this viewpoint it would be best to list the using up of these rights not as a negative item on the left-hand side, but as a positive one on the right-hand side. Table 9.4 would thus be replaced by Table 9.5. Thus bank money would be described as a liability of the bank in the basic sense that it represents a deduction from its assets.

Assume now that there is a single rate of interest in the economy, say, 5 percent. Then the income statement of the bank is that of Table 9.6. Thus the bank will be earning the market rate of interest, 5 percent on its common stock.

Table 9.5

<table>
<tr><td colspan="4">Balance Sheet of Nonfinancial Private Sector</td></tr>
<tr><td>Assets</td><td></td><td>Liabilities</td><td></td></tr>
<tr><td>Government fiat money</td><td>$ 25,000</td><td>Debt to bank</td><td>$ 5,000</td></tr>
<tr><td>Bank money</td><td>5,000</td><td></td><td></td></tr>
<tr><td>Common stocks of bank</td><td>5,000</td><td></td><td></td></tr>
<tr><td>Other assets</td><td>100,000</td><td>Net worth</td><td>130,000</td></tr>
<tr><td></td><td>$135,000</td><td></td><td>$135,000</td></tr>
</table>

<table>
<tr><td colspan="4">Balance Sheet of Bank</td></tr>
<tr><td>Assets</td><td></td><td>Liabilities</td><td></td></tr>
<tr><td>Debt of private</td><td></td><td>Bank money</td><td></td></tr>
<tr><td> sector</td><td>$ 5,000</td><td> produced</td><td>$ 5,000</td></tr>
<tr><td>Monopoly rights to</td><td></td><td>Net worth</td><td></td></tr>
<tr><td> produce money</td><td>5,000</td><td>Common stocks</td><td>5,000</td></tr>
<tr><td></td><td>$ 10,000</td><td></td><td>$ 10,000</td></tr>
</table>

What must now be emphasized is that, as Table 9.2 indicates, the increase in the net worth of the private sector takes place immediately upon its receipt of the monopoly issue rights—that is, before it actually issues the new money. This simply reflects the fact that at the moment the individuals receive these rights they take account of the present value of the future income stream they will be able to earn when they (or, what is equivalent, the bank they will establish) exercise the right to produce money in order to acquire interest-yielding assets.

Table 9.6

<table>
<tr><td colspan="2">Income Statement of Bank</td></tr>
<tr><td>Interest received from loans</td><td>$250</td></tr>
<tr><td>less Operating costs</td><td>0</td></tr>
<tr><td>Net Profits</td><td>$250</td></tr>
</table>

Correspondingly, we should expect that the real-balance effect (or, more accurately, real-financial-asset effect[5]—for the monopoly right to produce money is indeed a financial asset) will begin to operate and push prices upwards the moment the government grants the monopoly rights to the private sector. In the foregoing tables we have abstracted from this effect on prices—as is evidenced by the fact that the nominal value of "other assets" remains fixed throughout at $100,000. Actually, however, the 20 percent increase in financial assets will—in the absence of money illusion—generate a corresponding increase in the price level. Were we, then, to take

[5] See my *Money, Interest, and Prices*, 2nd ed. (New York, 1965), p. 290.

account of this effect, the final balance sheet would (in contrast with Table 9.5) show that the nominal value of "other assets" had also risen by 20 percent. Such a final balance sheet would also reflect the fact that the net *real* wealth of the private sector as obtained by consolidating the balance sheets of Table 9.5 (namely, government fiat money *plus* private monopoly rights to produce money *plus* other assets) was the same as it was in Table 9.1. Clearly, a corresponding equality would hold for the consolidated real net worth of the private sector. Thus here, as elsewhere, the role of the real-balance effect is to help explain the dynamic process by which a monetary change affects the price level.

It is also clear that under the foregoing assumption a (say) decline in the price level will generate a real-financial-asset effect that would reflect the increased real value of government fiat money in the hands of the private sector, as well as the increased real value of the latter's monopoly rights to issue $5,000.

Note that in the consolidation of balance sheets, the bank money held as an asset by the nonfinancial private sector is offset by the bank money listed as a liability of the bank. Equivalently, we could have taken Table 9.4 as our point of departure—with the starred entries (referring to monopoly rights) deleted. From this viewpoint the consolidation of balance sheets yields a definition of the net wealth of the private sector as equal to government fiat money *plus* bank money *plus* other assets. But as long as we remember that this bank money had its origin in the monopoly rights which the government granted to the private sector, there is no substantive difference between this definition of net private wealth and the preceding one. Similarly, there is no difference between saying that a decline in the price level affects aggregate demand by increasing the real value of the total money supply (government *plus* bank), or that it does so by increasing the real value of total net financial assets (government money *plus* private monopoly rights to produce money).

From this alternative viewpoint it would be quite correct also to say that—in so far as the real-balance effect is concerned—there is no difference between government money and bank money. This conclusion is not at all surprising. For under the foregoing assumptions banks are essentially agents of the government, producing money under exactly the same conditions (namely, zero costs) as the government itself. It can therefore make no difference whether the $5,000 of new money is produced by the government (and distributed by it as a gift) or by the bank (to whose owners the government has granted the monopoly right as a gift).

2. Let us now move one step closer to reality by assuming that holders of bank money have the right to present it to the bank and receive government money in exchange. Assume further that in order to meet this contingency the bank maintains a reserve of 20 percent. This ratio might be a legal minimum one imposed by the government; alternatively, it might be the one shown by experience to be necessary.

In any event, the immediate implication of these reserve requirements is that the right to produce $5,000 of bank money is now worth only $4,000; for these rights now enable their possessor to acquire only $4,000 of interest-yielding assets. Correspondingly, instead of Table 9.3 we would have Table 9.7.

Table 9.7

Balance Sheet of Nonfinancial Private Sector

Assets		Liabilities	0
Government fiat money	$ 25,000		
Common stocks of bank	4,000		
Other assets	100,000	*Net worth*	$129,000
	$129,000		$129,000

Balance Sheet of Bank

Assets		Liabilities	0
Monopoly rights to produce $5,000 subject to 20 percent reserve ratio	$ 4,000	*Net worth* Common stocks	$ 4,000
	$ 4,000		$ 4,000

Assume now that the bank begins to exercise its monopoly rights. Then in accordance with its reserve requirements, $0.20 of every dollar of bank money which it produces will be used to acquire government fiat money, and only $0.80 will be used to acquire debt instruments of the private sector. Correspondingly, Table 9.4 is replaced by Table 9.8.

It will be noticed that the government money which the bank acquires is not listed as one of its assets; it is instead subsumed under the entry "Monopoly rights used up $4,000." Indeed, the way in which these rights are used up would be clarified if we were to replace this entry by the joint entry

Bank money produced	$5,000
less Government fiat money acquired	1,000
	$4,000

Finally, substituting this joint entry into the bank balance sheet of Table 9.8 we obtain Table 9.9.

Assuming again that the market rate of interest is 5 percent, the income statement of the bank is that of Table 9.10. Thus in this case too the bank is earning—as it must—5 percent on its net worth.

Clearly, the interpretation of the balance sheets of Table 9.8 (or 9.9) parallels that presented in the preceding section. In particular, the net financial assets of the private sector relevant for the Pigou effect can be defined equivalently either as the total quantity of money held by the nonfinancial private sector (namely, government fiat money $24,000 *plus* bank money $5,000 = $29,000) or as the total net financial assets obtained from the consolidation of the balance sheets of Table 9.9 (namely, government fiat money

Table 9.8

Balance Sheet of Nonfinancial Private Sector			
Assets		*Liabilities*	
Government fiat money	$ 24,000	Debt to bank	$ 4,000
Bank money	5,000		
Common stocks of bank	4,000		
Other assets	100,000	*Net worth*	129,000
	$133,000		$133,000

Balance Sheet of Bank			
Assets		*Liabilities*	0
Debt of nonfinancial private sector	$ 4,000		
*Monopoly rights to produce money subject to 20 percent reserve requirement	4,000		
less *Monopoly rights used up	4,000	0	*Net worth* Common stocks	4,000
		$ 4,000		$ 4,000

Table 9.9

Balance Sheet of Nonfinancial Private Sector	
Same as Table 9.8	

Balance Sheet of Bank			
Assets		*Liabilities*	
Reserves (government fiat money)	$ 1,000	Bank money produced	$ 5,000
Debt of nonfinancial private sector	4,000		
Monopoly rights to produce money subject to 20 percent reserve requirement	4,000	*Net worth* Common stocks	4,000
	$ 9,000		$ 9,000

Table 9.10

Income Statement of Bank	
Interest received from loans	$200
Less Operating costs	0
Net profits	$200

$25,000 *plus* private monopoly rights to issue money subject to 20 percent reserve requirements $4,000 = $29,000).

3. Before leaving these simple examples we should note that the foregoing approach can also be used to interpret the "asset-liability" nature of government fiat paper money. There can be no doubt that the willingness to accept money as a means of exchange is one of those social conventions—together with such parts of the "social infrastructure" as honesty, willingness to adhere to laws, stable government, and the like—which greatly increases the potential productivity of an economy and hence its wealth. From this viewpoint we can think of the government's monopoly on the right to issue paper money as reflecting its expropriation (or, perhaps better, nationalization) of this component of the social wealth. Thus from the moment in which the "social contract" which creates it is concluded, the government has an asset—and a corresponding net worth—equal to the value of this social convention. The government then draws down on the value of this asset by printing money to finance (say) deficits on current account. Thus when it completes these operations, the government's balance sheet can (in analogy to that of the bank in Tables 9.5 or 9.9) be presented as in Table 9.11. Since the net worth of government is never a matter of operational significance, the terms below the dotted line in Table 9.11 are, in practice, never explicitly listed. What does, however, remain is the description of fiat money as a liability of the government.

Table 9.11

Balance Sheet of Government		
Cumulated deficits on current account	$ 25,000	Fiat money in circulation (value of nationalized social convention "used up") $ 25,000
Value of nationalized social convention of accepting fiat money	$ 25,000	*Net worth* $ 25,000

Clearly—and in accordance with what has already been noted at the end of Section 1 above—what the government determines is the nominal quantity of money. Its real value is determined by the demand of the private sector for money holdings. In brief, the real value of the social convention of using money is determined by society itself.

4. Our discussion until now has assumed that banks are costless firms, operating on the basis of monopoly rights granted to them by the government. Let us now go to the opposite extreme and assume that the banking industry has operating costs like any other industry; and that it is a fully competitive one, enjoying no monopoly rights and subject to no government restrictions. As in

Section 2, banks must hold reserves to enable them to redeem their money for government fiat money. In accordance with these assumptions, the amount of such reserves which the bank holds is determined by considerations of the optimum composition of a portfolio, and not by any government regulations.

Let us now provide our accounting description of the establishment and development of banks within this system. Like any other firm, the competitive bank cannot begin to operate unless it first acquires assets; and these assets are initially acquired by the sale of common stock. Taking Table 9.1 once again as our point of departure, we can then describe the establishment of banks by Table 9.12.

Table 9.12

Balance Sheet of Nonfinancial Private Sector			
Assets		*Liabilities*	0
Government fiat money	$ 20,000		
Common stocks in banks	5,000		
Other assets	100,000	*Net worth*	$125,000
	$125,000		$125,000

Balance Sheet of Banking Sector			
Assets		*Liabilities*	0
Reserves (government		*Net worth*	
fiat money)	$ 5,000	Common stocks	$ 5,000
	$ 5,000		$ 5,000

The banks begin to operate by using the fiat money which they have received—as well as the bank money which they produce—to acquire the productive assets (plant and equipment, debt instruments of the private sector, etc.) which will generate their net income stream. The major point which must now be emphasized is that this transformation in the composition of its balance sheet, from the initial one in Table 9.12 to the optimally composed one to which we shall turn in a moment, will not affect the net worth of the bank: for the $5,000 which the individuals have paid for common stocks represent the discounted value of the net income stream which they anticipated on the assumption that banks would earn the competitive rate of return (or, more accurately, the rate of return which makes individuals indifferent as between investing in banks or in alternative industries).

Consider now the consolidated balance sheet of the banking sector in its "final," profit-maximizing position. In this position, it will have produced bank money and acquired assets with this money until the marginal cost to the banks of selling bank money (in more usual language, of attracting demand deposits—and this includes the administrative costs of accepting deposits and processing checks for collection, the costs of the record-keeping services which the banks provide, the costs of advertising and other promotional schemes, and the possible payment of interest to those who hold bank money) equals the marginal revenue (net of the costs of making loans and obtaining their repayment) from the additional debt instruments which the bank acquires with its money. Thus in its ultimate optimum position, the relevant balance sheets might look like those in Table 9.13.

Table 9.13

Balance Sheet of Nonfinancial Private Sector

Assets		Liabilities	
Government fiat money	$ 15,000	Debt to banks	$285,000
Bank money	300,000		
Common stocks in banks	5,000		
Other assets	90,000	*Net worth*	125,000
	$410,000		$410,000

Balance Sheet of Banking Sector

Assets		Liabilities	
Reserves (government fiat money)	$ 10,000	Bank money	$300,000
Debt of nonfinancial private sector	285,000		
Plant, equipment, and other assets	10,000	*Net worth* Common stocks	5,000
	$305,000		$305,000

A comparison of Tables 9.12 and 9.13 shows that the banking sector has succeeded in selling $300,000 of bank money (i.e., in persuading the public to hold $300,000 of bank deposits)—partly in exchange for assets (including fiat money), and partly in exchange for increased liabilities of the private sector. (Once again, we are abstracting from the influence on the price level of this expansion in the money supply.) Table 9.13 also shows that under the prevailing conditions (including those which relate to the interest rates which the bank pays and receives) the bank's optimum reserve ratio is 3.33 percent.

For our purpose, the major aspect of Table 9.13 is that it lists bank liabilities equal in amount to bank money outstanding. This is not an additional assumption, but the unavoidable implication of our earlier argument that the bank's acquisition of additional assets (as described in the shift from Table 9.12 to 9.13) has not increased its net worth. Hence the increase in bank assets must have been accompanied by an equal increase in liabilities. And since (by assumption) the additional assets were acquired in exchange for bank money—and only in this way—the increased bank liabilities must equal the amount of bank money issued (or "produced").

Note the phrasing of this conclusion: It is not necessarily bank money *per se* (whatever that may mean) which is a liability; instead, all that has been established by our formal argument is that there must be liabilities equal in value to that of the bank money. The economic interpretation of this conclusion is that bank money represents a future flow of services which the bank has obligated itself to provide; the annual (imputed) market value of these services to the individuals who hold the bank money is the interest for-gone; and the present value of this future stream is precisely $300,000 = $r\left(\dfrac{\$300,000}{r}\right)$, where r is the market rate of interest per year. An alternative, and more direct, formulation[6] is that the market value of the aforementioned services (as evidenced by the amount which individuals have "paid" for it) is precisely $300,000.

Note that in neither of the foregoing interpretations do we take explicit account of the fact that the possessor of bank money can insist on its conversion into fiat money; for this is already included in the services of bank money which make him willing to hold it — or to "pay" for it. Alternatively, from the viewpoint of the banks, we can say that they consider the $300,000 of bank money as a perpetual liability: even if some individuals use their bank money to repurchase fiat money from the banks, the latter will (by assumption) be able to "sell" the returned bank money to someone else, thus maintaining the total stock outstanding at $300,000. Again, from the viewpoint of the banks the restriction which this convertibility requirement places on them is reflected in the fact that their portfolio of assets includes reserves.

In any event, our assumption that the banking sector in Table 9.13 is in competitive equilibrium implies that its current costs of providing the aforementioned services are such as to leave it with the normal rate of return on its net worth of $5,000. Assume that this rate equals the market rate of interest, taken once again as 5 percent per year. Then the net annual profits of the banking sector must be $250. Assume for simplicity that all of the banks' plant and equipment is used in connection with the "production" and servicing of bank money (demand deposits), as contrasted with the banks' lending activities; assume also that the annual rate of depreciation on these assets is 20 percent. Then the banks' income statement is given by Table 9.14. In other words, under these assumptions, the fact that banks are earning the normal rate of return implies that their costs of carrying out all the administration and bookkeeping costs connected with bank money (demand deposits) are (per annum) equal to 4 percent ($\dfrac{\$12,000}{\$300,000} \times 100$) of the volume of this money outstanding.

[6] Due to Peter Diamond.

Table 9.14

Income Statement of Banking Sector	
Net[7] interest from loans (= $285,000 × 0.05)	$ 14,250
less Depreciation	2,000
less Operating costs connected with bank money	12,000
Net profits	$ 250

Note that the foregoing suggests yet another interpretation of the liability "Bank money $300,000" in the balance sheet of the banking sector in Table 9.13. In particular, this can now be interpreted as the present value of the current operating costs of maintaining this stock of money ($280,000 = $\frac{\$14,000}{0.05}$) plus the present value of the imputed annual interest charge on the fixed assets (reserves and plant and equipment) which the banks also find it necessary to hold for this purpose [$20,000 = $\frac{0.05\,(\$10,000 + \$10,000)}{0.05}$].[8]

This is actually a general relationship which is an alternative statement of the existence of competitive equilibrium in the banking sector. For let $R, D, P, B,$ and C, respectively, represent the items Reserves, Debt, Plant and equipment, Bank money, and Common stocks in the bank balance sheet of Table 9.13. Thus

$$R + D + P = B + C. \tag{1}$$

The condition of competitive equilibrium (as exemplified by Table 9.14) can then be expressed symbolically as

$$rD - X = rC, \tag{2}$$

where r is the competitive rate of return and X is current costs (depreciation *plus* other operating costs). Dividing (2) through by r and substituting into (1) then yields

$$B = R + P + X/r, \tag{3}$$

which is the expression of the preceding paragraph.[9]

5.   Before going on to draw the general implications of the preceding, rather

---

[7] Net of the costs of making and collecting the loans; see Section 5.

[8] See Appendix I for the use of this paragraph to interpret and criticize the Pesek-Saving contention that bank money is a net asset of the economy.

[9] Note that a corresponding interpretation can be made of the bank's balance sheet in Table 9.9. The present value of the imputed interest charge of holding reserves in this case is $1,000, and the difference between this amount and the $5,000 listed as "Liabilities: Bank money produced" is precisely the value of the monopoly right of producing money subject to the reserve requirement. This is a specific instance of the more general case (of a banking system with monopoly profits) discussed in Section 6.

formalistic, argument, let me indicate some further economic aspects of the assumption that banks have operating costs.

In the discussion at the end of Section 1 it was pointed out that the assumption that banks—like government—produced money without cost implied that the two kinds of money were identical. (Indeed, an individual holding government money in this case could just as well be described as a bank with a 100 percent reserve ratio.) Conversely, the recognition in the preceding section that the production of bank money does involve operating costs implies that this money is of a different nature from government fiat money. In particular, the operating costs connected with bank money are a necessary condition for the distinctive services which it provides: namely, convenience of payment of large sums, convenience of payment over distances, safety, record-keeping, provision of automatic receipts, and the like. On the other hand, government fiat money provides its distinctive services of ease of transfer of small sums in face-to-face situations, usability in communities where one is not known, and anonymity.

Thus, it is not correct to describe bank money (demand deposits) as providing services *in addition* to those provided by fiat money (hand-to-hand currency). What we must instead say is that though both of these assets are—by definition—money, the liquidity services provided by them are of a different nature. There is, however, a relationship between them: for in equilibrium the net value of these services at the margin must, in each case, equal the rate of interest. And it is this condition which determines the optimum ratio of these two kinds of money.

It follows from this discussion that there is a fundamental difference between the monetary expansion represented by the movement from Table 9.7 to 9.9 in Section 1, and that represented by the movement from Table 9.12 to 9.13 in the preceding one. In the first case, the increased money supply is of the same nature as the original one; hence (as indicated on pp. 172–173 above) the price level will increase proportionately, leaving real money balances unchanged. In the second case, however, the new bank money is of a different nature; hence the monetary expansion will be accompanied by an increase in the demand for money; and hence the price level will increase less than proportionately. Thus, in the equilibrium position corresponding to Table 9.13 the real value of money balances will be greater than that of Table 9.12, reflecting the fact that part of the money supply (namely, that produced by banks) now provides a new type of liquidity service. Furthermore, the extent (in real terms) to which the total money supply increases is directly related to the scope of these new liquidity services, which is in turn determined by the scope of the costs incurred by the banks in providing these services. And this is yet another aspect of equation (3) above—rearranged so as to equate the increase in the nominal money supply generated by the banking system (i.e., the excess of bank money over bank reserves, or $B-R$) with the present value of the costs of inducing the public to hold the stock of bank money outstanding.

So much for the implications of the operating costs connected with bank money. Let me now turn briefly to the costs connected with bank loans, which I have so far ignored (see footnote 7 above). Consider the entry "Net interest from loans" in the income statement of Table 9.14. It would be more realistic to assume that there are two interest rates in an economy: what we have so far called the market rate of interest, and which represents the rate on relatively safe securities (5 percent); and a higher rate of interest (say, 6 percent) that the bank charges for its loans. This higher rate represents the higher riskiness of these loans, the costs of checking the credit-worthiness of the borrowers, the costs of collecting these loans, and the like. Now under the assumption of perfect competition the bank has the alternative of borrowing all the funds it lends out directly from the market at 5 percent, which means that it would have no net worth; hence—if such borrowings can be carried out costlessly—the assumption of competitive equilibrium implies that the net interest it earns on its loans must also equal 5 percent. In other words, the aforementioned costs must amount to approximately 1 percent of the amount of the loans.

Similarly, if we assume that the balance sheet in Table 9.13 reflects the banks' situation at the instant that the loans are made, then $285,000 is greater than the volume of these loans by the amount which the bank has spent on investigating credit-worthiness, etc. In other words, the banks lend at 6 percent; but the $285,000 is the present market value of the loan repayments which they will receive, discounted at the market rate of 5 percent. It is the price at which banks can sell these loans in the market today with a guarantee on their repayment; for this guarantee does not involve the banks in any greater risk than they would have by continuing to hold the loans to maturity.

In the present paper, I shall continue to abstract from this complication. To deal with it would require listing a figure for the liability of the nonfinancial sector to the banks which differs from the value of the corresponding asset which the banking sector holds—and to make yet another entry to take account of this discrepancy. More fundamentally—as already noted—it would require us to assume that there are two interest rates in the economy.

6. If we now consolidate the balance sheets of Table 9.13, we see that bank money as an asset of the nonfinancial sector is cancelled out by the same item as a liability of the banking sector—thus yielding Table 9.15. Actually, as will be shown in the next section, this cancelling out cannot really be carried out in such a mechanical manner when we come to analyze the real-balance effect of a price change. But for the moment let us take this as a reaffirmation of the usual conclusion that the net financial assets of the private sector as a whole (including the banking sector) consist only of government fiat money and not bank money.

It should be emphasized that this conclusion does not mean that the banking industry is not a productive sector of the economy. On the contrary, Table 9.13 indicates that it has a net worth of $5,000, representing the capitalized value of the income stream which it generates. Similarly, the standard procedure for estimating income originating in the banking

Table 9.15

Consolidated Balance Sheet of Private Sector			
Assets		*Liabilities*	0
Government fiat money	$ 25,000		
Other assets	100,000	*Net worth*	$125,000
	$125,000		$125,000

industry (viz., imputing interest income to holders of demand deposits, and an offsetting charge for bank services[10]) will show it to be making a positive contribution to the national income.

Similarly, it should be emphasized that the fact that bank money is not part of net wealth does not imply that it is not part of the money supply, or that changes in the banking sector will not affect monetary aspects of the economy. All that is implied is that such changes will *initially* generate only substitution effects, and not wealth (viz., real-balance) effects. This is a point which I have discussed in detail elsewhere.[11]

A word might also be said about the fact that the net worth of the economy as a whole does not change in the shift from Table 9.12 to Table 9.13. This reflects the assumption in all of the foregoing that technology is constant and that, accordingly, the productive activities of the banking sector are at the expense of those of other sectors. Thus, the discussion of Section 5 notwithstanding, the foregoing balance sheets should be interpreted as representing not the introduction of a new technology (i.e., the introduction of a banking system which hitherto did not exist at all), but potential shifts at the margin in the productive resources of an economy with a given technology. But this is the relevant viewpoint for the question at issue: namely, the proper measure of the wealth of an economy at a given point of time; or, more specifically, the proper measure of wealth for the analysis of the real-balance effect of a change in the price level.

On the other hand, if there should occur an exogenous technological improvement in the process by which bank money is produced (or, more generally, in the financial sector of the economy), then total wealth will increase. And this increase in wealth will accrue to those individuals who for one reason or another possess the rights to these improvements. Correspondingly, a monetary expansion which is generated by such a technological improvement will (just like a costless increase in government fiat paper money) initially generate a wealth effect.

There is, however, a question as to whether technological change should be considered as exogenous, or as an endogenous economic activity which is also carried to the point at which marginal revenues and costs are equal. To the extent that the latter approach is followed, the monetary

[10]Cf., e.g., R. Ruggles and N. D. Ruggles, *National Income Accounts and Income Analysis*, 2nd ed. (New York, 1956), pp. 60–64.

[11]*Money, Interest, and Prices, op. cit.*, Chapter XII: 5–6, especially pp. 299–301.

expansion once again does not generate a wealth effect. All this raises questions with which we cannot deal here.

Thus the analysis up to this point has generally supported the traditional exclusion of bank money from net national wealth. Let me, however, note that there are some fundamental differences in both approach and interpretation. First of all, the crux of our argument has been the effect of the operations of the banks on their net worth. The traditional argument, on the other hand, has been in terms of offsetting assets and liabilities, with no explicit reference to net worth. Indeed, in my own treatment of this subject in the past, the net worth of the banking sector did not even appear as an item in its balance sheet![12]

Second, a comparison of Section 4 with Sections 1–2 above shows that—for the purpose of measuring net wealth—the really relevant distinction between types of money is not between the "outside" and "inside" varieties, but between money which has no costs of production—or, more generally, whose marginal cost of production is less than its marginal value (and this has implicitly been assumed to be the case for government fiat paper money)—and money whose marginal cost of production equals its marginal value.

At first sight this last sentence would seem to imply that commodity money (say, gold) is also not part of net wealth. It should therefore be emphasized that the marginal cost referred to in the preceding paragraph (and in the discussion of bank money in the preceding section) is the marginal cost of *maintaining the stock of money constant at a given level* (i.e., the cost which corresponds to depreciation in the case of a physical asset). In the case of gold, these costs (generated primarily by the necessity of replacing worn-out coins) are negligible. In contrast, the costs of producing the stock of gold itself are significant—but they are historical ones; and here, as elsewhere in economic analysis, historical costs are irrelevant. On the other hand, the current costs of *increasing* the stock of gold are most relevant; indeed they lead to the conclusion that in competitive equilibrium such an increase—by diverting productive resources hitherto devoted to other ends—does not at the margin increase the total wealth of the economy. (Note that foreign exchange reserves are analogous to gold for the purpose of this argument.)

7. Let us now examine the real-balance effect of a price decline in the economy described by Table 9.13. Here—as throughout the argument—this must be done by analyzing the effects of this change on the net worth of the banking sector.

The crucial question in this analysis is what assumption the banking sector makes about the impact of this price decline on the physical volume of administrative operations (per unit of time) needed to maintain the stock of bank money constant at $300,000–and hence on the banks' costs. If,

[12]*Ibid.*, pp. 296 and 304. Cf. also above, p. 169.

for example, banks assume that this volume will remain the same, then the lowered price level means that the banks' nominal costs of operations per unit of time are lower, and hence their profits are greater. Hence the nominal net worth of the banking sector—that is, the capitalized value of these profits—increases; and this, of course, causes a corresponding increase in the net worth of the nonfinancial sector. This increased net worth is matched in the balance sheet of the banking sector by the introduction of an asset "Goodwill." Under this assumption (as will be shown later) a consolidated balance sheet of the private sector would show an increase in its real net worth which equals the increase in the real value of the total money holdings (bank as well as government) of the nonfinancial sector.

It does not, however, seem reasonable that the banking sector would make this assumption. For—in the absence of money illusion—it might well be expected to take account of the fact that if the price level is, say, 10 percent lower, then each individual transaction with the bank (namely, each deposit made and each check drawn) will also be roughly 10 percent less in nominal value.[13] Under these circumstances the banks will assume that the physical volume of bank operations connected with maintaining the nominal stock of bank money fixed at its original level will be roughly 11 percent $\{\approx [(1.00/0.90) - 1.00]\ 100\}$ greater than it was before the price decline. But since the prices of the factors of production engaged in these operations have (by assumption) declined by 10 percent, total nominal operating costs will remain more or less the same. Hence, net profits will remain the same and hence so will the nominal net worth of the banking system. In this case, as will be shown below, the increase in the real net worth of the private sector will equal the increase in the real value of government fiat money—in accordance with the traditional contention.

Note that the difference between these alternative assumptions is not necessarily related to different assumptions about the velocity of circulation. For in both cases the total physical volume of goods purchased per unit of time could remain the same, so that velocity could be lower. In terms of $MV = PT$, in both cases the constant level of M and lower level of P could be accompanied by a constant value of T per unit of time—and hence a lower value of V. What is instead at issue here is the effect of the lowered price level on the average physical quantity of goods purchased in a transaction: according to the first assumption, it increases in inverse proportion to the price level; according to the second, it remains constant. Clearly, it is this second assumption which is more in accordance with the absence of money illusion.

---

[13] This point can be usefully illustrated by the following data on the Israel economy: from 1954 to 1961 the index of wholesale prices rose roughly by 40 percent, while the implicit GNP price index rose by 54 percent; during the same period the average amount of a check drawn on overdraft accounts rose from IL758 to IL954, or by roughly 26 percent. In part, the differences between this percentage increase and that of the price level can be explained in terms of the structural changes which occurred in the Israel banking system during this period. Cf. Meir Heth, *Banking Institutions in Israel*, 2nd ed. (Jerusalem, 1966), pp. 120–122.

8.   The conclusions of this paper up to this point can be demonstrated formally quite simply. Consider for generality a banking system which may have monopoly rights and/or goodwill (whose capitalized value will be denoted by $G \geq 0$). The balance sheet of such a system is described by

$$R + D + P + G = B + C, \tag{4}$$

where, once again, R, D, P, B, and G, respectively, represent the reserves, debt holdings, plant and equipment, bank money, and common stocks of the system—all measured in money terms. Assume that the system earns the normal rate of return, r, on its common stock as valued by (4); that is, inclusive of goodwill. Thus equation (2) above continues to be valid. Substituting from (2) into (4) then yields

$$B = R + P + \frac{X}{r} + G, \tag{5}$$

where, as before, X represents nominal operating costs. In the case of perfect competition, $G = 0$ by definition, so that (4) and (5) reduce to (1) and (3), respectively.

Let us now define the total money supply, M, as

$$M = \bar{M}_H + B, \tag{6}$$

where $\bar{M}_H$ is the government fiat money in the hands of the nonfinancial private sector. The total quantity, $\bar{M}$, of this fiat (outside) money is then

$$\bar{M} = \bar{M}_H + R. \tag{7}$$

Finally, the balance sheet of the nonfinancial private sector can be written as

$$\bar{M}_H + B + C + T = D + W, \tag{8}$$

where T represents physical assets and W the net worth or wealth of this sector.

The consolidated balance sheet of the private sector is thus obtained by adding equations (4) and (8) to yield the following measure of the net real private wealth of the economy:

$$\frac{W}{p} = \frac{(\bar{M}_H + R) + G}{p} + (P^* + T^*), \tag{9}$$

where $P^* = P/p$ and $T^* = T/p$ represent the real quantities of physical assets, whose sum (though not sectorial distribution) is assumed constant. Thus, as explained in the preceding sections, net real financial assets consist only of outside money and the capitalized value of the monopoly bank profits (or goodwill). Correspondingly, the real-balance effect of a price change is determined by the change in the real value of these assets; that is, by

$$\frac{\partial \left(\dfrac{W}{p} \right)}{\partial p} = - \frac{\bar{M}_H + R}{p^2} + \frac{\partial \left(\dfrac{G}{p} \right)}{\partial p}. \tag{10}$$

Thus the extent to which the real-balance effect of a price change exceeds that generated by outside money alone exactly equals the extent to which the price change generates an increase in the real value of the asset goodwill—and hence in the real net worth—of the banking system.[14]

The application of this general principle to the two specific ones described in the preceding section is straightforward. Let us first re-write (5) as

$$\frac{G}{p} = \frac{B - R - pP^* - p\dfrac{X^*}{r}}{p},\tag{11}$$

where X^* represents the total real operating costs of the banking system (per unit of time) required for the maintenance of B nominal units of bank money in circulation. The common assumptions of both cases are (a) that the banking system is initially in a position of competitive equilibrium (in which, by definition, $G = 0$), and (b) that the volume of B (and hence R) remains constant in the face of a change in p. Differentiating (11) partially with respect to p under these assumptions then yields

$$\frac{\partial\left(\dfrac{G}{p}\right)}{\partial p} = -\frac{1}{rp}\frac{\partial[p(rP^* + X^*)]}{\partial p},\tag{12}$$

where the derivative has been evaluated at the point $G = 0$.

The crucial additional assumption of the second case described above is that total *nominal* operating costs, $p(rP^* + X^*)$, are invariant under a change in p (that is, *real* operating costs per nominal unit of bank money outstanding are inversely proportionate to p, which means that the *real* operating costs of the bank depend on the *real* volume of bank money—a relationship that accords with the absence of money illusion). Hence the derivative in (12)—and correspondingly the second term in equation (10)—is zero. [More directly, the assumption of constant nominal costs implies constant nominal profits and hence constant nominal goodwill at the initial level $G = 0$; hence $\dfrac{\partial\left(\dfrac{G}{p}\right)}{\partial p}$ in (10) is zero]. Thus the real-balance effect stems solely from outside money, $\overline{M} = \overline{M}_H + R$.

Consider now the first case. The crucial assumption here is that *real* operating costs per nominal unit of bank money, and hence $P^* + X^*$, are constant. Evaluating (12) under this assumption then yields

$$\frac{\partial\left(\dfrac{G}{p}\right)}{\partial p} = -\frac{rP^* + X^*}{rp} = -\frac{P + \dfrac{X}{r}}{p^2} = -\frac{B - R}{p^2},\tag{13}$$

<hr/>

[14] In tracing through the details of the balance-sheet variations generated by the price change, several fine points relating to the proper revaluation of assets arise. These are illustrated in Appendix II below.

where use has been made of (5) under the assumption $G = 0$. Substituting from (13) into the general expression (10) then yields

$$\frac{\partial\left(\frac{W}{p}\right)}{\partial p} - -\frac{\bar{M}_H + R}{p^2} - \frac{B - R}{p^2}$$

$$= -\frac{\bar{M}_H + B}{p^2} = -\frac{M}{p^2}.$$

(14)

Thus in this case it is the total money supply—inside as well as outside—which is relevant.

As indicated above, the implicit assumption of the cost function stipulated in this case is that there is money illusion in the system. We can accordingly conclude that in the absence of such illusion—that is, under the cost conditions stipulated in the penultimate paragraph—the real-balance effect of a price decline is determined solely by the volume of outside money in circulation.

From the viewpoint of long-run competitive equilibrium, however, this conclusion is valid even if there is money illusion in the system. For the above discussion has shown that bank money is part of net wealth for purposes of the real-balance effect only to the extent that the price decline increases the nominal net worth of the banking system. But if because of the banks' cost function such an increase should take place, the rate of return in the banking industry would rise above the competitive one. Hence new firms will be attracted into the banking industry until the profit rate is driven down once again to the normal level. Correspondingly, the increase in the net worth of the banking system that might be generated by a price decline is inversely related to the length of time that banks assume their above-normal profits will continue. The shorter this period, the better the approximation of the real-balance effect which defines it solely in terms of government fiat money, as distinct from bank money—no matter what the nature of the banks' cost functions.

I have so far discussed the real-balance effect of a price decline. What about the corresponding effect of an increase in the quantity of money? Let me first emphasize that it is meaningless to ask this question about the quantity of bank money; for in the present model this is an endogenous variable. One can therefore only ask about the effect of a change in (say) the reserve ratio which banks feel they must hold—or of any other change in their cost conditions; alternatively, one can ask about the effect of a change in the public's desired ratio of bank money to government money—or of any other change in the demand condition facing the banks. As has been shown elsewhere,[15] such changes influence the economy through their effect on the demand of the banking system for the debt instruments of the private

[15] On this and the following paragraph, see Patinkin, *Money, Interest, and Prices, op. cit.*, p. 300.

sector as well as their effect on the total supply of money (government and bank, the proportions of which will change). What the preceding analysis now shows is that there may be an additional effect: namely, the possible direct effect of the designated change on the net worth of the banking system.

Of particular theoretical interest is yet another—and simplistic—case in which the government distributes additional quantities of its own money as gifts to the nonfinancial and banking sectors, in the same proportion in which government money was originally held by them. In accordance with the traditional approach, the initial increase in net wealth is then equal to this increase in government money—which generates a real-balance effect to push prices upwards. In the final equilibrium position which will be re-established, all the entries in the balance sheets of Table 9.13 (including bank money) will have increased in the same proportion as the initial in-crease in the quantity of government money. Since, however, the price level will also have increased in the same proportion, all real quantities will have returned to their original respective levels (cf. pp. 172–173 above).

9. Let me now briefly sketch how the basic approach of this paper can also be applied to the far more realistic case of a banking industry which is not perfectly competitive. Thus assume that there is restricted entry into this industry in the form of (say) the necessity to obtain a government license to operate a bank. This case is a combination of the ones described above. Namely, if the government grants such a license as a gift to a group of individ-uals, then the net worth of the private sector is immediately increased by the value of the license—as in Section 1 above. On this increased net worth (assuming the salability of the license) banks will earn the market rate of return. As in the preceding section, the nature of the real-financial-asset effect in such an economy will then depend on the effects of a price decline on the net worth of the banking sector.

Alternatively, we can assume that there is free entry into the banking industry, but that the imperfect competition manifests itself in the form of an agreement among the banks (which may be government-imposed) not to compete with each other either with respect to the price of their product (i.e., not to sell bank money at a discount with respect to government fiat money— a restriction inherent in the banks' commitment always to exchange bank deposits and fiat money at a one-to-one ratio) or with respect to the price they pay to attract reserves (a restriction inherent in, say, the prohibition of interest payments on deposits). Thus the banking sector is effectively a cartel on both the buying and selling sides. Now, if the banks' cost curves are U-shaped, then firms will continue entering the industry until profits are driven down to their normal levels—in which case bank money will not be part of net wealth, in accordance with the argument of Sections 4 and 6 above.[16] Clearly, such a cartel could also operate without free entry—in

---

[16] For a general analysis of a cartel with free entry, see my "Multiple-Plant Firms, Cartels, and Imperfect Competition," *Quarterly Journal of Economics*, LXI (1947), Section 3.

which case the considerations of the preceding paragraph would continue to be relevant.

Analogous to the assumption of imperfect competition is that of imperfect foresight. As will be recalled from the discussion of perfect competition in Section 4 above, the basic fact that net worth remains unchanged in the shift from Table 9.12 to Table 9.13 reflects the assumption of such foresight. Accordingly, if we assume more realistically that there is initially some uncertainty as to the extent to which the banks will carry out their business successfully, then their net worth will increase as they show that they can do so. This increase in net worth is accompanied by an increase in the asset "Goodwill"—which, economically, is analogous to the value of the bank license discussed at the beginning of this section.

10.   I conclude this paper by recapitulating its major findings in terms of our initial question: is there a difference between outside and inside money from the viewpoint of the wealth concept relevant for the real-balance effect? What the foregoing analysis has, first of all, shown is that this is not the relevant distinction. For what really matters from the viewpoint of the real-balance effect is not whether the issuer of the money is the government or the private banking sector, but whether there are costs involved in maintaining constant the stock of money. More specifically, money is wealth from the viewpoint of the real-balance effect only to the extent that there is a difference between the value of the stock of money and the present value of the costs of maintaining that stock constant.

In general, such costs are negligible with reference to gold or government fiat money. On the other hand, they are definitely not negligible with reference to bank money. Indeed, it has been shown in Section 4 that if the banking sector is a competitive one, earning the normal rate of return, then these costs equal the value of the stock of bank money outstanding. Under this assumption, then, the hitherto accepted approach of measuring the real-balance effect only in terms of government money continues to be the correct one from the long-run viewpoint. And in the absence of money illusion. it will be correct from the short-run viewpoint as well (see Section 8).

Conversely, if because of restricted entry the banking sector enjoys monopoly profits, then bank money should be included in net wealth for the purpose of the real-balance effect to an extent equal to the capitalized value of these profits. For this value represents the difference between the stock of bank money and the costs of maintaining it.

We note finally that in general it is the government which restricts entry into the banking sector—usually by means of requiring a license (or its equivalent) in order to operate a bank. Thus the extent to which bank money is included in net wealth for the purpose of the real-balance effect can be interpreted as representing the value of the transfer by the government to the private sector of part of its (the government's) sovereign monopoly right to issue money.

Appendix I

The approach of p. 180 above makes it possible to provide a simple (and, at first sight, persuasive) interpretation of the Pesek-Saving argument that, in part, is implicit in their own presentation.[1]

In brief, individuals who hold bank money fully consider it to be an asset. On the other hand, the extent to which banks consider it as an effective liability, at any point in time, is indicated by their "revealed preference" for the volume of reserves that they choose to hold in order to be able to meet the (net) demand of their depositors for repayment in government (fiat) money during the subsequent time interval. (The level of these reserves is determined primarily by the banks' expectations about the stream of withdrawals and deposits during this interval, as well as their evaluation of the costs of being caught illiquid.) Hence the Pesek-Saving conclusion that bank money less reserves is a net asset of the economy.

This formulation also has the advantage of enabling an equally simple demonstration of the fallacy of the Pesek-Saving argument: namely, the holding of reserves is not the only liability incurred by the banks in maintaining their stock of money outstanding. Indeed, as shown on pp. 178–180, under competitive conditions these other liabilities will exactly equal the difference between bank money and reserves. Hence under these conditions bank money is not a net asset of the economy.

Appendix II[2]

The conclusions of Section 7 can be usefully illustrated by a detailed analysis of the effect of a 10 percent decline in prices on the balance sheets and income statement of Tables 9.13 and 9.14, respectively. Consider first the case in which banks assume that each individual transaction will also decline 10 percent in nominal value. As shown above, the income statement of the banking sector then remains the same as in Table 9.14. Let us turn now to the balance sheets described by Table 9.13. In the first instance the 10 percent decline in prices reduces the nominal value of the plant and equipment held by the banks by $1,000, and this capital loss initially causes a corresponding decrease in the value of their common stocks. But since the capitalized value of the banks' net income stream is still $5,000, the banks can sell another $1,000 of common stocks. Furthermore, the $1,000 so received will have to be used by the bank to acquire (from the nonfinancial sector) the additional 11 percent of plant and equipment now necessary to service the outstanding stock of $300,000 of bank money.

[1] See Pesek and Saving, *op. cit.*, pp. 85–87, 145–147, *et passim.*
Cf. also J. M. Buchanan, "An Outside Economist's Defense of Pesek and Saving," *Journal of Economic Literature*, VII (1969), 812–814.
[2] The following analysis could not have been carried out without the assistance and advice of Peter Diamond and Tsvi Ophir, to whom I am very grateful.

After all of these changes are recorded, the balance sheet of the banking sector will remain nominally the same as it is in Table 9.13—though the entry "Plant, equipment, and other assets $10,000" will now represent a physical quantity 11 percent greater. On the other hand, the balance sheet of the nonfinancial private sector will show a nominal decline of $10,000 in "Other assets" and a corresponding decline in net worth—with all other entries remaining the same. This decline in the nominal value of plant and equipment reflects two facts: first, the sale of $1,100 of plant and equipment (valued at their original prices) to the banking sector; second, the valuation of the remaining plant and equipment at a price level 10 percent lower. Thus the value of plant and equipment held by the nonfinancial sector is $80,000 ≈ ($90,000 − $1,000)0.90.

In real terms (i.e., valued at the original price level), however, the net worth of the nonfinancial private sector has increased by $2,778 = [($125,000 − $10,000) ÷ 0.90] − $125,000. But this is precisely the increase in the real value of the total quantity of government fiat money in the system [i.e., ($25,000 ÷ 0.90) − $25,000]. Clearly, this result would be obtained directly by consolidating—at the *original* price level—the balance sheets discussed in the penultimate paragraph, thus yielding Appendix Table 1. A comparison with Table 9.15 then shows that the only net asset whose real value has increased as a result of the price decline is government fiat money.

Appendix Table 1

Consolidated Balance Sheet of Private Sector (at constant prices)

Assets		Liabilities	0
Government fiat money	$ 27,778		
Other assets	100,000	Net worth	$127,778
	$127,778		$127,778

Let us now consider the alternative assumption indicated in Section 7 —namely, that the physical volume of administrative operations remains the same despite the 10 percent decline in all prices (including the prices of the factors of production employed by the banks). Then the banks' depreciation charges and operating costs in Table 9.14 decline by 10 percent, with a resulting increase in net profits (at current prices) to $1,650 (= $250 + $1,400). The capitalized value of these profits (at the competitive rate of return of 5 percent) is then $33,000—which must also equal the current value of the common stocks of the banking sector. Instead of Table 9.13 we would then have (at current prices) Appendix Table 2. The new asset of the banks, "Goodwill," represents the capitalized value of the reduced costs (including reduced imputed interest charges on plant and equipment) made possible by the 10 percent price reduction.

If we now consolidate the balance sheets of Appendix Table 2—and revalue the assets at the *original* price level—we obtain Appendix Table 3. A

Appendix Table 2

Balance Sheet of Nonfinancial Private Sector (at current prices)

Assets		Liabilities	
Government fiat money	$ 15,000	Debt to banks	$285,000
Bank money	300,000		
Common stocks of banks	33,000		
Other assets	81,000	Net worth	144,000
	$429,000		$429,000

Balance Sheet of Banking Sector (at current prices)

Assets		Liabilities	
Reserves (government fiat money)	$ 10,000	Bank money	$300,000
Debt of nonfinancial private sector	285,000		
Plant, equipment, and other assets	9,000	Net worth	
Goodwill	29,000	Common stocks	33,000
	$333,000		$333,000

comparison with Table 9.15 then shows that the 10 percent price reduction has increased the real net worth (wealth) of the private sector by $35,000—which equals (as it must) the increase in the real value of the *total* money supply held by the nonfinancial private sector [($315,000 ÷ 0.90) − $315,000 = $35,000].

Appendix Table 3

Consolidated Balance Sheet of Private Sector (at constant prices)

Assets		Liabilities	0
Government fiat money	$ 27,778		
Other (physical) assets	100,000		
Goodwill	32,222	Net worth	$160,000
	$160,000		$160,000

We might note that an alternative interpretation of the foregoing can be made by valuing the banks' liability with respect to bank money—not at the market price of the services provided by this money, but at the banks' costs (including imputed interest charges on reserves and plant and equipment). Correspondingly, there would be no asset "Goodwill" appearing among the assets of the banking sector in Appendix Table 2 and, instead, the liabilities connected with bank money would be listed at $271,000 = $300,000 − $29,000. Clearly, this would not affect the net worth of the banking sector.

From this viewpoint, however, it would be more appropriate not to cancel out the item "Bank money," but instead to write the original consolidated balance sheet of Table 9.15 in the form of Appendix Table 4. The balance sheet corresponding to Appendix Table 3 would then have the form of Appendix Table 5—where the banks' increased real costs of $1,111 of maintaining their money outstanding represents the increased real burden of maintaining the same nominal reserves, despite the reduced price level [$1,111 = ($10,000 ÷ 0.90) − $10,000]. Needless to say, the increase in the real net worth of the consolidated private sector is exactly the same as it was before.

Appendix Table 4

Consolidated Balance Sheet of Private Sector (at constant prices)

Assets		*Liabilities*	
Government fiat money	$ 25,000	Capitalized value of costs of maintaining the nominal stock	
Bank money	300,000	of bank money outstanding	$300,000
Other (physical) assets	100,000	*Net worth*	125,000
	$425,000		$425,000

Appendix Table 5

Consolidated Balance Sheet of Private Sector (at constant prices)

Assets		*Liabilities*	
Government fiat money	$ 27,778	Capitalized value of costs of maintaining the nominal stock	
Bank money	333,333	of bank money outstanding	$301,111
Other (physical) assets	100,000	*Net worth*	160,000
	$461,111		$461,111

10

Money and Growth in a Keynesian Full-Employment Model[1]

The purpose of the present paper is to analyze the influence of monetary changes on growth under assumptions which will enable us to make use of a simple diagrammatic technique analogous to the one originally developed by Lloyd Metzler[2] and subsequently used extensively in my own work.[3] Though the following analysis will be carried out throughout under the assumption of a growing economy with full employment, I have for simplicity denoted the underlying model as a Keynesian one: for it has the major attribute of a Keynesian model of being based on a simultaneous equilibrium analysis of the commodity and money markets.

1. A FISHERINE ANALYSIS

As a preliminary step, let me present a Fisherine analysis of the effect of anticipated inflation on the rate of investment in an economy. My point of

---

Based on lectures given in the Seminar on Monetary Theory at the Hebrew University of Jerusalem in 1968. A version of this paper was also delivered as a lecture at Osaka University in July 1969.

[1] In the writing of this paper, I have benefited greatly from reading Robert Mundell's two stimulating articles on "Inflation and Real Interest," *Journal of Political Economy*, LXXI (1963), 280–283, and "A Fallacy in the Interpretation of Macroeconomic Equilibrium," *Journal of Political Economy*, LXXIII (1965), 61–66. I have also benefited from reading an unpublished paper by Phillip Cagan on "The Channels of Monetary Effects on Interest Rates" (National Bureau of Economic Research, July 1966).

[2] Lloyd Metzler, "Wealth, Saving, and the Rate of Interest," *Journal of Political Economy*, LIX (1951), 93–116. Metzler's diagram in turn is analogous to the well-known Hicks *IS–LM* diagram.

[3] Indeed, I would now use the analysis of Sections 2–3 below to replace the quite inadequate—and on some points even incorrect—analysis of money and growth which appears in Chapter XIV: 5 of my *Money, Interest, and Prices*, 2nd ed. (New York, 1965).

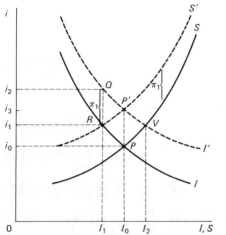

0   I_1 I_0 I_2 I, S **Figure 10.1.**

departure will be Fisher's well-known distinction[4] between the money and real rate of interest, represented respectively by i and r. If π represents the rate of change in prices, then (in terms of instantaneous rates of change)

$$r = i - \pi, \tag{1}$$

where in each case the anticipated rate is assumed to be equal to the prevailing one. Thus the real rate of interest is the money rate corrected for the rate of change in the value (purchasing power) of money.

Assume first that the price level is constant and (for a given level of real income) draw in Figure 10.1 the real investment (I) and savings (S) curves of the economy as a function of the real rate of interest. Since by assumption $\pi = 0$, there is no difference in this case between the money and real rates of interest; hence the vertical axis in Figure 10.1 is designated as i. The curves in Figure 10.1 are drawn with the traditionally assumed slopes. Their intersection at point P determines the equilibrium levels of interest (i_0) and real investment (I_0), respectively.

Assume now that for some reason (and I shall be more explicit on this point in the next section) the actual—and hence anticipated—rate of price change in the economy becomes $\pi = \pi_1 > 0$. By assumption, investors are concerned only with the real rate of interest. Hence—since it is the money rate of interest which is represented in Figure 10.1—this change in anticipations will reflect itself diagrammatically in a uniform upward shift of the investment curve by the distance π_1. For this will reflect the fact that the money rate of interest at (say) point Q on the new curve I' corresponds to the same real rate of interest as that represented by point R on curve I—so that the level of real investment corresponding to these two points is also the same (viz., I_1).

[4] Irving Fisher, *The Rate of Interest* (New York, 1907), pp. 77–86 and 358–360; *The Theory of Interest* (New York, 1930), Chapters 2 and 19.

Thus at first sight it would seem that—in accordance with the contention sometimes voiced—inflation stimulates investment and thus brings the economy to the intersection point V, corresponding to the level of real investment $I_2 > I_0$. But it can immediately be seen that this is an unwarranted conclusion, stemming from the asymmetric assumptions that whereas investors are rational individuals concerned with the real rate of interest, savers continue irrationally to be concerned with the money rate, despite the anticipated inflation. Correspondingly, if we were to assume that savers too are concerned only with the real rate of interest, then the anticipated inflation would cause the curve S in Figure 10.1 also to shift upwards by the distance π_1 to S'. Hence the new equilibrium position in the economy, P', would be one in which the money rate of interest would exceed the original one by π_1, so that the real rate of interest—and hence the real level of investment—would remain unchanged.

Thus the foregoing analysis brings us to the traditional-sounding conclusion that a fully anticipated inflationary process affects only the money rate of interest, while leaving invariant the real variables of the system.[5] But what we must now note is that this conclusion rests on an analysis which has been restricted to the equilibrium condition in the commodity market as represented by the savings = investment condition. The question which must now be raised is the effect on this conclusion of extending the analysis —in Keynesian-like fashion—to a simultaneous analysis of equilibrium conditions in the commodity and money markets. It is to this task that we now turn. At the same time, we shall not remain within the framework of the stationary economy considered by Keynesian economics, but shall explicitly present the analysis within the context of a growing full-employment economy.

2. A KEYNESIAN ANALYSIS

Consider a growing money economy which (in accordance with Solow's assumptions[6]) has two factors of production, physical capital (K) and labor (L), generating the output Y in accordance with the production function

$$Y = F(K, L) \qquad (2)$$

assumed to be linearly homogeneous. Thus the intensive form of the production function is

$$y = f(k) , \qquad (3)$$

[5]This, for example, is Abba Lerner's conclusion; see his *Essays in Economic Analysis* (London, 1953), pp. 329–330.

Actually, Fisher himself did not believe that the money rate would increase by the full extent of the rate of price increase—but only because he attributed imperfect foresight to individuals; see his *Theory of Interest, op. cit.*, pp. 43–44.

[6]Robert M. Solow, "A Contribution to the Theory of Economic Growth," *Quarterly Journal of Economics*, LXX (1956), 65–94.

where $y = Y/L$ and $k = K/L$. The marginal productivity of capital is thus represented by $f'(k) > 0$, which in equilibrium must equal the real rate of interest, r. Finally, let M represent the nominal quantity of money in the economy, p the price level, and

$$m = \frac{M/P}{L},$$ (4)

the per capita quantity of real money balances.

Following Solow, assume that the quantity of labor in the foregoing economy is growing exogenously at the rate n, and that it is always fully employed. Define the steady state of this economy as one in which both per capita capital, k, and per capita real balances, m, are constant. It then follows from (2) that in the steady state K and Y are each growing at the rate n. Similarly, it follows from (4) that in the steady state total real money balances, M/p, are also growing at the rate n. Letting μ represent the rate of change (assumed to be exogenous) of total nominal money balances, M, this condition can be formulated as

$$\mu - \pi = n.$$ (5)

That is, in the steady state the rate of change of prices equals the rate of change of the nominal money supply, corrected for the rate of increase of output. Note that this is *not* a statement of the quantity theory, but simply part of the definition of the steady state. Correspondingly, whether or not the quantity theory holds in this model in the long run depends on whether or not it converges to the steady state. In this paper we shall assume that this convergence does indeed take place.

In what follows we shall be interested only in the steady states of the economy as just defined. More specifically, we shall be concerned with the effect of a change in μ on the values of k and m in this state.

Consider now the commodity market. Instead of describing the equilibrium condition in this market by $S = I$ (as in the preceding section), let us do so by the equivalent condition $E = Y$, where E is the aggregate real demand for consumption and investment commodities combined. For simplicity, assume that this demand is a certain proportion, α, of total real income, Y. Assume further that this proportion depends inversely on the rate of interest and directly on the ratio of real money balances to physical capital. The second relation is a type of real-balance effect,[7] reflecting the assumption that the greater the ratio of real money balances to physical capital in the portfolios of individuals, the more they will tend (for any given level of income) to shift out of money and into commodities. With reference to the first relation, assume—as in the Fisherine analysis of the preceding section—that both investment and saving (and hence consumption) are affected only by the real rate of interest, and not the money rate. The equilibrium condition in

[2]Cf. above, pp. 155–157.

the commodity market is then represented by

$$\alpha\left(i - \pi, \frac{M/p}{K}\right)\cdot Y = Y, \tag{6}$$

where use has been made of equation (1). By assumption, $\alpha_1(\ )$ is negative and $\alpha_2(\ )$ positive, where $\alpha_1\ (\alpha_2)$ is the partial derivative of $\alpha(\ )$ with respect to its first (second) argument.

Let us now turn to the money market. Following Tobin,[8] let us assume that the demand in this market depends on the volume of physical capital and on the rate of interest. More specifically, assume that the demand for money is a certain proportion, λ, of physical capital, K. Thus the larger K, the greater (other things equal) the total portfolio of the individuals and hence the greater the demand for money: this can be designated as the scale effect of the portfolio. Assume further that the proportion λ depends inversely on the rate of interest. That is, the higher the rate of interest, the smaller the proportion of money relative to physical capital which individuals wish to hold in their portfolios: this can be designated as the composition effect. What must now be emphasized is that the rate of interest relevant for this effect is the money one. For the alternative cost of holding money instead of a bond is precisely this rate. The same is true if we measure this cost in terms of the alternative of holding physical capital: for the total yield on this capital is its marginal product (equal in equilibrium to the real rate of interest) *plus* the capital gain generated by the price change (π): that is, it is $r + \pi = i$. Alternatively, if we measure rates of return in real terms, the rate of return on money balances is $-\pi$ and that on physical capital r; hence the cost of holding money is the difference between these two rates, or $r - (-\pi) = i$. Thus we can write our equilibrium condition in the money market as

$$\lambda\ (i)\cdot K = \frac{M}{p}, \tag{7}$$

where by assumption the derivative $\lambda'(\ )$ is negative.

Dividing equations (6) and (7) through by Y and K, respectively—and transforming them into per capita form—we then obtain the system of equations.

$$\alpha\left(i - \pi, \frac{m}{k}\right) = 1 \tag{8}$$

$$\lambda(i) = \frac{m}{k}. \tag{9}$$

Now, in steady states there is—by (5)—a one-to-one correspondence between μ and π; indeed, they differ only by the constant n, representing the

[8] James Tobin, "Money and Economic Growth," *Econometrica*, XXXIII (1965), 679. See also Miguel Sidrauski, "Inflation and Economic Growth," *Journal of Political Economy*, LXXV (1967), 798–799.

rate of growth. Hence since μ is assumed to be exogenously determined, the same can be said for π. Thus—in steady states—equations (8)–(9) can be considered as a system of two equations in the two endogenous variables i and m/k, and in the exogenous variable π. Assuming solubility of these equations, the specific value of k (and hence m) can then be determined by making use of the additional equilibrium condition that the marginal productivity of capital equals the real rate of interest, or,

$$f'(k) = i - \pi. \tag{10}$$

In accordance with the usual assumption of diminishing marginal productivity, we also have

$$f'(k) < 0. \tag{11}$$

The solution of system (8)–(9) can be presented diagrammatically in terms of Figure 10.2. The curve CC represents the locus of points of equilibrium in the commodity market for a given value of π. Its positive slope reflects the assumption made above about the respective influences of the real rate of interest $(i - \pi)$ and of the real-balance effect (as represented by m/k) on α. Namely, a (say) increase in i increases the real rate of interest and thus tends to decrease α: hence the ratio m/k must increase in order to generate a compensating increase in α and thus restore equilibrium to the commodity market. On the other hand, LL—the locus of points of equilibrium in the money market—must be negatively sloped: an increase in the supply of money and hence in m/k must be offset by a corresponding increase in the demand for money, which means that i must decline. The intersection of the two curves at W thus determines the steady-state position of the economy.

Assume for simplicity that the given value of π for which CC and LL are drawn is $\pi = \pi_2 > 0$, corresponding to the rate of monetary expansion μ_2. Assume now that this rate is exogenously increased to $\mu = \mu_3$, so

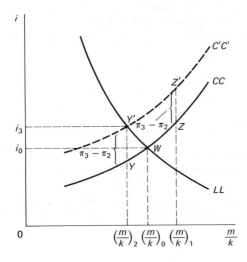

Figure 10.2.

that [by (5)] the steady-state value of π is increased accordingly to $\pi_3 = \mu_3 - n > \pi_2$. How does this affect the steady-state position in Figure 10.2?

From the fact that π does not appear in (9), it is clear that LL remains invariant under the foregoing change. On the other hand, by the same argument made above in connection with Figure 10.1, it can be shown that the curve CC must shift upwards—in a parallel fashion—by the distance $\pi_3 - \pi_2$: for at (say) the point Z' on the curve $C'C'$ so constructed, the money/capital ratio m/k and the real rate of interest $i - \pi$ are the same as they were at point Z on the original curve CC; hence Z' too must be a position of equilibrium.

We can therefore conclude from Figure 10.2 that the increase in the rate of monetary expansion (and hence rate of price increase) shifts the steady-state position of the economy from W to Y'. From the construction of $C'C'$ it is also clear that the real rate of interest at Y' is $r_3 = i_3 - \pi_3$, which is less than the real rate at W, namely, $r_0 = i_0 - \pi_2$. Thus the policy of increasing the rate of inflation decreases the steady-state value of the real rate of interest, and also the money/capital ratio.

Because of the diminishing marginal productivity of capital [see equation (11) above], the decline in r implies that k has increased. Thus the fact that m/k has declined does not necessarily imply that m has declined. This indeterminacy reflects the two opposing influences operating on m which are reflected in equation (7), rewritten here in the per-capita form as

$$\lambda(i) \cdot k = m. \tag{12}$$

To use the terminology indicated above (p. 199), the increased inflation increases the steady-state stock of physical capital, and thus exerts a positive portfolio-scale effect on the quantity of real-money balances demanded. At the same time, the increased inflation means that the alternative cost of holding money balances (for a given level of k and hence r) has increased, and this exerts a negative portfolio-composition effect on the demand for these balances; that is, individuals will tend to shift out of money and into capital. Thus the final effect on m depends on the relative strength of these two forces. In any event, it is clear that even if m should increase, it must do so proportionately less than k.

Note that the only exogenous variable which appears in system (8)–(10) is the rate of change of the money supply, as represented by $\pi = \mu - n$. In contrast, the absolute quantity of money, M, does not appear. It follows that once-and-for-all changes in M will not affect the steady-state values of m, k, and i as determined by the foregoing system for a given value of π.

Thus system (8)–(10) continues to reflect the neoclassical property of being neutral (insofar as the value of the real variables are concerned) with respect to once-and-for-all changes in M. On the other hand, because of the Keynesian-like interdependence between the commodity and money markets, it is not neutral with respect to changes in μ.

Note that in the absence of this interdependence, the system would be neutral (at least insofar as the steady-state value of k is concerned) with respect to changes in μ as well. This would be the case either if the demand for commodities depended only on the real rate of interest, and not on m/k; or if the demand for money depended only on k, and not on the money rate of interest.

The first of these cases is analogous to the dichotomized case of stationary macroeconomic models.[9] It would be represented in Figure 10.2 by a CC curve which was horizontal to the abscissa. Correspondingly, the upward shift generated by the rate of inflation would cause the new CC curve to intersect the unchanged LL curve at a money rate of interest which was $\pi_3 - \pi_2$ greater than the original one, and hence a real rate of interest (and hence value of k) which was unchanged. The second of these cases would be represented in Figure 10.2 by a vertical LL curve. Hence the upward parallel shift in the CC curve generated by inflation would once again shift the intersection point to one which represented an unchanged real rate of interest. Note that full neutrality with respect to the change in μ—that is, neutrality with respect to all the real variables—exists only in this second case. For in the first case there is a decrease in the steady-state value of m/k—and hence of m.

We might finally note that the ease with which the results of this section have been reached stems from the crucial assumption[10] that behavior in the commodity market is influenced only by real rate of interest, while that in the money market is influenced only by the money rate. The definiteness of the results would be lost if we were to make the more general assumption that both markets were influenced by both rates of return.

3. THE TRANSITION PERIOD

We have so far restricted ourselves to a comparison of stationary states. Let us now describe diagrammatically the manner in which the economy moves from one such state to another. Figure 10.3 depicts the situation analyzed in Figure 10.2, in which the nominal money supply is initially (i.e., until time t_0) increasing at the rate μ_2, and the price level at the rate $\pi_2 = \mu_2 - n$. The vertical difference between the two curves over this range thus represents the initial steady-state level of per capita real money balances, m_2. At time t_0 the rate of expansion of the money supply is increased to μ_3. Assume that the economy reaches a new steady-state position at time t_1, and that per capita real money balances in this state are less than they were in the original one. This is reflected by the fact that the vertical distance between the two curves is now log m_3, which is less than log m_2. It is clear from Figure 10.3 that in order to achieve such a lowering of real balances, the price level during the transition period $t_0 - t_1$ must have increased at a rate greater than $\pi_3 = \mu_3 - n$, which is the rate prevailing in the new steady state. This greater rate of increase can be interpreted as reflecting the operation of the real-balance effect during the transition period, stemming from the fact that the

---

[9] Cf. my *Money, Interest, and Prices, op. cit.*, 242, 251 (note 19), and 297–298. See also the discussion of a dichotomized growth model, *ibid.*, pp. 362–363.

[10] Due to Mundell; see note 1 above.

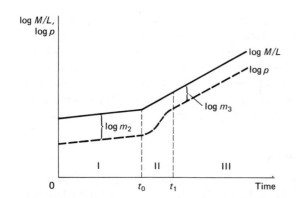

Figure 10.3.

value of $\dfrac{M/p}{K}$ —or, equivalently, m/k in equation (6)—is above its optimum level throughout this period.

It might be noted that instead of the curve log (M/L) in Figure 10.3 we could alternatively draw a curve representing log (M/Y). Since in the steady state L and Y grow at the same rate, n, these two curves (in the regions I and III, referring to the steady states) have respectively the same slope. In the case of curve log (M/Y), however, the vertical distance between it and the curve log p represents the inverse of the velocity of circulation—or the Cambridge K.[11] Correspondingly, the narrowing of the distance between the two curves in region III, as compared with I, would represent the increase in the velocity of circulation which, by assumption, is generated by the increased rate of inflation.

It is also instructive to compare the situation in Figure 10.3 with the one which would obtain if instead of a change in μ at point t_0 there were to take place a once-and-for-all change in the nominal quantity of M, with the subsequent rate of expansion of the money supply remaining unchanged. As

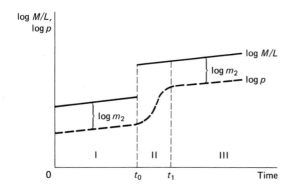

Figure 10.4.

[11] From the Cambridge equation $M = KPY$, we have log $K = \log (M/Y) - \log P$.

shown above (p. 201), this does not affect the steady-state values of the real variables of the system. This conclusion is represented by Figure 10.4. Except for the discontinuity at time t_0, the slope of the curve log (M/L) in this diagram remains unchanged. Similarly, the slope of log p in the new steady state (region III) is the same as in the original one (region I). Finally, and most important, the vertical distance between the respective curves in these two regions—representing per capita real balances, m—is also unchanged.

4. CONCLUDING REMARKS

The main purpose of this paper has been to analyze the effect of monetary policy on growth within a simple Keynesian-like model. It is hoped that placing the analysis within such a familiar framework will lend an intuitive appeal to the conclusions reached. But this objective has been attained at the price of significant oversimplification. Thus the production function—a basic ingredient of any growth model—has been left in the background. Similarly, no attempt has been made to examine the stability of the system. Finally, I have not really explained how the increased quantity of money is injected into the system and the effect that such an injection has on the disposable incomes of individuals. These questions are dealt with in the next essay.

11

The Role
of Money
in a Simple
Growth Model[1]

Increasing attention has been devoted in the recent literature to the role of money in growth models. In Part I of this paper we shall summarize Tobin's basic analysis of this question.[2] We shall then show that this analysis is deficient in that it does not really assign a meaningful role to money—either

Written jointly with David Levhari. Reprinted by permission from American Economic Review, *LVIII (1968), 713–753.*

[1] The authors wish to express their indebtedness for helpful suggestions and criticisms of earlier drafts of this paper made at seminars and workshops at the Hebrew University, M.I.T., University of Illinois, and University of Chicago. They have also benefited greatly from the criticisms and suggestions of Yigal Greif, Miguel Sidrauski, Jerome Stein, and an anonymous referee.

The authors are also indebted to the Israel Academy of Sciences and Humanities for a research grant for technical assistance.

The work on this paper was completed when I was visiting at M.I.T., under a grant from the National Science Foundation (NSF Grant GS 1812).

[2] James Tobin, "Money and Economic Growth," *Econometrica*, XXXIII (1965), 671–684; and "The Neutrality of Money in Growth Models: A Comment," *Economica*, XXXIV (1967), 69–72. Other contributions to this question have been made by Alain C. Enthoven, "A Neo-classical Model of Money, Debt, and Economic Growth," Mathematical Appendix to J. G. Gurley and E. S. Shaw, *Money in a Theory of Finance* (Washington, D.C., 1960); A. L. Marty, "Gurley and Shaw on Money in a Theory of Finance," *Journal of Political Economy*, LXIX (1961), 56–62; Don Patinkin, *Money, Interest, and Prices*, 2nd ed. (New York, 1965), Chapter XIV:5; Jerome L. Stein, "Money and Capacity Growth," *Journal of Political Economy*, LXXIV (1966), 451–465; and H. G. Johnson, "The Neo-Classical One-Sector Growth Model: A Geometrical Exposition and Extension to a Monetary Economy," *Economica*, XXXIII (1966), 265–287; *idem*, "The Neutrality of Money in Growth Models: A Reply," *Economica*, XXXIV (1967), 73–74. The authors have also benefited from reading in mimeographed form Miguel Sidrauski's doctoral thesis, which has since been summarized in Miguel Sidrauski, "Rational Choice and Patterns of Growth in a Monetary Economy," *American Economic Review (Proceedings)*, LVII (1967), 534–544, as well as a paper of his which has since appeared as "Inflation and Economic Growth," *Journal of Political Economy*, LXXV (1967), 796–810. See also R. A. Mundell, "Inflation and Real Interest," *Journal of Political Economy*, LXXI (1963), 280–283, and "A Fallacy in the Interpretation of Macroeconomic Equilibrium," *Journal of Political Economy*, LXXIII (1965), 61–66.

as a consumer's or a producer's good. Parts II and III of the article then analyze models in which money is assumed to fulfill these respective functions. Part IV presents some concluding observations.

Our main concern in this paper will be with comparative dynamics: that is, with the analysis of the effects of different monetary policies on the steady-state or long-run-equilibrium properties of the model. We shall also briefly discuss the stability properties of the model, though only under additional simplifying assumptions.

I. THE TOBIN ANALYSIS[3]

1. Consider a Solow[4] growth model with a linearly homogeneous production function $Y = F(K, L)$, where Y, K, and L respectively represent net output, capital, and (effective) labor. Dividing the production function through by L yields the per capita or intensive form $y = f(k)$, where $y = Y/L$ and $k = K/L$. As usual, assume that the marginal product of capital is positive and diminishing; i.e., $f'(k) > 0$ and $f''(k) < 0$. Assume also that the (effective) quantity of labor grows exogenously at the constant per period rate of n.

Into this model Tobin introduces a government which spends a fixed proportion of the national income, and which finances this expenditure either by levying taxes or by printing money. For the purpose at hand, this is analytically equivalent to the simpler assumption (which we shall now use) that the sole function of the government is to issue paper money which it injects into the economy by means of transfer payments—or withdraws by means of taxes. These payments (or taxes) are assumed to be independent of the individual's holdings of money—so that they do not affect his decisions with respect to the level of these holdings. Note that, by definition, this money is of the outside type: that is, it represents the debt of a unit external to the private sector of the economy, and hence a net asset of this sector. We shall also assume that there are no direct storage costs of holding money. Similarly, as long as we deal with outside money, we shall assume that there are no costs of administering the monetary system.

The major path through which money affects the workings of the economy in the Tobin model is through its effect on the real disposable income which determines the consumption (or, equivalently, savings) behavior of the individuals. According to Tobin, this disposable income is now

$$Y_D = Y + \frac{d\left(\frac{M}{p}\right)}{dt} = Y + \frac{M}{p}(\mu - \pi),\tag{1}$$

---

[3] We make use here of Johnson's convenient presentation of the Tobin analysis in terms of an adapted Solow model. It should, however, be noted that—as Tobin (*op. cit.*, 1967) has already shown, and Johnson acknowledged (*op. cit.*, 1967)—Johnson's main conclusion, that money is neutral in the Tobin model, is incorrect; see note 17 below.

[4] Robert M. Solow, "A Contribution to the Theory of Economic Growth," *Quarterly Journal of Economics*, LXX (1956), 65–94.

where M represents the quantity of money supplied (and hence existing) in the system, p the price level, $\mu = \dot{M}/M$ the rate of change of the money supply, and $\pi = \dot{p}/p$ the rate of change of the price level. Thus real disposable income in this model is defined as real net national income (Y) *plus* the real value of the increase in the nominal quantity of money ($\mu M/p$—which in turn represents the real value of the transfer payments actually made by the government) *less* the decrease in the real value of existing cash balances caused by a price increase $[\pi(M/p)]$.

Note that in order to maintain consistency of the national accounts in real terms, this definition of real disposable income makes it necessary to define the real deficit of the government as also equal to $\mu(M/P) - \pi(M/p)$; for only then will it be true that (in real terms) savings = investment + government deficit. This means that, for example, the government will be recorded as incurring a real deficit even if it does not issue new money, but instead experiences an increase in the real value of its outstanding debt in the form of money as a result of a price decline.

The model just described has two assets—physical capital and real money balances. The rates of return on these assets are $r = \partial F(K, L)/\partial K = f'(k)$ and (by the assumption of zero storage costs) $-\pi$, respectively, where r is the real rate of interest, equal to the marginal productivity of capital, and $-\pi$ is the rate of decrease of the price level.[5] In accordance with the usual approach of monetary theory, we shall also assume that there exist "market frictions" and/or uncertainties with respect to the timing of payments which generally cause individuals to hold a portfolio which consists of both of these assets. In deciding on the optimum composition of this portfolio, the individual is actually concerned with the *anticipated* rates of return from the two assets. For simplicity, however, we shall assume that these are always equal to the *existing* rates. In view of the greater liquidity of money balances, it then follows that equilibrium cannot prevail unless the yield from these balances is less than that on physical capital; i.e., $-\pi < r$.

---

[5]Note that $-\pi$ is the rate of return per unit of time on a unit of *real* money balances. For consider an individual holding a given nominal quantity of money. The increase in his wealth generated by a price change is

$$d\left(\frac{M}{p}\right) = -\frac{M}{p^2}\,dp.$$

The corresponding increase in his wealth per unit of time (i.e., the increase in his income) is

$$\frac{d\left(\frac{M}{p}\right)}{dt} = -\frac{M}{p^2}\frac{dp}{dt} = -\frac{M}{p}\pi.$$

Hence the increase per unit of real money balances (i.e., the rate of return on real balances) is

$$\frac{\dfrac{d\left(\frac{M}{p}\right)}{dt}}{\dfrac{M}{p}} = -\pi.$$

2.   Assume now that individuals save a certain proportion, s, of their disposable incomes. Assume also that they hold a certain proportion, λ, of the national income, Y, in the form of real money balances (actually, Tobin assumes that the relevant variable here is physical capital, K; this difference does not, however, affect the nature of the steady-state path); and that this proportion is inversely dependent on the anticipated alternative cost of holding these balances: i.e., on the difference between what could have been earned from the holding of a unit of physical capital and what will be earned from the holding of real money balances. By our assumption that anticipated and actual rates of return are equal, this cost is $r - (-\pi) = r + \pi$, or Fisher's money rate of interest. Thus we assume that $\lambda = \lambda(r + \pi)$, where $\lambda'(\ )$ is assumed negative. As noted above, in any equilibrium situation we must have $-\pi < r$, which means that the money rate of interest must be positive.

The Tobin model is thus one in which the rate of capital accumulation is

$$\dot{K} = F(K, L) - (1 - s)\left[F(K, L) + \frac{M}{p}(\mu - \pi)\right], \qquad (2)$$

where the second term on the right-hand side represents the amount of commodities consumed. Under the assumption that the demand for real money balances

$$\frac{M^d}{p} = \lambda F(K, L) \qquad (3)$$

is always equal to the supply M/p (an equality which we shall assume to be maintained by the instantaneous adjustment of the price level), Tobin shows that the steady-state value of the capital-labor ratio, k, of this model is determined by the condition

$$[s - (1 - s)\lambda n]f(k) = nk.^{6} \qquad (4)$$

In terms of Figure 11.1, the equilibrium value of k is determined by the intersection of the solid curve with the ray nk at k_0. Since s is less than unity, this is necessarily less than the equilibrium ratio k_1 that would be determined by the intersection of $sf(k)$ with nk in the usual Solow barter model. [For the moment, the dotted curve $\sigma f(k)$ should be ignored.] In Tobin's words, "equilibrium capital intensity is lower in the monetary model."[7]

On further reflection, however, this conclusion seems unreasonable. For if the sole result of introducing money into an economy were to reduce k and hence per capita output and consumption, why should it be introduced? Where are the vaunted advantages of a monetary economy?

This paradox leads us to the observation that though equation (3) does

[6]This is equation (9) in Tobin (*op. cit.*, 1967). Its derivation and interpretation will become clear from the discussion in Part II below; see especially note 17. Tobin also uses this equation to show that an increase in the rate of inflation increases the equilibrium value of k; this, too, will be discussed below.

[7]*Ibid.*, p. 71.

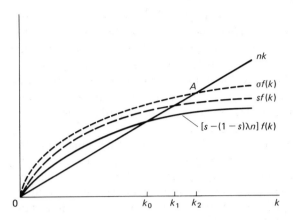

Figure 11.1.

describe a positive demand for real money balances, the preceding model does not really provide a rationale for the holding of these balances. For such a rationale must interpret money balances either as a consumer's good or as a producer's good.[8] In the first case, the services rendered by money balances should appear in the individual's utility function and hence in his (imputed) disposable income; whereas in the second they should reflect themselves in the production function. Neither of these approaches, however, is reflected in the preceding model. For on the one hand, its production function is the same as that of a barter economy; while on the other, its definition of disposable income includes only the actual increase in the real value of cash balances, not the imputed value of their liquidity services. Thus the foregoing model is not really consistent with the existence of money.

II. MONEY AS A CONSUMER'S GOOD

3. Let us now see how these difficulties are obviated by treating money as a consumer's good. Conceptually, this means that money enters the utility function and its imputed services are included in disposable income. In accordance with the principles of welfare economics, these services must clearly be valued at the alternative cost at the margin of holding money balances which, as shown in the preceding section, is the money rate of interest, or $r + \pi$. The relevant definition of disposable income is then

$$
\begin{aligned}
Y_D &= Y + \frac{M}{p}(\mu - \pi) + \frac{M}{p}(r + \pi) \\
&= Y + \frac{M}{p}(\mu + r),
\end{aligned}
\tag{5}
$$

---

[8] Cf. Patinkin, *op. cit.*, pp. 146–147. An attempt to clothe this somewhat formalistic statement with more economic meaning is provided (*ibid.*, pp. 79–80, 117–119, 147–148, and 154). Cf. also the beginning of Section 10 below.

where once again M/p represents the real quantity of money in the system.[9] Thus real disposable income is defined as net national income (Y) *plus* the real value of the increase in the nominal quantity of money ($\mu \, M/p$) *plus* the imputed real interest on real money balances $[r(M/p)]$. Thus in contrast with (1), the decrease in the real value of money balances caused by a price increase $[\pi(M/p)]$ does not appear as a deduction from disposable income; for it is offset by the fact that $\pi(M/p)$ also represents part of the imputed income from the holding of real balances.

It should be noted that a critical role in this offsetting is played by the assumption that the anticipated rate of price change (which is one of the components by which we value the liquidity services of the money balances) equals the actual rate (by which we measure the decrease in the real value of these balances). This also provides a key to an intuitive understanding of the offsetting. In brief, the quantity of real balances which the individual holds is, by assumption, the outcome of a decision made under the certain knowledge that prices will increase at the rate π; hence the advantages of holding such balances must at least offset the loss generated by the price change. Alternatively, we can say that, in an economy in which everyone foresees with certainty a given price change and adjusts his money holdings accordingly, such a price change cannot—by definition—be said to generate the "capital losses" on these holdings which are assumed by the definition of disposable income presented in equation (1).[10]

Another point that should be made with reference to the foregoing definition of disposable income (and the one of the preceding section as well) is that they treat the increase in real cash balances as part of income; in principle, however, it should be treated as an increase in wealth, which in-

[9]This definition has recently been criticized by Johnson on the grounds that it leads to the allegedly paradoxical result that if the money rate of interest is zero, money balances will be at their satiety level—but real income "from this source" will then be zero [H. G. Johnson, *Essays in Monetary Economics* (Cambridge, 1967), p. 171, footnote 1]. This, however, is simply a specific instance of Adam Smith's "water-diamond paradox"—arising, as is well known, from the difference between marginal and total utility. Correspondingly, if Johnson's "paradox" should lead us to measure the contribution of liquidity services to real national income by the area under the demand curve (as suggested in *ibid.*), it should lead to a similar procedure with respect to water—or, for that matter, any other good.

At the same time it should be noted (as has been indicated in a discussion of this paper by Jürg Niehans at the Conference on Money and Economic Growth which took place at Brown University in June 1968) that what we have called here "real income" is not the "real income" relevant for considerations of welfare economics in a world in which money enters the utility function; not because of the marginal evaluation of liquidity services, but because this definition measures "real income" only in terms of physical commodities, instead of in terms of an initial optimum basket consisting of both commodities and liquidity services. Correspondingly if by an appropriate quantity index we were to measure "real income" in terms of the number of such baskets that individuals can acquire, it would always be true that larger holdings of real balances would, *ceteris paribus*, imply a higher level of real income (but see below, Section 9).

These considerations do not invalidate the definition of real income adopted here; but they do preclude our interpreting the "income effect" of the resulting functions in terms of the Slutzky (or Hicks) income effect.

[10]All this is analogous to the familiar conclusion of demand theory that if an individual comes to market with a basket of goods which is an optimum one at the prevailing prices, then a change in these prices will generate a substitution effect, but not an income effect.

creases disposable income only by the permanent income stream which corresponds to it.[11] As has, however, already been noted, our major concern in this paper is with the steady-state growth path; and, as we shall see, the quantity of real cash balances along such a path increases at a constant rate per period; correspondingly, we can properly treat the increase during any given period as part of the income of that period. On the other hand, this definition is not, strictly speaking, valid for positions off the growth path and, in particular, for the stability analysis of this path. But we shall not deal with these complications here.

Let us now revise model (2)–(3) in the light of these considerations. Total consumption will now be represented by $(1 - s) [F(K, L) + (M/p) (\mu + r)]$. But what should now be deducted from total commodity output in order to obtain investment in commodities is not *total* consumption, but *physical* consumption—which is the term we shall use (for want of a better one) to denote all consumption, except that of liquidity services. Thus condition (2) above is replaced by

$$\dot{K} = F(K, L) - \left\{ (1 - s) \left[F(K, L) + \frac{M}{p} (\mu + r) \right] - \frac{M}{p} (r + \pi) \right\}, \quad (6)$$

where once again we have made use of the assumption that the price level instantaneously adjusts itself so as to equate the demand and supply for real balances; that is,

$$\frac{M^d}{p} = \lambda F(K, L) = \frac{M}{p}. \quad (7)$$

It should be noted that the *desired* level of physical consumption, C_P, should be represented not by the second term on the right-hand side of (6), but by

$$C_P = (1 - s) \left[F(K, L) + \frac{M}{p} (\mu + r) \right] - \frac{M^d}{p} (r + \pi). \quad (8)$$

That is, in measuring the disposable income which determines desired total consumption, the relevant quantities are the volume of transfer payments *actually* received by individuals (viz., $\mu M/p$), and the imputed income from the real balances *actually* held (viz., rM/p); for whether or not the latter balances are at their desired level, the individual can always consider them as convertible into physical capital yielding the (for him) given rate of return r. On the other hand, in determining the desired level of physical consumption, it is the amount of liquidity services which individuals *desire* to consume which is the relevant deduction from total *desired* consumption. Thus the form of (6) depends on assumption (7) that actual and desired quantities are equal.

[11] Cf. Patinkin, *op. cit.*, pp. 658–659.

We can also see from (8) that the real-balance effect on C_p—that is, the effect on this consumption of an exogenous increase in the amount of real balances actually held by individuals—is determined by differentiating (8) partially with respect to M/p, keeping all other variables (K, L, μ, π, r—and hence M^d) constant. Thus the real-balance effect implicit in (8) is $\partial C_p/\partial (M/p)$ $= (1 - s)(\mu + r)$.

Two further observations might be made about model (6)–(7). First, in contrast with model (2)–(3), even in the extreme case of a stationary economy in which $\mu = \pi = 0$, real balances would continue to appear in the definition of income. Indeed, the real-balance effect in (8)—properly modified—would then stem from the term $(1 - s)r(M/p)$, which is also one of the ways in which the effect can be represented in short-run Keynesian models.[12] From this it is clear that the influence of $(M/p)(\mu - \pi)$ on consumption in equation (2)—or of $\mu(M/p)$ in equation (6) or (8)—cannot be identified with the real-balance or Pigou effect in the usual sense of the term.

Second, it would be more consistent with general considerations of economic theory if the demands for both consumption commodities and money balances were represented as depending upon disposable income as defined by (5). This, however, would greatly complicate the comparative-dynamic analysis which follows, so that we continue to use the simpler equation (7). Note that this observation is equally relevant for the Tobin model.

4.   Let us now consider the steady-state—or long-run-equilibrium—growth properties of model (6)–(7). Assume that the effective labor supply and the nominal quantity of money grow, respectively, at the constant rates n and μ, where μ (though not n) can be negative. Define the steady-state growth path of the system as one in which both per capita physical capital and per capita real money balances (to be denoted by m) are constant—and assume that such a path exists and that the system converges to it.

From the constancy of $k = K/L$ along the steady-state path, it follows that

$$\frac{\dot{k}}{k} = \frac{\dot{K}}{K} - \frac{\dot{L}}{L} = \frac{\dot{K}}{K} - n = 0. \tag{9}$$

Similarly, the constancy of $m = M/pL$ implies

$$\frac{\dot{m}}{m} = \frac{\dot{M}}{M} - \frac{\dot{p}}{p} - \frac{\dot{L}}{L} = \mu - \pi - n = 0.^{13} \tag{10}$$

---

[12] *Ibid.*

[13] Even though this equation equates the rate of increase of the price level with the rate of increase of the quantity of money (net of the rate of increase of output), it should not be interpreted as an expression of the quantity theory. For equation (10) does not depend on the behavior functions of the model, but is simply part of the definition of the steady state. Correspondingly, the long-run validity of the quantity theory in the model can be established only by showing that its behavior functions are such that it does indeed converge to a steady state.

Thus total physical capital and total real money balances both expand at the constant rate n along the path. It is also clear from (10) that π is constant along the path. Similarly, from the fact that $r = f'(k)$ it is clear that the real rate of interest is constant.

Let us now determine the steady-state value of k. Substituting from (7) into (6), dividing through by K, and collecting terms we obtain

$$\frac{F(K,L)}{K}\{\lambda n - s[1 + \lambda(n + \pi + r)]\} + n = 0, \tag{11}$$

where use has been made of (9) and (10). Dividing numerator and denominator of the first term by L and transposing them yields the steady-state condition that must be satisfied by k,

$$\{s[1 + \lambda(n + \pi + r)] - \lambda n\}f(k) = nk. \tag{12}$$

The coefficient of $f(k)$ in this equation can be given a straightforward economic interpretation. As Tobin has emphasized, the distinguishing feature of a money economy in a growth context is that not all of savings (S) need be devoted to augmenting the stock of physical capital; instead some can be devoted to the accumulation of real money balances. That is, if savings devoted to the capital stock—or "physical savings"—are denoted by S_P, we have

$$S_P = S - \frac{d\left(\frac{M}{P}\right)}{dt}, \tag{13}$$

which in our model can be rewritten as

$$S_P = s\left[Y + \frac{M}{P}(\mu + r)\right] - \frac{M}{P}(\mu - \pi).^{14} \tag{14}$$

In the steady state, this becomes

$$S_P = sY[1 + \lambda(n + \pi + r)] - \lambda Yn, \tag{15}$$

where once again use has been made of (7), (9), and (10). Correspondingly, what we shall define as the "physical savings ratio" is

$$\sigma = \frac{S_P}{Y} = s[1 + \lambda(n + \pi + r)] - \lambda n, \tag{16}$$

which is seen to be the coefficient of $f(k)$.

---

[14] As the reader can verify, this result can also be obtained from the alternative definition

$$S_P = Y - C_P,$$

where C_P represents physical consumption; i.e., consumption exclusive of that of the services of money balances.

It is clear from this definition that even in the case where the overall savings ratio s is constant, σ is not: for it depends on λ, which in turn depends on the money rate of interest $i = r + \pi = f'(k) + \pi$. Thus σ is a function of k and π; and this functional dependence exists a fortiori in the more general case that will concern us, in which s too is assumed to be a variable, directly dependent on the respective rates of return which can be earned on the two assets in which form savings are held. That is, we shall assume that

$$s = s[f'(k), -\pi] \qquad\qquad s_1 > 0 \quad s_2 > 0, \qquad (17)$$

where $s_1(s_2)$ represents the partial derivative of function (17) with respect to the first (second) argument. As we shall see in the next section, it is this dropping of the assumption of a constant s—rather than the differing definitions of disposable income—which causes our model to yield results which are qualitatively different from those of the Tobin model.

Thus the condition for steady-state growth in the present model is seen to be completely analogous to the one in the original Solow model: for equation (12) states that a steady state will exist when (in per capita terms) the amount of new physical capital provided by savers (as represented by the left-hand side) equals the amount of new physical capital necessary in order to maintain a constant capital-labor ratio (as represented by the right-hand side). From this interpretation it follows that if a steady state exists, then σ must be greater than zero: for since the labor supply is growing, there must be positive physical savings in order to maintain a constant capital-labor ratio.

It is also clear from (16) that σ is not necessarily less than s. Correspondingly, the dotted curve $\sigma f(k)$ in Figure 11.1 can intersect the ray nk rightwards of k_1. Thus unlike the situation in the Tobin model, the capital-labor ratio in the steady state of the monetary economy is not necessarily less than the barter one. And even when it is, this does not mean that the individuals in the economy are worse off; for they now derive utility from money balances as well as from physical consumption.

5.   Consider now the comparative-dynamic properties of the system. For this purpose let us first rewrite the steady-state condition (12) as

$$\frac{f(k)}{k} = a(k) = \frac{n}{\sigma(k,\pi)}, \qquad (18)$$

where $a(k)$ represents average output per unit of capital. As will be shown below (note 19), under certain assumptions as to the form of the production function, this equation has a unique strictly positive solution for k, as of any given value of π. The basic question which now concerns us is the effect on this solution of a change in the rate of monetary expansion μ. From (10) we see that in the steady state, μ and π differ only by the constant n. Hence the answer to our question can be determined by implicitly differentiating k with respect to π in equation (18).

Carrying out this differentiation, we obtain

$$a'(k)\frac{dk}{d\pi} = -\frac{n}{\sigma^2}\left(\sigma_k\frac{dk}{d\pi} + \sigma_\pi\right),$$ (19)

and therefore

$$\frac{dk}{d\pi} = \frac{\sigma_\pi}{-\dfrac{\sigma^2}{n}a'(k) - \sigma_k},$$ (20)

where σ_k and σ_π are the partial derivatives of σ with respect to k and π, respectively.

Under the assumption of a linearly homogeneous production function with positive marginal products for each factor, the average product $a(k)$ must be declining; that is, $a'(k) < 0$. The signs of σ_π and σ_k, however, cannot be specified a priori. For differentiating (16) partially, we obtain

$$\sigma_k = f''(k)\{s_1[1 + \lambda(n + \pi + r)] + s[\lambda'(n + \pi + r) + \lambda] - \lambda'n\}$$ (21a)

$$= s_1 f''(k)[1 + \lambda(n + \pi + r)] + \lambda s\left[1 + \frac{\lambda'}{\lambda}(\pi + r)\right]f''(k)$$ (21b)

$$- (1 - s)\lambda' f''(k)\,n$$

and

$$\sigma_\pi = -s_2[1 + \lambda(n + \pi + r)] + \lambda s\left[1 + \frac{\lambda'}{\lambda}(\pi + r)\right] - (1 - s)\lambda'n.$$ (22)

Consider now the signs of these expressions. By assumption, $0 < s < 1$, $s_1 > 0$, $s_2 > 0$, $f''(k) < 0$, $\lambda' < 0$, and $r + \pi$ (the money rate of interest) > 0. Hence each of the terms in (21b) is negative with the possible exception of the second one. Consider now the expression $(\lambda'/\lambda)(\pi + r)$. This is the partial elasticity of the demand function for real balances (7) with respect to the money rate of interest. In accordance with the findings of most empirical studies,[15] this can be assumed to be less than unity in absolute value. Hence σ_k can be assumed to be negative. On the other hand, even under the assumption of an inelastic demand, the sign of σ_π is indeterminate.

These results can be given a straightforward economic interpretation. An increase in k or π affects the physical-savings ratio in two ways: first, by changing the total savings corresponding to a given level of physical output (and this will be called the "overall-savings effect"); second, by

[15] Cf., e.g., the summary of such studies in R. Teigen, "Demand and Supply Functions for Money in the United States: Some Structural Estimates," *Econometrica*, XXXII (1964), 505. See also Frank de Leeuw, "A Model of Financial Behavior," in J. S. Duesenberry and others (eds.), *The Brookings Quarterly Econometric Model of the United States* (Chicago, 1965). p. 493; S. M. Goldfeld, *Commercial Bank Behavior and Economic Activity* (Amsterdam, 1966), pp. 77–78; and D. Laidler, "The Rate of Interest and the Demand for Money: Some Empirical Evidence," *Journal of Political Economy*, LXXIV (1966), 543–555.

changing the proportion of the two forms—physical capital and real money balances—in which these savings are held (and this will be called the "composition effect"). The overall-savings effect, in turn, is directly dependent on the changes in two factors: the overall-savings ratio and the level of imputed income from money balances. These two components of the overall-savings effect are respectively represented by the first two terms in (21b) and (22), whereas the composition effect is represented by the last term. (Note that the overall-savings and composition effects do not correspond to the wealth and substitution effects, respectively. For one component of the overall-savings effect is the change in s caused by a change in the rate of return, which thus reflects a substitution between present and future consumption.)

Thus the three terms of equation (21b) can be interpreted as follows: An increase in k reduces the real rate of interest $r = f'(k)$ and hence reduces the overall-savings ratio [i.e., $s_1 f''(k) < 0$]. Similarly, it reduces the money rate of interest and hence increases the holdings of real money balances, but (by the assumption of inelastic demand) less than proportionately, so that the imputed disposable income from these balances decreases [i.e., $(1 + \eta)f''(k) < 0$, where η is the elasticity of demand for money balances]. Hence the overall-savings effect is unequivocally negative. At the same time, the composition effect is also negative: for no matter what the elasticity of demand, the fact remains that the reduction in the money rate of interest has diverted a larger proportion of savings to the accumulation of real money balances [i.e., $- (1 - s)\lambda' f'' (k) < 0$]. Hence an increase in k necessarily decreases σ.

In contrast, the three terms of equation (22) imply that the effect of an increase in π cannot be specified a priori. For though the resulting increase in the money rate of interest generates a positive composition effect, the overall-savings effect is indeterminate. For on the one hand (assuming inelastic demand) the increased money rate of interest increases the imputed disposable income from money balances; but on the other, the increase in π means a decrease in the rate of return from money balances $- \pi$ and hence in the overall-savings ratio s.

Let us now summarize the implications of this discussion for equation (20). Most reasonably, this equation states that a change in π will affect the steady-state value of k if and only if it affects the physical savings ratio σ. Furthermore, if the demand for money balances is inelastic, then k will change in the same direction as σ: for then the denominator of (20) is positive, so that sign $dk/d\pi = $ sign σ_π. In the special case in which the overall-savings and composition effects of an increase in π exactly offset each other, $\sigma_\pi = 0$, so that k is not affected by a change in the rate of monetary expansion. If the composition effect should predominate, then σ_π is positive and hence so is $dk/d\pi$. The more insensitive the overall-savings ratio to changes in $- \pi$ (i.e. the smaller s_2), the more likely is this predominance to occur. Indeed, in the extreme case in which $s_2 = 0$ (and a fortiori in the case where s is constant with respect to both r and π), the overall-savings effect of an increase in π will reinforce the composition effect in causing k to increase.[16,17]

By making use of the correspondence principle, we can derive these results without making any direct assumptions about the elasticity of demand for money. For as will be shown in Section 7 below [see especially equation (33)], stability of the system implies that the denominator of (20) is positive. Hence if the system is stable, sign $dk/d\pi = $ sign σ_π.

In terms of Figure 11.1—and this will also be shown below—stability of the system implies that the curve $\sigma f(k)$ cuts the ray nk from above. Hence if an increase in the rate of monetary expansion (and hence π) should cause $\sigma f(k)$ to shift upwards at the initial equilibrium position A in Figure 11.1 [and this is the graphical meaning of $\sigma_\pi > 0$ in equation (20)], then the new point of intersection will be rightwards of A, which means that the long-run-equilibrium value of k will increase. Conversely, this value will decrease if the increase in π causes a downward shift in $\sigma f(k)$ in the neighborhood of point A.

It should now be emphasized that the foregoing analysis has been based on a savings function whose form has been postulated, and not derived from considerations of utility maximization. If, however, the latter (and surely preferable) approach is followed, and if the individual is assumed to maximize his utility over an infinite horizon at a constant rate of subjective time preference δ, then it can be shown[18] that the steady-state value of k is

---

[16] Note that the overall-savings effect will cause k to increase even if we assume that λ is constant, so that there is no composition effect. It is, however, somewhat inconsistent to assume that real balances are valued at the money rate of interest, while at the same time assuming that the demand for these balances is unaffected by this rate.

[17] The reader can readily verify that in the Tobin model of Section 2 above, equations (23), (21b), and (22) reduce respectively to

$$\sigma = s - (1 - s)\lambda n$$

[which is, of course, the coefficient of $f(k)$ in equation (4)],

$$\sigma_k = f''(k) \left[s_1(1 + \lambda n) - (1 - s)\lambda'n \right],$$

and

$$\sigma_\pi = - s_2(1 + \lambda n) - (1 - s)\lambda'n.$$

Here the sign of σ_k is unequivocally negative; but the sign of σ_π—and hence, by equation (20), of $dk/d\pi$—remains indeterminate. Thus the indeterminacy remains even with the Tobin definition of disposable income.

Actually, however, Tobin restricts his analysis to the case in which s is constant, and so concludes that $dk/d\pi$ is unequivocally positive (op. cit., 1967, pp. 70 and 71–72). This conclusion is also reached by Stein (op. cit., p. 461–463), though under somewhat different assumptions.

[18] See the excellent article by Sidrauski (op. cit., American Economic Review 1967). The utility function must satisfy some additional restrictions.

In connection with the following argument, note that the assumption of a constant δ is a very strong one, implying the existence of other invariances in the system as well. In particular, it implies that no matter what the form of the production function (assuming constant technology), the steady-state real rate of interest (though generally not the level of k) remains constant and equal to $\delta + n$. Similarly, it implies that a shift in liquidity preference which does not affect the rate of time discount will not affect the steady-state value of k, and hence will also leave the rate of interest invariant.

unaffected by a change in μ and hence π. This is the immediate consequence of the fact that under these assumptions the system cannot be in equilibrium unless the marginal productivity of capital equals the rate of time preference plus the rate of population growth; that is unless $f'(k) = \delta + n$. And for a given δ and n, this uniquely fixes k. This invariance of k would remain true even if δ were not constant, but depended on k. But it would not remain true if δ depended in some way on m—as would, for example, be the case if it depended on the ratio of wealth to disposable income. Nor, as we shall see at the end of Section 11 below, would it be true if money entered the production function.

We have so far concentrated our attention on the effect of an increase in the rate of monetary expansion on the steady-state capital-labor ratio. Let us now consider its effect on the corresponding money-labor ratio, or $m = M/pL$. For this purpose let us divide (7) through by L and rewrite it as

$$m = \lambda[f'(k) + \pi] \cdot f(k). \tag{23}$$

In the case in which $dk/d\pi < 0$, the effect of an increase in π is unequivocally negative; for it generates a decrease in both λ and $f(k)$, where the decrease in the former is caused by an increase in both components of the money rate of interest, $f'(k) + \pi$. If, however, $dk/d\pi > 0$, then the effect is indeterminate: for on the one hand $f(k)$ increases; whereas, on the other, because of the decline in $f'(k)$, there may be a net decrease in the money rate of interest, thus causing λ to increase. The nature of this indeterminacy can be seen more rigorously by differentiating (23) with respect to π to obtain

$$\frac{dm}{d\pi} = \lambda' \cdot [f''(k)\frac{dk}{d\pi} + 1] f(k) + \lambda f'(k)\frac{dk}{d\pi}. \tag{24}$$

The foregoing technique can also be used to analyze the effect of a shift in liquidity preference. For this purpose we assume that λ also depends directly on a taste parameter α. That is, $\lambda = \lambda [f'(k) + \pi, \alpha]$ where λ_1 (corresponding to λ' above) is again negative and λ_2 positive. From (16) it is then clear that the physical-savings ratio σ also depends on α, and that its partial derivative with respect to this variable is $\sigma_\alpha = [s(\pi + r) - (1 - s)n] \lambda_2$, whose sign is indeterminate. This indeterminacy reflects the fact that an increase in α will, *ceteris paribus*, increase money balances, hence the imputed income from these balances, and hence total savings; but at the same time it will increase the amount of these savings diverted to the accumulation of real balances.

It is clear from (10) that an increase in liquidity preference will not affect the steady-state value of π—for, by definition, it does not affect μ. Hence the effect of such an increase on the steady-state value of k can be obtained by replacing the denominator of equation (18) by $\sigma(k, \pi, \alpha)$, and implicitly differentiating this equation with respect to α, while keeping π constant. This yields an expression identical with equation (20), except for the replacement of $dk/d\pi$ and σ_π by $dk/d\alpha$ and σ_α, respectively. Thus the sign of $dk/d\alpha$ is indeterminate.

By using an argument analogous to that of equation (24), one can then show that $dm/d\alpha$ is indeterminate if $dk/d\alpha < 0$, and positive if $dk/d\alpha \geq 0$. Thus a priori one cannot even say whether an increase in liquidity preference will increase long-run-equilibrium real balances. Note that this indeterminacy holds in the Tobin model as well. For disregarding the imputed income from liquidity services only enables us to infer unequivocally that σ_α, and hence $dk/d\alpha$ are negative; but this decrease in k causes interest to rise and output to fall—thus tending to decrease the amount of money demanded. Hence, if this tendency is sufficiently strong, it can offset the initial rightward shift in the demand function for money caused by the increase in liquidity preference.

6. Even though the effect of a change in π on the steady-state value of k is indeterminate in the small, it can be shown that under the assumptions of the preceding section a sufficiently large decrease in π must decrease k.

The argument will be carried out with the aid of Figure 11.2. The curve EE represents the relation between the steady-state value of k and the rate of price change π as given by (18). The slope of this curve is represented as positive in some regions and negative in others, to reflect the indeterminacy which was shown to exist in the preceding section. If the production function has the "neo-neoclassical" form, then for each value of π there exists one nonzero steady-state value of k—and the curve EE has been drawn accordingly.[19]

Let us now also represent on the left-hand portion of the abscissa the real rate of interest, r. Under perfect competition this equals the marginal productivity of capital, which has been assumed to be a decreasing function of k. Accordingly, we can represent this function in the left-hand quadrant of Figure 11.2 by the upward-sloping curve QQ. Under the assumption about the form of the production function made in the preceding paragraph,

---

[19] The proof is as follows: Assume π constant at π_0 in steady-state condition (18) and form the function

$$\phi(k) = a(k) = \frac{n}{\sigma(k, \pi_0)}.$$

[Since $a(k) \equiv f(k)/k$, this function is defined only for $k \neq 0$.] The derivative of this function with respect to k is

$$\phi'(k) = a'(k) + \frac{n}{\sigma^2}\sigma_k.$$

Now, we have seen in the preceding section that both $a'(k)$ and (under the assumption of an interest-elastic demand for money) σ_k are negative; hence $\phi'(k)$ is negative. Hence $\phi(k)$ is monotonically decreasing, so that there can at most be one value of k for which the steady-state condition $\phi(k) = 0$ is satisfied. Under the assumption that the production function has the "neo-neoclassical" form, $a(0) = \infty$ and $a(\infty) = 0$; hence $\phi(0) > 0$ and $\phi(\infty) < 0$, so that a solution must exist.

In graphical terms this means that for every value of π a point of intersection A exists in Figure 11.1, and the curve $\sigma f(k)$—drawn as of the given value of π—must be above the ray nk leftwards of this point, and below it rightwards.

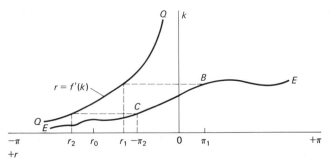

Figure 11.2.

$f'(0) = \infty$ and $f'(\infty) = 0$, so that the curve QQ approaches each of the axes asymptotically.

Now, as indicated in Section 2, in any equilibrium situation with zero storage costs of money—and a fortiori in the steady state—the yield on money, $-\pi$, must be less than the yield on physical capital, r; for otherwise liquidity considerations would cause everyone to shift out of the latter and into the former. This means that the steady-state level of k corresponding to any given value of $-\pi$ must have a marginal productivity greater than this value; in graphical terms, EE must be to the right of QQ. If we now make the further assumption that for every level of π there does indeed exist a steady-state value of k, then it follows that, as π approaches $-\infty$, the curve EE must also approach the horizontal axis asymptotically. Thus a sufficiently large price decline must necessarily cause a decrease in k.

This conclusion has implications for the possibility, discussed by Tobin, that the steady-state value of k might correspond to a marginal productivity and hence real rate of interest which lies below some minimum level (say, r_0) insisted upon by potential investors, while potential savers are quite willing to continue saving at this rate. In such a Keynesian situation (represented by point B in Figure 11.2) full employment could not prevail. But the preceding argument implies that the monetary authorities could always solve this unemployment problem by carrying out a sufficiently deflationary policy. Thus, for example, if they were to cause prices to decline at the rate π_2, the resulting decrease in k would raise the real rate to r_2, safely above the critical minimum.[20]

In brief—and in somewhat oversimplified terms—by carrying out a deflationary policy, the monetary authorities siphon off savings into the accumulation of real money balances; hence by choosing a deflation of the appropriate severity, they can leave an amount of savings for physical-capital accumulation which is consistent with the minimum rate of return (and hence maximum capital intensity) insisted upon by investors. If unemployment is caused by people "wanting the moon," then the monetary authorities can indeed provide them with the moon.

[20] Tobin, *op. cit.*, 1965, pp. 675, 680–681.

7.   We have until now assumed that the system converges to a steady state, i.e., that it is stable. Let us now examine this assumption. The general analysis of the problem yields complicated expressions which can be evaluated only by placing additional restrictions upon the system.[21] For simplicity, then, we shall limit our stability analysis to the case in which the monetary authorities decide upon a constant rate of price change, π_0, that they wish always to maintain (i.e., out of the steady state as well), and carry out this policy by making continuous adjustments in the rate of change of the money supply.[22] From the logarithmic differentiation of the money excess-demand equation (7) we have

$$\frac{\dot{\lambda}}{\lambda} + \frac{\dot{Y}}{Y} = \mu - \pi; \tag{25}$$

hence the foregoing policy requires that the rate of change of the money supply at any instant of time be

$$\mu = \pi_0 + \frac{\dot{\lambda}}{\lambda} + \frac{\dot{Y}}{Y} = \pi_0 + \frac{\lambda f''(k)\dot{k}}{\lambda} + \frac{f'(k)\dot{k}}{f(k)} + n. \tag{26}$$

In the steady state $\dot{k} = 0$, so that the necessary rate is constant at $\mu = \pi_0 + n$, as in (10).

   In order to analyze the stability of the system under this assumption we substitute from (7) into (6) (again reflecting the assumption that the equilibrium condition in the money market is always satisfied), divide through by K, and rearrange terms to yield the differential equation

$$\frac{\dot{K}}{K} = \frac{\dot{k}}{k} + n = \frac{f(k)}{k}\{s[1 + \lambda(\mu + r)] - \lambda(\mu - \pi)\} \tag{27}$$

or

$$\frac{\dot{k}}{k} = a(k)\{s[1 + \lambda(\mu + r)] - \lambda(\mu - \pi)\} - n, \tag{28}$$

where μ is no longer constant, but instead varies in accordance with (26). Substituting, then, from this equation and rearranging terms yields

$$\frac{\dot{k}}{k} = \frac{\sigma(k; \pi_0)a(k) - n}{G(k; \pi_0)} = \frac{\sigma(k; \pi_0)f(k) - nk}{kG(k; \pi_0)}, \tag{29}$$

where

$$G(k; \pi_0) \equiv 1 + (1 - s)a(k)k\lambda f''(k) + (1 - s)\lambda f'(k) > 1, \tag{30}$$

---

[21] See the references in note 23 below.
   The reader who is not interested in the technical analysis of stability conditions can omit this section without loss of continuity.
[22] This is the useful device employed by Johnson, *op. cit.*, 1966, p. 281.

where s and λ are functions of k and π_0, as above. Note that setting $\dot{k} = 0$ in equation (29) reduces it (as it must) to steady-state condition (18).

Stability of the system in the small means that any chance increase (decrease) in k above (below) its steady-state level generates automatic market forces to return it to this level. Thus a necessary and sufficient condition for this stability is that $d(\dot{k}/k)/dk < 0$ in the neighborhood of the steady-state position. Carrying out this differentiation in (29) yields

$$\frac{d\left(\frac{\dot{k}}{k}\right)}{dk} = \frac{G(\ )\dfrac{d[\sigma(k;\pi_0)a(k) - n]}{dk} - [\sigma(k;\pi_0)a(k) - n]\dfrac{dG(\ )}{dk}}{[G(\ )]^2}, \quad (31)$$

which is to be evaluated at steady-state values. Since $\sigma a(k) - n$ is then zero, it follows that

$$\text{sign}\,\frac{\left(d\,\dfrac{\dot{k}}{k}\right)}{dk} = \text{sign}\,\frac{d[\sigma(k;\pi_0)a(k) - n]}{dk}$$

$$= \text{sign}\,[\sigma_k a(k) + \sigma a'(k)] \quad (32)$$

$$= \text{sign}\,\left[\sigma_k \frac{n}{\sigma} + \sigma a'(k)\right]$$

$$= \text{sign}\,\left[\sigma_k + \frac{\sigma^2}{n} a'(k)\right]$$

in the neighborhood of the steady state. Hence the system is stable under our present assumptions if, and only if, $\sigma_k + (\sigma^2/n)a'(k)$ is negative. Thus, as already indicated in our discussion of equation (20), the assumption that the system is stable provides information about the comparative-dynamics properties of the system.

The economic interpretation of the foregoing stability condition is straightforward. A chance increase in k above its steady-state value will affect the level of capital intensity both by affecting the physical-saving ratio and by affecting the output (per unit of capital) out of which such savings are made. Hence if these influences are on balance negative, the degree of capital intensity k will be forced back to its original level. If, however, the increase in k causes σ to increase (as will be the case if the demand for money is sufficiently elastic), and if this effect is strong enough to overcome the negative effect on average output, then the degree of capital intensity will be further increased, thus rendering the system unstable. On the other hand, it is clear that under the assumption of an inelastic demand as made in Section 5, the system is stable.

It should, however, be emphasized that this stability depends in a crucial way on the assumption that π remains constant throughout the adjustment process. For assume that π increases. This causes a shift out of money and into commodities, tending to increase π even further. There is, of course, the countervailing force that the increase in the price level decreases

the real value of cash balances, and thus tends to restore portfolio equilibrium. But in the absence of special assumptions, there can be no assurance
as to which of these two forces will prevail.[23]

We now note that the foregoing mathematical development implies
that the basic dynamics of the system can actually be analyzed in the usual
manner in terms of the curves $\sigma(k;\pi_0)f(k)$ and nk in Figure 11.1—even
though these curves do *not* take account of the compensatory monetary
policy described by (26). In particular, equation (29) implies that the
sign of $\dot{k}$ is always the same as that of the difference between these two
curves; the compensatory changes in μ do influence $\dot{k}$, but only to make it
smaller in absolute value than this difference.

Again, the stability condition described by (32) will be satisfied if,
and only if, $\sigma(k;\pi_0)f(k)$ cuts nk from above. For form the function $z = \sigma(k;\pi_0)f(k) - nk$, divide it through by k, and differentiate $w = z/k = \sigma(k;\pi_0)a(k) - n$ with respect to k. Evaluating the resulting derivative at
equilibrium point A in Figure 11.1—at which $z = 0$—we then have

$$\text{sign } \frac{dw}{dk} = \text{sign } \frac{k\frac{dz}{dk} - z}{k^2} = \text{sign } \frac{dz}{dk} \tag{33}$$

$$= \text{sign } [\sigma_k a(k) + \sigma a'(k)].$$

Hence, z will be positive immediately to the left of A, and negative immediately to the right—if and only if dz/dk is negative when evaluated at point
A; that is, if and only if a negative sign obtains in (32).

An immediate implication of this argument is that under the assumptions of Section 5, the system is stable in the large as well as in the small.
For, by the argument of note 19, $\sigma(k;\pi_0)f(k)$ then lies above (below) the
ray nk at any point to the left (right) of point A in Figure 11.1. Hence
there always exist forces pushing k toward the steady-state value, which must
exist.

8. Let us now consider the implications of the foregoing discussion for
the question of the neutrality of money in the context of the steady state. By
such neutrality we mean that monetary changes do not affect the steady-
state value of k and hence real rate of interest. As we shall, however, see
below, there are some problems with reference to this definition.

As has already been emphasized in the literature,[24] there are two
different aspects of this question: the influence of the *absolute* quantity of
money (and hence the absolute price level) on the steady-state path, and
the influence of the *rate of change* of money (and hence the rate of change of

---

[23] Cf. Tobin, *op. cit.*, 1965, pp. 682–684. For a detailed discussion of stability conditions
in a model with a variable π, see both of Sidrauski's articles cited earlier. For a corresponding
discussion with respect to a somewhat different model, see Stein, *op. cit.*, pp. 458–461. In the
Sidrauski analysis a vital role is played by another factor from which we have here abstracted—
namely, the way in which price expectations are formed.

[24] See Marty, *op. cit.*, p. 56, and Tobin, *op. cit.*, 1967, p. 69.

this price level) on the path. From steady-state condition (12) we see that the long-run equilibrium value of k depends only on the latter. From this it follows that if at any point on the steady-state path the quantity of money should (say) double, and if subsequently the monetary authorities should continue with the same rate of monetary expansion as before—then the long-run equilibrium value of k will not be affected. Hence, by (23), neither will the corresponding equilibrium value of m. All that will occur is that immediately after the doubling of the quantity of money there will, by (6), be a positive real-balance effect which will increase the demand for commodities and thus cause the price level to rise faster than usual with consequent effects on k; but if the system is stable, this more rapid rise in prices will continue only until it has reduced the real value of cash balances (and hence demand for commodities) to what they otherwise would have been—at which point the system will have returned to a long-run equilibrium with the same value of π, and hence k and m, as before, but with an absolute price level twice its previous height.

Thus in this sense—which corresponds to that of the traditional quantity theory, with its emphasis on the fact that there can be no real consequences of a change in the monetary unit—money is neutral. On the other hand, as equation (20) shows, money will not generally be neutral in the second sense. Basically, this is a reflection of the fact that different rates of expansion of the money supply imply different rates of return on the holding of real balances, and hence different decisions as to the optimum combinations of the assets (real balances and physical capital) which the individual chooses to hold. Hence the equilibrium amounts of these assets in the economy will in general also be different.

Only if the overall-savings and composition effects of equation (20) exactly offset each other will money be neutral in the second sense too. In this special case the increase in μ leaves k and hence the real rate of interest unaffected, and merely causes the money rate of interest to increase by the same amount that π does. This is the conclusion associated with the traditional discussions of the neutrality question.[25]

But what must now be emphasized is that even in this "neutral" case the increase in μ and hence π will affect the steady-state level of some of the real variables of the system. For it is clear from (24) that it is impossible for both k and m to remain invariant under a change in π. Thus in the case just discussed the increase in the money rate of interest will decrease the demand

---

[25] Cf. e.g., Abba P. Lerner, *Essays in Economic Analysis* (London, 1953), pp. 329–330. Fisher himself did not believe that the money rate increased by the full extent of the rate of price increase—but only because he attributed imperfect foresight to individuals [Irving Fisher, *The Theory of Interest* (New York, 1930), pp. 43–44].

The fact, shown above, that the real rate of interest will generally be affected by a monetary expansion has been instructively demonstrated within the framework of the more familiar *IS–LM* diagram by Mundell, *op. cit.*, 1963 and 1965. [This framework has also been used in the preceding chapter.]

for money and hence m.[26] Correspondingly, by (5), it will change real disposable income. Conversely, if we define "neutrality" as a change which does not affect per capita real disposable income, then it is clear from (5) that it must affect either k and/or m. More specifically, substituting $\mu = \pi + n$ into (5), converting it to the intensive form $y_D = y + m(\pi + n + r)$, and differentiating with respect to π yields

$$\frac{dy_D}{d\pi} = f'(k)\frac{dk}{d\pi} + m\left[1 + f''(k)\frac{dk}{d\pi}\right] + [\pi + n + f'(k)]\frac{dm}{d\pi}. \quad (34)$$

Hence, taking account of (24), it is possible to have a case in which $dy_D/d\pi = dm/d\pi = 0$ and $dk/d\pi > 0$; it is also possible to have a case in which $dy_D/d\pi = dk/d\pi = 0$ and $dm/d\pi < 0$; but it is not possible to have a case in which $dy_D/d\pi = dk/d\pi = dm/d\pi = 0$.

In sum, once we include money services in the definition of income, it is impossible for a variation in the rate of change of the money supply to be neutral in the sense of leaving invariant all the real variables of the system.

We conclude with some brief comments on shifts in liquidity preference. As we saw at the end of Section 5, such a shift will generally affect the steady-state level of k. This, however, should not really be interpreted as a deviation from the neutrality of money. For in system (6)–(7)—as in most growth models—physical savings and investment are assumed to be identical. More specifically, individuals are assumed to make decisions only as to savings, which are then transferred directly and without any friction into investment. Now, it is clear from (6)–(7) that a shift in λ represents not only a shift in the demand for money, but also [through the influence of M/p in equation (6)] a shift in physical consumption and hence savings. Hence it is perfectly in keeping with the classical and neoclassical tradition to conclude that such a shift will generally affect the real rate of interest.

Conversely, a neutral shift in liquidity preference could take place in a growth model which permitted individuals to make independent savings and investment decisions, and which assumed that the shift in liquidity preference simultaneously and directly affected these decisions in offsetting ways. This, of course, is what would take place in such a model if the shift in liquidity preference were to be accompanied by simultaneous and equiproportionate shifts in the demands for consumption and investment commodities, respectively.

9. We consider finally the implications of the foregoing analysis for one aspect of the problem of optimum growth: namely, the choice of a path with

---

[26] More specifically, substituting $dk/d\pi = 0$ in equation (24) yields

$$\frac{dm}{d\pi} = \lambda' f(k) < 0.$$

the highest *constant* level of utility per unit of time. As has been emphasized in the literature, such a steady-state path is not necessarily an optimum one in the sense of maximizing total utility over the entire economic horizon: for if there exists positive subjective time preference, total utility could be increased by consuming some of the capital in this initial steady-state path, and then settling down to another such path at a lower level of consumption. Nevertheless, since the problem has been much discussed in the literature, it is worthwhile commenting briefly upon it.

Just as in the preceding discussion of the nature of neutrality, the major point here is that this utility now depends not only on physical consumption, but also on real money balances. By definition, per capita physical consumption is

$$c(k) = f(k) - \sigma f(k), \tag{35}$$

which in the steady state reduces to

$$c(k) = f(k) - nk. \tag{36}$$

Hence the relevant representative utility function is

$$U = U(c,m) = U[f(k) - nk, m], \tag{37}$$

and the necessary condition for utility maximization is that

$$dU = U_1 \cdot [f'(k) - n] \, dk + U_2 dm = 0 \tag{38}$$

for all possible differential movements dk and dm. Assuming nonsatiety of commodity consumption (i.e., $U_1 \neq 0$), this condition will be satisfied if and only if the equations

$$f'(k) - n = 0 \tag{39}$$

$$U_2[f(k) - nk, m] = 0 \tag{40}$$

are simultaneously satisfied.

In the usual discussion of optimum policy, it is assumed that the policy authorities are free to fix certain parameter(s) so as to satisfy the appropriate utility-maximizing conditions. So far we have assumed that the only policy parameter is μ, or, equivalently, π. Let us, however, now assume that the authorities control yet another parameter, β (representing, say, fiscal policy), which also affects the overall-savings ratio s. This means that this ratio is now represented not by (17), but by $s = H[f'(k), -\pi, \beta]$. In principle, then, equations (18) and (23)—with σ now assumed to depend also on β—could be solved out for k and m as a function of the policy parameters β and π; and these solutions could then be substituted into equations (39)–(40). This would give us two equations to be solved out for the two parameters π and β, whose solutions would, of course, be the optimum values of these parameters.

Thus these assumptions lead to the usual Golden Rule (39); namely, that the optimum policy is that which generates a level of k whose marginal product equals the rate of growth of the economy. The assumptions also lead to the conclusion that the optimum real quantity of money is that which renders its marginal utility equal to zero—which, under the present assumptions, is also the marginal cost to society of producing real outside-money balances. This satiety level of balances can be assumed to be achieved when the alternative cost of holding money, as measured by the money rate of interest, i, is also zero. Since $i = f'(k) + \pi$, it follows that the optimum rate of price change under these conditions is $-\pi = f'(k) = n$. That is, the optimum rate of price decrease equals the rate of growth of output. Correspondingly, optimum monetary policy calls for a constant quantity of money: i.e., $\mu = \pi + n = 0$.[27]

Within the context of our model, however, a more interesting question is the nature of optimum policy when—as in the analysis of the preceding sections—the authorities are free to determine only the parameter π. Formally, this means that (39)–(40) could be reduced to two independent equations in the single parameter π; correspondingly, it would not generally be possible to fix a value for this parameter which could simultaneously satisfy both equations.

The economic implications of this argument can be made clearer by first rewriting maximum condition (38) as

$$\frac{dU}{d\pi} = U_1 \left[f'(k) - n \right] \frac{dk}{d\pi} + U_2 \frac{dm}{d\pi} = 0. \tag{41}$$

From (24) it is clear that $dm/d\pi$ generally differs from zero; hence it is equally clear that the rate of price change π that the monetary authorities must impose in order to satisfy (41) is not generally the one that will generate the steady-state capital-labor ratio k specified by Golden Rule (39). Conversely, and more to the point, the authorities would not generally be acting in an optimum manner if they made use of their policy parameter π to bring the economy to a position in which this Rule would be satisfied. In brief, since by assumption the individual also derives utility from the holdings of cash balances, the proper choice of π must take account of its influence on these holdings as well as on the level of physical consumption.

In a similar way condition (41) implies that, if $dk/d\pi \neq 0$, then the optimum is reached at a point where $U_2 \neq 0$; that is, at a point where real balances are not at their satiety level. This reflects the fact that in the present context—in which the individual is constrained to remain at a constant level of utility—there is, in fact, a social cost attached to increasing m by decreasing π; for the latter decrease may also decrease k, hence $f(k)$, and hence per capita physical consumption. This argument, however, cannot be carried over to the case in which the individual is free to maximize his utility over the entire time horizon without being subject to the foregoing restraint.[28]

[27] Cf. Marty, *op. cit.*, p. 57, and Johnson, *op. cit.*, 1966, p. 284.

[28] We are indebted to Miguel Sidrauski for very helpful comments on this section. We are also indebted to Milton Friedman and Hirofumi Uzawa for pointing out an erroneous interpretation of the optimum which appeared in an earlier draft.

III. MONEY AS A PRODUCER'S GOOD

10. Let us now briefly consider the alternative of treating money as a producer's good. By this we mean that money is held only because it enables the economic unit in question to acquire or produce a larger quantity of commodities, in the usual sense of the term. On the other hand, money holdings per se are assumed not to generate any utility.[29]

One way of carrying out this approach is to analyze the demand for money by means of the usual techniques of optimum-inventory theory.[30] However, though we are now indeed considering money as an inventory, we shall adopt the analytically simpler (though less precise) technique of directly introducing the real quantity of money into the production function. In particular, we shall assume that all money balances are held by the business sector of the economy, whose production function has the form $Y = G(K, L, M/p)$, which is again assumed to be linearly homogeneous in all the variables. This function can be interpreted as reflecting the assumption that just as production depends on fixed capital, so it depends on working capital. Thus real money balances can be considered just like any other inventory which enters into the productive process. Note that within the context of steady-state growth (in which the increase in total output is the result of an increase in the number of firms in the economy, each producing the same amount) the assumption of linear homogeneity can hold even if there should be intrafirm economies of scale in connection with money balances.[31]

In somewhat more concrete—and more familiar—terms we can assume that an economy without money would have to devote effort (read: labor and physical capital) in order to achieve the multitude of "double coincidences"—of buyers who want exactly what the seller has to offer—on which successful barter is based. Hence the entrance of money into the production function reflects the fact that it frees labor and capital for the production of commodities proper. This is an alternative expression of the greater specialization and exchange which money makes possible. At the same time, we continue with the assumption that money is of the outside type, without any costs of production or administration.

In any event, an immediate implication of our present approach is that the imputed services of money balances should *not* be included in disposable income. For these services are already reflected in the increased output of commodities which these balances make possible, so that it would be double counting to take account of them again in our definition of income.[32] On the other hand, the changes in the real value of cash balances

---

[29] For further clarification of this distinction see Patinkin, *op. cit.*, pp. 146–147.

[30] Cf. W. J. Baumol, "The Transactions Demand for Cash: An Inventory Theoretic Approach," *Quarterly Journal of Economics*, LXVI (1952), 545–556; James Tobin, "The Interest-Elasticity of Transactions Demand for Cash," *Review of Economics and Statistics*, XXXVIII (1956), 241–247; and Patinkin, *op. cit.*, Chapter VII. Note that this approach is applicable to households as well as to firms.

[31] Cf. Patinkin, *op. cit.*, pp. 87–88.

[32] *Ibid.*, pp. 160–161.

generated by changes in the price level should be reflected in disposable income; for even though all money balances are assumed to be held by firms, these gains and losses can be assumed to be passed on to households. Hence the definition of disposable income is once again that specified in equation (1) above. Similarly, and in analogy to (2), the rate of capital accumulation is

$$\dot{K} = G\left(K, L, \frac{M}{p}\right) - (1 - s)\left[G\left(K, L, \frac{M}{p}\right) + \frac{M}{p}(\mu - \pi)\right]. \tag{42}$$

Under steady-state assumption (10), this can be written in the intensive form

$$sg(k, m) + (s - 1)mn = nk, \tag{43}$$

where $y = g(k, m)$ is obtained from the foregoing production function by dividing it through by L. Note that equation (43) can be rewritten as

$$\left[s + \frac{(s - 1)mn}{g(k, m)}\right]g(k, m) \equiv \sigma^*(k, \pi)g(k, m) = nk, \tag{44}$$

where, as the reader can readily verify, $\sigma^*(k, \pi) = s + (s - 1)mn/g(k, m)$ is the appropriate physical-savings ratio. Thus (44)—and hence (43)—are entirely analogous to (4).

On the other hand, we are no longer free to describe the demand for money balances by equation (3). For the treatment of these balances as a factor of production implies that the demand for them is determined by the marginal productivity principle. Now, the marginal advantages which a firm obtains from holding a unit of real money balances consists not only of its marginal physical product, but also of the marginal capital gains, $-\pi$, that can be earned by virtue of any anticipated price decline.[33] Hence, since the prices of physical capital and real balances are, by definition, equal, the relevant marginal condition is

$$g_k(k, m) = g_m(k, m) - \pi \tag{45}$$

where $g_k(\,)$ and $g_m(\,)$ are the partial derivatives of $g(\,)$ with respect to k and m, respectively.

In general—and even in the case of a simple, Cobb-Douglas production function—equation (45) cannot be solved explicitly for the demand for real balances m as a function of k and π. Nevertheless, by implicit differentiation of (45) it is possible to show that the partial slopes of m with respect to these variables have respectively the same signs as in (3)—or, rather, (23).

For this purpose let us first define the function

$$\psi(m, k, \pi) \equiv g_k(k, m) - g_m(k, m) + \pi, \tag{46}$$

---

[33] Cf. note 3 above.

whose partial derivatives are thus

$$\phi_m = g_{km} - g_{mm}$$
$$\phi_k = g_{kk} - g_{mk} \tag{47}$$
$$\phi_\pi = 1,$$

where g_{km}, g_{kk}, etc. are the respective second-order partial derivatives of $g(\ )$, and where by the assumption of continuity $g_{km} = g_{mk}$. By the assumption of diminishing marginal productivity, g_{kk} and g_{mm} are both negative. Under the further assumption that the factors are cooperant (as is, for example, the case with a Cobb-Douglas function), $g_{km} = g_{mk}$ is positive. Using these assumptions in (47) implies $\phi_m > 0$ and $\phi_k < 0$. Differentiating (46) partially implicitly then yields

$$\frac{\partial m}{\partial k} = -\frac{\phi_k}{\phi_m} > 0 \tag{48}$$

and

$$\frac{\partial m}{\partial \pi} = -\frac{\phi_\pi}{\phi_m} < 0. \tag{49}$$

As the reader can verify, these are also the signs of the corresponding slopes of demand function (23).

Returning now to the definition of disposable income in the present case, we note that from one viewpoint it is actually closer to definition (5). For substituting from (45) into (1) we obtain

$$Y_D = Y + \frac{M}{p}(\mu - \pi)$$
$$= Y + \frac{M}{p}(\mu + g_k - g_m) = Y + \frac{M}{p}(\mu + r - g_m). \tag{50}$$

Thus just as in the case where money is treated as a consumer's good, the definition of disposable income can be written without explicit reference to π. The interpretation of this is analogous to that presented in connection with definition (5): since the price rise is anticipated, the loss it generates in the real value of money holdings must (at the margin) just equal (and hence be representable by) the net gains in production that these holdings make possible—which in the present case equals $g_m - g_k$.

The steady-state values of k and m—for any given value of π—are, of course, obtained by the simultaneous solution of (43), (45). Clearly, per capita output in this steady state will be greater than or equal to the corresponding output in a barter economy with the same level of k: for firms in the monetary economy always have the option of carrying out production without the use of money.

11.   As before, our major concern is to analyze the effect on the steady-state values of k and m of a change in μ and hence π. If (45) could be solved for the demand for m as a function of k and π, then this function could be substituted in (43) and the analysis could proceed as in Sections 4–5 above. As we have however already noted, in general such a solution cannot be obtained. We can therefore only resort to an implicit differentiation of system (43), (45) with respect to π.

Assuming for simplicity that s is constant and carrying out this differentiation, we obtain the system of equations

$$[sg_k - n]\frac{dk}{d\pi} + [sg_m + (s - 1)n]\frac{dm}{d\pi} = 0, \tag{51}$$

$$[g_{mk} - g_{kk}]\frac{dk}{d\pi} + [g_{mm} - g_{km}]\frac{dm}{d\pi} = 1. \tag{52}$$

Solving by use of determinants then yields

$$\frac{dk}{d\pi} = \frac{sg_m + (s - 1)n}{-\Delta} \tag{53}$$

and

$$\frac{dm}{d\pi} = \frac{sg_k - n}{\Delta}, \tag{54}$$

where

$$\Delta = [sg_k - n][g_{mm} - g_{km}] - [sg_m + (s - 1)n][g_{mk} - g_{kk}]. \tag{55}$$

As the reader can readily verify, the assumptions made in connection with (47) above are not sufficient to determine the signs of the expressions $sg_k - n$ and $sg_m + (s - 1)n$, and hence of the derivatives (53)–(54). This indeterminacy is interpreted graphically in Figure 11.3. The curve mm in this diagram represents the locus of all points which satisfy (45) for a given value of π. By (52)—or (48)—its slope is positive. On the other hand, the

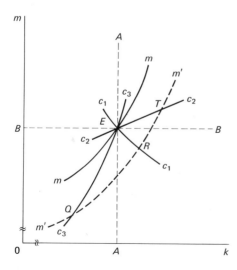

Figure 11.3.

slope of the curve representing (43)—which can be seen from (51) to be equal to $-[sg_k - n]/[sg_m + (s - 1)n]$—cannot be specified a priori. Correspondingly, in the neighborhood of the original long-run equilibrium position E, the slope of curve (43) can be either negative (c_1c_1) or positive—and in the latter case it can cut mm from either above (c_2c_2) or below (c_3c_3). Now, by (49) an increase in π causes a downward shift in mm to (say) $m'm'$. On the other hand, it is clear from (43) that it does not affect the cc curve. Hence the effect of such a shift on the steady-state values of the system depends on the shape of cc, and on whether accordingly the system is brought to point Q, R, or T. Furthermore, as we shall see below in terms of a different graphical analysis, the correspondence principle does not enable us to eliminate any of these alternatives.

Despite this indeterminacy, there are two analogies that might be noted between the foregoing results and those obtained in the case where money was assumed to be a consumer's good. First, we saw from (20) and (22) that even for a constant s, the sign of $dk/d\pi$ could not be determined without making some assumption as to the elasticity of demand for money, and this is analogous to the influence of g_m on the sign of $dk/d\pi$ in (53). Second, from the fact (demonstrated in the preceding section) that the slopes of the demand function for money have the same signs, whether it is considered a consumer's or producer's good, it follows that there are also certain common relationships between the signs of $dm/d\pi$ and $dk/d\pi$. In particular, differentiating the excess-demand equation for money, $\psi(m, k, \pi) = 0$, totally with respect to π, we obtain

$$\psi_m \frac{dm}{d\pi} + \psi_k \frac{dk}{d\pi} + \psi_\pi = 0, \tag{56}$$

which we rewrite as

$$\frac{dm}{d\pi} = -\frac{\psi_k}{\psi_m} \frac{dk}{d\pi} - \frac{\psi_\pi}{\psi_m}. \tag{57}$$

The equality between the signs of the slopes of the money-demand functions as shown in (48)–(49) means that in both cases $-\psi_k/\psi_m > 0$ and $-\psi_\pi/\psi_m < 0$. Hence in both cases if $dk/d\pi \leq 0$, then $dm/d\pi < 0$; and if $dm/d\pi \geq 0$, then $dk/d\pi > 0$. On the other hand, if $dk/d\pi > 0$, then the sign of $dm/d\pi$ is indeterminate; similarly, if $dm/d\pi < 0$ then the sign of $dk/d\pi$ is indeterminate.

These relationships have already been noted in the preceding case in connection with the discussion of equation (23). They can also be directly derived from Figure 11.3. If the increase in π decreases k (i.e., generates a new equilibrium position on $m'm'$ leftwards of the vertical line AA), then it must also decrease the equilibrium value of m. On the other hand, if it shifts the system to an equilibrium position rightwards of AA, then nothing can be said about the direction of change in m. Corresponding statements can be made, *mutatis mutandis*, for shifts to equilibrium positions above and below the horizontal line BB.

Let us now see if it is possible to make some additional "reasonable" assumptions that will enable us to determine the signs of derivatives (53)–(54). Consider first $sg_m + (s - 1)n$ and let us divide it through by g_m, thus yielding $s + (s - 1)n/g_m$. From (42) and (10) we know that total steady-state physical savings in the present model are

$$\dot{K} = S_p = Y - (1 - s)\left(Y + \frac{M}{p}n\right)$$
$$= sY + (s - 1)\frac{M}{p}n. \tag{58}$$

The addition to physical savings when physical income increases is then

$$\frac{\partial S_p}{\partial Y} = s + (s - 1)\frac{\partial\left(\frac{M}{p}\right)}{\partial Y}n. \tag{59}$$

This can be assumed to be positive, though—unlike the situation with respect to the physical-savings ratio σ—this is *not* a necessary characteristic of the steady state. Now the derivative $\partial (M/p)/\partial Y$ can be interpreted as the additional real balances needed for an additional unit of output, which is nothing else but the reciprocal of g_m. It then follows that $s + (s - 1)n/g_m$, and hence $sg_m + (s - 1)n$, can be assumed to be positive.

This, however, does not enable us to determine the signs of the derivatives in (53)–(54). Because for different—though quite "reasonable"—values of the variables, the expression $sg_k - n$—and hence the slope of cc in Figure 11.3—can be either positive or negative.

We also note that this indeterminacy is not removed by assuming that the system is stable. As will be shown in the next section, under the assumption of a compensatory monetary policy which keeps π constant, such stability once again means (in terms of Figure 11.1) that the physical-savings curve $z = \sigma^*(k;\pi_0)g(k, m)$ [see equation (44)] cuts the ray nk from above. Hence at the level of k corresponding to long-run equilibrium position A in Figure 11.1, a change in π will cause the physical-savings curve to shift vertically by an amount equal to

$$\frac{dz}{d\pi} = \sigma_\pi^*(k, \pi)g(k, m) + \sigma^*(k, \pi)g_m(k, m)\frac{\partial m}{\partial \pi}. \tag{60}$$

From the definition of σ^* in (44) we obtain $\sigma_\pi^* = [(s - 1)s/g^2] (g - mg_m) \cdot \partial m/\partial \pi$. Since this expression is being evaluated for a fixed value of k, it follows from (49) that $\partial m/\partial \pi < 0$. By the assumed nature of the production function, we also have that output g exceeds factor-share mg_m. Thus σ_π^*—and hence the first term of (60)—is positive. In terms of Section 5, this reflects the fact that under our present definition of disposable income and assumed constancy of s, an increase in π causes only a positive composition effect. But in contrast with Section 5 it is no longer true that sign $dz/d\pi = $ sign σ_π^*. For the decrease in m generated by the increase in π also decreases the output out of which physical savings are made; and this is represented by the second—and negative—term in (60). Thus whether the physical savings curve $\sigma g(k, m)$ rises or falls in the neighborhood of point A—and whether, accordingly, $dk/d\pi$ is positive or negative—depends on which of these two forces predominates.

For much the same reason it can be shown that, unlike the situation in Section 6 above, this indeterminacy continues to prevail even for a "large" price decrease. For the equality between the real rate of interest and the marginal productivity of capital is now expressed by the relation $r = g_k(k, m)$; hence there exists a curve QQ for every value of m. Once again, as shown by (49), the greater the rate of price decrease, the greater the demand for money m as of any given level of k; hence (assuming the factors to be cooperant) the more the marginal productivity curve QQ shifts left-wards in Figure 11.2. Hence the fact that QQ is asymptotic to the X-axis as of a given value of m does not enable us to draw any inferences about the behavior of EE as π decreases indefinitely.

In a similar way it can be shown that—in contrast with the situation at the end of Section 5 above—the steady-state level of k will be affected by a change in π even in the case in which the savings function is derived from maximizing utility over an infinite time horizon at a constant rate of subjective time preference δ. For the necessary equality between the marginal productivity of capital and $\delta + n$ in this case is expressed by the equation $g_k(k, m) = \delta + n$, which no longer fixes the value of k.[34]

12.   Let us continue to assume that s is constant, and consider the stability properties of the model. Dividing (42) through by k and converting it to the intensive form yields the differential equation

$$\frac{\dot{k}}{k} = s\frac{g(k,m)}{k} + (s - 1)\frac{m}{k}(\mu - \pi) - n. \tag{61}$$

For simplicity, let us again restrict the analysis to the case in which the monetary authorities continuously adjust μ so as to keep π constant through-out the dynamic process. The implications of this policy in the present case can be seen by first differentiating (45) with respect to time under the assumption that π is constant at π_0 to yield

$$(g_{kk} - g_{mk})\dot{k} + (g_{km} - g_{mm})\dot{m} = 0, \tag{62}$$

and then making use of the fact that, by definition,

$$\frac{\dot{m}}{m} = \mu - \pi - n. \tag{63}$$

---

[34] Since writing this section we have learned that Uzawa has presented a growth model in which money enters the production function. Uzawa derives savings behavior from utility maximization and is thus able to determine the sign of $dm/d\pi$ as negative and $dr/d\pi$ as positive; but the sign of $dk/d\pi$ remains indeterminate. Hirofumi Uzawa, "On a Neo-Classical Model of Economic Growth," *Economic Studies Quarterly*, XVII (1966), 1–14.

Substituting accordingly from (62) into (63) we see that the necessary rate of change of the money supply at any instant of time is

$$\mu = \pi_0 + n + \frac{\dot{m}}{m}$$

$$= \pi_0 + n + \frac{k}{m}\frac{g_{kk} - g_{mk}}{g_{mm} - g_{km}}\frac{\dot{k}}{k} \tag{64}$$

Substituting from (64) into (61) and collecting terms then yields the differential equation of the system as a whole

$$\frac{\dot{k}}{k} = \frac{s\dfrac{g(k, m)}{k} + (s - 1)\dfrac{m}{k}n - n}{H(k, m)}, \tag{65}$$

where

$$H(k, m) \equiv 1 + (1 - s)\frac{g_{kk} - g_{mk}}{g_{mm} - g_{km}}, \tag{66}$$

Once again, the system is stable in the small if and only if

$$\frac{d\left(\dfrac{\dot{k}}{k}\right)}{dk} < 0 \tag{67}$$

when evaluated at the steady-state position. Now, by (44) the numerator of (65) is zero at this position, while the denominator is always positive. Hence, by the same argument as in Section 7 above, we have

$$\text{sign}\,\frac{d\left(\dfrac{\dot{k}}{k}\right)}{dk} = \text{sign}\,\frac{d\left[s\dfrac{g(k, m)}{k} + (s - 1)\dfrac{m}{k}n - n\right]}{dk} \tag{68}$$

$$= \text{sign}\left[s\frac{kg_k - g}{k^2} + \frac{sg_m + (s - 1)n}{k}\frac{\partial m}{\partial k} - \frac{(s - 1)mn}{k^2}\right],$$

where $\partial m/\partial k > 0$ by (48). Since the share of any factor is assumed to be less than the whole (i.e., every factor has a positive marginal product), the term $kg_k - g$ is negative. [This is actually the argument which also lies behind the negative sign of $a'(k)$ assumed in Section 5 above.] But this is not enough to determine the sign of the right-hand side of (68), which might be positive. Thus the stability of the present model cannot be unequivocally affirmed even under the simplifying assumptions of a constant s and π.

This possible instability can be interpreted economically as follows: A chance increase in k (m constant) will decrease average output in the usual manner, and thus tend to be self-corrective; this is represented by the negative expression $s(kg_k - g)/k^2$ in (68). But m cannot remain constant; for the increase in k decreases the real—and therefore money—rate of interest and thus generates an increase in the input of m [see equation (48)]. Hence average output and hence physical savings will tend to increase. It follows that if this latter influence is sufficiently strong (i.e., if g_m is sufficiently large), k will be driven ever farther away from its original steady-state value.

We note finally that the foregoing stability condition is once again capable of a simple graphical interpretation. In particular, by applying the argument at the end of Section 7 above, it can be shown that the right-hand side of (68) will be negative if and only if the physical savings curve $z = \sigma^*(k; \pi_0)g(k, m)$ defined by (44) intersects the ray nk from above. As we have seen, however, in our discussion of equation (60), this fact does not enable us to determine the comparative-dynamics properties of the system.

13. Consider finally the implications of the present model for optimum growth in the sense of Section 9. As in the analysis of that section we distinguish between the case in which the policy authorities control both μ (and hence π) and s, and the case in which they control only μ.

The entrance of money into the production function does not change the basic fact that the level of per capita investment (physical saving) necessary to maintain a constant capital-labor ratio is nk. Hence any steady-state level of consumption, c, must satisfy the relationship $c = g(k, m) - nk$. By taking the differential of this function, the reader can establish (along the lines of Section 9 above) that a government which has at its disposal the policy parameters π and s will maximize c by choosing values of these parameters—and thereby k and m—which simultaneously satisfy the Golden Rule [which in the present case has the form $g_k(k,m) - n = 0$], and bring money balances to their satiety level [i.e., $g_m(k, m) = 0$]. Equation (45) then implies $-\pi = n$, from which it follows once again that optimum policy calls for keeping the quantity of money constant.

As before, a more interesting question is the nature of optimum policy when the authorities control only π. The necessary condition for maximum steady-state consumption, namely

$$\frac{dc}{d\pi} = g_k \frac{dk}{d\pi} + g_m \frac{dm}{d\pi} - n\frac{dk}{d\pi} = 0 \tag{69}$$

which is seen to be similar to (41), then implies that the ordinary Golden Rule will not be valid except in the special case where $dm/d\pi = 0$. Generally, however, per capita consumption can be increased when $g_k = n$ by changing π so as to increase m and thereby per capita production. Similarly, only in the case in which $dk/d\pi = 0$ will maximum welfare imply the holding of cash balances which are so large that $g_m = 0$. The interpretation of these results is entirely analogous to the one of the corresponding results presented in Section 9 above—including the restrictive sense in which "optimum" is being used here.

Actually, equation (69) can be interpreted as a generalized form of

the Golden Rule.[35] Specifically, a necessary condition that a policy parameter be at its optimum steady-state value is that any differential change in
the parameter generate an increase in per capita capital and hence output
(dy) which is just equal to the increased output that must be devoted to maintaining a constant capital-labor ratio (ndk): for if the former should exceed
(fall below) the latter, it would be possible to increase steady-state consumption by changing the parameter so as to increase (decrease) k. It is this
necessary condition which is reflected in the requirement of (69) that
$dy/d\pi = g_k(dk/d\pi) + g_m(dm/d\pi) = n(dk/d\pi)$.

By making use of the results of Section 11 we can greatly simplify equation (69). In particular, substituting from (53)–(54) into (69) reduces the
latter to $g_k - g_m = n$. From (45) it then follows that $-\pi = n$, which in turn
implies $\mu = 0$. Thus constancy of the nominal quantity of money represents
optimal monetary policy even in the case in which the government controls
only μ! On the other hand, this constancy does not have the same connotation in this case as in the preceding one. For since under our present
assumptions the Golden Rule $g_k - n = 0$ does not generally obtain, neither
does satiety of money balances $g_m = 0$. Correspondingly, the real rate of
interest at this optimum will generally be greater than n, and hence the money
rate of interest greater than zero.

If we now make use of the relation $g_k - g_m = n$ in (69), we see that it
implies that $dk/d\pi = -dm/d\pi$ in the optimum steady state. This in turn
reflects a more basic relationship that obtains in the present model (as well
as, *mutatis mutandis*, in the ordinary Solow model) for any steady state. In
particular, substituting $g(k, m)$ from steady-state condition (43) into the
definition of steady-state consumption $c = g(k, m) - nk$ yields

$$c = \frac{1 - s}{s} n(k + m).$$

(70)

That is, per capita steady-state consumption is proportionate to per capita
total wealth, $k + m$. Hence c is maximized with respect to π when this wealth
is also so maximized, which means $dk/d\pi + dm/d\pi = 0$. And from this fact
we could then directly deduce from (69) that the optimum steady state is
characterized by the relation $g_k - g_m = n$.

Note that this relation obtains only on the assumption that s is constant. In the more general case in which s depends on $r = f'(k)$—and a
fortiori in the case in which it depends also on $-\pi$, as in (17) above—
maximum consumption would not generally coincide with maximum wealth
in (70). Correspondingly, we would then have to remain with the general
optimum relationship described by (69).

[35] The remainder of this section represents the outcome of extremely helpful discussions
at M.I.T., in which James Mirrlees first pointed out how (69) could be simplified by substitution
from (53)–(54), and Robert M. Solow and C. Christian von Weizsäcker then interpreted the
result by showing that the model was characterized by the underlying relationship (70). We
are greatly indebted to them for their most valuable help.

We note finally that since the analysis of Section 9 deals with the maximization of utility derived from two separate goods, the foregoing argument cannot be carried over to it—even under the assumption of a constant s.

IV. SOME CONCLUDING REMARKS

14. The analysis of this paper has been presented as dealing with the effects of the rate of monetary expansion on the growth path of the system. Actually, however, its concern has been with a monetary expansion used by the government in one specific way—namely, to finance transfer payments. Indeed, these transfer payments, $\mu(M/p)$, appear as a component of disposable income both in definition (1) and in definition (5).

This suggests that the effects of a monetary expansion differ in accordance with the use which the government makes of the money which it prints. Let us illustrate this point by considering the model of Part II and assuming that the government uses the newly issued money for three different purposes: transfer payments, consumption (expenditures from the current budget on goods and services), and investment (corresponding expenditures from the development budget). Let the respective proportions in which the money is spent for these purposes be q_T, q_C, and q_D, where, of course, all the q's are greater than or equal to zero and $q_T + q_C + q_D = 1$. (We deal only with the case of a monetary expansion; in the case of a monetary contraction, $q_C = q_D = 0$ and $q_T = 1$, by definition.)

An immediate implication of these assumptions is that the definition of disposable income is now

$$
\begin{aligned}
Y_D &= Y + q_T\mu\frac{M}{p} - \pi\frac{M}{p} + \frac{M}{p}(r + \pi) \\
&= Y + q_T\mu\frac{M}{p} + r\frac{M}{p}.
\end{aligned}
\tag{71}
$$

That is, income from transfer payments is only $q_T\mu(M/p)$; on the other hand, the loss on real balances generated by a price change and the imputed income from the services of these balances remain the same as before. It follows that the equilibrium condition in the commodity market is now— instead of (6)—

$$
\begin{aligned}
(1 - s)&\left[F(K, L) + q_T\mu\frac{M}{p} + r\frac{M}{p}\right] \\
&+ q_C\mu\frac{M}{p} - \frac{M}{p}(r + \pi) + \dot{K} = F(K, L),
\end{aligned}
\tag{72}
$$

where $q_C\mu(M/p)$ represents the government's real demand for consumption commodities. Note that the government's demand for investment commodities does not appear separately in the equation, for it is already included in $\dot{K}$.

Substituting the money demand function (7) into (72) and carrying out similar operations to those used in Section 4, we can reduce (72) to the form (18), which we rewrite as

$$\frac{f(k)}{k} \equiv a(k) = \frac{n}{\sigma(k; \pi, q_T, q_C)}, \tag{73}$$

where

$$\sigma = s\{1 + \lambda[q_T(n + \pi) + r]\} - \lambda[(q_T + q_C)(n + \pi) - \pi]. \tag{74}$$

Correspondingly, the effect of a change in π on k is again given by (20), which we rewrite for convenience as

$$\frac{dk}{d\pi} = \frac{\sigma_\pi}{-\frac{\sigma^2}{n} a'(k) - \sigma_k}, \tag{75}$$

where now

$$\sigma_k = f''(k)\left(s_1\{1 + \lambda[q_T(n + \pi) + r]\} + s\{\lambda'[q_T(n + \pi) + r] + \lambda\} \right. \tag{76}$$
$$\left. - \lambda'[(q_T + q_C)(n + \pi) - \pi]\right)$$

and

$$\sigma_\pi = -s_2\{1 + \lambda[q_T(n + \pi) + r]\} + s[\lambda'[q_T(n + \pi) + r] + \lambda q_T] \tag{77}$$
$$- \lambda'[(q_T + q_C)(n + \pi) - \pi] - \lambda[q_T + q_C - 1].$$

Clearly, these last three expressions reduce respectively to (16), (21a), and (22) for the special case in which $q_T = 1$ and $q_C = q_D = 0$. As the reader can verify, the assumptions made above in connection with the latter equations are not sufficient to determine the signs of σ_k and σ_π here.

The foregoing expresses the obvious fact that under the stated assumptions both the sign and magnitude of $dk/d\pi$ depend on the policy parameters q_T, q_C, and (by implication) q_D. A much more significant (though equally obvious) fact is that by *changing* these parameters, the government can generate a monetary expansion with any desired effect on k. Thus assume that the government accompanies the monetary expansion with a change in the proportion of the new money devoted to current and development expenditures, respectively, while keeping constant the proportion devoted to transfer payments. Then the effect of such a policy is determined by differentiating (73) implicitly with respect to μ to yield

$$\frac{dk}{d\mu} = \frac{\sigma_\pi + \sigma_{q_C}\dfrac{dq_C}{d\mu}}{-\dfrac{\sigma^2}{n}a'(k) - \sigma_k}, \tag{78}$$

where from the partial differentiation of (74)

$$\sigma_{q_C} = -\lambda(n + \pi) \tag{79}$$

and where we have made use of the assumption that $dq_T/d\mu = 0$ and of the fact that, by (10), $d\pi/d\mu = 1$ in the steady state. Clearly, then, $dk/d\mu$ depends on the way in which the government simultaneously changes q_C, as represented by $dq_C/d\mu$.

Thus consider the case in which the government wishes to generate a neutral monetary expansion, in the sense of leaving k invariant. The required change in q_C (and hence q_D) can then be derived from (78) by setting the left-hand side equal to zero and obtaining

$$\frac{dq_C}{d\mu} = -\frac{\sigma_\pi}{\sigma_{q_C}} = \frac{\sigma_\pi}{\lambda(n + \pi)}. \tag{80}$$

Thus if σ_k is negative so that—in the absence of any change in q_C—sign $dk/d\tau$ would equal sign σ_π by (75); and if σ_π is positive, so that k would otherwise increase with an increase in μ; then equation (80) makes the obvious statement that the government must increase the proportion of its expenditures on consumption goods (i.e., decrease the proportion on investment goods) in order to keep k constant in the face of a monetary expansion.[36]

Note that the government can influence k even if it does not have a development budget. For assume that $q_T + q_C = 1$. This does not affect (78); but it does cause (79) to be replaced by

$$\sigma_{q_C} = -\lambda s(n + \pi), \tag{81}$$

and (80) accordingly by

$$\frac{dq_C}{d\mu} = \frac{\sigma_\pi}{\lambda s(n + \pi)}. \tag{82}$$

Since $s < 1$, this means that in order to increase μ and yet leave k constant, the government will have to increase its expenditures on consumption goods relatively more in the present case than in the preceding one. The explanation is straightforward: An increase in government consumption in the preceding case meant a corresponding decrease in government investment; but the increase in government consumption in the present case is solely at the expense of transfer payments, and hence is in part offset by the resulting reduction in disposable income and hence private consumption.

In brief, even if the government does not itself carry out investment, it can affect the level of capital intensity in the economy by varying the proportion of its budget devoted to the consumption of goods and services as against transfer payments. For by shifting from the latter to the former it essentially transfers disposable income from units (households) whose marginal propensity to consume is less than unity to a unit (the government) whose propensity is unity; hence it increases the overall ratio of physical consumption (decreases the overall ratio of physical savings) and thus tends to decrease the level of k.[37]

[36] Note that a necessary condition for such a policy to be feasible is that the economy is not initially at a position in which $q_C = 1$.

[37] There is an obvious analogy here to the balanced-budget-multiplier argument.

We note too that the entire argument of this paper has been based on the assumption that all money is issued by the government and is therefore of the outside variety. In order to analyze an economy with inside money as well, we would have to introduce into the model a bond (or loan) market which would reflect the deposit-creating activities of the banking sector. We would also have to take account of the costs of these activities. In particular, whether money was considered a consumer's or producer's good, the production function would have the general form

$$H\left(K, L, \frac{M}{p}, Y\right) = 0, \tag{83}$$

reflecting the fact that capital and labor were also used up in maintaining the financial structure which generated real money balances.

Of particular theoretical interest is the case of a pure inside-money economy: that is, one in which the entire money supply is created by the credit-extending activities of the banking system.[38] From our observations of the real world, it seems only reasonable to assume that the bonds of any economy experiencing a constant rate of price change would have an "escalator clause" tying the principal and interest payments to the price index. And just as the banks would insist on such a clause on the loans they made, so individuals would insist upon it with reference to their demand deposits—thus assuring that they would not suffer any capital losses as a result of price increases. In more formal terms, these capital losses would be automatically offset by the *explicit* rate of return π which demand deposits would earn. Correspondingly, under these assumptions the alternative cost of holding money would be r, and not $r + \pi$. More generally, there would be no asset in the economy with a real rate of return of $-\pi$. Furthermore, in such an economy, the government—by definition—issues no money; hence the component of disposable income which represents government transfer payments made with newly issued money ($\mu M/p$) would be zero.

From all this it follows that in a pure inside-money economy, the behavior of individuals would not be affected either by the rate of expansion of the money supply, μ, or by the rate of price change, π. Hence the system is neutral—with respect to *all* real variables—in the second sense indicated in Section 8 above. Similarly, the system is neutral in the first sense: for its dependence on M/p means that if the nominal quantity of money is (say) twice as high as before, then a price level which is also twice as high will enable the system to return to equilibrium with all the real variables having the same values as before.

We note finally that we have dealt in this paper with two extreme cases: one in which money is only a consumption good and one in which it is only a producer's good. However, money can be assumed to fulfill both these roles simultaneously. In particular, whereas money holdings of firms lend them-

---

[38] Cf. on this discussion John G. Gurley and Edward S. Shaw, *Money in a Theory of Finance* (Washington, D.C., 1960); Patinkin, *op. cit.*, Chapter XII: 5.

selves to analysis via the production function, those of households lend themselves—at least in part[39]—to analysis via the utility function. Hence a truly general model would analyze the total demand for money from both these viewpoints.

---

[39] The proviso is necessitated by the comment in note 30 above.

BIBLIOGRAPHY

CHAPTER 1. ON STOCKS AND FLOWS

ALLEN, R. G. D. *Mathematical Analysis for Economists*. London: Macmillan, 1938.

EVANS, G. C. *Mathematical Introduction to Economics*. New York: 1930.

JOHNSON, HARRY G. "Monetary Theory and Policy," *American Economic Review*, LII (June 1962), 335–384.

PATINKIN, DON. *Money, Interest, and Prices*. Evanston, Ill.: Row, Peterson, 1956; 2nd ed. New York: Harper & Row, 1965.

CHAPTER 2. PRICE FLEXIBILITY AND FULL EMPLOYMENT

DEWHURST, J. and associates. *America's Needs and Resources*. New York: Twentieth Century Fund, 1947.

HABERLER, G. *Prosperity and Depression*. 3rd ed. Geneva: League of Nations, 1941.

HICKS, J. R. *Value and Capital*. 2nd ed. Oxford: Clarendon Press, 1946.

KALECKI, M. "Professor Pigou on 'The Classical Stationary State': A comment," *Economic Journal*, LIV (April 1944), 131–132.

KEYNES, JOHN MAYNARD. *The General Theory of Employment, Interest and Money*. New York: Harcourt Brace Jovanovich Inc., 1936.

KLEIN, LAWRENCE R. "The Use of Econometric Models as a Guide to Economic Policy," *Econometrica*, XV (April 1947), 111–151.

LANGE, OSCAR. *Price Flexibility and Employment*. Bloomington, Indiana: Principia Press, 1945.

MINTS, LLOYD W. "Monetary Policy," *Review of Economic Statistics*, XXVIII (May 1946), 60–69.

PATINKIN, DON. "Involuntary Unemployment and the Keynesian Supply Function," *Economic Journal*, LIX (September 1949), 360–383.

PATINKIN, DON. "A Reconsideration of the General Equilibrium Theory of Money," *Review of Economic Studies*, XVIII, No. 1 (1950), 42–61.

PIGOU, A. C. "The Classical Stationary State," *Economic Journal*, LIII (December 1943), 343–351.

PIGOU, A. C. "Economic Progress in a Stable Environment," *Economica*, XIV (August 1947), 180–188.

Samuelson, P. A. "The Stability of Equilibrium: Comparative Statics and Dynamics," *Econometrica*, IX (April 1941), 97–120.

Shackle, G. L. S. "Interest-Rates and the Pace of Investment," *Economic Journal*, LVI (March 1946), 1–17.

Simons, Henry C. *Economic Policy for a Free Society*. Chicago: University of Chicago Press, 1948.

Stein, Herbert. "Price Flexibility and Full Employment: Comment," *American Economic Review*, XXXIX (June 1949), 725–726.

CHAPTER 3. FINANCIAL INTERMEDIARIES AND THE LOGICAL STRUCTURE OF MONETARY THEORY

Friedman, Milton. *A Theory of the Consumption Function* (National Bureau of Economic Research: General Series No. 63). Princeton: Princeton University Press, 1957.

Gurley, John G. and Shaw, Edward S. *Money in a Theory of Finance*. Washington, D.C.: The Brookings Institution, 1960.

Modigliani, Franco. Postscript to "Liquidity Preference and the Theory of Interest and Money," in H. Hazlitt (ed.), *The Critics of Keynesian Economics*. Princeton: Van Nostrand, 1960, pp. 183–184.

Patinkin, Don. *Money, Interest, and Prices*. Evanston, Ill.: Row, Peterson, 1956; 2nd ed. New York: Harper & Row, 1965.

CHAPTER 4. MONETARY AND PRICE DEVELOPMENTS IN ISRAEL: 1949–1953

Gross, Nachum. "Inflation and Economic Policy in Israel: First Phase, 1949–1950" (unpublished M.A. thesis, The Hebrew University 1954, Hebrew).

Kochav, David. "Imports without Allocation of Foreign Exchange in Israel: 1949–1952" (unpublished M.A. thesis, The Hebrew University, 1953, Hebrew).

Mints, Lloyd W. *A History of Banking Theory*. Chicago: University of Chicago Press, 1945.

Patinkin, Don. "Keynesian Economics and the Quantity Theory," in K. Kurihara (ed.), *Post-Keynesian Economics*. New Brunswick, N.J.: Rutgers University Press, 1954, pp. 123–152.

Viner, Jacob. *Studies in the Theory of International Trade*. New York and London: Harper & Row, 1937.

CHAPTER 5. WICKSELL'S CUMULATIVE PROCESS IN THEORY AND PRACTICE

Cagan, Phillip. *Determinants and Effects of Changes in the Stock of Money, 1875–1960*. National Bureau of Economic Research: Studies in Business Cycles No. 13. New York and London: Columbia University Press, 1965.

De Leeuw, Frank. "A Model of Financial Behavior," in J. S. Duesenberry and others others (eds.), *Vhe Brookings Quarterly Econometric Model of the United States*. Chicago: Rand-McNally, 1965, pp. 464–530.

Goldfeld, Stephen M. *Commercial Bank Behavior and Economic Activity*. Amsterdam: North-Holland Publishing Co., 1966.

Klein, Lawrence R. *The Keynesian Revolution*. 2nd ed. New York: Macmillan, 1966.

Patinkin, Don. *Money, Interest, and Prices*. 2nd ed. New York: Harper & Row, 1965.

Wicksell, Knut. *Lectures on Political Economy*. Vol. II: *Money*. Trans. by E. Classen. London: Routledge & Kegan Paul, 1935.

Wicksell, Knut. *Interest and Prices*. Trans. by R. F. Kahn. London: Macmillan, 1936.

CHAPTER 6. THE CHICAGO TRADITION, THE QUANTITY THEORY, AND FRIEDMAN[1]

ANGELL, JAMES W. "Money, Prices and Production: Some Fundamental Concepts," *Quarterly Journal of Economics*, XLVIII (November 1933), 39–76.

ANGELL, JAMES W. *The Behavior of Money*. New York: McGraw-Hill, 1936.

ANGELL, JAMES W. *Investment and Business Cycles*. New York: McGraw-Hill, 1941.

BRONFENBRENNER, M. "Observations on the 'Chicago School(s)'," *Journal of Political Economy*, LXX (February 1962), 72–75.

BROWN, A. J. "Interest, Prices, and the Demand Schedule for Idle Money," *Oxford Economic Papers*, II (May 1939), 46–69, as reprinted in T. Wilson and P. W. S. Andrews (eds.), *Oxford Studies in the Price Mechanism*. Oxford: Oxford University Press, 1951, pp. 31–51.

DAVIS, J. R. "Chicago Economists, Deficit Budgets, and the Early 1930s," *American Economic Review*, LVIII (June 1968), 476–482.

FISHER, IRVING. *The Rate of Interest*. New York: Macmillan, 1907.

FISHER, IRVING. *The Purchasing Power of Money*. 2nd rev. ed., 1922. Reprint. New York: Kelley, 1963.

FISHER, IRVING. *The Theory of Interest*. 1930. Reprint. New York: Kelley, 1954.

FRIEDMAN, MILTON. "The Quantity Theory of Money—A Restatement," in Milton Friedman (ed.), *Studies in the Quantity Theory of Money*. Chicago: University of Chicago Press, 1956, pp. 3–21.

FRIEDMAN, MILTON. *A Program for Monetary Stability*. New York: Fordham University Press, 1960.

FRIEDMAN, MILTON. "The Monetary Theory and Policy of Henry Simons," *Journal of Law and Economics*, X (October 1967), 1–13.

FRIEDMAN, MILTON. "Money: Quantity Theory," in David L. Sills (ed.), *The International Encyclopedia of the Social Sciences*. Vol. X. 1968, 432–447.

FRIEDMAN, MILTON, and MEISELMAN, DAVID. "The Relative Stability of Monetary Velocity and the Investment Multiplier in the United States, 1897–1958," in *Stabilization Policies*. (Commission on Money and Credit.) Englewood Cliffs, N.J.: Prentice-Hall, 1963.

HICKS, J. R. "A Suggestion for Simplifying the Theory of Money," *Economica*, II (February 1935), 1–19, as reprinted in Friedrich A. Lutz and Lloyd W. Mints (eds.), *Readings in Monetary Theory*. Philadelphia: 1951, pp. 13–32.

KAHN, R. F. "Some Notes on Liquidity Preference," *The Manchester School*, XXII (September 1954), 229–257.

KEYNES, JOHN MAYNARD. *A Treatise on Money*. London: Macmillan, 1930.

KEYNES, JOHN MAYNARD. *The General Theory of Employment, Interest and Money*. New York: Harcourt Brace Jovanovich, Inc. 1936.

KLEIN, Lawrence R. "The Use of Econometric Models as a Guide to Economic Policy," *Econometrica*, XV (April 1947), 111–151.

KLEIN, LAWRENCE R. *Economic Fluctuations in the United States, 1921–1941*. Cowles Commission for Research in Economics Monograph No. 11. New York: Wiley, 1950.

KNIGHT, FRANK H. "The Business Cycle, Interest, and Money: A Methodological Approach," *Review of Economic Statistics*, XXIII (May 1941), 53–67, as reprinted in *On the History and Method of Economics*. Chicago: University of Chicago Press, 1956, pp. 202–226.

KNIGHT, FRANK H. "Economics," *Encyclopaedia Britannica*, 1951, as reprinted in *On the History and Method of Economics*. Chicago: University of Chicago Press, 1956, pp. 3–33.

---

[1]This bibliography does not include the Ph.D. theses listed in Appendix III to this chapter (p. 116 above).

KNIGHT, FRANK H. *Risk, Uncertainty and Profit.* New York: Kelley, 1957.

MAKOWER, HELEN, and MARSCHAK, JACOB. "Assets, Prices and Monetary Theory," *Economica*, V (August 1938), 261–288, as reprinted in George J. Stigler and Kenneth E. Boulding (eds.), *Readings in Price Theory.* Chicago: Irwin, 1952, pp. 283–310.

MARKOWITZ, HARRY. "Portfolio Selection," *Journal of Finance*, VII (March 1952), 77–91.

MINTS, LLOYD W. *A History of Banking Theory.* Chicago: University of Chicago Press, 1945.

MINTS, LLOYD W. "Monetary Policy," *Review of Economic Statistics*, XXVIII (May 1946), 60–69.

MINTS, LLOYD W. *Monetary Policy for a Competitive Society.* New York: McGraw-Hill, 1950.

MODIGLIANI, FRANCO. "Liquidity Preference and the Theory of Interest and Money," *Econometrica*, XII (January 1944), 45–88, as reprinted in Friedrich A. Lutz and Lloyd W. Mints (eds.), *Readings in Monetary Theory.* Philadelphia: 1951, pp. 186–239.

PATINKIN, DON. "An Indirect-Utility Approach to the Theory of Money, Assets, and Savings," in F. H. Hahn and F. P. R. Brechling (eds.), *The Theory of Interest Rates.* London: Macmillan, 1965, pp. 52–79.

PATINKIN, DON. *Money, Interest, and Prices.* 2nd ed. New York: Harper & Row, 1965.

ROBINSON, JOAN. "The Rate of Interest," *Econometrica*, XIX (April 1951), 92–111.

SELDEN, RICHARD T. "Monetary Velocity in the United States," in Milton Friedman (ed.), *Studies in the Quantity Theory of Money.* Chicago: University of Chicago Press, 1956, pp. 179–257.

SIMONS, HENRY C. "Banking and Currency Reform" (unpublished memorandum, 1933).

SIMONS, HENRY C. *Personal Income Taxation.* Chicago: University of Chicago Press, 1938.

SIMONS, HENRY C. "A Positive Program for Laissez Faire," 1934. As reprinted in *Economic Policy for a Free Society.* Chicago: University of Chicago Press, 1948, pp. 40–77.

SIMONS, HENRY C. "Rules versus Authorities in Monetary Policy," *Journal of Political Economy*, XLIV (February 1936), 1–30, as reprinted in *Economic Policy for a Free Society.* Chicago: University of Chicago Press, 1948, pp. 160–183.

SIMONS, HENRY C. "Hansen on Fiscal Policy," *Journal of Political Economy*, L (April 1942), 161–196, as reprinted in *Economic Policy for a Free Society.* Chicago: University of Chicago Press, 1948, pp. 184–219.

SNYDER, CARL. "New Measures in the Equation of Exchange," *American Economic Review*, XIV (December 1924), 699–713.

SNYDER, CARL. "The Influence of the Interest Rate on the Business Cycle," *American Economic Review*, XV (December 1925), 684–699.

SNYDER, CARL. "The Problem of Monetary and Economic Stability," *Quarterly Journal of Economics*, XLIX (February 1935), 173–205.

STIGLER, GEORGE J. *Production and Distribution Theories.* New York: Macmillan, 1941.

TOBIN, JAMES. "A Dynamic Aggregative Model," *Journal of Political Economy*, LXIII (April 1955), 103–115.

VINER, JACOB, *Studies in the Theory of International Trade.* New York and London: Harper & Row, 1937.

VINER, JACOB. "International Aspects of the Gold Standard," in Quincy Wright (ed.), *Gold and Monetary Stabilization.* 1932. As reprinted in *International Economics.* Glencoe, Ill.: The Free Press, 1951, pp. 137–140.

VINER, JACOB. "Schumpeter's *History of Economic Analysis*," *American Economic*

Review, XLIV (December 1954), 894–910, as reprinted in *The Long View and the Short*. Glencoe, Ill.: Free Press, 1958, pp. 343–365.

VINER, JACOB. "The Necessary and the Desirable Range of Discretion to be Allowed to a Monetary Authority," in Leland B. Yeager (ed.), *In Search of a Monetary Constitution*. Cambridge, Mass.: Harvard University Press, 1962, pp. 244–274.

WARBURTON, CLARK. "The Volume of Money and the Price Level Between the World Wars," *Journal of Political Economy*, LIII (June 1945), 150–163.

WARBURTON, CLARK. "Quantity and Frequency of Use of Money in the United States, 1919–45," *Journal of Political Economy*, LIV (October 1946), 436–450.

WARBURTON, CLARK. "Monetary Velocity and Monetary Policy," *Review of Economics and Statistics*, XXX (November 1948), 304–314.

WARBURTON, CLARK. "The Secular Trend in Monetary Velocity," *Quarterly Journal of Economics*, LXIII (February 1949), 68–91.

CHAPTER 7. INTEREST

BAILEY, MARTIN J. "Saving and the Rate of Interest," *Journal of Political Economy*, LXV (August 1957), 279–305.

BARKAI, HAIM. "A 'Recoupment Period' Model of Investment and Pricing in a Socialist Economy," in D. C. Hague (ed.), *Price Formation in Various Economies*. New York: St. Martin's Press, 1967, pp. 183–202.

BEAR, DONALD V. T. "The Relationship of Saving to the Rate of Interest, Real Income, and Expected Future Prices," *Review of Economics and Statistics*, XLIII (February 1961), 27–35.

BERGSON, ABRAM. *The Economics of Soviet Planning*. New Haven: Yale University Press, 1964.

BOULDING, KENNETH E. *Economic Analysis*. 2nd ed. New York: Harper & Row, 1948.

BROWN, ARTHUR J. *The Great Inflation 1939–1951*. London: Oxford University Press, 1955.

BURNS, ARTHUR F. "New Facts on Business Cycles," in Geoffrey H. Moore (ed.), *Business Cycle Indicators*. Princeton: Princeton University Press, 1961, pp. 13–44.

BURNS, ARTHUR F. and MITCHELL, WESLEY C. *Measuring Business Cycles* (National Bureau of Economic Research: Studies in Business Cycles No. 2). New York: The Bureau, 1946.

CAGAN, PHILLIP. *Determinants and Effects of Changes in the Stock of Money, 1875–1960* (National Bureau of Economic Research: Studies in Business Cycles No. 13). New York and London: Columbia University Press, 1965.

CAGAN, PHILLIP. "Changes in the Cyclical Behavior of Interest Rates," *Review of Economics and Statistics*, XLVIII (August 1966), 219–250.

CASSEL, GUSTAV. *The Theory of Social Economy*. New rev. ed., trans. by S. L. Barron. New York: Harcourt Brace Jovanovich, Inc., 1932.

CONARD, JOSEPH W. *An Introduction to the Theory of Interest*. Berkeley: University of California Press, 1959.

EINZIG, PAUL. *Primitive Money in its Ethnological, Historical and Economic Aspects*. London: Eyre and Spottiswoode, 1949.

ENTHOVEN, ALAIN C. "A Neo-classical Model of Money, Debt, and Economic Growth." Mathematical appendix to J. G. Gurley and E. S. Shaw, *Money in a Theory of Finance*. Washington, D.C.: The Brookings Institution, 1960, pp. 301–359.

FINCH, DAVID. "Purchasing Power Guarantees for Deferred Payments," *International Monetary Fund Staff Papers*, V (February 1956), 1–22.

FIRTH, RAYMOND. "Capital, Saving and Credit in Peasant Societies: A Viewpoint from Economic Anthropology," in Raymond Firth and B. S. Yamey (eds.),

Capital, Saving and Credit in Peasant Societies. Chicago: Aldine, 1963, pp. 15–34.

FISHER, IRVING. *The Theory of Interest.* New York: Kelley, 1930.

FRIEDMAN, MILTON. *A Theory of the Consumption Function* (National Bureau of Economic Research: General Series No. 63). Princeton: Princeton University Press, 1957.

GURLEY, JOHN G. and SHAW, EDWARD S. *Money in a Theory of Finance.* Washington, D. C.: The Brookings Institution, 1960.

HEICHELHEIM, FRITZ M. *An Ancient Economic History: From the Palaeolithic Age to the Migrations of the Germanic, Slavic and Arabic Nations.* 2 Vols. Rev. English ed. Leyden: Sijthoff.

HICKMAN, W. BRADDOCK. *Corporate Bond Quality and Investor Experience* (National Bureau of Economic Research: Studies in Corporate Bond Financing No. 2). Princeton: Princeton University Press, 1958.

HICKS, J. R. *Value and Capital.* 2nd ed. Oxford: Clarendon Press, 1946.

HOMER, SIDNEY. *A History of Interest Rates.* New Brunswick, N.J.: Rutgers University Press, 1963.

JORGENSON, DALE W. "The Theory of Investment Behavior," in Robert Ferber (ed.), *Determinants of Investment Behavior* (Universities-National Bureau Conference Series No. 18). New York and London: Columbia University Press, 1967, pp. 129–155.

KAPLAN, NORMAN. "Investment Alternatives in Soviet Economic Theory," *Journal of Political Economy*, LX (April 1952), 133–144.

KESSEL, REUBEN A. *The Cyclical Behavior of the Term Structure of Interest Rates* (National Bureau of Economic Research: Occasional Paper No. 91). New York and London: Columbia University Press, 1965.

KEYNES, JOHN MAYNARD. *A Treatise on Money.* London: Macmillan, 1930.

KEYNES, JOHN MAYNARD. *The General Theory of Employment, Interest and Money.* New York: Harcourt Brace Jovanovich, Inc., 1936.

KNIGHT, FRANK H. *The Ethics of Competition and Other Essays.* New York: Kelley, 1935.

KNIGHT, FRANK H. "The Quantity of Capital and the Rate of Interest," *Journal of Political Economy*, XLIV (August 1936), 433–463 and *ibid.* (October 1936), 612–642.

KNIGHT, FRANK H. "Diminishing Returns from Investment," *Journal of Political Economy*, LII (March 1944), 26–47.

KUZNETS, SIMON. *Modern Economic Growth: Rate, Structure, and Spread.* New Haven: Yale University Press, 1966.

LEONTIEF, WASSILY W. "Theoretical Note on Time-Preference, Productivity of Capital, Stagnation and Economic Growth," *American Economic Review*, XLVIII (March 1958), 105–111.

LERNER, ABBA P. *Essays in Economic Analysis.* London: Macmillan, 1953.

LIVIATAN, NISSAN. "Multiperiod Future Consumption as an Aggregate," *American Economic Review*, LVI (September 1966), 828–840.

MACAULAY, FREDERICK R. *Some Theoretical Problem Suggested by the Movements of Interest Rates, Bond Yields and Stock Prices in the United States since 1856* (National Bureau of Economic Research: General Series No. 33). New York: 1938.

MARSHALL, ALFRED. *Principles of Economics.* 8th. ed. London: Macmillan, 1920.

MARTY, ALVIN L. "The Neoclassical Theorem," *American Economic Review*, LIV (December 1964), 1026–1029.

NELSON, BENJAMIN N. *The Idea of Usury: From Tribal Brotherhood to Universal Otherhood.* Princeton: Princeton University Press, 1949.

NOONAN, JOHN T. *The Scholastic Analysis of Usury.* Cambridge, Mass.: Harvard University Press, 1957.

NOVE, ALEC. *The Soviet Economy: An Introduction.* New York: Praeger, 1961.

PATINKIN, DON. *Money, Interest, and Prices.* 2nd ed. New York: Harper & Row, 1965.

PHELPS, EDMUND S. "Second Essay on the Golden Rule of Accumulation," *American Economic Review*, LV (September 1965), 793–814.

PIGOU, A. C. *The Economics of Stationary States.* London: Macmillan, 1935.

PIRENNE, HENRI. *Economic and Social History of Medieval Europe.* London: Routledge & Kegan Paul, 1936.

ROBERTSON, D. H. *Essays in Monetary Theory.* London: King and Son, 1940.

ROBINSON, JOAN. "The Rate of Interest," *Econometrica*, XIX (April 1951), 92–111.

ROBSON, PETER. "Index-Linked Bonds," *Review of Economic Studies*, XXVIII (October 1960), 57–68.

SOLOW, ROBERT M. "A Contribution to the Theory of Economic Growth," *Quarterly Journal of Economics*, LXX (February 1956), 65–94.

STEIN, JEROME L. "Money and Capacity Growth," *Journal of Political Economy*, LXXIV (October 1966), 451–465.

SWAN, T. W. "Economic Growth and Capital Accumulation," *Economic Record*, XXXII (November 1956), 334–361.

TOBIN, JAMES. "Liquidity Preference as Behavior Towards Risk," *Review of Economics Studies*, XXV (February 1958), 65–86.

TOBIN, JAMES. "Money and Economic Growth," *Econometrica*, XXXIII (October 1965), 671–684.

WICKSELL, KNUT. *Lectures on Political Economy.* Vol. II: *Money.* Trans. by E. Classen. London: Routledge & Kegan Paul, 1935.

WICKSELL, KNUT. *Interest and Prices.* Trans. by R. F. Kahn. London: Macmillan, 1936.

CHAPTER 8. ON THE NATURE OF THE MONETARY MECHANISM

ANDO, ALBERT, and MODIGLIANI, FRANCO. "The 'Life Cycle' Hypothesis of Saving: Aggregate Implications and Tests," *American Economic Review*, LIII (March 1963), 55–84.

ANDO, ALBERT, and MODIGLIANI, FRANCO. "The 'Life Cycle' Hypothesis of Saving: A Correction," *American Economic Review*, LIV (March 1964), 111–113.

CAGAN, PHILLIP. *Determinants and Effects of Changes in the Stock of Money, 1875–1960* (National Bureau of Economic Research: Studies in Business Cycles No. 13). New York and London: Columbia University Press, 1965.

FISHER, IRVING. *The Purchasing Power of Money.* 2nd rev. ed., 1922. New York: Kelley, 1963.

FRIEDMAN, MILTON, and MEISELMAN, DAVID. "The Relative Stability of Monetary Velocity and the Investment Multiplier in the United States, 1897–1958," in *Stabilization Policies.* (Commission on Money and Credit.) Englewood Cliffs, N.J.: Prentice-Hall, 1963.

FRIEDMAN, MILTON, and SCHWARTZ, ANNA JACOBSON. *A Monetary History of the United States 1867–1960* (National Bureau of Economic Research: Studies in Business Cycles No. 12). Princeton: Princeton University Press, 1963.

GÅRLUND, TORSTEN. *Life of Knut Wicksell.* Trans. by Nancy Adler, Stockholm: Almqvist and Wiksell, 1958.

GOLDFELD, STEPHEN M. *Commercial Bank Behavior and Economic Activity.* Amsterdam: North-Holland Publishing Co., 1966.

GURLEY, JOHN G. and SHAW, EDWARD S. *Money in a Theory of Finance.* Washington, D.C.: The Brookings Institution, 1960.

LANDSBERGER, MICHAEL. "Windfall Income and Consumption: Comment," *American Economic Review*, LVI (June 1966), 534–540.

LINDBECK, ASSAR. *The "New" Theory of Credit Control in the U.S.* Rev. ed. Stockholm: Almqvist and Wiksell, 1962.

MUNDELL, R. A. "The Public Debt, Corporate Income Taxes, and the Rate of Interest," *Journal of Political Economy*, LXVII (December 1960), 622–626.

PATINKIN, DON. *Money, Interest, and Prices.* 2nd ed. New York: Harper & Row, 1965.

PHILLIPS, C. R. *Bank Credit.* New York: Macmillan, 1928.

SUITS, DANIEL B. and SPARKS, GORDON R. "Consumption Regressions with Quarterly Data," in J. S. Duesenberry and others, (eds.), *The Brookings Quarterly Econometric Model of the United States.* Chicago: Rand-McNally, 1965, pp. 202–223.

TOBIN, JAMES. "Money and Economic Growth," *Econometrica*, XXXIII (October 1965), 671–684.

UNITED STATES Bureau of the Census, *Historical Statistics of the United States, Colonial Times to 1957* (Washington, D.C.: U.S. Government Printing Office, 1960).

WICKSELL, KNUT. *Lectures on Political Economy.* Vol. II: *Money.* Trans. by E. Classen. London: Routledge & Kegan Paul, 1935.

WICKSELL, KNUT. *Interest and Prices.* Trans. by R. F. Kahn. London: Macmillan, 1936.

CHAPTER 9. MONEY AND WEALTH

BUCHANAN, J. M. "An Outside Economist's Defense of Pesek and Saving," *Journal of Economic Literature*, VIII (September 1969), 812–814.

GURLEY, JOHN G. and SHAW, EDWARD S. *Money in a Theory of Finance.* Washington, D.C.: The Brookings Institution, 1960.

HETH, MEIR. *Banking Institution in Israel.* 2nd ed. Jerusalem: Falk Institute, 1966.

KALECKI, M. "Professor Pigou on 'The Classical Stationary State': A Comment," *Economic Journal*, LIV (April 1944), 131–132.

PATINKIN, DON. "Multiple-Plant Firms, Cartels, and Imperfect Competition," *Quarterly Journal of Economics*, LXI (February 1947), 173–205.

PATINKIN, DON. *Money, Interest, and Prices.* 2nd ed. New York: Harper & Row, 1965.

PATINKIN, DON. "Money and Wealth: A Review Article," *Journal of Economic Literature*, VII, No. 4 (December 1969), 1140–1160.

PESEK, BORIS P. and SAVING, THOMAS R. *Money, Wealth, and Economic Theory.* New York: Macmillan, 1967.

PIGOU, A. C. "The Classical Stationary State," *Economic Journal*, LIII (December 1943), 343–351.

RUGGLES, R. and RUGGLES, N. D. *National Income Accounts and Income Analysis.* 2nd ed. New York: McGraw-Hill, 1956.

CHAPTER 10. MONEY AND GROWTH IN A KEYNESIAN FULL-EMPLOYMENT MODEL

CAGAN, PHILLIP. "The Channels of Monetary Effects on Interest Rates." National Bureau of Economic Research, New York: The Bureau, July 1966. (Mimeograph.)

FISHER, IRVING. *The Rate of Interest.* New York: Macmillan, 1907.

FISHER, IRVING. *The Theory of Interest.* New York: Kelley, 1930.

LERNER, ABBA P. *Essays in Economic Analysis.* London: Macmillan, 1953.

METZLER, L. A. "Wealth, Saving, and the Rate of Interest," *Journal of Political Economy*, LIX (April 1951), 93–116.

MUNDELL, R. A. "Inflation and Real Interest," *Journal of Political Economy*, LXXI (June 1963), 280–283.

MUNDELL, R. A. "A Fallacy in the Interpretation of Macroeconomic Equilibrium," *Journal of Political Economy*, LXXIII (February 1965), 61–66.

PATINKIN, DON. *Money, Interest, and Prices.* 2nd ed. New York: Harper & Row, 1965.

SIDRAUSKI, MIGUEL. "Inflation and Economic Growth," *Journal of Political Economy*, LXXV (December 1967), 796–810.

SOLOW, ROBERT M. "A Contribution to the Theory of Economic Growth," *Quarterly Journal of Economics*, LXX (February 1956), 65–94.

TOBIN, JAMES. "Money and Economic Growth," *Econometrica*, XXXIII (October 1965), 671–684.

CHAPTER 11. THE ROLE OF MONEY IN A SIMPLE GROWTH MODEL

BAUMOL, W. J. "The Transactions Demand for Cash: An Inventory Theoretic Approach," *Quarterly Journal of Economics*, LXVI (November 1952), 545–556.

DELEEUW, FRANK. "A Model of Financial Behavior," in J. S. Duesenberry and others (eds.), *The Brookings Quarterly Econometric Model of the United States.* Chicago: Rand-McNally, 1965, pp. 464–530.

ENTHOVEN, ALAIN C. "A Neo-classical Model of Money, Debt, and Economic Growth." Mathematical appendix to J. G. Gurley and E. S. Shaw, *Money in a Theory of Finance.* Washington, D.C.: The Brookings Institution, 1960, pp. 301–359.

FISHER, IRVING. *The Theory of Interest.* New York: Kelley, 1930.

GOLDFELD, STEPHEN M. *Commercial Bank Behavior and Economic Activity.* Amsterdam: North-Holland Publishing Co., 1966.

GURLEY, JOHN G., and SHAW, EDWARD S. *Money in a Theory of Finance.* Washington, D.C.: The Brookings Institution, 1960.

JOHNSON, H. G. "The Neo-Classical One-Sector Growth Model: A Geometrical Exposition and Extension to a Monetary Economy," *Economica*, XXXIII (August 1966), 265–287.

JOHNSON, H. G. "The Neutrality of Money in Growth Models: A Reply," *Economica*, XXXIV (February 1967), 73–74.

JOHNSON, H. G. *Essays in Monetary Economics.* Cambridge, Mass.: Harvard University Press, 1967.

LAIDLER, D. "The Rate of Interest and the Demand for Money: Some Empirical Evidence," *Journal of Political Economy*, LXXIV (December 1966), 543–555.

LERNER, ABBA P. *Essays in Economic Analysis.* London: Macmillan, 1953.

MARTY, A. L. "Gurley and Shaw on Money in a Theory of Finance," *Journal of Political Economy*, LXIX (February 1961), 56–62.

MUNDELL, R. A. "Inflation and Real Interest," *Journal of Political Economy*, LXXI (June 1963), 280–283.

MUNDELL, R. A. "A Fallacy in the Interpretation of Macroeconomic Equilibrium," *Journal of Political Economy*, LXXIII (February 1965), 61–66.

PATINKIN, DON. *Money, Interest, and Prices.* 2nd ed. New York: Harper & Row, 1965.

SIDRAUSKI, M. "Rational Choice and Patterns of Growth in a Monetary Economy," *American Economic Review, Proceedings*, LVII (May 1967), 534–544.

SIDRAUSKI, M. "Inflation and Economic Growth," *Journal of Political Economy*, LXXV (December 1967), 796–810.

SOLOW, ROBERT M. "A Contribution to the Theory of Economic Growth," *Quarterly Journal of Economics*, LXX (February 1956), 65–94.

STEIN, JEROME L. "Money and Capacity Growth," *Journal of Political Economy*, LXXIV (October 1966), 451–465.

TEIGEN, R. "Demand and Supply Functions for Money in the United States: Some

Structural Estimates," *Econometrica*, XXXII (October 1964), 476–509.

TOBIN, JAMES. "The Interest-Elasticity of Transactions Demand for Cash," *Review of Economics and Statistics*, XXXVIII (August 1956), 241–247.

TOBIN, JAMES. "Money and Economic Growth," *Econometrica*, XXXIII (October 1965), 671–684.

TOBIN, JAMES. "The Neutrality of Money in Growth Models: A Comment," *Economica*, XXXIV (February 1967), 69–72.

UZAWA, HIROFUMI. "On a Neo-Classical Model of Economic Growth," *Economic Studies Quarterly*, XVII, No. 1 (September 1966), 1–14.

Index
of Names

Index
of Subjects

Absolute price level. *See* Price level, absolute

Aggregate demand, 39, 87, 89–90, 96, 138, 139, 144
  for commodities, 137
  full employment level of, 97

Aggregate expenditures, 57

Aggregate real behavior, 50

Agricultural prices, 64–65

Anglo-Palestine Bank, 56

Anti-depression policy, 22

Asset bonds, 48

Asset-debt positions, mixed, 34 n

Asset money, 48

Assets, 109, 120
  financial, 37
  influence of on savings, 156–157, 158, 160
  liquid, 64
    volume of, 104 n
  portfolio of, 156–157, 158, 160

Balance of payments, 57, 64

Balanced-budget-multiplier argument, 240 n

Balanced-growth process, 36

Bank borrowing, 57

Bank credit, 57, 65, 66, 70
  authorized, 66
  distribution of, 67

  expansion of, 73 n, 85, 146
  outside liquidity restrictions, 67
  real value of, 62

Bank Leumi Le-Israel, 56 n

Bank of Israel, 56 n

Bank reserves, 68, 84, 85, 86, 88–89, 137, 173–174

Banking system, 59, 66, 85, 86, 88, 97, 169–191
  credit extending activities of, 241
  currency conversion effect on, 69
  government borrowing from, 58
  portfolio of, 50
  reserves of, 146
  supply of money, 51

Banking theory, 53

Bankruptcies, 16, 23, 70

Banks, 61, 62
  establishment of, 177

Black-market, 57
  dollar rate, 60, 62, 63, 70
  prices, 60, 62, 70

Blocked account, 70

Bond market, 54

Bonds, 40, 43 n, 49, 101
  demand for, 47, 138
  excess demand for, 44
  excess supply of, 43
  market purchase of, 138
  open-market purchase of, 44, 138

72 73 74 75 76   9 8 7 6 5 4 3 2 1